It [...]

y [...]

great institution [...] image of
the richness of our state.

Sincerely,

Beverly W Hogan

President
Tougaloo College
February 19, 2003

Mississippi:
The View From Tougaloo

The 1966 Meredith March led by Dr. Martin Luther King, Jr.

MISSISSIPPI:
THE VIEW FROM TOUGALOO

Second Edition

Clarice T. Campbell and Oscar Allan Rogers, Jr.

This volume is sponsored by
Jackson State University

Library of Congress Cataloging in Publication Data

Campbell, Clarice T.
  Mississippi: the view from Tougaloo

  Bibliography: p.
  Includes index.
  1. Tougaloo, Miss. Southern Christian College.
I. Rogers, Oscar A., joint author. II. Title.
LC2851.T6C35   378.762′51   78–10229
ISBN 0–87805–091–4
ISBN 0–87805–092–2 pbk.

To
L. Zenobia Coleman
Librarian at Tougaloo for thirty-four years

This second edition of **Mississippi: The View from Tougaloo** *is dedicated to alumna Maggie Burkhead Drake '46. With her encouragement, hundreds of individuals have gone to Tougaloo College and many other schools to gain an education and begin productive lives. She brought out the best in everyone she touched. Treasured memories of her as a motivator, counselor, helper, and friend continue to inspire countless relatives, former students, and friends. It is in her honor that this book's financial supporters have committed proudly their personal resources to extend this published record of our Alma Mater's legacy.*

Acknowledgments

THOSE WHO EXPECT of history a public relations document may be disappointed in this work. Frankly, in the study of Tougaloo from its founding in 1869 to the present, we found neither angels nor demons at the college. We did find many conscientious people dedicated to an ideal—people who tried hard, sometimes failing, more often succeeding. Many connected with the college held views ahead of their time in regard to race, but few were entirely free of racial bias. This was as true of black as of white. Surely, any fair-minded reader will make allowances for the social, political, and economic climate in which the characters of this story acted their parts.

We could have omitted all references that imply imperfection, but we deliberately chose to include some. Historians do a disservice to the public when they edit their findings to tell only good about those whose reputations they prefer untarnished. To exaggerate, or to be inordinately selective of the praiseworthy in some, places others in a worse light than they deserve.

Examples are the histories of Reconstruction. Historians, attempting to further rapprochement between the North and the white South around the turn of the century, emphasized the bad and overlooked the good in Reconstruction. Subsequent generations have presumed Congressional or Radical Reconstruction a total failure. As a result of this rationale, white America delayed further experimentation in achieving racial equality. Using facts previously omitted, modern historians have presented a more balanced picture of Reconstruction. One eminent white southern historian, Francis Butler

Simkins, concluded after reexamining the evidence that the greatest failure of Reconstruction was its abrupt ending. America might have been saved many of today's problems had early historians presented a more representative selection of facts.

In this first extensive story of Tougaloo College we have tried to organize fragmented information from primary sources into a meaningful whole without too much concern for Tougaloo's image. The college is not on trial. It has proved its worth over the past century. It is strong enough to stand the light of truth.

This is not to say that we have always found the truth—an elusive quality at best. Many facts were not available to us, because of fire and some carelessness in preservation of official records, or our inability to find all extant material. We have devoted more than a decade to study of the college from the perspective of a black author who graduated from Tougaloo in the forties and a white author who taught at Tougaloo during the sixties. We hope our work will stimulate others to delve into the records of Tougaloo's fascinating history.

No history of this size and scope could be written without the help of many persons. We are indebted to L. Zenobia Coleman, Tougaloo's librarian for thirty-four years, and to her successor, Jeannetta Roach, and her assistant, Virgia L. Shedd, for their interest and cooperation. Of equal importance has been Dr. Clifton Johnson, archivist of the American Missionary Association Collection and director of the Amistad Research Center in New Orleans. Dr. Jessie Carney Smith, librarian at Fisk University, and her staff were helpful. Personnel in the Mississippi Room at the University of Mississippi in Oxford and in the Mississippi Department of Archives and History at Jackson cheerfully located old government reports and letter files of governors for our use. Ken Lawrence, Program Director of the Mississippi Surveillance Project of the American Friends Service Committee, has been of inestimable help, particularly in the writing of those parts that deal with the Federal Bureau of Investigation. Tougaloo College and Rust College have been

viii   *Acknowledgments*

generous with the use of their photocopying machines and other equipment.

We are indebted for whatever human interest may be found in this history—something not readily extracted from official reports—to those who through interviews and letters recalled experiences at Tougaloo College. Though it is impossible to mention all, some were Rosalie McKee Shelton, Felix Moman, I. S. Sanders, Lillian Voorhees, Helen Griffith, Lilybel Wilson King, Annie Hamilton, Doris Tharpe Hall, Julia Bender, Mahala Irvin Smith, Edith Knight Hussey, Lionel and Lucile Fraser, Stella Molette, William and Naomi Townsend, Cawthorn A. Bowen, John Lee, George and Ruth Johnson, Henry Briggs, John Dixon, Ernestine Holloway, Beulah Marr, Homer Larsen, Eleanor Cobb Rogers, Harold Warren, Samuel Kincheloe, A. D. Beittel, George and Ruth Owens, Arvarh and Willie Pearl Strickland, Mrs. Washington Cole, Al Johnson, Robert Smith, James Brown, Edwin King, John Dittmer, James Loewen, John Garner, and Richard Porter.

Our appreciation also extends to Dr. Margaret DeChamps Moore, Dr. Allen Cabaniss, and Dr. Arthur W. Calhoun, all of whom encouraged us to write Tougaloo's history and gave practical suggestions.

And finally we are grateful to the Southern Fellowships Fund whose grant enabled one of us to give a full year's time to research and writing, unhampered by financial distractions.

Though we have tried to do our research carefully and to be accurate, it is inevitable that some important omissions, possibly errors of fact, and questionable interpretations will be picked up by readers, especially those who lived a part of Tougaloo's history. We shall welcome any corrections or additional information. Any comments sent us (c/o *Tougaloo News*, Tougaloo College, Tougaloo, MS 39174) will be printed in the *Tougaloo News*. This kind of interchange should be of value to those who write future histories or articles on Tougaloo College.

CLARICE T. CAMPBELL
OSCAR ALLAN ROGERS, JR.

Acknowledgment II

WHAT A DIFFERENCE two decades made in the life of Tougaloo College and the state of Mississippi! Since 1978, the College has inaugurated three presidents and has utilized administrative services of three interim presidents. College alumni increased by some 3,000 graduates. Three major buildings were constructed after 20 years of no new buildings. Graduates were elected to the state legislature and an alumnus chaired the Board of Trustees of Institutions of Higher Learning. A graduate was appointed to the Mississippi Supreme Court, and another elected three times to the U.S. Congress. Budgets and endowments increased by millions of dollars.

Substantial alumni giving matched that of major supporters. The United Negro College Fund's innovative projects provide increased revenue, as do the Federal Title III grants. Some 250 faculty and staff of the College are the best qualified ever. Beard Hall built in 1898 was demolished, as were several faculty dwellings.

These and other changes, good and some not good, took place! Berkshire Cottage, built in 1894 burned, and Kincheloe Science Hall suffered a major explosion. Death came to the campus with the demise of the Vice President of Academic Affairs, a *summa cum laude* graduate of the class of 1950.

These changes took place in a more enlightening racial climate in Mississippi. Legal segregations and overt discrimination ended. The disposal income of African Americans was at an all time high. Increased second and third generation of their children enrolled at Tougaloo.

This year (2001) several alumni decided to publish a revised edition of *Mississippi: the View from Tougaloo*, which is out of print. They realized the increasing impact of Alex Halley's *Roots* and other genealogical interests are having on family reunions and gatherings. Thus, there is a noticeable demand for the 1978 edition of the history. Tougaloo alumni and enrolled students seek to acquire written sources that list their family members.

Thus the revised edition extends the struggles of Tougaloo (1869) from the administration of the Rev. J.K. Nutting (1873) of Glenwood, Iowa, the College's first president, to that of Interim President Dr. James H. Wyche (2001) of Brown University. It treats recent visions of the presidents, the growth and development of the College, and the stellar contributions of the graduates and faculty make to Mississippi and the nation.

For this edition, we are indebted to many researchers, but especially to the memory and legacy of Dr. Clarice T. Campbell, who in 1994 rekindled interest in an expanded edition of the 1978 work. She desired that copies of the history be available to all graduates.

H. T. Drake '50, National Alumni Association President 1988-91, spear headed the drive to publish and finance the second edition. Drake since 1947 lived across County Line Rd, a stone throw from the campus. He remains involved in the life of the campus, the Tougaloo community and alumni chapter. We had the professional service of Clarence W. Hunter, archivist, for his role in the production of Chapter 22. Hunter's career as an archivist was influenced by Carter V. Woodson. From 1990-1999 he was an archivist at Tougaloo and at the Amistad Research Center in New Orleans from 1999-2001.

The staff of the Zenobia Coleman Library: Charlene Cole (Director of Library Services), Alma Fisher, Annie Harper, Tony Bounds, Lavinia Hutchins, Allie Jackson, Bernice Smith, and Minnie Watson provided us with documents and resources. Other help came from Mary-Margarette Butler and staff members of the computer laboratory at Jackson State University; Patricia Murray, Beverly Hogan, and others.

Ethel Lewis Rogers contributed toward the structure and narrative of the text.

The following Tougaloo alumni provided the finance for this 2002 publication of *Mississippi: The View From Tougaloo*:

> Dr. Van S. Allen '50
> Mrs. Charlene Cole '54
> Attorney Constance Slaughter-Harvey '67
> Dr. Roy L. Irons '72
> Precious T. '94 & Crystal Wise Martin
> Congresssman Bennie G. '68 & London Johnson '68 Thompson
> The H.T. Drake Family '50
> Tougaloo College National Alumni Association

Oscar A. Rogers, Jr.

Table of Contents

Foreword

THE AUTHORS OF *Mississippi: The View from Tougaloo*, Clarice T. Campbell and Oscar Allan Rogers, Jr., have dramatized one of the most significant developments in higher education in America. They have told the story of Tougaloo College, beginning with its inception in 1869.

The American Missionary Association, the founding body of Tougaloo College, was responding to the educational needs of the newly emancipated blacks immediately following the end of the Civil War. The endeavors of the A.M.A., and of similar institutions throughout the South, display the very best expression of human concern and kindness, especially since the movement was initiated soon after a time when one could lose his hands to the chopping block for teaching enslaved blacks to read and write.

These white men and women from the Northeast served as administrators, faculty and staff members. They and their friends also served as trustees, spokesmen and fund raisers for the College. And thousands have followed in their train for better than a hundred years now. The continuity, strength and beauty of this spirit is seen in those who are presently supporters of the College, especially when one examines the relationships that clearly tie the supporters of the past with those who fulfill this role for Tougaloo in A. D. 1978.

The following account begins with a history of the formation of the American Missionary Association, in part through the efforts of Lewis and Arthur Tappan, the well-known abolitionists, who established the Amistad Committee in 1839 to defend the slaves who mutinied aboard the *Amistad* as they

xiii

were being taken to America. The magnitude of the A.M.A. commitment led to the establishment of some five hundred schools in the South "primarily for freedmen, but open to illiterates regardless of color." The phrase "open to illiterates regardless of color" formed the model for democratic education that the American system of higher education would not really follow until a hundred years later. Though policies and practices of discrimination in education were to increase for a time, Tougaloo graduated its first white student, Luella Miner, daughter of the school's treasurer, in 1879.

The Tougaloo experience reflects, through the account of its battles to survive and be effective, the shifts and changes in the attitudes of those in control of the political, social, and economic affairs of both the state of Mississippi and the A.M.A. itself. The Tougaloo story is a story of compassionate individuals, and groups of individuals, imbued with Christian principles and steeped in the concepts of the dignity of the human being and the right to equal treatment and justice under the law. All those who believe in these concepts can find in the amazing Tougaloo story at least some hope and courage to face the many challenges yet to come.

DR. VAN ALLEN
JACKSON, 1978

Mississippi:
The View From Tougaloo

1

Exploring the Roots

IN GOOD BIBLICAL STYLE one might say the *Amistad* begat the American Missionary Association, and the American Missionary Association begat Tougaloo College and her five sister institutions: LeMoyne, Talladega, Straight, and Tillotson colleges, and Fisk University.[1] With a pride in their heritage, college leaders recount the dramatic story of the *Amistad* at orientation programs for incoming students and faculty.

In 1839 two Cubans bought a group of Africans at auction in Havana and tried to take them on the schooner *Amistad* to a remote island. Enroute the Africans, under the leadership of Cinque, mutinied and forced the Cubans to steer eastward toward their native land. At night, however, the navigators headed north by west and eventually reached Long Island, where American naval officers released the Cubans and sent the Africans in chains to New Haven.

President Van Buren, to placate Southerners and their northern sympathizers, and to avoid trouble with Spain, favored returning the prisoners to their purchasers. But Lewis and Arthur Tappan, the well known abolitionists, organized the Amistad Committee to assure the prisoners a fair trial. The case was important not only because of the bitter slavery controversy but also because of international complications. Spain had abolished slavery in 1830 except for ladinos (property already owned). The Cubans had affidavits stating these Africans were ladinos.

---

1. Straight is now Dillard, Tillotson is Huston-Tillotson, and LeMoyne is LeMoyne-Owen.

3

In spite of the 1837 depression, the Amistad Committee raised money to obtain able lawyers for the blacks. John Quincy Adams added his prestige and legal competence to the defense, which proved that the affidavits were fraudulent and that the Africans had been in Cuba only ten days; so they were freed and returned to Africa along with two missionaries. This story is dramatically portrayed in a mural which stretches across one full wall of the library at Talladega College in Alabama.

Before long the Amistad Committee recognized the inconsistency of a concern for blacks in Africa without a concern for blacks enslaved in America. Thus, the committee evolved into the American Missionary Association (A.M.A.), nonsectarian and independent of church control. The A.M.A. determined from the start to "speak the truth in love" and refused to compromise with slavery. Members "convenanted" not to obey the federal fugitive slave laws, which required free states to return slaves who were trying to escape.

With the advent of the Civil War, the Association felt education of freedmen was a "work meet for repentance." Several denominations, notably the National Council of Congregational Churches, adopted the A.M.A. as their agent to work with the freedmen. Gen. O. O. Howard, director of the war department's Freedmen's Bureau, which was established to meet the immediate needs of Negroes as well as whites in distress, offered government aid to any church board willing to teach Negro children and train Negro teachers for prospective public schools.

Thus, the American Missionary Association established over five hundred schools in the South, primarily for freedmen but open to illiterates regardless of color. Because slave codes forbade the teaching of slaves to read or write, the educable potential of blacks was for many whites an open question. Most white people were unaware of the faith blacks had in education and their determination to get it. House slaves had sometimes learned their ABC's along with the children of a master who defied the law by permitting his young slaves to learn. When masters strictly observed the law, clever black children often learned by listening and observing their master's children at study. What one slave learned in this way he or she might teach others surreptitiously. Young George W. Albright, who later became a state senator, obtained his elementary education through his mother, the cook for the master's house. While the white children studied at her kitchen table, she absorbed what she could and passed it on to her small son. In a sense, blacks were so hungry for education that they "bootlegged" it, at the risk of being caught and punished. So it was not surprising that the A.M.A. found adults as well as children eager to learn.

In the Mississippi Reconstruction Convention of 1868, eighty-four whites and sixteen Negroes wrote a new constitution which provided free public schools for all children between five and twenty-one—a new departure for Mississippi. Before the war little was done to promote public education even for white children. For the most part, mismanagement had wasted federal grants for education. A notable exception was Franklin Academy in Columbus, financed by income from sixteenth-section lands in the district. But it remained for the maligned Reconstruction Convention realistically to attack the educational problem.

Negro teachers had to be trained if only because ex-Confederates were strongly opposed to education of the Negro by Yankee teachers, under whose tutelage the Republican Party could garner the Negro vote. Moreover, northern teachers who were refused lodging in respectable white homes lived in Negro homes and thus forfeited the respect of white Southerners. In short, the Yankee "schoolmarm" was a "carpetbagger."

Though some thoughtful white Southerners saw the importance of teaching the blacks, to instill in them a reverence for the South's way of life, local white teachers were hard to find. The idea of white ladies teaching in black schools was repugnant to most white Southerners, who probably agreed with the editorial:

A lady who is capable of teaching at all must be in sore need if she has to resort to a colored school to eke out a precarious existence and we hope the time will never come when any true daughter of the South will ever be put to that necessity.

Anyway, the June election of 1868 rejected the new constitution. Whites resented not only the section on schools but also the disfranchisement of "rebels."

In the meantime the American Missionary Association was phasing out its work in primary schools to concentrate on higher education for training teachers to supply the public schools which it believed would be established throughout the South.

Early in 1869 the American Missionary Association commissioned Allen P. Huggins, a former Union officer who had settled in Mississippi, to look for suitable land for a normal-agricultural school. Near the Tougaloo railway station seven miles north of Jackson, he found the old Boddie plantation of 2,000 acres, with a spacious antebellum mansion. The home had been built for John Boddie's fiancée who specified that it should have a cupola from which she might view the city of Jackson. Before the mansion was complete, the lady married another. Some said she was fickle; others said she was repulsed by the harsh way Boddie used his slave labor. Disappointed in love, Boddie used the mansion to store his cotton and the cupola to observe, not Jackson, but the progress of his field hands.

After the war, the plantation was unprofitable. There was daily liability of theft or destruction. Boddie sold the place to pay his debts. The new owner, about to lose the place for taxes, offered it to Huggins for $15,000. However, with so much Mississippi land for sale at that time, the A.M.A. played a waiting game.

By mid-February 1869, the political situation was beginning to change. When Mississippi Democrats had the choice of military rule under General Gillem who was sympathetic to them, or a reconstruction government with Negro suffrage, they chose military rule. But on March 4, 1869, Grant became President and gave Gen. Adelbert Ames, from a New England family of abolitionists, command over the Fourth Military District. Ames's appointments to office included blacks as well as whites who were sympathetic to the freedmen. The Democrats quickly recognized that a civil government over which they might have some control would be a better choice under these circumstances. Huggins accurately anticipated that the state constitution, with the "rebel" clause deleted, would be ratified; he, therefore, urged the A.M.A. to push forward with the plans for a school.

Meanwhile another former Union officer, George McKee, had bought the plantation to subdivide for sale to freedmen. Knowing a school would enhance values, McKee offered to sell Huggins the mansion with about 500 acres for $12,000. After some negotiation, Huggins obtained them for $10,500, which was paid by the Freedmen's Bureau.

Because the donor of the right of way to the Illinois Central had stipulated that all trains should stop at the Tougaloo crossroads, transportation to Jackson was a matter of only forty minutes, even at the slow pace of the wood-stoked locomotives. The rutted road from the station to the mansion passed through a dense forest of pines, massive hickories, and oaks festooned with Spanish moss. The convergence of two brooks had given the name Tougaloo (pronounced Toó-ga-loo), an Indian name meaning "at the fork of the stream." Beyond stood the mansion, set against vast rolling fields of cotton.

Nearby on the McKee property were the former slave quarters. They were occupied by rough and unruly blacks given to brawling. Families were haphazard, and Huggins was appalled at the fornication and adultery that constituted a way of life, even for many church members. These were ways learned in slavery when masters discouraged family ties as impediments to the free transfer of property and when emotional religious orgies were considered a safer outlet for pent-up feelings than more aggressive forms of expression.

Huggins longed to be a minister so that he might instruct from the pulpit. A Baptist of deep religious conviction, he was repelled by corruption in Mississippi Baptist congregations, black and white. The feeling was evidently mutual, as the white Baptists later denied him membership because he refused publicly to apologize for having been a Union officer.

Huggins considered joining the Congregationalists who, not having any established churches in Mississippi, could "commence from the groundwork." He believed it necessary to "lay a foundation of correct Christian living" and to keep out all the sensational, confusing doctrines.

Where, thought Huggins, might he better attack superstition, immorality, and ignorance than in a Christian boarding school? All his efforts to find the right site for a manual labor school and all the long tedious hours of negotiating to obtain the property were but preparation for the real work ahead. Passionately desiring to have a part in building the school, he wrote Gen. C. H. Howard, brother of O. O. Howard of the Freedmen's Bureau. C. H. Howard was the A.M.A. secretary in the Chicago office; his influence in the A.M.A. would continue long after his brother O. O. left the Bureau. Huggins told C. H. Howard of his deep interest and offered his services. No one, he felt, could collect the "proper set of work hands" and manage the plantation any better than he, with his "enterprise and energy and practicability." Furthermore, he had the friendship of Captain Pease, the superintendent of education in Mississippi, and of General Ames. Huggins was making $2,000 a year in the Internal Revenue Service and did not expect to "better his purse," but he wanted the satisfaction of working for a cause in which he was interested. He sent a similar letter to Edward P. Smith, A.M.A. secretary in the New York office.

The American Missionary Association secretaries evidently did not share Huggins's high estimate of his qualifications for the superintendency of the school. Gen. C. H. Howard's comment to Smith was simply, "It is not best to retain him." One can but wonder why Huggins was unacceptable to the A.M.A. He was dedicated to the cause of the freedmen. Frustrated in his desire to build Tougaloo University, he worked to promote public state schools for all, in accordance with the new constitution.

The Ku Klux Klan took such offense from his activities that on one occasion its members threatened to burn the home of a Negro who was giving Huggins a night's lodging. To save his host's family, Huggins surrendered himself to the hooded Klansmen and came near to losing his life in the ensuing struggle. Later, Huggins was made a trustee of Tougaloo University, but he was never to have the leadership role he so coveted.

2

Moral Uplift

ON OCTOBER 12 OF 1869 H. S. Beals of Angelica, New York, who had previously opened two schools for the American Missionary Association, arrived to take charge of the project at Tougaloo. With the cooperation of his wife and daughter Sarah, he had earned a reputation for pioneering with a minimum of capital. Although listed on the Tougaloo record as teachers, the three workers assumed responsibility for the many unexpected tasks associated with the new project.

During the arduous journey of seven days from Chicago the Beals family had been delighted with the veritable fairyland of the country. Nor did the beauty end with their arrival at Tougaloo. The woodland of the school's property with its "boundless contiguity of shade" Beals found well balanced with broad acres of open land. From these fields forty bales of cotton had already been picked and were expected to bring $7,500 at market.

Other features of the property were less pleasing. Beals feared the outside repairs to the residence would cost at least $250 besides the expense of roofing an area of about 500 square feet. This work would have to be done immediately to save the building from complete ruin. Beals noted great discrepancies in the structure. He thought the glass was fit for a palace while the brick hearths were scarcely fit for a cabin. What Beals did not know was that when Boddie's fiancée lost interest in him,

10

he lost interest in the mansion and completed it as cheaply as possible. Beals estimated that furnishing the massive living room, which measured twenty by thirty feet, and the other large rooms would require a minimum of $500. Part of the farm would have to be enclosed with a fence. Teams, wagons, plows, harrows, cultivators, hoes, shovels, harness, and other equipment needed on a model farm would swell the initial investment. The school would require a recitation room at a cost of $3,500 more. With nothing in his pocket and no sign of the check Beals expected on his arrival, the obstacles appeared insurmountable.

Except for the missionary boxes which had followed them, Beals and his family would have felt almost forgotten. He wrote the Rev. E. P. Smith in the New York office that his ladies sent thanks for all the nice things in the boxes and asked that next time bolts of sheeting and children's clothing be included.

By April of 1870 Beals, with the help of his family and one teacher sent by the A.M.A., had made a good beginning of his tasks. In the faith that money would come, he wasted no time starting the repair work on the house. Also he surveyed one hundred sixty acres which he divided into thirty-acre sections. Selling homesites had a two-fold advantage: It brought money for the school's needs, and it attracted to the community stable families from which good students could be expected.

Dormitories were started for both boys and girls. The first was a story-and-a-half frame structure, thirty-two by seventy feet, located to the north of the mansion. The upper level was planned to house twenty-five to thirty boys, while the first floor was designed for recitation rooms and an assembly hall that could be used on Sundays as a church. This building came to be known as the men's hall or the normal building. To the south of the mansion a two-story frame structure was erected, thirty-four by seventy feet. The dining room, kitchen, laundry, and sitting room were on the first floor, while the second floor could accommodate from twenty-five to thirty girls.

To encourage contributions for furnishing the building Gen. C. H. Howard issued a circular:

Is there not something humanizing and closely allied to a Christian influence, in a neatly furnished room? There is no more doubt of it than that there was something degrading and brutalizing in the old slave-hovels, slave pens and "quarters" where sometimes a hundred or more human wretches were herded together like cattle, having merely stalls to separate families.

Not waiting for the new buildings, Beals started a day school in the mansion within a month of the day he and his family arrived. Of necessity, the classes were conducted without adequate seating or other facilities and supplies, but the pupils showed interest and their numbers increased.

However, the primary concern to the A.M.A. was the establishment of a normal (teacher training) school. The state constitution, ratified in November 1869, shortly after Beals's arrival at Tougaloo, required the state to establish free public schools, and the need for qualified teachers to staff them was urgent. Under the new constitution, Capt. H. R. Pease, who, as superintendent of education for the Freedmen's Bureau, had supported the purchase of the Tougaloo property, was elected as the first state superintendent of public education. He, as well as George McKee, member of Congress from the district, and several state legislators promised their support for a normal school.

A threat to state financial aid for Tougaloo arose in the spring of 1870 when some Negro legislators insisted that either the University of Mississippi at Oxford must accept Negro applicants or the state must establish a university for blacks. Gov. James L. Alcorn doubted that the Negroes would be satisfied with a school operated by the American Missionary Association. He predicted that the blacks would demand Negro administrators and teachers. Officials of the A.M.A. feared loss of support for Tougaloo if the state built a university for Negroes.

With little hope of state support, E. P. Smith of the New York office felt the A.M.A. would do well to sell the property. On the other hand, he believed it would be better for the blacks of Mississippi if the A.M.A. were to hold on and make Tougaloo a model school. He had little faith that a school under Negro

management would succeed. He feared that the colored trustees would use the state money "for the appointment of
some Dinah and Sambo." In any event, Smith thought a school
administered by blacks would soon fold. Captain Pease advised
retaining the institution and asking for more aid from the
Freedmen's Bureau. He believed that even if a state Negro college were founded elsewhere, the A.M.A. might persuade
the legislature to accept some responsibility for Tougaloo's
finances.

Faith that the money would be forthcoming proved justified. In June of 1870 the Freedmen's Bureau granted Tougaloo
$5,000. That same month the legislature approved a system of
scholarships which would allow each state representative to
name every term one student whose tuition and weekly allowance of fifty cents would be paid by the state. The recipients of
the scholarships were required to be of good moral character,
to pass an examination, and to agree to teach three years in
Mississippi's common schools. Tougaloo received about $1,000
from this source during the first year. The state also appropriated money to assist in payment of salaries and to purchase
equipment. Altogether, the state contributed about $4,000 for
the year 1870–1871.

With improved financial prospects, Pease proceeded to
carry out the A.M.A.'s request for a charter. Though he doubted
that Tougaloo was the most euphonious name for a college, he
was overruled. The charter was drawn for Tougaloo University
and granted by the state legislature on May 13, 1871. Many
persons scoffed at the title of university (common usage for
many schools of the day). But Augustus F. Beard of the A.M.A.
later defended the name, saying that when parents name a
baby they give it an adult name; "the universities were named
all right. Now you bring them up." But subsequent administrations were more realistic, and Tougaloo's name was officially
changed in 1916 to Tougaloo College. In the intervening years
students were met at the level of their needs. The faculty never
tried to force higher education on students unprepared for it.
No bachelor's degree was conferred until 1901 and then to only
one student who comprised that first graduating class of the
college program.

Though Tougaloo University was to serve primarily Negro students, no mention of race was written into the charter. The first normal school graduating class in 1879 included a white student, Luella Miner, daughter of the school treasurer. The school has always been legally open to whites, but their own prejudice has prevented many from attending.

The charter specified the powers and limitations of the board of trustees, which has always been composed of both blacks and whites. Upon nomination by the A.M.A. the board could appoint a president and such teachers as were necessary. It was also given the power to organize new departments. The total value of the university property was limited to $500,000.

The normal department, organized in October 1871, became a state sponsored normal school on January 3, 1872, by act of the Mississippi legislature. A fair understanding of the fundamentals of arithmetic, geography, and grammar were required for admittance to it. Both elementary and advanced courses of study were offered, of two years each, except that both could be completed in three years. Each school year consisted of three terms: October through December, January through March, and April through June.

The normal school was equipped to train students in the most modern methods of teaching, with primary and intermediate departments conducted as a model school. What students learned in their theory classes they could observe and experience through practice teaching in the model school. The library had a fair selection of books, though the claim to a thousand, made in the catalogs and other official reports, was misleading since many of the books were obsolete before they were given to the school and should have been discarded. Other teaching helps included maps, charts, globes, some science equipment and musical instruments.

Few students could pay all their expenses in cash, though the charges were nominal. Tuition was one dollar, board and room were ten dollars, and rental of texts needed was thirty cents. Total cost for a student was less than twelve dollars a month. Even if he paid full tuition, each student was required to work one hour a day under supervision not only to give service to the school but also to develop his own work skills and habits. Some fortunate students received state scholarships of two dollars a month; but they, like most of the other students, usually found it necessary to work for at least part of their expenses.

The plantation school offered a variety of work opportunities. Housekeeping duties occupied the girls. Depending on the season, boys plowed and performed such chores as cleaning, digging, fencing, and planting. Frequent rains and a shortage of tools and teams made it difficult to get the most return from the boys' work.

The amount of corn harvested from the first year proved insufficient for the big school family and the several teams of mules, and Beals had to purchase additional quantities. He tried the next year to prevent another such outlay of cash by setting off forty acres to be planted on shares, then planting fifty acres in corn himself. Ten or fifteen acres were planted with broom corn so that the girls could pay some of their expenses by working on small brooms and brushes.

Loneliness and a feeling of isolation depressed all the missionary workers laboring in this strange land where differences in basic philosophy precluded any close relationships with the white population. Lack of publications, irregular mail service, and delayed answers from the home offices made them feel they were "beyond civilization." When, after thirty days, a check promised him by Gen. C. H. Howard finally came, Beals wrote the New York Office, "I wot not what had become of him. But now he has come out of the cloud, I hope I shall not lose sight of him again." Other letters complained that with no magazines or newspapers, the workers were destitute of news. Most letters to the home office or to friends included a plea for some reading material—even if it were only last year's almanac. "Can you afford," one writer pleaded, "the *Advance*, *Congregationalist*, or any newspaper for your mission family at Tougaloo?" Being so far from civilization, he said, they were likely to forget what little they knew. One teacher was so overjoyed when she received the weekly *Congregationalist* that she offered the good Massachusetts deacon who sent it a thousand thanks.

Beals was as dismayed as Huggins had been by the immor-

ality and low morals of the community. The Sabbath was
scarcely known by either whites or blacks; licentiousness and
ignorance were widespread. It seemed that everyone used
whisky intemperately. In thanking a friend for a temperance
tract, Beals wrote that he could scatter a thousand of them to
advantage, but he doubted he could sell even one; for what the
people needed most, they were unwilling to buy. Violence was
common. During the fall election shortly after Beals arrived, at
least two Negroes were killed near the school, one in Jackson
and one in Canton. Beals reported to the New York office that in
other places people had been responsive to help when it was
offered them, but here they acted as though they were just
awakening from a Rip Van Winkle sleep not of twenty years,
but of fifty. They were uninspired, with no apparent ambition
but to raise more cotton. To them cotton was more than
King—it was Lord, he said.

Beals wrote Gen. C. H. Howard that it would cost more to
rouse the people in Mississippi than elsewhere to feel their
moral and intellectual needs. "It will take money and work and
prayer." Then, reverting to his characteristic optimism, he
added that he did not read the signs of Providence aright if this
were not the propitious time to thrust in the sickle. Beals, in
November 1869, interpreted the election of Republican Gov.
James L. Alcorn, a large plantation owner who had never favored secession, as the triumph of free principles and the end of
the rebels' last hope. He and those who came after him had yet
to learn of what toughness the rebels were made.

Of great help to Beals in raising the moral standards of the
community was the arrival of Ebenezer Tucker. An Oberlin
graduate who had taught from 1859–1868 at Liber College, a
Christian reformatory in Indiana, Tucker was sent to Tougaloo
in the summer of 1870 to become principal of the normal and
manual training departments. An ebullient gentleman, he
threw himself wholeheartedly into the work and the lives of his
students. "You can scarcely ever realize . . . the feeling of a
teacher for his pupils," he once wrote a former student. "Yes,
indeed, I take pride in the welfare and success of 'my boys and
girls.' Aha! that was one of my troupe, I exclaim."

Tucker, even more than most of the workers, saw Negroes as just people. "Educate not the Negro, but the child," he advocated, "not for his place but that he may find his place." He took pride in the achievements of the freedmen. They "are making steady progress," he wrote, "though there is much debasement. Their worst foes are intemperance and licentiousness." Like Thaddeus Stevens of the U. S. Congress, Tucker felt it a great mistake that the large estates had not been confiscated and given to the freedmen. It troubled him that the wealth for which the Negroes had labored as slaves should not have been shared with them at the time of their emancipation. "We have the spectacle of a people, poor, ignorant, helpless, at the mercy of the arrogant and hostile landholders. . . ." Even so, working against all odds, many Negroes did buy land in Jackson, Clinton, Raymond, and around the school.

Tucker was one who inculcated moral values with every formal school subject. "Stick to unsullied honor and Christian integrity," he admonished a student. "Do you envy the Tweeds, the Fisks, the Stokes, nay even the Vanderbilts, the Jay Cookes? I do not, for my part. The Day of Judgment comes even here below, much more in the world to come. 'Honor bright' is worth all it costs."

While many things in the South caused an honest man to blush and hang his head, Radicalism, he thought, had done quite well in Mississippi—much better than in Louisiana, South Carolina, and Florida. However, he said it was unfortunate that offices were multiplied so as to make a good thing out of it, at a time when strict economy and integrity were needed more than ever before. The deluded, crushed, impoverished South, he said, needed all her resources for rejuvenation, and none should be spared for fat offices and unprincipled jobbers. He declared it was one of the curses of this world that selfish, reckless, unprincipled men should cling to the car of progress, and sometimes well nigh stop her onward course.

After serving a year and a half as principal, Tucker left to take a small school of about seventy students in Raymond, Mississippi. Why he left is not known, but Gen. C. H. Howard was evidently displeased with him. He wrote the New York office that Tucker was recommended to him by the president of Oberlin College and a minister, both of whom he thought the less of for the fact. Evidently Tucker was still considered fit to lead the students in their moral and spiritual development, as he returned every five weeks to conduct church services.

The church and the Sabbath School, located on the first floor of the men's hall, constituted an integral part of the school program and served the community as well. Before the end of 1869 the Sabbath School attendance, composed mainly of adults who often came from a distance of five to ten miles, approached two hundred in number, according to Beals. He described their attentiveness, their earnest eyes, their whispered responses during the prayers as indications that "Jesus was there." These people convinced Beals and the other school workers that a few congenial souls were in sympathy with Christ.

Nellie M. Horton, an A.M.A. teacher from New Orleans who visited Tougaloo in April of 1871, found the religious teaching was working an improvement in the lives of the people. Writing from the cupola of the old slaveholder's mansion where nearby "little wooly heads" were playing around the cabin doors of the quarters, she observed in a letter:

Ah! The Missionary Association has changed the aspect of this plantation life. I never *felt* the contrast between the "then and now" more than ... the other morning when after listening to some tales of brutal cruelty, and the horrors of old plantation life from those who felt what they were telling, I came up the quiet beautiful path past the little cabins in the "quarters" and stepped into a clean little house to help a woman read one of the Psalms and saw her husband come in from his work, reading a story in his paper about I'll fetch it yet. I thought we *would* just give them the helping hand and *trust them* to "fetch it yet."

Beals reported a steady work of grace had been following the school since the first scholars began spelling out the divine messages of the New Testament. Numbers continued to increase, and every communion season brought additions to the church. This report, like others of Beals, may have been a bit exaggerated, for the church was never very large.

Perhaps it would not be unfair to say that Beals often wrote with A.M.A. donors in mind. His expressions appear calculated to open a man's purse. An unfavorable situation was described as making "the eye moisten and the heart bleed." He could not keep back the tears at the memory that three days before he had sent "five noble young men" from the college doors in a single day because there was no room for them and no work for them to pay their expenses. Scores, Beals declared, were waiting until new buildings were erected. "We have done something, only to learn that we must do more," he said. Beals could not believe that the "charities of God's dear children" would be given "sparingly" for this work in Mississippi. Having been sent hundreds of miles away to pitch their "tents amid the shadows of semi-barbarianism," the missionaries wanted money and prayers to "rear the altars and light the fires of freedom and righteousness." He believed the needs of the missionaries would be met so that they might become "sanctified instrumentalities" through which these "children of ignorance and want and suffering" could be brought to the "meaning of Infinite mercy."

Though Beals was called in the spring of 1873 to work with the Indians before his dreams for Tougaloo had been fully realized, his achievements were impressive. Tangible evidence of his work could be seen in the repaired mansion and the two new buildings which served the needs of around sixty boarding scholars and a hundred day students. Work opportunities on the plantation made an education possible for many who otherwise would not have aspired so high. With the model and normal schools well organized, the university already had a reputation for quality teaching. The religious work was well begun, and the community felt its impact.

The reasons for terminating Beals's services were as cryptic as were those for the dismissal of Huggins and Tucker before him. Some believed A. J. Steele, the principal of the normal school who had succeeded Tucker, was responsible. Gen. C. H. Howard wrote the New York office that he still believed in Beals's integrity. Nevertheless, the fulfillment of Beals's dreams for Tougaloo had to be left to his successors.

Frank G. Woodworth gave twenty-five years of his life to the advancement of Tougaloo University.

The Illinois Central station at Tougaloo no longer gives daily passenger service, but formerly it was a lifeline to the outside world.

Some of the jobs available to work-aid students were serving meals and cleaning up in the old dining hall.

Strieby Hall was built almost wholly by students from Tougaloo and other A. M. A. schools.

Mindful of the maxim that a poor man cannot afford a poor cow, Tougaloo made its prize bull available to local farmers.

Commencement exhibits of useful articles made by the students in the Tougaloo shop.

In days past the workshops provided Tougaloo men important training as well as service to the college.

Washington Hall served as chapel (below) and young men's dormitory (above) until destroyed by fire in 1881.

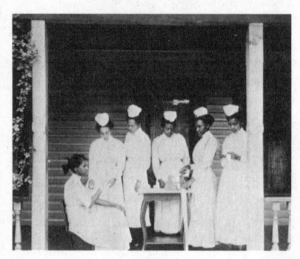

Class in nurse training

The Old Dining Hall built in 1900

The Daniel Hand School was used as a practice school for normal students at Tougaloo.

Beard Hall

The Sarah A. Dickey Memorial Hospital replaced the old hospital which had been destroyed by fire.

The dean comes to dinner. Dorothy Gordon beams with pride as her students entertain Dean Fraser in the Home Economics Practice House (Thelma Caldwell Sanders next to dean).

3

Bricks Without Straw

THE REV. J. K. NUTTING OF GLENWOOD, IOWA, was chosen by the American Missionary Association to be Tougaloo's first president. At least Nutting understood his position to be that of president, and his stationery carried the title. He was never given the authority of a president, and some later records refer to G. Stanley Pope as the first president. But on the abrupt departure of Beals, Gen. C. H. Howard assigned Nutting to Tougaloo in April 1873, though he was not fully prepared for the job.

In May, before Nutting was well established in his position, the Tougaloo family was besieged by some fifteen cases of measles, several of pneumonia, and about twenty of diphtheria. One student died. Fearing further contagion, some parents took their children out of school. Perhaps their withdrawal was for the best, as it reduced the number sleeping in a bed to no more than two.

School opened in the fall of 1873 with an enlarged staff. Whereas Tougaloo had been operating under the direction of Gen. C. H. Howard of the A.M.A. Chicago office, in the fall of 1873 the New York office took over. Important changes were made in policy. No longer would students be encouraged to work in order to pay their expenses and to develop habits of industriousness and thrift. The school was advised to accept primarily students who could pay in cash or do work of a "pecuniary" nature. The A.M.A. did not intend to have Tougaloo remain a drain on its treasury.

21

Reaction was immediate and intense. Though there was work "aching to be done" on shabby buildings, on grounds overgrown with weeds, and with pigs "uninhibited" by fences, this kind of work produced no money. Nor was any profit realized from chopping wood for fourteen fireplaces and five or six stoves. Teams required care but, again, such work did not bring in any cash. Working girls assigned to housekeeping produced no money, but the school could not operate without them. Only those boys who worked in the cotton fields produced a monetary income. Nutting asserted that unless students were paid for their services, Tougaloo might as well put up the shutters. No student ever had paid his way otherwise; and none could, he said.

Another policy change dealt with food. The school community was urged to eat off the plantation. With beef at only nine cents a pound, Nutting asked if the school family was expected to eat "interminable bacon," which was distasteful and unwholesome for most. The president, whose nerves were taut because of the illness of his two small children, instructed the superintendent to serve beef at four meals each week. This order, which bordered on defiance, he deemed necessary in an exhausting climate.

With dissatisfaction breeding more dissatisfaction, the school administrators, Nutting, A. J. Steele (school principal), and S. C. Osborn (farm superintendent) became increasingly critical of some procedures which they had never before seriously questioned. The A.M.A. had always required that all monies received for the school be sent to the Association's treasury. In theory disbursements were then made to cover the needs of the school; but in practice the Association did not return enough money to operate the school. Tougaloo received from the Association only $1,000 of the state's annual appropriation of $3,700 for the principal of the normal school. Steele suggested to E. M. Cravath of the New York office that the remainder of the amount be used at the school for improvements in the kitchen and dormitories, both of which offered an open invitation to disease. He thought such a policy would encourage further appropriations from the state.

The common treasury also received monies which had

been given by individuals for specific purposes. Contributions toward an intermediate building, which Nutting received from his speaking tour of several states during the summer of 1873, were sent to the A.M.A. office, but not enough money was forwarded to Tougaloo to meet the expenses of labor and materials for the new building. When school opened in the fall, it was over $1,200 in debt. Since more lumber and labor were needed for the building, and the dining room and kitchen had to be stocked for the beginning of the school year, the debt mounted higher.

As the national depression hit a new low in the fall of 1873, the A.M.A. encountered financial problems from which it did not recover for a decade. Jackson merchants, pressed to meet their own accounts, were forced to demand payment from their debtors. Previously, merchants had allowed some of Tougaloo's thirty-day accounts to run as long as three and four months. Also, merchants were hesitant to continue extending credit because of their fear that the A.M.A., which they associated with the two Howard brothers, might fold as a result of the widely publicized "defalcations" of Gen. O. O. Howard.

Because the Freedmen's Bureau symbolized military occupation and Negro equality, the white South continually sought to find irregularities in Gen. O. O. Howard's administration. At the conclusion of each investigation, General Howard was exonerated. Yet Confederate sympathizers were only too glad to believe the worst.

By mid-October either substantial amounts had to be paid on the accounts or the school could not buy a barrel of flour or a pound of meat except for cash, and of that it had none. Osborn, observing that patience ceased to be a virtue, wrote Cravath, the current secretary, that he must have $1,000 within ten days. Even the cotton crop, he explained, could not be counted on to help the school through this crisis. With business conditions as they were, cotton was worth only two-thirds of what it had brought the year before. In any event, it could not be marketed without a press. Previously the school had used General McKee's press; but it, together with his gin-house and his cotton, had been destroyed by fire.

One hundred mouths attacked the diminishing food supply

three times each day while Nutting and Osborn watched the mails for a check. Osborn telegraphed his old friend, Gen. C. H. Howard, for advice, but received no answer. The school was by then entirely out of flour, sugar, and tea, and had enough meat to last only two or three days. With no word from the A.M.A. except a request for a more detailed accounting of expenses, Osborn telegraphed again: "IF POSSIBLE SEND ME ONE THOUSAND DOLLARS TO SAVE CREDIT OF INSTITU- TION." Then, a full eleven days after mailing his first plea for funds, with the school on half rations and the students having no meat at all, he sent another: "I WILL CLOSE INSTITUTION UNLESS I GET MONEY THIS WEEK."

Despairing of ever hearing from the Association, Osborn refused to give the school up until he had exhausted the power of prayer. On the night of October 28, he and his wife dropped to their knees in earnest petition for a special blessing. The next morning, almost before their prayer was ended, Tougaloo re- ceived a check from the A.M.A. for $500, and within a few days another came in the same amount.

The immediate financial crisis had been weathered, but the experience left cleavages that would be long in healing. Cravath was irked that he had not been told earlier of the de- teriorating finances; Nutting and Osborn felt it was the respon- sibility of General Howard in the Chicago office to have briefed the New York office on the situation when it assumed supervi- sion of Tougaloo University.

Discord among the staff grew to greater proportions as Cravath insisted on further retrenchments. Osborn felt that Steele and Nutting had panicked when students were late en- rolling in the fall because unusual weather had delayed cotton picking. Fearing there would be no students, they had ad- mitted small boys who could not earn their board. He also complained that his suggestions for economies had usually been overruled by Nutting and Steele to whose "better judg- ment" he deferred. In several letters he implied that the school was not running smoothly and that nothing but Cravath's presence and advice would "obviate the difficulty."

Personal finances were a never ending source of irritation.

Those in administrative positions at Tougaloo often had running accounts with the A.M.A. office. Loans were frequently given to them by the A.M.A. or made by them to it. For some, board was charged to their accounts; for others it was included as a part of their salary. The A.M.A. did not operate on written contracts for services, on any fixed salary scale, or with any definite arrangement for pay. The money compensation was intertwined with irregular fringe benefits and the expected rewards from the Lord for services rendered in his name. Teachers promised fifteen dollars a month were required to send a requisition to New York to collect it. If the school were out of forms, collection was delayed.

Such a system, or lack of system, placed the workers in the humiliating position of feeling they must justify requests for salary payment by a recital of their obligations. On one occasion Nutting found it embarrassing, he wrote, to have to ask for mercy, but his funds were exhausted. At the time of writing, he said he could not raise enough money to buy a dozen eggs for the baby, and the medical bills for the child he lost were still unpaid. This hurt his pride, as the doctor was a "Southerner pure." With no time or energy to "eke out with his pen" as he had often done in other situations, he must ask Cravath to take only fifty dollars a month out of his salary to be applied on his debt to the Association. He was sorry he could not say, "Let my salary wait;" this he hoped to do if he ever escaped from the present pinch.

Deering, one of the teachers, wrote Cravath in November: "I am needing a little money very much." He asked that thirty-five dollars be sent to his daughter at Oberlin and ten to him. He was sorry to call for money but seemed compelled.

Of all the workers at the school, Steele expected the most in fringe benefits. Osborn, who was never notified that Steele had made a special arrangement with Howard, refused to accept bills for extra food purchases eaten in the Steeles' room. Nor was Osborn happy with the slight upward adjustment made in his salary when he became business manager in addition to his duties as superintendent of the plantation. If the six hundred dollars were all the A.M.A. could pay, he said he would have to be satisfied, but he thought that if it could "pay Prof. Steele $1000 a year and doctor bills and freight bill and extra board for five hours" of work a day, he certainly should have an equal amount for from ten to fourteen hours, when he paid his own extras.

To be held responsible for the welfare of the school, while all authority over major and minor details was centered in New York, placed Nutting in a difficult position. The mansion's roof that leaked like a sieve, flooding with each rain the students who slept on the upper floor, did not have the importance in New York that it had in Tougaloo. Tarpaper, laid four years before over the original gravel and tar, under the direction of Beals, was now hopelessly broken. Every wind blew ten to forty more feet of paper to the ground. The cost of a new roof would be considerable, but delay would be hazardous for the students and would further rot the cornice and the main timbers. The carpenters estimated that it would take at least $1,000 to put the outside of the building in order. Approval from New York was not granted.

The cistern, another matter subject to New York's order, was a point of friction. The year before, the household was driven to drink water from the pond. Again in the past summer the school was reduced to one foot of water before unseasonal rains replenished the supply. An additional cistern, authorized by Gen. C. H. Howard and dug at great labor, had never been bricked for lack of money. It had begun to cave in and would endanger the foundation of the men's hall. Nutting asked Cravath if he could authorize forty dollars to brick it or if it should be filled at nearly equal expense in labor. Approval was given to brick it but no money was sent. With the school's credit exhausted, the work was not done.

At the height of the financial worries, Miss Ferguson, one of the school's most robust lady teachers, fell ill while attempting to help the overworked matron. She barely escaped brain fever, Nutting wrote, and required rest for some time. Unless the matron, Miss E. M. Evans, who had won "golden opinions" for her work, got another assistant, she herself would almost certainly break under the double strain. Duties to the kitchen and dining room required her full attention, while the girls' dormitory needed constant vigilance from five-thirty in the morning until ten-thirty at night and "one eye open all night." When Miss Evans threatened to quit, Nutting, without waiting for Cravath's approval, engaged as her assistant Mrs. Grover, the bride of one of the carpenters working on the grounds. She asked only a teacher's wage of fifteen dollars a month, and Nutting could only hope Cravath would approve.

Dissensions did not absorb all of the staff's attention. Nutting inaugurated the department of theology with a broad range of courses. The Greek books he ordered were, after a long delay, sent by the New York secretaries with some misgivings regarding the appropriateness of a study of Greek in a labor school for freedmen. But Nutting assured them that only the best scholars would be allowed to study Greek and that, were the secretaries to see the way he used his books, they would approve. Because of the A.M.A.'s nondenominational policy, Nutting could not actively recruit students to enter the ministry of the Congregational church. Since Congregationalism was practically unknown in the South, and the students were "either Baptists, Methodists, or nondescripts," he was, he said, manufacturing a ministry for every denomination except the one he loved best.

Nutting submitted to the secretaries several suggestions for changes in the school and the plantation. Among them was one to decrease the number of courses a student could take concurrently. Previously he had followed the procedure already in effect, not realizing at first the difference in capacity of these "adult children" and the long-trained youth of the North.

Another suggestion, with which Osborn heartily concurred, was to rent or lease most of the land for sharecropping, retaining only sufficient acreage to provide for the school's consumption of garden, orchard, poultry, and stock products. This change, Nutting contended, would avoid the problems involved in raising cotton. In addition to the usual cotton farmer's problems of unpredictable weather and fluctuating prices, Tougaloo had no labor supply during the summer recess. Abolishing cotton planting would diminish interference with the school's educational program and assure a good table in the boarding hall.

To encourage the Negroes of the state to assume more responsibility for Tougaloo University, Nutting planned a library and music hall to be financed by them. Miss A. W. Underwood, a black employee, and two students were sent out to their own people to solicit $500–$1,000 necessary for its construction. J. K. Deering, who had recently taken over the religious and missionary work as an added assignment, was happily surprised when his congregation gave $86 toward the building.

With a natural talent for mechanics, Nutting developed several labor-saving contrivances. In this way he hoped to reduce the number of working girls needed in the kitchen and boarding hall and to make room for more paying scholars. "A simple sliding cupboard, raised by a wheel cable, saves an amount of time equal to the labor of three working girls. . . . A winch and pulley at the cistern, discharging water in the kitchen and pantry above, saves one girl's labor."

A more spectacular success was his washer. It was attached to an engine and enabled four or five girls to do the washing which previously employed twenty or more. At the same time it eliminated the need of two boys to carry water in buckets. The white neighbors, upon learning that seventeen hundred pieces had been washed between breakfast and supper, were so impressed that they asked the school to do their laundry for a fair price. Nutting thought such an arrangement might provide enough money to employ a laundress and thereby relieve the matron for whom the washing was rather too much anyway.

By repairing the turning lathe Nutting hoped to be able to produce more of the school's furniture and to develop some marketable items to give the school an added source of revenue. He had experimented during the previous spring with a few neat and supposedly durable camp stools, but he had "calculated on white usage." As rocking chairs they came to grief. Henceforth he would build, he said, with a view to endurance.

Another item which Nutting hoped to market was moss. Moss, which could be found in unlimited supply in the

Tougaloo forests, was selling in Jackson for six cents a pound. Since the process of curing was relatively simple, Nutting thought the younger class of boys could be set at the task. If Cravath approved, the president was ready to give this experiment a trial.

Notwithstanding all Nutting's ideas to eliminate labor and to produce some salable items, Cravath was adamant in his demand that the expenses be cut. Having already reduced expenditures to the bare necessities, the staff saw no place to retrench further unless work were stopped on the intermediate building. Osborn wrote Cravath that, while he had originally advised against the building, he now felt that with all materials on the ground the carpenters should be retained to finish the work. Nutting stated that his summer speaking had brought in money which was earmarked for the building. He reminded Cravath that, even with the new building and the old slave pen at the rear of the mansion which was being remodeled to house some boys, students would still be crowded to a point endangering their health. The boys, he said, were much disappointed to be put three in a bed.

Nevertheless Cravath ordered the carpenters who were working on the intermediate building discharged and the number of students who did not pay cash or whose work did not produce an income reduced. With heavy heart Nutting sent some ten students home. Several had come long distances and had no money for the return trip. "Not one but wept," and some "seemed to be almost in despair feeling that they had lost their only chance of an education." They were willing to work and there was work enough needed to employ fifty men all winter, he wrote, but it would bring in no money. For this reason, he said, from one to six applicants were turned away daily because they could not pay.

The several appeals from Osborn and Steele and the invitation from Nutting, asking that Cravath visit Tougaloo, resulted in the arrival at the end of November, of James F. Claflin, a special representative of the A.M.A. When he compared Tougaloo with the noble work being done at Fisk, Talladega, Atlanta, and other A.M.A. institutions which he visited en route to Mississippi, Claflin was extremely indignant over the "criminal imbecility" of the work at Tougaloo. The disease was too serious, he wrote, to be cured by correspondence. If Cravath could not come to Tougaloo before Christmas, Claflin announced, he intended to return to New York to lay before the secretaries a full statement of affairs.

Claflin professed to find a state of mutual dissatisfaction among the teachers. Nutting responded: "When you load a team too heavily, the horses will snarl." Everyone at the school, he said, was forced to attempt impossibilities for lack of means. The matron was trying to keep a boarding house under indescribable disadvantages. The manager was asked to provide well and cheaply with neither money, credit nor a wholesale trade. Both were expected to keep everything in order, while all labor which did not bring in a profit was eliminated. The primary teacher was asked to work with her lips "blue and her teeth chattering and her pupils' ditto." Until that term all the teachers had taught in a room having no heat. Nutting said that when he attempted it, he took a chill and immediately bought a stove. Under such conditions, he thought, one could expect to find only disheartened and cross people.

Claflin's departure for New York on December 15 was followed by a rash of resignations sent to Cravath. The matron, Miss Evans, at first merely stated she was not capable of managing the household at Tougaloo. Gen. C. H. Howard had promised her thirty dollars a month if she succeeded. "You will have to inquire of others," she wrote, "in regard to my success and pay me according to my work."

To be sure that Cravath understood what her job entailed, she explained her duties: She was responsible for the students' and teachers' tables, for sending meals to the Nutting and Steele families, and to Mrs. Osborn since her confinement. Mrs. Nutting, herself as "helpless as a baby," required the laundry of her babe's things to be specially done. In short, Miss Evans claimed, she had a school and three families to look after. If peace were to be maintained these families should be put by themselves. Her washing averaged nearly two thousand pieces each week. She was grateful for a good washing machine, but it was off in a shop where there was no place to leave the clothes. She had to receive them in the dining room and kitchen. Her irons had to be heated on a small cook stove where the greater part of the cooking was done. "Indeed," she wrote, "the confusion has made me nearly crazy if not entirely so and will make anyone you send to take my place the same."

Steele wrote Cravath that for two years he had worked hard and had thought he might make the normal department a model of its kind. But since he could no longer do satisfactory work, he asked to be relieved at the end of the semester. He attached no blame to President Nutting who, under the circumstances, had perhaps done all he could.

Other staff members gave notice. Both H. E. and M. E. Smith resigned, stating it was impossible to do good teaching under the existing circumstances and adding that the corruption of morals and manners among the faculty was fearful. E. D. Hart tendered her resignation and suggested that the A.M.A. should send no one to the primary department until there was a decent classroom. On December 15 Hattie Ferguson sent in her resignation, and Celestia A. Bailey followed suit three days later. Osborn wrote Cravath that, while he was willing to remain, he would not want to do so if anyone thought he was not satisfactorily filling his position.

Nutting, wanting the Association's secretaries to be free to act according to their best judgment, offered to yield without opposition or hard feeling and to assist a new man, should one be found for the institution. He admitted he was disappointed to have Claflin go back to New York rather than to have Cravath come to Tougaloo. "We have not so far lost confidence in the secretaries as to expect less from your coming than from his going," he wrote. He closed his letter with an urgent appeal for help which should be given quickly but not rashly. He thought no person could decide what ought to be done at Tougaloo on the basis of one day of observation. "Blame me if I deserve it," he concluded, "but let me understand the ground of censure."

4

Claflin's Revolution

AFTER A SERIOUS ILLNESS, James F. Claflin, member of a law and land office in Chicago, determined to devote the balance of his life to God and humanity. Long an admirer of the American Missionary Association's work, he offered his services to Gen. C. H. Howard without salary but with the option of drawing expense money if his own private funds proved inadequate. General Howard suggested that he be commissioned by Cravath as a professor of mathematics and as a general investigator to visit several A.M.A. schools for a period of two or three months each. It was under this arrangement that he had first visited Tougaloo University in November 1873. After a short visit, he went to New York in December to confer with Cravath. The executive office of the A.M.A. then sent him back to Mississippi with authority to make such changes as he desired in the operation of Tougaloo University.

When Claflin returned on December 31, Nutting found himself in a difficult and humiliating position with his authority superseded by Claflin. He considered resigning but decided to leave his fate in the hands of the New York secretaries. Insisting that the problem was not one to be solved at a glance, Nutting asked Secretary Cravath to come south to see for himself before he rushed to extreme action.

Nutting remained until the middle of April, but with Claflin's decision to "assume the reins until *the New Pres.*

should arrive," personnel changes were made with rapidity. The resignation of Professor Steele was accepted, and he was reassigned by the A.M.A. to LeMoyne College in Tennessee. Osborn's halfhearted resignation was refused on the recommendation of Claflin, who found him "a good fellow . . . working as well as he knows how," though he probably could never be made to be systematic. Claflin thought that Osborn's dissatisfaction with his salary could be overcome if the secretaries would "put it to him" on the basis of mutual sacrifice. He dismissed Mrs. Grover, Miss Evans's assistant, as an inefficient person.

Miss Evans acquiesced in Cravath's urgent request that she remain and she agreed to do her work faithfully, trusting in God for strength of mind and body until she could be relieved. She asked, however, to know what her pay would be for the time already served. Again she reminded Cravath that her day began at five in the morning and lasted until ten at night. In the country, she observed, she would be paid forty dollars a month for teaching in the public schools and charged only eight for board.

J. K. Deering, who was serving as pastor, was surprised to be dismissed, for Claflin had given him no intimation that his work was unsatisfactory. He thought he had done all that could be expected on the pastoral charge, and his missionary work promised openings for Sabbath Schools in the country where he planned to take some students as assistants. He was eager to continue working among the freedmen whom he believed he could help, and he wanted to remain in the South where his health had improved even under the pressure of his assignments. His most taxing work was the supervision of thirty to forty young men and boys from five-thirty in the morning until ten at night, a duty that Gen. C. H. Howard had not stipulated in his terms. In an attempt to satisfy both Deering and Claflin, the A.M.A. appointed Deering to Straight University in New Orleans. This change prompted Claflin to write New York: "I conclude you are about to bring Straight into as good condition as I found Tougaloo." Claflin volunteered the advice that Deering might be able to establish a Sabbath School, but he doubted he had "enough milk to nurse the infant." Whatever Claflin's estimate of Deering's ability, his departure left the school without a pastor, a supervisor for the difficult assignment of the men's hall, or a superintendent for the model school which consisted of primary and intermediate departments. Claflin was reduced to the necessity of putting an advanced student in charge of the model school.

While five teachers left Tougaloo, only two new teachers came. One decided after the first weekend that he could not accept the position. Of the other, Harrington, Claflin's first written comment was, "I like him." Five days later, however, he concluded that Tougaloo needed a *strong* man to supervise the men's hall. "Mr. Harrington is willing," he wrote Cravath, "but his head begins to trouble him already. He is likely to cave in any time."

While the staff decreased, the enrollment increased. Two more teachers were needed immediately. Claflin was willing to rehire Mrs. Grover or hire Mrs. Osborn for one. The other employee should be a man who was "good for something" and who could take charge of the model school. Claflin declared that no one at the school was fit to run it for a month should he be called away—always a possibility because of the illness which the year before had given him such a "narrow squeak" for his life. It was imperative, he said, that a president, not a cheap, second-hand man, be sent as soon as possible. Only a practical business man of good culture, willing to make noble sacrifices, could do this job. As a labor school, Tougaloo needed, he said, an abler man than might be tolerated in a strictly academic school. He offered to give personally five hundred dollars per annum toward the salary of a good man, but he would not give one cent to support shiftlessness.

Within the first week of Claflin's return a severe storm of three days' duration covered everything with sleet and ice. Water coming through the unrepaired roof and the paneless windows thoroughly drenched the inside of the mansion. With no wood cut ahead, the occupants were wet and cold. They were also low on staples because of the uncertainty of the school's future and Osborn's inability to pay existing debts.

Food which the railroad promised to deliver never arrived. At this inopportune time Claflin discovered that the two-thousand-bushel harvest of sweet potatoes had entirely disappeared within the past hundred days. Teachers and students alike were reduced to a diet of bacon and bread.

Claflin assured Cravath that an atmosphere of cheerfulness prevailed despite these trying hardships, and all laughed good naturedly over his inauspicious beginning. But for his part he could not understand how apparently rational men could have stayed year after year acquiescing to such conditions. He resolved never again to be caught in such a predicament.

The transportation of supplies had never been solved by Nutting. While the school owned four pairs of mules and horses, it had no wagon. During the storm, however, even if a wagon had been available, no team could have drawn supplies over the washed out roads. When the sun came out after the freeze, a horse which Osborn had earlier taken in on a debt was traded for a pair of oxen and some sweet potatoes. Claflin then laid in two hundred dollars' worth of provisions and bought a new wagon.

When the money to make good his promises of payment failed to arrive, Claflin was initiated into the worries which had beset every administrator at Tougaloo. He blamed the mails for the delay and himself for calculating too closely. He determined to sell his watch and clothes if necessary, for he resolved that the word of Tougaloo would be made to mean something.

To operate with efficiency and economy, Claflin revised the purchasing system. With the boarding department reduced to a regular bill of fare for each day of the week, it was a simple matter to plan ahead and to assure a steady stock of provisions. By keeping a list of needs, the school team and its new wagon could bring all supplies from Jackson in one weekly trip and save little freight bills of several dollars each. Some items were purchased as far away as New Orleans or Chicago when prices were advantageous.

All the while Claflin was pushing the building program, and the intermediate building was finished. The old slave pen, where in antebellum days manacled slaves were said to have been kept at night and fractious slaves were punished, was completely remodeled to serve as a dormitory. It was given the name of Boston Hall. The mansion received a new roof, some remodeling, and general repairs. The roof of the men's dormitory was raised to make two full floors which Claflin said not only gave more dormitory space but also improved the outside appearance. Thereafter the building was called Washington Hall. An extension of forty-two feet made to the rear of the boarding hall gave more space for dormitory rooms on the second floor and a dining room on the first floor which could accommodate one hundred and sixty students.

Students were made to conform to simple rules. Mats and scrapers were provided at the doors, and all doors were given latches. Any youth who failed to make proper use of them was quickly convinced that he had "better never been born." Noise was no longer tolerated at the tables in the dining room. Tools on the plantation were not allowed to "peep . . . from the leaves of every secluded corner," but hoes, shovels, and all tools looked as though they were on company drill in the tool house. Midnight rambles to fancy plantations and gatherings for the light fantastic were strictly prohibited. Under the new regime, Claflin boasted, the pigs were obedient, the calf restrained his appetite and the stock was shut up. Fences prevented the prodigal cow from living on husks in the next plantation. So docile had the animals become, he assured Cravath, that "If system could accomplish it, the very pigs would lay eggs and the rooster give milk."

For accounts contracted before January 1, 1874, Claflin accepted no responsibility, leaving them with Osborn. He assigned all new accounts and the general bookkeeping to Harrington, the normal school teacher. Students were required to pay half their ten-dollar monthly board and room expense in cash. This method assured funds to cover the actual food purchases which Osborn figured at five dollars a month per student. A teacher's board was somewhat more.

The students who worked for half their expenses—nearly the whole student body—were divided into gangs and put under a foreman of their own choosing. They all worked two and a half hours each afternoon and five and a half hours on Saturday, with Osborn or Claflin supervising. If tardy, lazy, or neglectful, a student had his pay docked accordingly. Claflin claimed that more work was done for half board than formerly was done for full board. The team's time was also economized by the systematic labor of the students. The chopped wood was hauled to the shed to satisfy the voracious appetite of the school's fourteen fireplaces; stoves would have been more economical but would have required an initial outlay of cash.

While the workers were on duty, the rest of the students were under the eye of a teacher. In the evening, study hours were observed from seven to nine-thirty in the schoolroom, eliminating study in the students' rooms which Claflin said amounted to nothing. Also in the evenings classes were conducted for a few railroad hands.

Fridays were set aside for miscellaneous activities. Before intermission there were rhetorical exercises. After intermission the girls received instruction in sewing, cutting, mending, and making their own clothes. The boys meanwhile were drilled in the common facings, positions, and marchings to cure them of their "cringing manners, slouchy postures, and shuffling gait" inherited from the old plantation days. Over all the work Claflin kept a close check, with each department reporting daily attendance, tardinesses, and absences to him.

Because Claflin's days at Tougaloo were so full that, as he once said, he had not even time to trim his corns, he was unable to do as much missionary work as he desired. Sunday, however, he rounded up nineteen miscreants playing marbles and took them to Sabbath School. Regular Bible readings were conducted at the old slave quarters by the school; and whenever the weather permitted, one of the faculty members held services at Lake Church several miles out in the country. With more hands the missionary work could have been greater, but Claflin emphasized he would rather have no more hands than to "have shiftless or lazy or sick or gossipy ones." Anyone coming down here, he wrote, who "counts his hours of work will never build up this school; a person must come here . . .

[to] work for one greater than the A.M.A. and be willing to work till the blood comes without whining. . . . Thank God, we are rid of all Drones." The church services conducted by Claflin or G. R. Warner, a new teacher, were instrumental in converting a number of students, among them the son of I. D. Shadd, Speaker of the House of Representatives in Jackson. Miss M. E. Smith attested to the outpouring of the Holy Spirit in a way she had never seen before at the school. Without excitement, she said, the deep and silent workings of the Spirit had been felt and the students who were leaving at the end of the term to teach would go with new determination and a desire to work for their Master.

Although Nutting "tried to behave" as a "weaned child," he could not entirely overcome his resentment at Claflin's high-handed manner. Most of the important changes Claflin made, Nutting conceded, were good. In fact, they had been included in his own plan of reorganization drawn up in the previous October. Money required for their execution, which Cravath could never find for Nutting, was somehow available to Claflin. Less obvious factors had also militated against changes during the fall. Nutting had lost his sunny-haired little boy, and Mrs. Osborn had been so critically ill before and after the birth of her child that Nutting could not worry Osborn with major changes on the farm. Claflin had the good fortune, Nutting thought, to arrive just as these troubles were clearing and was therefore free to effect constructive changes.

Two things which Claflin did, however, Nutting declared he would not have done. He would not have been so harsh in dealing with the students and faculty. He could never see the wisdom, he added, in "battering a man's teeth out to drive a fly off his chin." Nor would he have worked for appropriations from the state. Nutting could not understand why the A.M.A., which had always opposed state support of Catholic schools in New England, should feel it right to seek state support for its school in Mississippi.

With an enthusiasm suggesting an interest in political manipulation, Claflin worked to increase the state appropriations for the normal school. In February 1874, while the senatorial contest was at its height and no one wanted to offend anyone, he "shoved persistently" to get several bills approved and to get the treasurer to pledge him the funds. Governor Ames's economy drive made it doubtful for a while that anything would be appropriated for Tougaloo, but Claflin determined at least to make the legislators familiar with his features before they adjourned.

Unavoidably absent on March 18, when the debate on the bill was most heated, Claflin returned the next day to receive the congratulations of his friends in the legislature on the passage of an appropriation bill in the Senate. When Claflin insisted on seeing the bill before it went to the governor, he discovered the clerk of the House had failed to add the amendment which Claflin had sent to the desk of the Speaker and which was passed by the House and duly recorded in the Journal. Without this amendment, Claflin felt, the entire appropriation would go to the Holly Springs Normal School. Tougaloo's friends in the Senate were chagrined and tried unsuccessfully to recall the bill. Claflin then struck with all his force for a new bill of $10,000–15,000 although he knew the difficulty of getting it passed since many members of the legislature believed that Tougaloo would share in the previous bill. On March 28, by a majority of ten in the House and only one in the Senate, the bill was passed, giving Tougaloo $10,000 for a normal school building conditional on the A.M.A.'s providing $15,000 for the same building. Claflin also succeeded in arranging for a supplemental bill which divided the former appropriation of $9,000, which otherwise would have gone to Holly Springs Normal School.

After his six days in Jackson to guide the bills through the legislative process, Claflin took the train to Chicago where his immediate appearance was demanded in a court case. Upon his return to Tougaloo he found a letter from the none-too-happy secretaries in New York who questioned the wisdom of the fight in the legislature, which might in the long run lose friends for Tougaloo. They asked for an explanation of the close vote. Claflin wrote in reply that it was due to the bad "oder" (sic) of the institution. Even Senator Warner, one of Tougaloo's trustees, had said he considered it his duty to vote against even one dollar for Tougaloo. Claflin claimed he afterward convinced Warner so thoroughly that he voted for the bill and also for the second and third bills which passed by increasing majorities, indicating there were no lasting hard feelings. He added that Sen. H. Cassedy, a leading Democrat, and several other Democrats were favorably impressed by an address that Claflin made on education and voted for one or more of the appropriation bills. While it was true, as the New York secretaries had heard, that the auditor vowed he would not issue the warrants, Claflin thought he would change his mind. If not, Claflin believed, since he had made a friend of the attorney general and also of the leading judge of the supreme court, he could get a favorable decision from the attorney. If that proved not enough, he would get a mandamus which the auditor would have to honor. However, Claflin had already had a pleasant talk with him and believed he had "found the right string to pull to relieve his scruples. . . . I am on the pleasantest terms with the Governor [Ames] now," Claflin wrote, "whose reception I attended . . . and though he was a little facetious over our getting the $15,000 when he told us we could have but $5,000 yet he is square and will help me I think." Claflin felt it prudent to add, however, that while there was no time limit on the $10,000 it should be used before the legislature met again, lest it revoke the act.

Lack of a clear line of authority plagued Claflin no less than the earlier administrators and worked to undermine his effectiveness as superintendent and to increase his disenchantment with the A.M.A. When Harrington on April 14 came to take his leave for the train, Claflin learned for the first time of his resignation. Harrington gave no reason except private and family affairs. Claflin could only conclude Harrington had been relieved of his duties by the New York office which had not consulted Claflin. He was further offended by Cravath's letter claiming the right to discuss his actions with the teachers under his charge. This claim seemed so contrary to the agreement made when Claflin accepted his commission as to relieve him from all further obligation to the A.M.A. But because he did not want to interrupt the students' educational and religious progress, he determined to remain. Though his health was steadily worsening, he hoped "these poor simpletons" might not suffer a great loss.

During the second week of June 1874, Claflin was again called to testify in a court case in Chicago, and a return to Tougaloo so close to the end of the term seemed inadvisable. Claflin, in terminating his commission, felt some summary of the vast changes of the past six months should be attempted, but he thought those who had not seen the school as it was when he came to it could not understand the improvement. Nevertheless, a few simple facts stood out. The legislature had enlarged the appropriations, the boarding hall had become self-supporting, and fortunately the cisterns had been put in order or the school would have been compelled to close during the spring drought. The roof of the mansion and the enlargement of the building were nearing completion, leaving Osborn, Claflin thought, little work on them beyond following the instructions he was leaving. The bills were paid except for current items and debts incurred before Claflin came. The changes in the intellectual, religious, and moral training, while not as great as he had hoped, were not less important than the physical improvements. In a final word of advice, he admonished the New York secretaries to delay no longer in obtaining an efficient president, adding that their failure to provide one was to him unaccountable.

In a spirit of humility seldom seen in this energetic man, he wrote that none was more aware than he of the faults in his work or of his personal unworthiness of the blessings God had granted. He laid the work down, he said, with gratitude that he had been permitted to carry it so far. He took satisfaction, he concluded, in the knowledge that he had tried to do all faithfully and well, and he thanked the secretaries for their courtesy to him.

Miss E. M. Smith, speaking for those on the faculty and staff who were truly sorry to see Claflin leave, wrote New York that if there were any misunderstanding between Mr. Cravath and Mr. Claflin, she hoped it would be settled soon, as the school needed this noble Christian. He was stern, but just, she explained, and was respected and loved by the students.

Osborn might have pictured another side as he struggled with business that Claflin had described as all but finished. The bills for the buildings mounted, and Osborn had to wangle payment from the home office, which reverted to its old idea that the school's proceeds should suffice. Because the New York secretaries did not authorize the painting of the new roof and the new structures, these investments were open to deterioration from the weather. A law suit which Claflin had instigated over a mule went against the school after the expenditure of much time and money, and more threats of suits were received. The legislature was disaffected over the $10,000 appropriation which Claflin had pressured it to pass and eventually rescinded it. "Mr. Claflin," Osborn observed, "seemed to be unfortunate in getting the ill will of a great many men here."

Osborn wrote the secretaries in New York that "Enemies" of education for the colored circulated rumors that Tougaloo University had broken up and would not reopen in the fall. The report seemed credible because Claflin had been too busy to get out a catalog. But as people learned of the new building and grounds improvements, Tougaloo's prestige and desirability increased. Lt. Gov. A. K. Davis, a black, remarked on visiting the campus that Tougaloo would soon have the nicest school in the state. New student applications came in greater numbers than ever, and former students were eager to return.

The entire faculty was on hand for the opening of school on October 6, 1874. Of the new president, Osborn wrote that all were well pleased with "Proff Darling." With improved physical facilities, a full faculty, more students, and a new president, the coming school year looked promising.

5

"Hanging in There"

THOUGH L. A. DARLING HAD BEEN DISAPPOINTED in his assignment to Tougaloo, he wrote the A.M.A. upon arrival in the fall of 1874 that the school was well organized and under perfect control. Teaching was thorough and systematic, and moral training was strict. Darling judged G. R. Warner, whom the A.M.A. secretaries had returned with some misgivings, to be the right man for the right place.

The new administrator regretted that he could not report as favorably about the plantation, but he found it unprofitable. The livestock ate too much produce without benefit to the school. Darling's suggestions regarding farm operations were spurned by Osborn, who claimed full control of business and farm management. Darling wrote New York for confirmation of his authority and the exact position that Osborn held.

Making matters worse for Darling, Warner supported Osborn's assertion with his own claim to control over the normal school. These two men declared that no president had been appointed and that they were capable of managing their departments without one. Actually, though Darling had specifically asked the A.M.A. before he went to Tougaloo whether he would be president, the A.M.A. had never given him an unequivocal answer.

Osborn and Warner had their supporters, some of whom were high ranking. T. W. Cardozo, State Superintendent of Education, and James Hill, Secretary of State (both black),

43

wrote the A.M.A. that Professor Warner and Mr. Osborn had given the state members of the board of trustees entire satisfaction and if untrammeled in their work would make Tougaloo an honor to Mississippi and to the Association. With so much political excitement brewing in the state, the board desired to keep the schools free from turmoil and confusion. Because Osborn and Warner had thus far succeeded, it would be regrettable, the board believed, for anyone to be placed above the two men. Hill reminded the A.M.A. that state support would depend on continuance of a harmonious relationship. Isaiah Mitchell of Jackson wrote Cravath that Warner was a most excellent man and universally liked.

Osborn wrote the A.M.A. secretaries his "unbiased" view of the controversy between Darling and Warner, carefully avoiding any mention of his own involvement. He said that ill feeling between the two was detrimental to the school, especially when political affairs were so turbulent. The problem as Osborn analyzed it was that Darling felt the A.M.A. had given him absolute control of the school. At the same time Warner felt that the board of trustees expected certain results which he could not give under Darling's direction, inasmuch as their ideas regarding education were at variance. Osborn suggested that one man should be at the head of both the normal school and the institution.

Darling and Warner agreed to ask the A.M.A. to reassign one or the other of them. Darling believed that a female teacher sent in Warner's place would promote efficiency, economy, and harmony. However, he urged the secretaries not to wait until a lady teacher was found before removing Warner. "We'll be happier doing extra duty than living as we do."

Rather than the quick action requested by Darling, there were weeks of drifting. Cravath of the New York office held out hope that he would visit the school soon. Each train was anxiously awaited with everyone hoping to see Secretary Cravath step off it. On December 28 Darling telegraphed in desperation, "COME THIS WEEK WITHOUT FAIL ABSOLUTELY NECESSITY DEMANDS IT."

Cravath had not yet arrived when the board of trustees met on January 6, 1875. Though Warner had left two days before, the board refused to accept his resignation, insisting that it should have been consulted. Darling persuaded the members to take no action until Cravath came. At stake was the school's appropriation from the state.

Cravath sent Secretary George Whipple to Tougaloo in his stead. Whipple's hurried visit somewhat relaxed tensions at the school, and Cardozo and Hill took what Osborn described as a more sensible view. They seemed ready to confirm Darling as principal. Friends from the legislature who visited the school expressed their satisfaction, and the regular appropriation was anticipated. Darling exulted, "You have commissioned me to make this the best school in the state. I have done so and today it is acknowledged by those who are competent to judge."

This eminence which Darling attributed to the school was hard won. Besides his struggle for the right to direct the school, he had to develop a cooperative and efficient staff on a meager budget and less than full cooperation from the New York office. When Warner left, Darling insisted that only a competent music teacher would be acceptable as his replacement. Such a teacher failing to arrive, Darling suggested the employment of his seventeen-year-old daughter who could play the piano and, with study and practice, might meet the school's need. The cost of bringing her to Mississippi would be around $150, as someone would have to accompany her on the trip; in the meantime the school made out with Sadie Wilson at the organ.

Eventual arrival of Fannie Freeman to fill the position of music teacher provoked an indiscreet outburst from Darling. Secretary Whipple took offense at the tone of Darling's letter criticizing Miss Freeman and demanded an apology. Darling admitted he wrote under the influence of a strong feeling of disappointment but said he meant no disrespect. He felt some mistake had been made because Miss Freeman had not been told she would be expected to be proficient in leading group singing and teaching music. "This statement of facts must be my apology for any seeming implication of blame, together with the feeling we had that other institutions were cared for while we were left to the last."

By autumn of 1875 Darling had resigned himself to getting along with the forces assigned him. With political turbulence and physical violence rampant in the community as Democrats sought to overthrow the Reconstruction government, student enrollment had dropped too low to justify employment of a music teacher. The school no longer owned band instruments, as Osborn and Cravath had arranged for their sale, ironically, because they were not being used. Miss Freeman could teach beginning piano, and Darling's daughter, Miss Lena, managed quite well with vocal music. Darling took satisfaction in the spirit of the teachers. They were willing, earnest, and united; thus the work prospered even under adverse conditions.

Severing Osborn's relationship with the school was more difficult than severing Warner's. Osborn had been at the school longer, had control of business management as well as the farm, and was enmeshed with politicians at the state capital.

With Osborn and Darling both trying to economize in compliance with A.M.A.'s request, each blamed the other for extravagances. Osborn complained that family (boarding school) expenses were greater than receipts because of better living than the school could afford or than was necessary. Darling, however, attributed the budget imbalance to Osborn's extravagance. "If I am to control please give him instructions. If he is to be supreme in finances, then I must not be held responsible." The two men reached a modus vivendi which lasted until April 1876. Then Darling exploded with, "What are you intending to do in regard to Mr. Osborn?" It was absolutely necessary, he wrote, that Osborn's connection with the school cease during the coming summer. Darling did not write his reasons, stating only that Secretary Strieby already knew how unsuitable Osborn was for the position.

Darling's feeling toward Osborn was shared by students. Robert Martin, the Granberry brothers, and those students who had been in the school longest circulated a petition demanding Osborn's removal for being incompetent and lacking sympathy for the colored people. Darling granted Osborn's request for an opportunity to meet with the students, hear their charges, and explain any misunderstanding. Many of the charges proved false and frivolous. Students prepared another petition, and they were about to send it to New York when Darling positively forbade their doing so. He told them that if a change were made, it ought not to be done in a way that would give their political enemies power to do them injury.

Darling's sympathies, however, were with the students. He too believed Osborn incompetent. If a man were to manage his private affairs as loosely, he would soon come to poverty. Under Osborn's control the farm had never been an integral part of the educational program. To make it so, Darling thought, it would be easier to direct the work himself than to act through Osborn. Darling did not want to face the students in the fall of '76 having done nothing. Once he had stood in the gap, but to do it again because of administrative inaction was unthinkable. It pained Darling to write these things, and he would be in a delicate position should Osborn learn of it. But he felt that unless a change were made he could not direct the institution.

Osborn again turned to his political friends for support. The board of trustees passed a resolution (May 2, 1876) saying it was not bound by any society, corporation, or individual for the selection of teachers. Osborn assured the A.M.A. there would be no difficulty. "I know the appointed members of the board are willing to continue the same as usual. I took pains to get their views before they were appointed and requested the Governor to make the appointment of the men we have. The opposition all came from ex-officio members." Because members of the board were among his personal friends, Osborn was certain that they would comply with any request he made.

Letters sent to the New York office by men from the state capital strengthened Osborn's claim to political influence. Thomas L. Gathright, State Superintendent of Education, wrote that the state board of trustees would look upon removal of Mr. Osborn as a calamity. He said Osborn's judgment, industrious and temperate habits, and strict business integrity had

gained for him the confidence and friendship of the community. F. B. Pratt, senator from Canton and a board trustee, wrote
that it would be bad policy to remove Mr. Osborn. The previous
year's liberal appropriation of $3,000 had been largely the re-
sult of Osborn's influence and the confidence which southern
men had in his management. Democrats who came into office
in November 1875 did not favor state aid for institutions which
were under financial control of northern men. Anyone coming
from the North to supersede Mr. Osborn, however well qualified, would displease the prejudiced legislature. Men in the
legislature were especially opposed to outsiders having financial control of schools for colored people. Yet because the legislature had gone on record as favoring education for the colored
race, Pratt thought it might be generous in appropriations for
Tougaloo University if it were allowed a voice in selection of
the superintendent.

Faced with a choice between state aid and retention of Osborn, Darling conceded defeat. Men indebted to Osborn for
their appointment to the board would naturally rebel against
his removal. Also, Darling knew that Democrats in the flush of
full power would be glad for any excuse to withdraw state appropriations to a school for colored. Grateful that he still maintained a warm personal friendship with Osborn, Darling determined to work harmoniously with him. He would attempt
to control feeling among students for as long as necessary.
More than ever before, he felt his dependence upon God and
looked to Him who alone could guide the school through days
of darkness and doubt.

But Darling was soon to reverse his decision. Student actions showed such strong feelings against Osborn that Darling
decided it imperative that he leave. Darling pushed Osborn
into sending New York his resignation. This accomplished,
Darling left the school in Osborn's charge while he went to the
Nation's Centennial celebration in Philadelphia during the
first part of July.

When in the East, Darling had a conference with the A.M.A.
secretaries in New York, which left him bewildered. Unknown
to him Osborn had written them undermining Darling still

further and requesting that they make no positive arrangements regarding Tougaloo until he visited New York about the middle of July. The governor had commissioned him to find and arrest former Superintendent of Education Cardozo (black) who had embezzled $2,000 of Tougaloo's funds. Though Osborn's last year at Tougaloo had been most unpleasant, he said he was still using his influence to the advantage of the school.

With heavy heart Darling left New York. The secretaries had not reappointed him; they had, in fact, advised him to delay taking his family back to Mississippi, and he knew that the Mississippi state school board might repudiate him. Yet, believing his influence was needed at Tougaloo, he hastened back, accompanied by his family, to protect the school property which Osborn had left.

Except for some petty thefts, Darling found the physical property in better condition than the emotional climate. Osborn had prejudiced the trustees against Darling. Miss Freeman had exacerbated the trustees by accusing Darling of having forced teachers to join in student socials where she had been grossly insulted by young men who asked her to march with them. (Dancing not being permitted, marching formations were used as entertainment.) Furthermore, she had gone to Superintendent Gathright and berated him for wanting to send a "Nigger Teacher" to Tougaloo, saying he could count her out if that happened.

At the board meeting on August 1, 1876, Gathright presented for consideration all charges filed against Darling by Osborn and Miss Freeman. Some of the men who were previously resisting Darling's return were among the four Democrats and one Republican at the meeting over which the governor presided. Darling explained that in former years teachers did not feel degraded for having mingled with students at social gatherings. Teachers during the past year were allowed to mix or not as they preferred. After Darling's explanation, Miss Freeman's charge was discounted as an effort to set the "anti-color part of the trustees" against him. Superintendent Gathright called the meeting a complete triumph for Darling. The board unanimously elected him as principal of the normal school, and the governor signed the certificate of election. To Darling the about-face of the board was nothing less than the triumph of right and a work of the Lord.

Obtaining the confidence of the A.M.A. secretaries proved more difficult for Darling. They were more inclined to believe Osborn, who declared the trustees were opposed to the appointment of a colored teacher, than to believe Darling's assertion that the trustees wanted to appoint Miss Smith, a Negro, and would have done so with Darling's approval had she not accepted another position. They continued to fret over the possibility of losing state appropriations, as Osborn predicted, and wrote Darling that if the $1,500 still due and all further state aid depended on a new school management, the A.M.A. would be obliged to find a new man.

In view of what Miss Freeman had said to Gathright and the trustees during his absence, Darling was shocked when the A.M.A. nominated her to teach during the ensuing year. Darling wrote the home office that pupils held strong sentiments against her for what she had said in July and that colored people in general considered her no friend of the race.

An exchange of letters between Darling and the New York office carried some incriminating remarks. Darling condemned the secretaries for taking counsel of an enemy (Osborn) while rejecting that of a friend (Darling). He thought the secretaries should have encouraged him when Osborn was trying to undermine him rather than leaving him to fight alone. Darling said he did not ask that the secretaries always accept his judgment, but he believed his faithfulness to the cause during the past two years qualified him to have their confidence in his integrity. "I have *fought* and *won* and now if you wish me to retire, I am ready."

Culminating these exchanges, Osborn was removed, and Darling threw himself wholeheartedly into management of the farm. Thinking it should be an integral part of the educational program, he tried to make it a model of efficiency. From daybreak until sunset he worked in the fields with farm hands and thus got about double the work out of them. He attempted to eliminate the waste which made the department a bill of expense.

By the opening of school Darling could exult over his accomplishments. He had gathered fodder in greater quantity than the school had ever known. This harvest would release the farm's corn for use in the boarding hall. The large room opposite the parlor held barrels of chips picked up from the grounds. He effected an economy by directing the matron, Miss Farrand, to boil rather than bake the sweet potatoes.

So pleased was Darling with his smooth and economical operation of the farm that he offered the New York office a proposition. If his wife, a very efficient woman, were made his assistant, she could do whatever was most needed—take his classes when his presence was required on the farm, assist in correspondence, or work on the accounts. She would enable him to do without another man and still do all things well. The A.M.A. could save expense, though Mrs. Darling should receive some compensation. If paying her was contrary to A.M.A. rules, the Association could increase his salary instead. Darling was willing that Strieby ask Miss Farrand, the matron, what she might think of such an arrangement.

Had Darling seen the letters Miss Farrand and others of the staff wrote New York he would have been less than pleased. The consensus was that he made a better farmer than teacher. With his outside duties he could not do justice to the school even if he had known modern methods. Students complained of the dull classes and longed for someone like Professor Steele to wake them up. The boys should have someone in charge of their hall at night. Understandably jittery since a robbery in Miss Dora Ford's room a few months past, the staff felt a man should be on the place when Darling was away. The New York secretaries were sufficiently impressed by the staff letters to decline Darling's proposition.

M. E. Burnham arrived from Maine on the first Saturday of November 1876, and he was everything Darling, the ladies, and the students could ask for except that he lacked the sine qua non—health. He had accepted the position hoping outdoor work in a southern climate would improve his physical condition. Because Darling expected another lady teacher soon, he placed Burnham temporarily in the classroom. However, Burnham's condition indicated he must be given an outside assignment. His performance there was just as satisfactory. Mrs. Darling took his classes except a few which he continued to hear.

Though Darling but six weeks before had advised making Mrs. Darling his assistant, he now urged that another teacher be sent immediately, as it was difficult for his wife to be away from her little one. But he assured the New York office that she would carry on until a replacement could be found. The school hoped for Miss Angell whom Burnham had recommended as a good Christian, a well educated, successful teacher, and a good musician. "We need a corps of teachers imbued with the missionary spirit and free from race prejudice," he wrote. "Such we have not had. Some we now have."

Burnham's popularity increased. The boys liked him because he did not "fly all to pieces" but was patient with them both in class and about their work. Teachers hoped New York would give him full charge of the school so they would not have to "drag longer in the same groove." Miss Farrand cheerfully prepared his special diet, denying the secretaries' contention that its extra expense should involve a salary adjustment. Darling praised Burnham for carrying out directions and running the farm as perfectly as Darling himself. Darling's one disappointment was that Burnham's limited strength precluded his supervising the boys' hall, a responsibility which continued to devolve upon Darling.

Yet Burnham needed to make no apology for the size of his assignment. He carried out Darling's frequent specific directions, oversaw the farm work, and trained the boys to be efficient in their labor on the farm. He had a class in calisthenics as well as senior classes in Latin, philosophy, and chemistry. Darling and Burnham alternated responsibilities for the Sunday services. When one preached, the other superintended the Sabbath School, heard a class, and took charge of the evening meeting.

Unfortunately Darling's increasing satisfaction with Burnham was not reciprocated. Near the close of the term, Burnham wrote Strieby that some changes should be made for the second term. He felt, as did the teachers, a need for classification of students. Contention was rife, he wrote, under the absolute and somewhat peculiar authority of Professor Darling. Some teachers were needlessly overworked; others busied themselves in work that were better not done. Burnham urged Strieby to investigate the situation personally when he made his contemplated visit to the school.

Except for the arrival of Miss Orra Angell on December 31, the new term got off to a poor start. Students and teachers grieved over the resignation of Miss McGrath, a highly esteemed teacher, though they were soon to find Miss Angell equally fine. Miss Harris, another well liked teacher, was piqued over too much work, so Mrs. Darling took some of her classes. The A.M.A.'s refusal to pay an administrator's wife irked Mrs. Darling. A faculty meeting, called at the request of Strieby who hoped that a frank discussion of differences would bring about understanding and harmony, opened old wounds and caused new ones. Ill feeling among faculty members had a demoralizing effect upon students. The entire senior class (four students) applied for teaching positions in public schools.

Through all the turbulence Miss Farrand, though opposed to the general school management, could report improved relations between Darling and herself. "If his pudding is too hot, he only shows it by drinking hastily of cold water. Indeed! I think he tries very hard to show consideration . . . for me; which he did not do last year." Again she wrote, "Mr. D. treats me beautifully—polite, since our plain talk."

Secretary Strieby arrived on the night of January 23 in the midst of all this dissension. Within twenty-four hours he presented a plan, the success of which he admitted would depend on Burnham's health. Darling was to be pastor and manager of the farm and of business. Burnham was to be principal of the school. The duties of both Burnham and Darling were to be drawn up by them and submitted to the A.M.A. office for approval. Strieby returned to New York, pleased that all problems had been so readily resolved.

Darling found difficulty in confining himself to his limited roles. No sooner had Strieby left than he proposed to the teachers a change of texts and a rearrangement of some classes, without consulting the new principal. Darling strayed again from his departments when he asked the four senior class members if they would be willing to transfer to Fisk or Talladega where, with larger classes, they might have better instruction. The idea appealed to the four young men. Darling promised to explore the possibility of having their scholarships transferred.

Unfortunately at this critical moment in the school's life, Burnham's disease threatened to become serious. It was felt that if he were to reach home alive he should leave immediately. Darling arranged to accompany him as far as Cleveland where his brother would meet them. With his heart full of sorrow on account of his regard for Burnham, and disappointment at not having him as a co-laborer, Darling wrote Strieby to ask that Burnham's salary be continued through the term, for he would have many expenses. Darling added a statement of advantages in transferring the senior boys' English scholarships to other institutions.

In Darling's absence the faculty panicked upon learning of his offer to the seniors. Before Darling's letter was delivered, Strieby received a telegram: "MR. DARLING GONE NORTH WITH MR. BURNHAM DARLING ADVISED SENIORS TO ENTER FISK THEY AND OTHERS WILL LEAVE UNLESS COMPETENT TEACHERS SENT IMMEDIATELY." Signed, "FACULTY."

At Strieby's request the Rev. H. W. Carter rushed to Tougaloo from Selma, Alabama. Carter telegraphed on February 2: "SENIORS ARRANGING TO TEACH AND ENTER HIGHER INSTITUTION NEXT YEAR OTHERS QUIET." Miss Harris submitted her resignation as preceptress and teacher. From the course pursued in regard to the senior class, she deduced that the normal school enrollment would decline.

Darling returned on the night of February 2 and tried to convince Carter of the advisability of sending senior students to another institution. Darling conceded that he might have been indiscreet in suggesting the idea of transfer to the young men before speaking to New York of it, but he thought he should be credited for immediately placing the matter before the secretaries, even before embarking on his emergency journey with Burnham.

After giving Darling a polite hearing, Carter advised Strieby to carry out the plan he had devised while at Tougaloo the week before. Darling was well liked as a man, considered a good disciplinarian, and able to manage the farm and accounts. As a pastor he was satisfactory. A new principal should be sent who was capable of teaching Latin and grading the classes—two areas in which the ladies felt Darling had failed. Because of diminished enrollment, the new principal might get along with fewer teachers.

Darling was particularly sensitive over the small attendance, feeling he was unjustly censured for situations beyond his control. Some students had not the means to return; many who might have attended Tougaloo as day scholars were going to public schools taught by former Tougaloo students; unqualified assistant teachers, necessary as an economy measure, were detrimental to the school's image; and senior boys would probably have gone into teaching even if the transfer had not been suggested.

Darling also felt that, while spite on the part of Miss Freeman had disaffected his faculty, he could have kept the teachers under control had he been on the grounds. His absence was caused by a mistake of the secretaries in appointing a man in poor health. Darling asked the secretaries to review his case to see if withdrawal of their censure, which cut him to the heart, were not justified.

Carter felt himself in an awkward position when he was placed temporarily in charge of Tougaloo. He could not keep the boys from teaching, though both he and Darling offered to lend money if they would stay. As a temporary officer he was limited to a holding action, for a new principal would have his own ideas regarding changes to be made. Impatient to shake off the responsibilities of Tougaloo and wanting to see New Orleans before he returned to his Selma duties, Carter left (February 24) as soon as he was assured that Thomas Chase had accepted the appointment. Chase's arrival, however, was delayed by a sudden illness in his family.

One familiar with the history of Tougaloo University can readily guess the nature of Chase's first problem. "I do not feel quite sure," he wrote Strieby, "that Mr. Darling feels . . . his work is to be subordinate to the general management and would suggest that you make this plain to him. . . ." It was unfortunate, Chase thought, that a deposed principal should remain on the grounds. Unless his moral and religious nature were unusually well developed, he would be troubled at improvements upon his administration, pleased at failures, and tempted to increase difficulties.

Initially Chase was favorably impressed by the welcome given him and his family, but before long he discovered the school had on its Sunday clothes during those first few days. He soon found a painful lack of system and a great want of application among students. The girls were rude specimens addicted to boisterous laughing, singing, and shouting. Lying, cheating, laziness, and stupidity were as natural to them as breathing. Keeping them awake during the hour and a half of study time in the evening was almost impossible. How much was due to the "nature of the beast" and how much to lack of discipline and thoroughness Chase could not say.

While Chase had originally intended making few early changes, he found it necessary to turn things upside down. Darling, in accepting changes, seemed as "placid as a May morning," and teachers "wore smiling countenances"; but Chase imagined they cursed him inwardly. Though pupils thought his new rules harsh, he believed they would come to like a tight hold on them.

Boys needed a housemother, but obtaining one would require a building which she could properly supervise. When Claflin remodeled the men's hall, economy had been carried to an extreme. Neither inside stairs nor an anteroom had been provided. In fact, Chase said there was not enough "waste room" to hang a broom. Builders had dispensed with sash-cord and window weights, allowing some of the sashes to sag more than an inch. This sag might have occurred in any event, as the peculiar soil of the area caused irregular sinking of buildings.

By May, Chase had evaluated the faculty and staff. He found Darling's mind too illogical and his education inadequate for a university pastor; he might make a good pastor of an A.M.A. church. Miss Angell was above average as a teacher and a good disciplinarian. While Miss Farrand did not come up to the standard required at Atlanta University, teachers and pupils respected her. Miss Ford had an excellent spirit but tended to be easy and conservative in her teaching. Miss Freeman was eager to do well and cheerfully accepted advice but was too old when she began teaching to be very successful. Miss Harris, of unusually good mind and heart, would be a good preceptress if she were well and strong. She was a superior nurse. Her moral and religious influence was an asset to the school but she did not want to return, and Chase thought it better that she not do so.

Chase's taut administration earned the respect and gratitude of teachers and students. Teachers enjoyed their well defined, purposeful, and more nearly equal duties. Students were less inclined to sulk or to be saucy, and they prepared their lessons with a zest not known in recent years. Miss Freeman summed up the change when she wrote Miss D. E. Emerson at the A.M.A. office, "There is a new atmosphere. . . . Teachers and scholars . . . work with renewed energy."

Darling was to be principal in name only, until the close of the term, with Chase holding the office in reality. While Chase doubted Darling had any extensive influence with the trustees, or that Darling was thinking of the good of the school, as he often said, this procedure would allow time for developments. At the May 9 board meeting Chase handed the trustees his resignation, but Darling failed to present his.

Darling's discharge reached him near the end of May. Disappointed but not yet defeated, he wrote Strieby in an attempt to persuade him of the injury his dismissal would cause the school. A stranger would need time to get acquainted with the thousand and one things that required attention. Darling said he would willingly stay another year at a greatly reduced salary. This was a new tune for Darling. During his tenure he had persistently attempted to get more money for his wife's services, for his own extra work, and even twenty-five dollars or more to cover the clothes he wore out while engaged in farm work after Osborn left. Later he offered to give up the pastorate if he could be the farmer. He wanted to remain where the Lord had owned and blessed his labors by using him to convert more than fifty souls and enabling him to strengthen and encourage the hearts of many Christians. He and Mrs. Darling wanted "to sink self out of sight" that they might do good for the people and smooth the way for those who came to labor.

Students rallied to the support of Darling. Angie Williams wrote the A.M.A. in behalf of the young ladies of the university, asking that all teachers be returned, including Professor Darling and his family. A petition was signed by fourteen students saying Professor Darling was their minister: "We cannot possibly give him up. We love him and his family." Though students echoed Darling's claim that he had no part in promoting the petition, there were obvious indications that he gave influence and cooperation. Darling announced from the pulpit that the young men would meet after the evening service. It was there that the petition was drawn up. Granberry, after telling Mrs. Chase that he had not talked with Darling about the petition, said, "Mr. Strieby is at Atlanta . . . so we shall send it there." He could hardly have known about Strieby had Darling not told him. Mrs. Chase told Granberry that the greatest need was for materials to build up a school. Granberry replied that he and the rest would like to stay if things went right but that they did not like so much quarreling among the teachers.

Reflecting on all the dissensions plaguing the school, Mrs. Chase thought it a great pity that people could not love one another better, but if all evil is universal good, she supposed, "We shall see the good of it on the other side."

6

Early Years in Retrospect

SURPRISINGLY, THE DIFFICULTIES OF THE EARLY years did not usually stem from the white community which was generally expected to be hostile toward Northerners interested in educating the former slaves. Instead, they originated in the school itself and in its parent organization, the American Missionary Association. Without ascribing fault, an analysis of the basic causes for some of the more common problems may be revealing. They might be considered under three headings: (1) the thin spread of resources, (2) the A.M.A. policies of administration, and (3) the peculiarities of a plantation school.

1) The heart of the A.M.A. was ever bigger than its resources, causing it to rely heavily on various outside sources for financial help. The difficulty in obtaining the Tougaloo property and putting up the first buildings was resolved only when the Freedmen's Bureau came to the school's aid.

The state of Mississippi made annual appropriations of from three thousand to forty-five hundred dollars during the years 1871–1877. These figures are deceptive, however, as the appropriations were paid in state warrants which fluctuated in value from sixty-five to eighty cents on the dollar. Debate ran continuously between the A.M.A. office and Tougaloo's administrators as to when these warrants should be cashed to realize the most on them. In some instances when they were held for a higher value, they actually fell in value. The case was such that the school·never could benefit from their immediate

59

use. On other occasions the delayed transaction was more rewarding, especially if a sale could be made to a landholder who could get face value in payment of his state taxes. If deterioration to property caused by postponement of the new roof, painting of a building, or bricking a cistern were considered—not to mention the delayed education and health safeguards—net increase, if any, was probably minimal. Warrants could be converted into state bonds which were worth more, but bonds could not be used to meet the school's current needs.

The superintendent of schools in Madison and Hinds counties each could usually be counted on for the support of one teacher at sixty dollars a month for five months, the length of the county school term. County warrants, however, were sometimes of even less value than state warrants. After Hinds and Madison counties built their own schools within a mile and a half on either side of Tougaloo, each superintendent reduced his contribution to around forty dollars per month for the county school term.

Tougaloo's plantation produced some revenue from rental of land or share cropping and, in the first years, from cotton. The time to sell cotton was as unpredictable as the time to sell warrants, with the result that the school could be in want while cotton was held in the hope of a rising market. In some cases friends of the A.M.A. loaned money on the cotton at no interest, to enable the school to wait for a better price.

Individuals and organizations sent special-purpose gifts. One man gave three hundred dollars to be used for student aid, but not for an endowment fund. Another man offered two thousand to a normal school which did not teach a dead language. Tougaloo qualified. Seeds for the garden valued at sixty-nine dollars, butter knives worth twelve, and a box of "duds" were typical ways friends in the North remembered the school. Some sent twenty-five or thirty dollars to furnish a room and one sent seventy-five to furnish the parlor.

Numbers gave at great sacrifice. A post office clerk sent fifteen dollars with a note saying it should have been paid earlier but he had been sick. One contributor wrote, "I wish it were possible for me to increase this little sum $1.00. . . . I am an aged and feeble woman with a small income." A ten-dollar money order was received with a note saying "I am poor but God has given me privileges of which the colored . . . are deprived." A contributor who, obviously, lacked the education which he wanted for the freedmen wrote, "Pleas find two Dollars for Freedmen it is not so much as usealy (but it is according to my means at presant). . . . You must except the will for the Deed this time." Literally thousands of such sacrificial gifts were received, most, no doubt, for the same underlying reason as expressed in a notation on a used envelope enclosed with the sender's donation of a dollar, "for Christ's cause."

Life membership in the A.M.A. at thirty dollars was recognized with a certificate which one might hang on the wall to encourage others to obtain one. The donor also received a life subscription to the *American Missionary*. Anyone reading this monthly journal was sure to respond to the vivid description of the work and its needs with additional donations.

An attractive certificate in legal language acknowledged gifts of money on which the Association assumed the obligation of paying interest during the donor's lifetime. People were also encouraged to remember the American Missionary Association in their wills.

Every month the *American Missionary* listed by states each donation from the smallest twenty-five cents to the largest, which might run into the thousands of dollars. The total amount of all gifts for a year amounted to about $300,000. The listing encouraged others to contribute and acted as a check of the receipts. The A.M.A. office was sure to receive a complaint if any gift was omitted.

No figures are available relative to the cost of soliciting and collecting this money, but a businessman in Chicago, who described himself as a regular contributor and firm believer in the work, suggested that fifteen percent of all gifts was used for administrative purposes. "I should feel more liberal towards the 'A.M.A.' if it did not take so much to 'run the machine,'" he wrote.

Gen. O. O. Howard of the Freedmen's Bureau, himself a Congregationalist and supporter of the A.M.A., believed that the Association had more schools than it could handle successfully. He contended that too many of its schools were not first class, largely because of a lack of competent administrators for whom the Association would have to pay better salaries. Salaries could be no higher if resources continued to be spread over too many projects. The big heart of the A.M.A. constantly led it to do just that—spread its limited resources over too many projects.

2) Given good administrators, which Gen. O. O. Howard believed was the A.M.A.'s great need, it is hard to conceive of Tougaloo's doing much better under the policies of the home office. Never did the A.M.A. delegate to Tougaloo's administrators authority commensurate with the responsibility laid upon them. No doubt the Association believed that a centralized control would safeguard the expenditure of the donor's money and assure wise administration of the schools. But to be forced to submit every decision to men in New York unacquainted with local problems proved impractical. Because the overworked secretaries assumed responsibility for so many details, they were often forced to delay decisions, adding to the confusion and apprehension at the school and contributing to the deterioration of morale.

Most defeating of all the administrative policies was the confused line of authority. Nutting, Claflin, and Darling each understood he was in full charge of A.M.A. interests on the campus, but the heads of the Tougaloo departments were not notified of such an overriding authority. Thus the principal of the normal school could insist he was responsible to the state, which provided his salary, and the business manager/farm superintendent could feel he was responsible only to the home office. Indeed, the A.M.A. secretaries encouraged this attitude by consulting and directing department heads—even teachers and staff members—completely bypassing the administrator of the school. (One of Claflin's laments was that the New York secretaries discussed him in their correspondence with other members of the school and actually defended their right to do so.) One might almost conclude that the New York secretaries favored having members of the faculty and staff in competition with one another as a check on their behavior. The administrators, with no power to hire or fire, to set salaries or other benefits, were at the mercy of their faculty and staff, who with impunity appealed every unpopular ruling to New York.

The policy of maintaining a common treasury for all the A.M.A. work, however good in theory, was difficult for the workers to accept when insufficient funds were received at the school. After funds had been solicited for a specific purpose, school officials naturally felt resentment at the suspension of the project midway for lack of money. Or when the state and counties were known to have appropriated money for certain salaries, it was hard for the teachers to accept in good grace their low salaries which, after adding fringe benefits of room and board, insurance, retirement, and travel, scarcely reached the figure allowed. Furthermore, misgivings regarding this fiscal policy of the A.M.A. were held by public officials who voted the appropriations, and their questions encouraged faculty discontent.

Another perpetual problem arose from the hazy verbal arrangements with each staff and faculty member regarding the terms of his employment. Irregular payment of compensation, the wide disparity in salaries and a similar disparity in fringe benefits caused further ill feeling. Written contracts and at least a rough salary scale with regular fringe benefits could have avoided many difficulties.

3) Finally, the very nature of a plantation school gave rise to problems not found in a more traditional school program. The home office could never divest itself of the notion that the plantation supplemented by state funds should make the school financially independent of A.M.A. support, while at the same time it was difficult to find anyone to direct the school who was knowledgeable in both school and plantation administration. Though the former owners of the plantation had sold it because it was not a profitable enterprise, the A.M.A. expected inexperienced men and young students to make it pay. Vain attempts to realize this desire complicated management of the school to the extent that even the educational program was interrupted when the plantation required immediate attention.

Also, a plantation school was by necessity isolated from all
the amenities of the community. The women rarely went into
Jackson. Faculty and staff were obliged to associate with themselves day after day. They did not even have separate dwellings
to which they could escape at night. Overworked, underpaid,
unequally treated, and often unappreciated, they sometimes
succumbed to petty bickering. Had they been within reach of a
town, even an unfriendly town which ostracized them, they
could have turned some of their hostility toward the local citizens rather than toward one another.

For all Tougaloo's problems and shortcomings, Nutting's
claim that a steady influence for good already emanated,
penetrating to the farthest corners of the state, had foundation
in fact. The success of the school's graduates, even its students
who left without completing the normal school, prompted
Pease, state superintendent of education, to recommend that
the legislature increase its annual support of the normal school
to $5,000.

Extant letters written by students to the New York A.M.A.
secretaries attest to their ability to write with a penmanship, a
sentence construction, a content and an organization comparable with the abilities of present college students. None of
them, however, was more than a normal-school student, since
the four-year college did not begin until 1897. Considering the
rough background of these students, most of whom had been
born in slavery, one must conclude that the school gave
superior instruction.

One young man's letter pointed up the kind of influence
that Tougaloo students had as they went out to teach. Of necessity he left school before completing his normal course, but he
proudly reported that the majority of his forty-nine scholars
could spell and read nicely while some could write and cipher.
His Sabbath School he claimed was even more interesting,
with eighty-three scholars in regular attendance, ranging in
age from nine to fifty-one. With Testaments in short supply, he
purchased cards on which Bible verses were printed, and occasionally he was able to buy Sabbath School papers for his students. Deploring the kind of preaching done by many who

pretended to be ministers of the gospel but who were really "recreants," he said he attempted to deliver a lecture each Sunday on something that would be of help to his people. He felt his inadequacy, however, and his letter was to ask the A.M.A. for help in the furtherance of his education.

The school's success was perhaps made possible, in spite of all the vicissitudes of the early years, because the faculty and staff never lost sight of the importance of their work. The elevation and the enlightenment of the entire four million freedmen were dependent, they believed, on normal schools. One teacher wrote that there was great need for educated and well trained colored teachers, to fill the school houses in every part of Mississippi. Their very earnestness in the cause was in a way responsible for the interpersonal strife. With so much at stake, it was difficult to condone imperfection, especially in others.

Close to the situation one saw the faults all too clearly, but looking back with the advantage of perspective one sees the virtues and contributions of each worker. Huggins gave yeoman service in finding and bargaining for the school property, while Beals prepared the property for its initial scholars. Tucker gave the school a buoyancy and confidence needed during those turbulent years in Mississippi. Nutting, whose innate kindliness led him as an administrator to be too lenient in his relationships with the personnel at the school and with the home office, had a personal integrity, a consistent and genuine goodness that any school of any age could cherish in its heritage. Steele, though never failing to look to his own advantage, was alert to the most modern methods of teaching, and few complaints were heard about the normal department when he was in charge; students later recalled him as a teacher who kept them awake. Though Osborn soon showed a tendency to undermine the other workers in his letters to the home office and was probably, as Claflin charged, not systematic with either his farm or book work, the school could scarcely have done without this plodder. When more brilliant but less enduring men dropped the work, it was he who until his dismissal in 1876 always picked up the pieces and carried on. Claflin, while inclining to be arrogant, making a fetish of system and leaving room for some question regarding his relationship with the legislature, must be credited with giving order to the school's operation and getting money from the A.M.A. Most pathetic of the early workers was Darling, who seemed to meet defeat at every turn. He faced all the problems of his predecessors plus the political revolution which removed Mississippi's Reconstruction government and catapulted the Bourbons, reemerging white leaders, hardly sympathetic to education, into state power. Sheer tenacity, at once Darling's weakness and his strength, enabled him to retain his position longer than had any previous head of the school. His contribution was mainly that of a holding action until a man who enjoyed the confidence of the A.M.A. took over. The women teachers and staff members, in an age when women were paid little, worked faithfully, resenting (and often protesting) that they received scant monetary return in comparison with the men, though they were doing as much work. Without their almost free services the A.M.A. could never have maintained the school.

Had Tougaloo's founders been saints they would deserve less credit than the ordinary human mortals they were. Through eight years of despair and hope, these people built a foundation of qualities—tangible and intangible—that lasted long into the future.

7

Tougaloo's First
Acknowledged President

G. STANLEY POPE, an Oberlin graduate and a Congregational minister whose family roots were deeply entwined in the pre-war abolitionist movement, arrived at Tougaloo in the fall of 1877 to become its first fully acknowledged president. As he surveyed the campus, its natural beauty, with moss-draped oaks, sweet gum, and hickory trees, must have stood in stark contrast to the old slave quarters, so close to the campus as to seem almost a part of it, and the deteriorating school buildings.

The condition of the mansion, the only building which held any claim to architectural pretensions, demanded Pope's first attention. After consultation with D. I. Miner, his farm superintendent and business manager, Pope decided this large building, which showed no more than patches of paint on its south and west sides, must be painted. Otherwise, it would deteriorate completely. The interior of the building required repairs, including carpentering, lathing, plastering, and painting.

Three rooms of the mansion claimed special attention. Besides the crumbling plaster and the splintered floors, Peoria room lacked all furniture. Pope reasoned that at some time in the past the church in Peoria must have furnished that room; either it should be refurnished or the plaque "Peoria" over the door removed. As it was, any visitor would surely wonder about unfair dealing. The straw matting in the room assigned to Miner might cause a fall. He replaced it with twenty-eight

67

yards of carpet from the Misfit Carpet Store—at a cost of one dollar per yard.

Concerned that the school's expensive apparatus was particularly useless because of its inaccessibility, Pope and Miner converted a large room on the first floor of the mansion to a recitation room. It had previously been occupied by a work bench and rats—a shame to the school. Walls and floors and woodwork had to be repaired, calcimined and painted. Cases were set up for the apparatus and for any geological specimens which might be collected. The addition of a large table and chairs made this an ideal room for natural philosophy and chemistry classes. Pope depended upon improvements of this kind to lure advanced students to remain.

If Pope were to have advanced students, he needed to build a corps of efficient teachers. Having requested that Catherine Koons be transferred to Tougaloo from Chattanooga, Pope promised not to be "sticklish" about the other appointments. Orra Angell, who had proved during the previous year to be all that her name implied, returned with some misgivings. She felt that her work merited a salary comparable to that of the males, and she disliked the spring term where Mississippi's weather was hard on the health of northern teachers. The A.M.A. made fortunate selections in Mary H. Scott, an associate of Miss Koons at Chattanooga, and, as matron, Sarah L. Emerson, sister of Miss D. E. Emerson in the New York office. Dora Ford was happy to be reappointed.

Though Pope had left Talladega under criticism, the A.M.A. was confident he could bring harmony to Tougaloo. This he determined to do. Most letters from Pope and his teachers to the A.M.A. office during the entire first year emphasized the harmony that prevailed. The music, which Darling had wanted, was provided in good measure by Miss Koons and Mrs. Pope. Their chorus work and singing at social gatherings gave an esprit de corps to the school. Pope seemed intuitively to recognize the ladies' need to get away occasionally from the narrow confines of the school. During their first spring break he took them all to New Orleans for a holiday. In some circumstances Pope's sensitivity to his teachers' feelings interfered with his effectiveness as an administrator. He found it impossible to dismiss a good Christian teacher such as Miss Ford, though she did not meet the need of the primary department. After considerable agonizing on the part of both Miss Ford and Pope, as each tried to communicate to the other, Pope in desperation called upon Secretary Strieby in the New York office to perform the unpleasant task.

Pope and Miner were disappointed in the small enrollment. About thirty came to board. A few enrolled in the day school for normal courses and about twelve in the primary. The large drop in the primary school could be attributed to Pope's policy of charging a dollar per month for tuition. He believed people should be encouraged to help themselves. Previously the school conducted the primary school as a laboratory in which the normal students gained practice in teaching. Pope later reverted to a free primary school, to have a good model class the year around. Those who came only part of the time had to pay as before.

Pope found the students more easily controlled than any he had encountered elsewhere in the South, and Miss Koons thought them superior to her Chattanooga pupils. Those students who started the year anticipating the customary fireworks in the faculty were surprised. One young man whose experience stretched back several years thought the students had never been more content.

However, the first year was not without some problems with the students. Pope immediately ran into scholarship demands from them. In keeping with his idea that students should be encouraged to help themselves, he planned to distribute the scholarship money to more students by reducing the amount any one person received to twenty-five dollars a term. Several claimed they had been promised more, and one threatened to write his benefactor. The three Granberry boys were on scholarships given by missionary-minded persons in England. Pope had to backtrack, for he could not afford to undermine the faith of the donors, especially those in England.

The students were not always the model of good behavior pictured at first. Miss Koons expected the matron, Sarah

Emerson, to find several jewels in her crown representing the good work she had done among these "wild girls." Others said, however, that they were angels compared to what they were the year before. Sometimes the teachers thought they had the worst class of any school, but Miss Scott supposed if they knew more of other schools they would not find their classes unusual.

The three Granberry brothers caused a disruption at the beginning of the second term, and F. C. Granberry, the talented and popular member of the graduating class, was expelled. When Pope wrote George C. Granberry, who had married and was then teaching near Tougaloo, asking him to pay something on his debt, George C. replied that he owed nothing to the institution—rather the institution owed him. George C. felt he should have his English scholarship while he was teaching, because he was keeping up with his studies and expected to take the examinations. J. N. Granberry, having used his English scholarship, wanted more financial help, to study theology the next year. In Pope's judgment the three Granberry boys had been helped too much for their own good. Difficult and, according to Chase, rather dull, as the two remaining Granberrys were, it was necessary to retain them, since the school needed a graduating class. At best it would number no more than three. In the end, three did graduate though not the same three Pope anticipated and possibly not in the year he expected. According to all the catalogs, Pope F. Tevault, J. N. Granberry, and Luella Miner constituted the graduating class of the normal school in 1879. Miss Miner, daughter of the business manager, was the only white graduate the normal school ever had. Not until 1964 did the college have any white graduates. George C. Granberry never graduated.

In planning the catalog for his second year, Pope and the teachers decided on some changes in the curriculum. They planned to revert to an earlier practice of offering a certificate for the completion of the normal course and a diploma for a higher normal course. The higher normal course (11th and 12th years) was expected to keep many in school, "not one in 15" of whom would go elsewhere for advanced work. Pope was satisfied to limit Tougaloo's offerings to a thorough and practical normal course which would speak to the need of the state for competent teachers. "We are willing to take the rough stone from a quarry and put on the heavy, telling strokes of the builder and leave the most artistic strokes of the sculptor to be given by some of our sister institutions." Darling's proposal of this idea had caused his downfall.

Because students were ignorant of the Bible, its systematic study was an integral part of the course of study for each grade. Pope planned only for a biblical department and not a theological department to train young men to preach. Having also a knowledge of the industrial arts, they would be fitted for a *practical* evangelism.

Systematic industrial instruction began with blacksmithing but rapidly expanded to other industrial arts. When Dr. Atticus G. Haygood approved Tougaloo for Slater Funds in the early 1880s, carpentry, shoe repairing, wheelwrighting, and tinning were added. All boys in the seventh grade were required to take one hour of instruction each day in carpentry, where they learned how to use tools and make common repairs. Eighth-grade boys received instructions in tinning and blacksmithing, taught by a former slave.

Those who showed special aptitude for mechanical work could be admitted after two years as apprentices to one of these trades. Apprentices became thorough workmen. They worked eight hours a day for two years and attended night classes. During their third and fourth years they worked a half-day in the shops and attended school in the other half-day.

Miner realized soon after his arrival in the summer of 1877 that the school could not gain materially from the farm during the coming year. Because the drought had shriveled whole acres of plants, the school would be compelled to purchase even potatoes and corn. Miner sowed new vegetable seed immediately and planted more sweet potatoes, trusting a rain would bring them on.

The farm needed fences to replace those destroyed during the war. Fences would restrain the school's stock and prevent neighboring cattle from grazing on the school pastures. They might also reduce theft, an ever present problem.

Miner's first year was plagued by excessive rain rather than
by drought as in the preceding year. Water in the submerged
creek bottom swept away the new fences and ruined ten acres
of corn. The higher land fared better, but the harvest produced
barely enough corn to make the school's own meal and feed its
stock.

Miner hoped to use scientific farming to implement the
A.M.A.'s original plan to make Tougaloo a school which could
eat from its plantation and in addition provide some cash income. He requisitioned from New York labor saving tools and
began a systematic improvement of the school's animals, starting with the purchase of an Ayrshire cow and calf from Talladega. Visitors soon remarked that blooded cattle were replacing the lean native kine.

The school's soil was improved according to the latest scientific knowledge. Miner carefully husbanded barnyard ma-
nure and cottonseed for the soil's enrichment. He planted and
turned under peavine. He rotated soil-depleting crops with
clover and other nitrogen-producing plants. To demonstrate
the value of rotation and deep plowing, Miner kept a few acres
planted in cotton.

Miner planted a good strain of strawberries. By spring
1878, the school enjoyed berries served in the dining room.
This success encouraged Miner to plant twenty-five to thirty
thousand more plants. Tougaloo soon became known for its
fine strawberries, and farmers in Madison County planted
hundreds of acres with plants obtained from the school. Being
on the line of the Illinois Central Railway, Tougaloo could ship
the berries directly to Chicago where they had a good market.

In 1886 Miner had seventy-five acres under cultivation. Besides the demonstration cotton and the strawberries, he raised
corn, oats, rye, peas, Irish and sweet potatoes, fruit trees, and
an extensive green garden to supply the school's kitchen.

The general farming was done almost entirely with student
labor. For work beyond the required hour a day, students received from five to eight cents an hour to apply on their board
and tuition up to a maximum of three dollars a month. Most
students worked the maximum. Pope claimed that even with

the inexpensive labor all farming and industry on the campus was an inconvenience and an expense to the school. Their chief value, he insisted, was in the training they gave the young people.

Pope's method of combatting the A.M.A.'s constant desire for retrenchment was to call for advance. Just one week after complaining of small enrollment, he wrote Strieby that he was having Osborn's house over the work shop—the upper story of the old slave pen—cleaned out to "crowd" fourteen boys in it. Though Miner felt the building not fit to house students, Pope wrote that this action was necessary because enrollment was increasing a little already and students predicted that the school would be overrun after Christmas. "Suppose we get entirely overrun with students after Christmas. What shall we do? . . . Shall they hang up in the trees or bivouac under them?"

In the spring of 1878 when the A.M.A. was harassed by a stubborn debt and Tougaloo was running in the red on its current expenses, Pope wrote Strieby suggesting a real room emergency would soon "envelop" the school. "We have had to put a bed in a recitation room which we need every day." Several students were expected the next week and others might come unannounced. "I see no way out but to put up barracks. Will you authorize?" He added that for the next year with the larger enrollment expected, the rooms over the shop and oil rooms (Osborn Hall, then used to house some of the boys) would be needed for recitations. The Peoria room, said at one time to have housed fourteen girls though it was large enough for only six, was needed as a sewing room.

Pope's tactic of "planning big" brought A.M.A. approval for the barracks, and the grounds began to hum with activity. Except for Alexander Moman, a carpenter who gave a few days of labor to apply on the rent of his farm, Miner and the students did the work. No sooner were the barracks begun than Pope advanced to a new position. "I wish we might make brick this summer for a new hall and so keep 6–8 faithful boys here to work." He recited the need to Strieby. Except for the mansion the foundations for all the buildings were warped and sinking.

Pillars were cracking, walls were settling, plaster was falling off. "We need $12,000 for a new boys' hall and $4000 for enlarging and repairing Ladies' Hall. Sorry we have cost you so much but we must cost you a great deal more. . . . We can slide down hill on very little. But if we must pull the load up hill we need help."

The years 1880 and 1881 would see both projects accomplished as well as a barn built for the fine breed of cattle Tougaloo was acquiring. Ladies' Hall, originally constructed hastily and cheaply, was destined to undergo several renovations and additions before it eventually burned to the ground in 1897. Pope was the second to try his ingenuity on it. He added a third story and a three-story ell on the south side. These changes permitted the building to accommodate about eighty girls and several teachers. Later Pope added a laundry. After Pope left Tougaloo, Ladies Hall received extensive repairs plus a small building in the rear for use as a bakery and a bathroom.

Though Pope used his pen to campaign through the *American Missionary* for a men's dormitory, he probably would not have been granted it so soon had not Washington Hall gone up in flames in January 1881. The young men, bereft of their quarters, preempted the nearly completed barn before the cattle took possession. They dubbed it Ayrshire Hall. Pope soon set the boys to work making brick from clay found in the Tougaloo creek bottoms. During the summer other A.M.A. students came to help the Tougaloo students in the construction of a new hall, 112 by 31 feet, three stories high, with a basement for laundry, storage, and bathrooms. Supervision was given by black mechanics. Secretary Strieby, who had laid the first brick in May, was present on Thanksgiving Day (1881) for dedication of the imposing brick dormitory which was to carry his name. In addition to housing sixty-five to eighty boys it had classrooms for the normal and higher classes, including science laboratories and a reference library.

Never one to rest on his oars, Pope began agitation for a new school building for the primary and intermediate departments with a chapel on the second floor. Stephen Ballard of Brooklyn responded with a gift of $5,000. With it Ballard Hall, constructed of wood, was built in 1886. Enough money was left after building Ballard Hall, regarded as a marvel in cheap construction, to build the Ballard Shops for the boys. Students trained in the industrial department did all the work on both buildings.

At the end of his ten years Pope could look upon the campus from his two-story home near the entrance to the campus, which he had built without the usual fanfare, and see gratifying changes. Strieby Hall was a much finer building than Washington Hall had ever been. Ballard Hall, the Ballard Shops, and the barn spoke eloquently of the school's work in training teachers, mechanics, and farmers. Ladies' Hall was enlarged, and it, as well as the mansion, had benefited from extensive repairs. Pope was, by his own admission, a poor beggar. He could not raise money by stumping the North as could some later presidents. But he knew how to get the most out of the A.M.A., namely by calling in a jovial, almost light handed manner for more and ever more construction for anticipated needs.

Pope's family underwent several important changes during his last five years at Tougaloo University. Mrs. Pope died in 1883 of malarial pneumonia, leaving two small boys. She was buried under the mossy oaks in the little cemetery on campus which had earlier been laid out by an intermediate teacher, Eliza Eldrige, who, as it turned out, was the first to be buried there. Pope later married Catherine Koons. After serving Tougaloo for ten years, longer than any of his predecessors, Pope and his family were transferred to do the Association's work in the Tennessee mountains.

8

A Long Chapter for the Longest Administration

FRANK G. WOODWORTH began in 1887 the longest tenure of any president in the history of Tougaloo College. A graduate of Iowa College where he also received his A.M. degree, a student at Yale and Hartford theological seminaries, a recipient of the D.D. degree from Knox College in Illinois, and a holder of the Phi Beta Kappa key, he dedicated twenty-five years of his life to the advancement of Tougaloo University.

Woodworth was the first president to find the school in a stable condition with a harmonious faculty and a student body engaged in a well defined program of study. The financial resources, while never enough, were adequate to assure the school's continuance. The buildings were in better condition than ever before, though buildings had a way of needing repairs and students of needing more buildings.

In Central Mississippi where the Mississippi Alluvial Plain rests three hundred feet deep, all the buildings tended to settle irregularly. The settling of Strieby Hall was presumably corrected in the summer of 1888 by running twelve anchors lengthwise and ten crosswise through the building, but in 1890 the foundations had to be entirely redone and the walls replastered. Southern contractors advised razing Ladies' Hall because it had settled so much into the treacherous soil that it could not be repaired safely. Unwilling to give up the building, the school's mechanics calculated the weight and the resulting strains and thrust. They drew up plans for concrete footings,

76

brick piers, and heavy timbering. During vacation enough students remained to do the work. They pulled on the forty-eight "jack-screws," lifted and blocked up the building, section by section, excavated exactly to the surveyors' stakes, mixed concrete and mortar and handled the huge pine timbers. These students, some very young and slight, undertook whatever was asked in this work which was new and strange to them. When finished, Ladies' Hall was considered as strong as any new building and much improved in plan.

Ten years after this extensive renovation, Ladies' Hall went up in smoke—just one day after school opened, later than scheduled because of quarantine. Fortunately the fire started when most were at prayer meeting. Only one teacher and three students were caught upstairs. The students escaped unscratched, but Miss Lynn was severely burned. Most occupants of the building lost everything except the clothes they wore. The dining room and kitchen provisions, all the fruit and vegetables canned at such effort by the students during the heat of the past summer, the smoke house, hen house, windmill house, and water tank went up in flames. One and a half hours after the alarm, the students and staff saw nothing but ashes where a large and strong Ladies' Hall had stood.

For a while the mansion next to Ladies' Hall was threatened. Had it burned, no doubt the rest of the buildings would also have gone. Students worked to keep the mansion wall wet—one of them using a little hand pump. A lady teacher on the mansion roof directed them. The heat was so intense that her hairpins burned her head, but she dared not loose her hair lest it catch fire. Another lady directed the saving of Bible Hall (the name given the old slave pen after the girls moved to Berkshire Cottage) at the rear of the mansion. While their efforts could not save the mansion and Bible Hall for long, they kept the buildings from catching fire until the wind shifted.

The next day was Thanksgiving. Faculty and students filled the chapel to give thanks that no lives were lost and no more buildings burned. Berkshire (see below) and the shops (called the Beehive) absorbed all the girls. Food cooked in the Berkshire kitchens was served in the study room of the boys' dormitory on the other side of the campus. School work resumed on Friday.

The loss of Ladies' Hall made Beard Hall, named for a venerable A.M.A. secretary, inevitable. Built in 1898, it was a large two-storied brick building, U-shaped, with an attic and a basement. Besides the fifty-eight girls' rooms, each of which bore the name of the donor who furnished it, and a few rooms for teachers, it had four music rooms, a Y.M.C.A. room, and space for a gymnasium in the basement. A building for the dining room was constructed between the mansion and Beard Hall. It seated two hundred students and thirty teachers. Behind it was a bake house.

Woodworth Church, a large brick structure, was built in 1901. Woodworth insisted it be called a church though later it was known as the Chapel. Walker Frazier, head carpenter at the school, directed construction while students again performed most of the labor. John Lee ('04) recalled in 1961 his pride in helping Mr. Frazier put up the stately tower with the fancy white shingles. Though the building had seats for about 350 people, it could accommodate nearly a thousand when the main room, lecture room and choir room were combined. Most of the furniture for the church was made in the shops. Mr. Lee made the pulpit, still in use today. In 1903 Murray M. Harris of Los Angeles gave the school a two-manual organ, thought to be the first of its type in the South. Neither electric nor waterpower being available, it was blown by manpower. Harris's sister, Mrs. Cyrus Hamlin, used the organ to make Tougaloo the most outstanding center for classical and sacred music in Mississippi.

Strieby Hall was declared unsafe, and the boys moved to the carpenter shop (the Beehive) until Galloway Hall was completed in 1907. This building was later called Old Galloway to distinguish it from its replacement which is still in use today. C. L. Wild, instructor in woodwork and masonry, directed the work, which was done by either students or former students. Designed in the shape of a T, the hall had two stories, and a basement almost wholly above ground. Including the furnishing, the cost was about $16,000. Because prosperity in the country had brought inflation with it, the money ran out before the basement was completed.

Bishop Charles B. Galloway, a Tougaloo trustee for whom the building was named, was ill and unable to attend the dedication, which assumed the characteristics of a rapprochement between North and South. Frank L. Bellinger, editor of the Jackson *Evening News*, looked upon the A.M.A. representatives from the North as an "earnest" that they were of a disposition to be helpful rather than critical. In that spirit, he said, the white South welcomed them. He reminded them, however, that southern people made no apologies for the actions of the fathers whose valor was the heritage of the whole land. Samuel Ward of Boston affirmed that both sections intended right. The evening concert, featuring Sullivan's Festival "Te Deum" sung by the Tougaloo chorus of more than a hundred voices, capped the spirit of harmony in the large mixed audience.

Connecting all the buildings were the boardwalks, lighted at night by lamps hung from posts. Constructed and kept in repair by the students, they were as romanticized as the boardwalks of Atlantic City. They continued in use until well into the 1920s and served a good purpose—that of keeping feet out of the Mississippi mud.

Notwithstanding all the building done in Woodworth's administration, students were continually turned away for lack of room. Of the A.M.A. colleges only Fisk boarded more students than Tougaloo at the turn of the century. Crowded conditions were alleviated in 1889 when the school restricted its boarding department to those of fifth grade or above, and again when the grade level was raised to the sixth in 1904. These restrictions were possible because the state was assuming greater responsibility for elementary teaching. More relief came to the boarding department when Mt. Hermon Seminary for girls at Clinton came under control of Tougaloo in 1904. Some of the younger girls could be sent there.

Pope, at his last commencement in 1887, promised the girls an industrial cottage. The alumni pledged the furniture for it. With further financial assistance from Mr. Ballard, Woodworth established temporary quarters over the original slave pen (then a wood and oil storage space), the second story of which had been successively Boston Hall for boys, Osborn's home, and Osborn Hall for boys. In 1890 Woodworth called upon the A.M.A. for money to build a new industrial cottage. The result was Berkshire Cottage. Besides the housekeeping suite, Berkshire had a music room, a kitchen for cooking classes, dormitory space for teachers and, after 1897, space for college women. Labor on this two-storied commodious home was done by students under supervision of the industrial arts faculty.

Whereas in the temporary quarters the girls returned to their dormitory rooms at night, in Berkshire Cottage they actually lived in the practice housekeeping suite. Before they were eligible for this experience the girls underwent thorough training in the several arts required of homemakers. The hour of daily work had given them experience in a variety of tasks, as their duties rotated each month. In a more formal way the girls from fifth to eighth grades received an hour and a half of instruction each day. They were taught to wash dishes, cook, can, and preserve. Beginning with darning, mending or the making of bedding and simple garments—often using materials sent them by A.M.A. friends in the North—some girls became proficient enough in sewing to make and sell shirts. Under the careful direction of their teacher the girls put into practice all they had learned about housekeeping. Scrubbing floors and washing windows were educational to girls who came from windowless cabins with crude floors or none at all. To plan and prepare nourishing meals within their budget allowance was a new experience to most students. Tougaloo was one of the first schools (if not the first school, as it believed) to give groups of four to six girls practical experience in homemaking (for four to eight weeks). Later many schools incorporated this practice into their home economics programs.

Agriculture and animal husbandry continued in importance for both their instructional value and their production of food for the boarding department. Besides the staple crops of corn, oats, sweet potatoes, and sugar cane, the school cultivated enough berries (strawberries, raspberries, and blackberries), garden produce, and fruit for a sizable market in Jackson and Chicago. As the demand for Tougaloo's products increased, the students learned the practical value of an attractive arrangement and a dependable quality.

Though Tougaloo had discontinued raising cotton as a money crop, in 1896 it planted one acre in cotton as an experiment. The land, only fairly good, was thoroughly prepared, using only barnyard fertilizers. Students carefully cultivated the plants. Despite a poor year for cotton, they gathered one and a quarter bales before an early frost cut off the top cotton. With a state average of one-third of a bale to an acre, both students and neighbors were excited. Farmers asked Tougaloo for seed.

In 1906 the U. S. Department of Agriculture made Tougaloo one of its demonstration centers. Under the Department's supervision two bales of cotton were raised to the acre when the state averaged only half a bale. Sixty-four and a half bushels of corn were raised to the acre when the state average was less than twenty.

Animal husbandry kept pace with the school's progress in agriculture. Usually from eighty to a hundred cattle were kept, as well as about the same number of swine and sheep of good breeds. In 1907 a beginning was made in raising horses, mules, and poultry. The school was practically self-sufficient for its meat, milk, butter, and eggs.

Tougaloo patterned its industrial courses after those offered at Massachusetts Institute of Technology, where its instructors had been trained. The purpose of the courses was not merely to produce physical objects but also to build character and stimulate the mind. Accurate drawings and lists of materials were required as a part of the course work. The thoroughness of this part of the training is indicated by the experience of a former student who gave the lumberman in his home town a drawing of a frame house. He attached to it a statement of the lumber required. The merchant asked who did it for him. "I told him I did and he hardly believed me."

From the beginning of universal free education, securing qualified teachers had been Mississippi's great problem. Importation of "aliens" (Northerners), relied upon during Reconstruction, was repugnant to most Southerners. Though Mississippi had two normal schools for blacks, it was the only state in the union in the 1880s with no normal to prepare white teachers. With no standards for teaching, appointments were at times awarded for political services or given to the highest bidder. Kindhearted superintendents often gave appointments to those who needed the positions, perverting the educational system into a charity for the support of "indigents" and "ignoramuses," as one superintendent expressed it.

In 1886 Mississippi made some long overdue revisions in its school laws. One of them required county superintendents to make regular visits to the schools under their jurisdiction. Another inaugurated a better system of financing, which enabled the state to pay teachers in cash rather than in depreciated state warrants.

Of the various changes made in 1886 none affected Tougaloo University more than the requirement for uniform state teacher examinations and the issuance of teacher certificates of three grades. While seventy percent of the teachers who took the state examination failed on the first year, those who had been trained at Tougaloo did very well—even those who had not taken the full normal course. One girl, unable to continue school at Tougaloo because of her mother's illness, took the examination with little hope of succeeding; she passed. The performance of Tougaloo's students in the state examinations added to its reputation for thorough training. The school's students were in demand by superintendents in Mississippi, Arkansas, and Louisiana.

To maintain this reputation and to improve the quality of teachers, the school raised its standards and lengthened the normal course. Though closing exercises were never skipped, there were no graduates between 1887 and 1892. When four normal students and one theological student qualified for graduation under the new standards in 1892, there was great excitement on campus. Tougaloo began in 1888 a six-week concentrated course for those who could not take the regular normal training. In the late 1890s Peabody funds financed the summer courses. These courses prepared students for the various grades of teacher certificates. Some attended to qualify for a higher certificate than they already had.

For some years Tougaloo had conducted night classes for its own plantation workers, railroad employees and other persons outside the school. By 1890 the night school was divided into two parts, one for the boarding students and one held in the Daniel Hand School, just outside the campus, for adults from neighboring areas. These night classes were taught by normal students.

Though agricultural, industrial, or normal training was usually considered enough for Negroes, Woodworth realized their need for a liberal arts education. If, he asked, the New England boy with all his cultural heritage and environment needed such an education, "how much more one whose heredity and surrounding have been the opposite?" A utilitarian education, while necessary, could not give a race the wider, nobler visions seen from the loftier heights, he said. A broad education was needed to develop Negro leaders. But there was another reason, peculiar to the black race, for providing the able Negro with the liberal arts. His soul, daily scarred by slights, insults, restrictions, discriminations, and contempt, needed to find solace in a "mind well stored with philosophy, science, history, literature, art, and in communings with the intellectual aristocracy of the past." Thus Tougaloo continually strengthened and extended its liberal arts program.

With less pressure on the boarding school from the lower grades, consideration could be given to the organizing of college level courses, for which the school was originally founded. The first college classes were offered in 1897. Tougaloo conferred its first A.B. on Traverse S. Crawford, the sole member of the class of 1901.

The music department flourished under the long and able leadership of Mrs. Cyrus Hamlin, wife of the dean. Aiming to produce not merely players and singers but also musicians who understood theory and harmony, she taught the students to write music and sing at sight. The advanced chorus studied the great works, such as Mendelssohn's "Elijah," Handel's

"Messiah," and Gounod's "St. Cecilia Mass," selected from a music library of twenty-five hundred titles. Disdaining popular music, Mrs. Hamlin allowed only the best to be heard in Woodworth Church where her fingers and feet brought majestic music from the organ her brother had given Tougaloo. From the primary grades through the college department students were exposed to good music; piano and organ recitals were frequent. Student choral groups were in demand by various conventions in Jackson as well as by some many miles away. As much as for its industrial instruction, Tougaloo won favor with the "best" white people in Mississippi for the quality of its music.

Tougaloo University felt its mission was not only to those who were relatively advantaged but also to those who had intellectual potential yet such poor background that without encouragement they might not attend any school. More than other A.M.A. schools, Tougaloo drew from the plantation Negroes, those who were "less tinged by white blood," at once the "most ignorant" and the "most hopeful." Some came from homes where as many as twenty might eat, sleep, and live in one room. Some had to be taught to undress before going to bed; some needed instruction in the use of a toilet. One girl, when faced with a stairway for the first time, climbed it on her hands and knees. (To judge from some descriptions of the outside stairs this may have been a sensible mode of climbing them!) As the number of second generation students increased, better home environment was evident.

Tougaloo tried to make the school a home for its students. Acting in place of parents it taught not only academic and industrial subjects but also personal hygiene, social arts, moral principles, and practical religion. Character was of prime importance. If by act or attitude a student was considered a bad influence, he or she was sent home.

To develop a sense of responsibility the students were subjected to a daily routine described in the *American Missionary* of May 1891. At 4:00 A.M. the baker, a student, began to prepare from forty to fifty three-pound loaves of bread, and cooks started breakfast in the kitchen. Farm boys who, like day girls,

George E. Rice, a much beloved and respected professor

Judson Cross Hall

Mr. George Owens, then business manager of Tougaloo College, presents a gift to Mrs. Annie Davis upon her retirement.

The Y. W. C. A. sorted clothing for the needy.

Dr. Samuel C. Kincheloe, president 1956-1960

Dr. Ernst Borinski's social science classes enriched the lives of several student generations.

Dr. Philip M. Widenhouse, General Secretary of the Division of Higher Education of the Board of Home Missions, May, 1958

Students dubbed this bus "The Panama Limited" after the Illinois Central crack train from Chicago to New Orleans. The bus brought students from Jackson to Tougaloo.

Mrs. Lucius Eastman's generosity helped elevate Tougaloo's library rating, an important requirement for accreditation. Tougaloo expressed its appreciation by naming the library in her honor in 1948.

Presidents Harold Warren, Samuel Kincheloe, and A. D. Beittel.

An annual Christmas party given for community children, held in Brownlee Hall, sponsored by Tougaloo community alumni with aid of churches

Fred L. Brownlee, General Secretary of the American Missionary Association completed thirty years of service in 1950.

Dr. A. B. Britton '48 receiving the "Alumnus of the Year" award for 1960 from Mrs. Maggie Dunson '45

Some of the most important religious, cultural, civil rights and community activities have been held in Woodworth Chapel, and many of the college's most distinguished visitors have spoken from its pulpit.

Tougaloo took pride in its 1937 champion football team. Coach Duke Williams, wearing the hat, stands on the right.

worked full time and attended night classes, went to milk the cows and care for other farm animals. When the bell at Strieby Hall rang long and loud at 5:00 A.M., the rest of the students were awakened. Some kindled fires, some did janitorial work, and some cleaned. Others might get in a few moments of study before breakfast.

At 6:00 a kitchen boy tinkled a large triangle bell which was answered by the Strieby bell and the howl of a dog. With this reminder of the imminence of breakfast, farm boys rushed their milk to the milk room where day girls strained it. All who had been doing their chores cleaned up; teachers struggled to wake from their last nap. A repeat of the triangle bell, Strieby bell, and the dog's howl started the boys—many in blue uniforms—marching two abreast from Strieby under the command of a sergeant; the girls, also in uniforms, marched from their dormitory rooms to the dining room. Five girls and five boys stood about each student table while teachers stood around the long table to sing the doxology.

Sustained by a hearty breakfast, the students marched out of the dining room to their various class assignments, including those in the shops, the girls' industrial house, and music practice. Farm boys and day girls began their work in field and house. Those with no specific assignment prepared their lessons in the supervised study room. At 8:45 a march was struck on the piano in Ballard Hall, and all students filed upstairs for the devotional exercises. These concluded, the students went to their classes, the first being in Bible study. At 9:00 normal students began taking their turns at observation or practice teaching in the Daniel Hand Primary School where children from the community had gathered.

Students enjoyed a free hour before beginning their afternoon classes, which gave more emphasis to the industrial arts. Twice a week the girls met with the nurse for a practical health talk while the boys had a talk on agriculture from the school's farmer. At 3:30 those who had not yet done their hour of daily service went to the woodyard, to the grounds to dig or rake leaves, to the halls to sweep or scrub, or to the laundry where from three to four thousand pieces were washed and ironed each week. Donning white caps, aprons, and sleeve protectors, the day girls left their household tasks in mid-afternoon for instruction in nursing and to give care to the sick.

The later afternoon allowed time for unprogramed activities and on occasion even recreation. The botany class might search the woods for specimens. If squealing were heard from the slaughter house, a class in physiology was sure to gather there for a practical lesson. Some played ball, croquet or other games. Others read in the reading rooms conveniently located in each dormitory. A team of girls might practice gymnastics while the quartet might practice for the coming Sabbath. Piano practicing was heard at all hours.

Supper was followed by evening devotion, chorus rehearsal, and study hours. Day girls and farm boys went to their night classes. At 9:00 classes and study hours came to a close. Calisthenics before lights went out at 10:00 P.M. consumed any remaining energy the students might have. This schedule gave the devil little opportunity to find idle hands, but in case he should there were rules to cover every contingency.

Each morning brought an inspection of rooms. The boys stood in the halls by their doors in an attitude of military salute. The inspector surveyed the beds with their quilts drawn smoothly over plump husk mattresses which had been made on campus. He scanned the open wardrobes containing the few garments and perhaps an extra pair of shoes. His fingers quickly detected any dust over door moldings or on top of wardrobes. If satisfied, the inspector saluted as he left the room, and the boys returned the salute, happy for a perfect mark. Girls' rooms were subjected to a similar routine minus the salute. It was a proud student who found his name listed for having a perfect room throughout the month.

Socials and dates held an important place in the students' lives. If a young man desired to escort a young lady to a program or a social, he sent her a written invitation. His letter was passed on by the matron who considered not only the substance but also the grammatical construction and spelling. The girl then wrote her answer, which had to pass the same kind of scrutiny. Invitations from the young men were delivered at the foot of a stairway in Beard Hall. The talk of the week among the young ladies was about who might or might not receive a letter at mail call. Marching at socials took the place of dancing, which was taboo. Dominoes, Old Maid, and checkers were popular indoor games. After a social or program the boys could escort their dates as far as the cedar tree, still standing, in front of the mansion. Sometimes, if the moon were not too bright, they sneaked a kiss.

An event that made a lasting impression on students was William H. Lanier's winning of his bride. Mr. Lanier had graduated from Tougaloo Academy in 1881; but with no college courses offered there until 1897, he went to Walden College. He became president of Alcorn College from where he came to Tougaloo looking for a wife. He quickly decided upon Elizabeth Dabney whom he courted and won though she had been considered Traverse Crawford's girl. In the vernacular of the students he "rolled" Crawford. Mr. Crawford, it is believed, never quite recovered from this loss though he did later marry.

The Athletic Club sponsored a variety of sports to celebrate Thanksgiving. Relay races, the potato race, and the jumping contest were always good for a lot of hilarity. Some, including teachers, played tennis. The highpoint of the day was the *intramural* baseball game.

*Inter*mural sports had their beginning in Woodworth's administration. The first practice basketball game was played in 1900. Tougaloo introduced football to southern Negro schools. Its first game was with Jackson College, then a Baptist school on the grounds presently occupied by Millsaps College.

Disciplinary problems were minimal. One faculty member writing many years later could recall no problems of discipline—the students were always "courteous, appreciative, and anxious to learn." A former day student, Lilybel Wilson King, however, remembers a time when she took a seat in a classroom which was folded up in the manner of the old stationary school seat-desk combination. The seat dropped with her on it, giving a loud clap. To help her remember that a "lady" always turns her seat down before sitting on it, she was given three extra hours of work in the laundry. Another former student recalls that a classmate was sent home for using tobacco. Any student found with liquor or firearms would have met an equally severe response. If disciplinary problems were few, it was likely because every little infraction was handled before larger difficulties arose and because the daily schedule left little room for mischief.

Students probably responded positively to the solicitude of the faculty. "Everybody loved President Woodworth," said Mrs. King. This sentiment took tangible expression when from their meager funds the students gave the president one hundred dollars to help meet a financial emergency. Perhaps many students would have been glad to echo a graduate's note handed to President Woodworth to be read after she left. While he and Mrs. Woodworth relaxed in the living room of their home on the second floor of the mansion, at the close of another year and another commencement, he drew the letter from his pocket and read:

Since I have been coming to Tougaloo, I have had quite a little help. Although it was a blessing from God, you are the agent through whom it came. These few lines are to let you know that I appreciate and thank you for your kindness.

9

Religion and Temperance

IN THE NINETEENTH CENTURY the American Missionary Association viewed its schools as instruments for the salvation of the people and the foundation of the church. Yet no A.M.A. school was narrowly denominational. In the 1880s Tougaloo's faculty represented six different denominations. At first, Tougaloo, like other A.M.A. institutions, was a week-long Sunday School with the Bible as a text in literally every department. It sought to give a "Thus saith the Lord" for everything from order, punctuality, and cleanliness to honesty, personal and social virtue, temperance, industry, and benevolence.

The church was organized at Tougaloo almost simultaneously with the school. Presidents Pope, Woodworth, and Holmes were as much pastors as school administrators, and they considered the Sunday School as important as the weekday classes. In the days when all Sunday School classes studied the same lesson, Woodworth made a practice of summing up the morning's lesson in the closing exercises. Faculty members, even if not Sunday School workers, came to church early, to listen to the president's masterly and helpful review. Dean Cyrus Hamlin, whose wife lifted the students' thoughts to God through music, was a leading force in religious activity during his twenty-year tenure (1896–1916). Later Traverse Crawford, John Lee, and two other young men from Tougaloo who settled in the Delta, conducted a young people's Sunday School class

89

which gained a reputation for vigor and interest. The four men readily gave credit to Dean Hamlin's inspiration and methods of instruction.

A teacher's duty usually included Sunday School teaching; and when President Holmes was on a fund-raising tour, teachers took their turn at preaching. On Sunday afternoons some faculty members rode out to the country in the school carriage to take a Sunday School lesson to the more distant children while advanced biblical scholars organized and conducted their own Sunday afternoon classes in the country. A Sunday School Institute was organized by Pope in 1878 to coordinate the Sunday School activities at the school with the areas served by Tougaloo's personnel. Friends in the North forwarded their Sunday School papers to the Institute. Tougaloo students felt a personal attachment to one particular girl whose neatly written name appeared on each week's paper.

Religious activities continued at Tougaloo during the summer vacations. Students who remained on campus to work taught the hundred or more children from surrounding farms who came to the campus Sunday School. Others substituted for the regular teachers in the country cabins. Though attendance was limited, the weekly meetings of the young people's society and the prayer meeting knew no interruption during vacations. Tougaloo students who fanned out into the country to teach day school during the summer were essentially an extension of the school's religious program. Organizing Sunday School often before their day schools, they taught in the aggregate some four thousand children each summer.

The church and Sunday School taught—and the school enforced—a strict observance of the Sabbath. Students were required to attend Sunday School as well as the church service. Girls, dressed in blue serge uniforms in winter, in white uniforms in spring or early fall, marched sedately to the church where they sat together on one side. Boys, dressed in dark suits, marched from their dormitories and sat on the other side. No complaints are recorded about the Sunday School or church services; but much was written, and many students living today recall the vital worth of both.

Sunday afternoon offered opportunity for various activities. One hour was allowed for visiting the library or for relaxing in other ways. Students read, wrote home, or meditated during "silent hour" which was observed from 2:00 to 4:00. No conversation was allowed during this period. Lilybel King tells of a student who looked out across the flower garden, waved, and softly called to a friend in the opposite wing of Beard Hall. Immediately the matron appeared to administer a reprimand. The Y.M.C.A. and the Y.W.C.A. were allowed to meet during "silent hour." For those who disliked enforced silence, this privilege must have been an inducement to join the Y. After silent hour, students might take an evening walk until supper. A boy and girl walked together only if chaperoned and if permission had been granted. College students were allowed a few more privileges. They could walk without chaperones the quarter of a mile to the Tougaloo station or enjoy other innocent pleasures such as picking plums and persimmons in season.

Sunday evening was filled with music and religious thought. Some students delighted in gathering after supper to sing the old songs, despite the school's emphasis on classical music. Sunday evening church services alternated weekly between preaching and class meeting. Preaching was always preceded by an organ service, and class meeting gave opportunity for students to tell of their Christian experience and growth. Students usually retired early at the conclusion of their "day of rest," to be ready for another week of study and work.

Like Allen P. Huggins in 1869, workers at Tougaloo were concerned for their black brothers and sisters who, while essentially religious, failed to associate religion with morals. A Tougaloo teacher calling on "one of the old aunties" might hear her expound on the glories of religion and visions of heaven and hell. But the auntie's religion failed to reduce her whisky consumption or to trouble her conscience when a lie served her purpose better than the truth. Many of Tougaloo's faculty looked upon most black ministers of the gospel as unfit to preach or lead. A large proportion of them was unlettered, and few were believed to be either intelligent or morally upright.

Some of the Tougaloo faculty, however, felt as did W.E.B.

DuBois that considering all the sins the white man had committed against the Negro both in and out of slavery, any white criticism of moral laxity in the Negro was presumptuous. One of the faculty admitted that "some of the most egregious sins of these old slaves" were probably "less in the eyes of God than many of our smaller ones."

To introduce a moral religion based on knowledge of the Bible and service to others, Woodworth conducted night classes for ministers already in the field. For long term improvement both Pope and Woodworth put their faith in the biblical department of the school. Slow to develop, it had but three members in 1889. Nevertheless this department, located in the inauspicious Bible Hall above the old slave pen, grew with the years, and out of it came some superior ministers. Men like Caesar Ledbetter and William A. Bender spread out across the state and beyond it, lifting in moral tone all who heard them.

Students of the biblical department were placed in charge of a branch of the Tougaloo church organized in 1887 at Sarah Dickey's Mt. Hermon School in Clinton. Traveling the fourteen miles over Mississippi's clay roads was always tedious and, in rainy weather, hazardous. Miss Koons wrote for the *American Missionary* of April 1887 a vivid account of one weekend's experience. She and President Pope, who was himself scheduled to preach the sermon at Mt. Hermon that weekend, were overtaken by darkness and a storm. At times the road could be seen only in a flash of lightning. The bewildered horse veered to one side, causing the right wheels to run up the bank, where a projecting root overthrew the buggy. Pope, out in an instant, gave his attention to the horse, leaving Miss Koons to disentangle herself as best she could. Stepping from the buggy into several inches of soft clay, she lost an overshoe. After some pawing in the darkness she recovered it and took her place at "poor Rob's" side. She stroked his head soothingly as Pope labored to release him from the shafts. This accomplished, the horse gave a couple of leaps up the slippery road and returned to stand close to Miss Koons.

Pope was tugging at the carriage with its two wheels in the

air when a flash of lightning disclosed two men on mules hurrying along the opposite bank. In response to Pope's "halloo" for help, they called out, "Who are you?" and hastened on. "The priest and the Levite having passed by on the other side, it was hoped that the Good Samaritan would appear next," but his not coming left Pope to right the buggy alone. Replacing the wet, muddy cushions and blankets, the passengers climbed into their seats and continued their journey. Dripping and muddy, they arrived at Mt. Hermon Seminary where they basked in a warm welcome and dried themselves by the glow of the fireplace.

The next morning Pope made good use of the experience in his sermon. He spoke of the need to take advantage of every "flash or even glimmer of the light of truth," not waiting to see all the way clearly mapped. He pointed to the joy which would be theirs when they safely arrived at the heavenly home where a warm welcome would be found.

Though the school constantly worked to convert the students and carefully reported each who gave his life to Christ, numbers were not the aim. It was important that the new Christian understand the responsibilities involved in his decision. Any emotional orgy was frowned upon. Tougaloo felt it had won a victory over ignorance and superstition when those at the funeral of Green Lemons, a Negro trustee of the college, laid aside "their usual wild and fantastic customs." They listened reverently. Evidently they were satisfied that this was a better way, as the next week the school was asked to conduct the service for a child who had died at the quarters.

Rather than emotional conversions, Tougaloo aspired to see a quiet working of the spirit accompanied by a desire for integrity of character. Aside from public and private worship and such personal qualities as honesty and kindness, character was judged by sexual purity and abstinence from use of profanity, tobacco, and alcohol.

To help students grow in these particulars, societies were organized. Greatest of these was the Temperance Society whose triple pledge saved many from profanity, tobacco, and "ardent spirits." At the beginning of Pope's term in office many of the best students resented his temperance preachments. But he and the faculty persisted, undergirding their arguments with printed tracts and articles in the school's publication. Each commencement gave them a wider audience to instruct in the evils of drink. One student gave a recitation during the commencement of 1879 in which he related an account of the death of a drunkard. The next morning he rushed to the office to sign the temperance pledge. Asked if he were not in the business of selling liquor, he answered, "Yes, but I shall bust it up. I felt as if I was bound for death." Another holdout who could not "give up the cup" finally signed. "You all got away with me last night. . . . I can't teach others what I won't do myself."

After students became loyal members of the Temperance Society, they crusaded for abstinence, distributing tracts purchased with Sunday School collections and circulating pledges with spaces for two hundred names. At the end of each summer they brought to Tougaloo a thousand to fifteen hundred signatures. When the students returned to their teaching posts for the next summer, they checked on their pledges to determine if they had kept the faith.

Some students met with strong opposition in their school districts. The old people set a poor example, buying whisky when they could not afford bread. They gave their children, even babies, whisky and ridiculed their young people when they signed temperance pledges. Both white and black thought it strange to see a young black man go to town and not enter a saloon. One girl was disheartened to find practically everyone at church snuffing or chewing and using the spittoons so thoughtfully provided. She did her best to influence them to "leave off" tobacco and whisky but found it a lost cause. Another student reported more success. He persuaded the pastor to give up drinking.

Probably the hardest temperance task which students undertook was that of reforming their own families. Two recently converted brothers returned to their home for the summer. Their stepfather, a heavy drinker, was accustomed to abusing the boys' mother. The young men, assuming control of the run-down farm, invited neighbors to join them and their parents every Wednesday evening in a prayer meeting. Before the boys went back to school in the fall their mother, their stepfather, and a "wicked" neighbor had accepted Christ. All three gave up drinking. "Oh Miss Koons," one rejoiced, "our home is a different place now."

Others than Tougaloo and its students were concerned about the liquor problem in Mississippi, a state known for heavy and almost universal drinking. The liquor interests had a stranglehold on politics through both Democratic and Republican parties. They influenced the blacks by telling them that without the proceeds from liquor licenses, which went to the common school fund, there would be no public schools. However, opposition was growing against the liquor interests. A convention of men from every county in the state met in 1881 and decided to work for prohibition. Southern Negroes in the professions, when polled by the New York *Independent* in 1887, were overwhelmingly of the opinion that the black race was hampered by intemperance, illiteracy, poverty, extravagance, and ignorance of everyday business principles. Tougaloo students argued in composition papers that poverty and most of the other named hindrances stemmed from intemperance. Money spent for liquor could not build a home or pay for an education. The temperance problem was national in scope, but though the North was "handicapped by German and Irish immigrants" a writer in the *Tougaloo Quarterly* (September 1885) saw hope for prohibition in the South. By 1887 over half the counties of Mississippi were legally dry.

Two societies closely related with the religious and temperance organizations were the White Cross for men and the White Shield for women. Knowing that if a black man attempted to defend a Negro woman by word or weapon he courted death or something worse, the White Cross taught that the best defense of the Negro woman was in the Negro man's virtue. It required of its men a pledge to treat all women with respect, to refrain from indecent jests and coarse language, and to hold personal purity as necessary for men as for women. Women were taught that their best defense was the "White Shield" of their own determined virtue and genuine modesty.

Other clubs added to the religious life of the school. The Young Men's Christian Association and the Young Women's Christian Association held meetings on every Sabbath. Composed of older youth, they used their influence to persuade those who had not yet accepted Christ to become Christians. Through missionary societies students learned that it is more blessed to give than to receive. The King's Daughters and the King's Sons, the two most prominent missionary societies on campus, interested themselves in local and foreign projects. Sunday School, too, was missionary minded. From the seventy dollars in its treasury at the end of the school year 1886–87, members voted to give forty to African missions, twenty-five to Tougaloo for library books, and five to the state temperance lecturer. Sharing what little they had with others enhanced the students' self esteem. One religious society of inestimable worth was the Covenanters. Without formal meetings, each member pledged himself to be prepared to take part in the regular Wednesday evening prayer service. The Covenanters assured lively and interesting meetings.

In retrospect some of the emphasis on temperance and religion appears extreme; but compared to the activity of other church colleges of that period, it was not out of line. It would be difficult to conceive of Tougaloo's success in developing well rounded, emotionally balanced students in a world organized to frustrate black people at every turn, without the undergirding of a strong religious teaching and its application to all of life.

10

Health and Health Services

BY COMPARISON WITH THE REST OF THE SOUTH, Tougaloo was thought to be a healthful setting. "We doubt if there is an institution in the South that can boast of less sickness than Tougaloo University," said one of its teachers. Yet one cannot read the fragmented accounts of life at Tougaloo without being impressed with the number of school deaths: the Nutting child, the nearly white boy who stuttered, Miss Eldrige who had selected the site for the cemetery, Mrs. Pope, the boy who drowned, a girl whose funeral sermon convinced I. S. Sanders he should transfer to Tougaloo, and others merely alluded to. Before medical science tamed many of the dread diseases that lurked in unsuspected corners, life was struck down without warning, leaving the bewildered survivors with the need to reconcile themselves to the unfathomable ways of God.

Prior to the Spanish-American War in 1898 which led to the discovery of the causes of malaria and yellow fever, Mississippi was considered an unhealthful place to live. Experience led people to conclude that high ground was safer than low and winter a more salubrious season than summer. They were right but for reasons they did not suspect. Mosquito breeding swamps were less likely to be found on high land, and mosquitoes multiplied in warm weather. Tougaloo, located on high ground, was acclaimed a healthful area. Yet even there the teachers complained in the spring of the oppressive heat and mosquitoes "so numerous and hungry that we all look as if we had the small pox."

Of the mosquito-carried diseases, malaria was endemic. Mrs. Pope died of malarial pneumonia in 1883, and several teachers gave up teaching at Tougaloo because they contracted malaria. Contrary to a popular belief, Negroes often suffered from malarial fever.

Tougaloo's first real bout with yellow fever came in the summer of 1878. The epidemic started as far north as Memphis and worked its way southward. Secretary M. E. Strieby of the A.M.A. urged D. I. Miner, Tougaloo's business manager, to leave, but Miner felt he could not forsake the skeleton crew of men, women, and students left to maintain the farm and prepare for the opening of school in the fall. People were already "panicky" because malarial fever sent one after another to bed. The less sick cared for the more sick and the recovered for the newly sick. Fortunately Miner and his family remained in as good health as the extremely hot weather allowed.

Miner was forced to make decisions, the responsibility for which he would have preferred to share with President G. Stanley Pope or Secretary Strieby, but both were too distant. He gave up all building operations thinking that even if workmen would come out from Jackson it would be unsafe for those at Tougaloo to have them on the grounds. Farming operations were curtailed almost to the necessary care of the stock. Should yellow fever break out in Jackson, Miner realized, it would be impossible to cash checks or get a bill changed, and mail service might be irregular. To meet such an emergency Strieby sent Miner a hundred dollars in small currency by registered mail.

Those on the grounds listened with alarm to reports of the advance of the fever. It reached Holly Springs where people were swiftly and often fatally struck down; it continued south another hundred miles to Grenada then to Canton, sixteen miles to the north of Tougaloo. It had not yet broken out in Jackson, seven miles to the south, but the city was like a deserted town. The few who remained were under strict quarantine. Miner closed the Sabbath School in the latter part of

August. Everyone hoped for an early frost before the yellow fever reached Tougaloo and Jackson.

In New York, the A.M.A. anxiously watched the telegraphic reports. Early in September when Jackson reported cases of yellow fever, the office sent what money it could for Tougaloo students and other black victims in Jackson. The poor, including most Negroes, were unable to leave the city and faced much hardship and suffering. Though cases of fever were numerous, about eighty percent of the Jackson victims recovered. This good record was attributed to cleanliness and disinfectants which Jackson urged upon all.

When in October a case of yellow fever occurred within a mile of the school, Miner took his family six miles into the woods. They settled in a cottage which he had secured earlier for just such an emergency. Making themselves comfortable, they prepared to stay until the first hard frost, which did not come until near the end of November. After that students slowly trickled back to school.[1]

Tougaloo took succeeding epidemics of yellow fever in stride. It imposed quarantine early. Supplies brought from Jackson were left at "Quarantine Oaks" or on the Moman grounds across the tracks, where they were picked up by the Tougaloo wagon. Since Tougaloo University had become known as safe ground, numbers of Jackson friends fled to the school's campus at the onset of an epidemic. School opening was delayed by several weeks at least five times between 1887 and 1899 before the fall frosts eliminated the danger of yellow fever.

In common with all schools of the nineteenth century, Tougaloo had its share of illnesses. Considering that water was drawn from cisterns, the existence of sluggish creeks and Molasses Lake, the use of outhouses as late as the 1950s, and the rats mentioned in letters, it is remarkable that the school never had a typhoid epidemic.

Pope and the teachers believed Negro students lacked the

---

1. The University of Mississippi, 180 miles to the north, had opened in the middle of November.

physical stamina of northern young people. The faculty encouraged students to endure hardships, but Pope felt improvement in dormitory heating was essential to decrease the number of pneumonia cases. When the insurance company refused approval of kerosene stoves throughout the school, Miner asked if they could be had for the sickrooms. He and Pope were in constant fear that teachers who sat up with the sick during the cold winter nights might come down with pneumonia.

Before Tougaloo had a hospital or sufficient buildings to permit effective isolation, measles, mumps, and other contagious diseases quickly swept throughout the student body. Only those immune because of prior exposure were left to care for the sick and continue the school work.

Epidemics of smallpox were not infrequent. Tougaloo was practically under quarantine from February 1900 to the end of the school year because of the prevalence of smallpox in the Jackson community. No new boarding students were accepted, and day students were excluded. Not wishing to risk unnecessary exposure, Tougaloo invited only a few guests to the commencement that year. Among them were Governor Longino, Secretary of State Power, ex-Congressman Hooker, and several pastors. No general invitation was given to the public. In 1918 smallpox combined with the influenza epidemic to claim the life of one teacher.

While care of the sick demanded immediate attention, Tougaloo was concerned with general improvement in the health of black people. The death rate among Negroes, according to those southern cities which maintained records, nearly doubled that of whites. The fact was not surprising in view of the poverty, ignorance, and high birthrate. Nearly half the Negro deaths were of little children. Tougaloo's carpenter shop often made coffins for the children of the neighborhood. Undoubtedly the death rate was higher after emancipation than before, though records are inadequate to afford proof. Much education was required to teach blacks to care for themselves as well as their former masters had cared for them when they had a high market value.

Tougaloo's curriculum included instruction in hygiene and home nursing, to replace widespread superstitions. One girl was discovered crying after she was forced to take her first bath. She feared she would be desperately ill from having "wet" all her skin at once. A woman who lived on the school's plantation attributed the good health of one of her children to dishwater baths. "Grease is good for her," she explained. To overcome such misconceptions, health principles were reduced to a set of rules. Among them were:

1. Avoid going into the presence of any contagious disease when perspiring or when the system is not fortified by food. An empty stomach and open pores increase the susceptibility to take disease.
2. It is best to bathe just before going to bed as any danger of catching cold is thus avoided, and the complexion is improved by keeping warm for several hours after leaving the bath.
3. Under no circumstances should a child be put to bed with cold feet. Sleep will be disturbed and sore throat or colds are apt to follow on account of the blood being drawn to the surface.
4. One of the best doctors we know is Dr. Rubber Hot Water Bag.
5. Milk should not be taken at, but between meals. It is a complete food in itself, containing all the necessary elements . . . but if taken with other foods tends to billiousness, because it gives the stomach too much to do.

When, despite preventive practices, students became ill, they were cared for in their respective halls by the tenth grade boys and girls assisted by the ninth. All had been trained in home nursing.

In 1890 a nurse training class taught by a trained nurse was added to the first and second years of the normal course. Special students, at least twenty years of age, who could present certificates of moral character, were also eligible. Lack of hospital practice precluded recognition as professional nurses, but the graduates qualified as trained attendants for the sick. They were competent to care for cases of fever, convalescents, chronic diseases, and other cases a physician might entrust to them.

In 1897 a prominent Jackson physician gave five young

women in nurse training a thorough written and oral examination similar to those given hospital nurses, covering far more than was expected of trained attendants. All five did so well that they were given certificates. Within three days after the story hit the Jackson papers, two were engaged in the new hospital connected with the state asylum for the insane and another was given work in Natchez.

The training of nurses was facilitated, and of greater benefit to Tougaloo students, after a small hospital of eight rooms was erected in 1901. Many later catalogs give 1889 as the date of construction. This date does not square with articles written in the 1890s referring to the lack of a hospital. A two-storied building, it had running water on the first floor, in a kitchen equipped with an iron sink. Improvements between 1920–26 included oil stoves, water piped to the upstairs, indoor toilets, and the addition of a bathroom. After the sudden and tragic loss of the hospital by fire in December 1926, the new Sarah A. Dickey Memorial Hospital was built.

By the end of Holmes's administration (1933) the school nurse was giving most of her time to preventive work. After the county health officer struck terror into the hearts of many students, causing widespread weeping and hysteria, the nurse obtained a permit to vaccinate against smallpox. She administered the vaccine to but a few each day and thereby maintained calm. All boarding students were examined by a doctor at the beginning of each year, and parents were notified of any abnormal conditions. The nurse examined students of the lower grades and the day students of the upper, though they too could have a doctor's examination upon payment of a fee of one dollar. Wasserman tests were given when recommended. Of the eight tests made in 1934 none was positive. A growth record indicating age, weight, and height was kept of each boarding student and pupil of Daniel Hand School.

With the school health program in effective operation, the next administration, in cooperation with the health offices of Madison and Hinds counties, was ready to launch a program to improve the health of the community.

11

Finances During the Administrations of Pope and Woodworth

ULTIMATE RESPONSIBILITY FOR THE FINANCES of Tougaloo University resided in the American Missionary Association, but it could not have operated without help from other sources. After the Freedmen's Bureau went out of existence in 1871, the state legislature made annual appropriations of from $1,500 to $4,500 every year except two until 1890.

Events leading to the withdrawal of state funds during those two years form an interesting chapter in Tougaloo's history. When, through violence and an appeal to racism, white antebellum leaders of the state ousted the Reconstruction government in the fall of 1875, economy became the watchword. However, public education had gained sufficient support to make it impossible to turn the clock back to pre-war days when there was no public education of any consequence for the white population and none whatever for the Negro. It is usually assumed that the legislature's interest in starving the public schools, especially those for Negroes, influenced its withdrawal of appropriations from Tougaloo in 1877. While probably true that the legislature did not favor state support of a school for Negroes controlled by northern men, extant letters give a more complicated picture.

The A.M.A.'s violation of the school's charter gave the state a legal basis for denying appropriations. Whereas the charter specified that the board of trustees should have power "upon the nomination of the A.M.A. to appoint a President of the Uni-

103

versity together with such professors and instructors as may be necessary to form an efficient faculty," the A.M.A. hired and fired at will and refused to consider Negro candidates proposed by the state members of the board.

The board of trustees was made up of both black and white state and A.M.A. appointments. During L. A. Darling's tenure the state members, most outspoken of whom were the Hon. James Hill, black secretary of state, and Col. J. L. Power, white chairman of the board and editor of the *Clarion*, urged appointment of two Negro teachers who they claimed were well qualified, Miss Smith and Mrs. Ireland. The state members of the board desired to encourage black youth by appointing blacks to the normal school faculty.

The desire for Negro appointees was not synonymous with a desire for integration. When Thomas Chase, representing the A.M.A., asked where a colored teacher would sit at meals, Colonel Power proposed that she be put at the head of a student table. Neither the state board nor the A.M.A. official was prepared for black and white to eat at the same table.

In proposing a Negro teacher the state trustees had openly challenged the A.M.A.'s practice of putting state money earmarked for teachers' salaries into a common fund from which teachers received as salary only fifteen dollars a month. No one but a missionary teacher could be expected to work for so little; and insurrection might be expected even from them, were a Negro colleague to receive the state rate of fifty dollars a month. Chase suggested to the A.M.A. that all lady teachers might be paid fifty dollars a month with fifteen deducted for traveling and medical expenses and twenty for board. Before the ink had dried on his proposal he recognized its weakness. A black teacher who lived in the South could not be charged traveling expense. Neither would she accept a charge of twenty dollars for board when the current rate was about half of that.

Already disgruntled because the A.M.A. had not acknowledged Hill's letter requesting the nomination of Mrs. Ireland, the state trustees were exacerbated by the dismissal of Darling and appointment of Chase without consultation with the board. Colonel Power reminded the A.M.A. of the school's charter, which specified that trustees were responsible for appointments of faculty and school officials. Chase proposed the New York office delay action until the board had time to cool off. Then, he thought, the A.M.A. could appoint teachers and be well into the term of 1877–78 before the matter of appropriations for the next calendar year came up. This arrangement would allow the new supervisor of Tougaloo to negotiate differences. If the school must accept a Negro teacher, the innovation would seem less a capitulation if the new administration did it. If no agreement could be reached which would give the A.M.A. the privilege of appointing teachers, the old maxim that custom makes law could be applied.

Thus G. Stanley Pope inherited the problem when he became president in 1877. Colonel Power wrote Strieby that while the state wanted to cooperate it could vote no further appropriations until the A.M.A. adhered to the terms of the charter. Though willing to allow the A.M.A. to nominate teachers, board members insisted on their right to elect and remove them. Colonel Power reiterated the trustees' desire to see a capable Negro teacher on the faculty.

Pope believed that if the A.M.A. yielded, it would soon be called upon to yield everything. If Mrs. Ireland, the Negro teacher, were employed—which Pope and Miner conceded might be good—the board would make other demands. Colonel Power had already stated that Pope could not be confirmed as principal until Darling submitted his resignation directly to the board. *This* Darling refused to do. Without ratification of A.M.A. nominations, the Association could not draw the remainder of the $1,000 due it from the 1877 appropriation. In making this deduction, Pope did the board an injustice. Though recommending no further appropriations, the board voted to pay the full balance, to avoid unnecessary detriment to the cause of education.

With no further aid in sight from the state, Pope wrote Strieby, ". . . do we live if we can or die if we must . . . ?" His answer came in the form of a cut in A.M.A. appropriations to such a low figure that Pope seriously questioned the Association's intention to continue the school.

In spite of economies devised by Miner and the matron, Sarah L. Emerson, the bills mounted. Virtually all the students paid half of their board in work. Students who had taught in the previous summer had state teachers' warrants in lieu of money. These could not be cashed until January. "What are we to do?" Miner plaintively queried. "Must the school 'go down' just when it is more prosperous than ever . . . ? When the school is full and increasing? When there is perfect harmony?" Pope wrote to New York, "What shall be done when we get to the end of our rope? Hang ourselves up?"

With an exaggerated flourish Pope informed Strieby that the students were collecting twenty dollars as a Christmas gift to the A.M.A. to help pay the Association's debt. He closed his letter with a postscript, "Can you send check for balance of my Dec. salary?" Two days later he wrote that thirty dollars had been collected rather than just twenty. "You will please take it from my salary and I will retain this." Obviously Pope favored a bird in the hand.

Some unexpected help came at the beginning of 1878 when Cardozo's bond paid $500. Cardozo was the black state superintendent of education who had absconded with $2,000 of Tougaloo's money.

Tougaloo always hoped for a financial return from its rentals, but more often they proved a liability. School funds had constantly to be diverted to meet renters' needs for cotton house floors, additions to homes, cisterns, and other essentials. These, together with taxes, almost equaled the income from the land. Because of excessive rains in the fall of 1877, renters were behind in cotton picking; and, because of the washed out roads, it was almost impossible to haul cotton to market. Thus all rent payments to the school were in arrears. Yellow fever in the summer of 1878 worked further hardship on the school's renters.

The Lemons farm posed a moral as well as a financial problem. The school had sold forty acres to Green R. Lemons, who was for several years a trustee of Tougaloo University. After paying $150 of the $500 he owed, Lemons died. Mrs. Lemons, paying $35 a year in interest (which amounted to 10% on the balance owed), remained on the farm. Darling had helped her to buy a house and groceries, for which she still owed $116. Having made only one bale of cotton in the fall of 1877, she defaulted on interest. "What shall I do?" pleaded Miner. "Turn her and her children away . . . ? Let her stay but refuse . . . further supplies . . . ?" Or should he continue to supply her, hoping for better seasons? Or let the indebtedness of $151 cancel her husband's payment of $150, putting her on the same rental basis as the others? Mrs. Lemons was not very faithful to the church, and she was so querulous in disposition that her neighbors would probably be happy to see her leave. Yet Miner did not want to oppress the widow and the fatherless—nor did he want to injure the A.M.A. either pecuniarily or morally. He wrote Strieby, "Don't . . . leave the decision to me. If the decision is made there that will be the end of it."

In the following summer (1878) conditions among the renters had not materially improved. Miner predicted that Jerry Nixon, with the best crop, and Alexander Castillo, who owed no previous rent, would probably be able to pay all indebtedness. Alexander Moman was making a good crop, from his twelve acres of bottom land. He would pay in work. Mr. Vincent, trying to tend fifty acres, would have done better had he properly cultivated twenty. His entire crop would not pay his indebtedness. He had a reputation for failing, Miner said. Mrs. Lemons was making her usual miserable failure and would be unable to pay any of her previous year's indebtedness.

Dr. J. H. McKay of Madison, who sometimes treated persons from Tougaloo, set off a flurry of excited hope for financial relief. Pope learned that McKay was a trustee for a fund of $10,000 provided by a man in Indianapolis who was interested in the Christian education of black people. McKay preferred to use it for an established school. Pope wrote immediately to Strieby suggesting that Dr. McKay be asked to visit Tougaloo ostensibly to make an impartial report to the A.M.A. on the work being done. It might be well, Pope added, to ask McKay to serve on the board of trustees.

Strieby either failed to understand Pope's strategy or opposed his devious course. In any case, he did not write to

McKay. In the meantime, at McKay's suggestion, Pope saw Mr. Musgrove of Jackson, another trustee of the Indianapolis fund. Musgrove did not have a high regard for Tougaloo because of the frequent turnover of teachers. He favored a new school at Edwards. Pope became apprehensive that both McKay and Musgrove might be Democrats and, being members of the Disciples of Christ church, would be "sticklish" on how the Bible should be taught. Discouraging as these two thoughts were, Pope still believed Strieby might write McKay and explain to him Pope's plan to make Bible study a regular and required course. It was an exciting dream while it lasted, but in the end the $10,000 built Southern Christian Institute at Edwards. Three quarters of a century were to elapse before the two schools would merge.

After two years, the state, whose officials never lost interest in the good work done at Tougaloo, resumed some financial responsibility for its success. Rather than appointing members to the board of trustees, it appointed a visiting committee to check on use of state money and progress of the school. This system continued until Mississippi's new constitution of 1890 forbade state appropriations to schools that were not free or that were under control of private agencies. Governor Stone, in his message to the legislature in 1892, said, "I do not hesitate to express the belief that no appropriation ever made for the education of the colored race has yielded as good returns, and if not prohibited by section 208 of the Constitution, I should cheerfully and earnestly recommend the usual appropriation."

Scholarships, usually administered through the A.M.A., were a source of income. An A.M.A. commission—sent to England in 1865 to raise funds for the education of the freedmen—obtained a number of pledges for annual scholarships. Scholarships were popular among donors because of the personal relationship which could be developed with the student. All recipients were expected to write their benefactors periodically. Pope learned on his first attempt that getting the letters written could be a difficult task. G. C. Granberry, on an English scholarship, was away teaching and did not write. Mason wrote "so poor a letter while trying hard to write a very good one" that Pope asked for him to be excused that year. H. T. Tanner wrote to his donor, Miss D. E. Emerson in the New York office of the A.M.A.: "Your donation to me was gratefully excepted. . . . your sister is well and seme to enjoy over hear. . . . I hope you the gratest success and ask you to pay for me that I may use the opertunity that God gave me." Had Pope been able to foresee the future attainments of these scholarship students—Tanner, for example, as a teacher at Alcorn College and a Tougaloo commencement speaker in 1888—he might have refrained from apologizing that he was not very proud of these letters but thought it best to send them as they were.

The A.M.A. vacillated between red and black ink in its financial statements. Repercussions from each business depression were felt in the Association's treasury, which needed $1,000 a day for general expenses. Not until 1879 did it find relief from a debt incurred during the panic of 1873. In 1885 it was again in debt but quickly recovered in 1887. The nationwide depression of 1893 was reflected in another stubborn deficit. Legacies fell off, and by 1895 the debt had mounted to more than $96,000. A Jubilee Fund composed of $50 shares sought to raise $100,000 beyond normal expenditures in commemoration of the A.M.A.'s fiftieth anniversary.

Wartime prosperity of 1898 accomplished what the "trumpet call of the Jubilee year" to those who "love our Lord and his needy poor" failed to do: it cleared the debt. Then, in a spirit of patriotism and compassion for the Puerto Ricans, the A.M.A. plunged into a program in America's newly acquired island. The Association's resources were spread more thinly than ever. Funds were required to cover work among the Mendis in Africa, the white mountain people in the Appalachians, the Chinese in California, the American Indians, the southern Negroes and now the Puerto Ricans. In 1903 the A.M.A. was again saddled with a debt of more than $19,000.

Whenever the A.M.A. was in debt, Tougaloo, like its sister institutions, was forced to retrench. Projects already started suffered. Strieby Hall, with its renovation for classroom use delayed, was only partially used for several years. Later declared unsafe, it was razed, leaving an ugly hole on the campus. In Old

Galloway Hall's entire twenty years of service, the basement was never finished. For want of repairs and an efficient sewer, plumbing in whole buildings had to be abandoned in favor of student carriers of water and outdoor privies. And what was worse, students were turned away for lack of facilities.

The high point of the 1888 annual meeting of the A.M.A. was the announcement of Daniel Hand's million dollar gift, believed to be the largest ever made up to that time in America by a living donor to a benevolent society. This large gift was recognition of the confidence Mr. Hand placed in the Association to use the money wisely. It was also recognition that despite years of "obloquy and danger" the A.M.A. had been true to the blacks. Daniel Hand, a businessman from the North who made his money as a merchant in Georgia, stipulated that only the interest on his gift of $1,000,894.25 should be used to educate colored people in the South. Drawing on money from the Daniel Hand Educational Fund for Colored People, Tougaloo started the Daniel Hand Primary School in 1890. It was located just outside the campus.

Two other important benefactors during this period were John F. Slater, a New England textile manufacturer, and Stephen Ballard. In 1884 the Slater Fund, established two years before, voted $2,000 for Tougaloo. In keeping with the policy of the Slater trustees who allocated the interest on the million dollar fund, Tougaloo used the money for industrial equipment and salaries of industrial arts teachers. In ensuing years the Slater Fund increased its grants to Tougaloo by several thousand dollars a year. Stephen Ballard gave $5,000 in 1885 for the building of Ballard Hall and Ballard Shops. Two years later he made another gift which enabled the girls to engage in practice housekeeping on a modest scale in temporary quarters over the old slave pen.

Endowments, continually sought, amounted to very little. By the end of Holmes's administration (1933), they totaled less than $50,000. Among alumni the school promoted a "living endowment"—an organization of persons who promised to contribute a regular sum to the college each year. A gift of $500 equaled an endowment of $10,000; a contribution of $800 equaled an endowment of $16,000.

Tougaloo's alumni were not the only black people from whom the school drew financial resources. As Tougaloo's enrollment increased, its income from tuition and board became a substantial amount. During the years 1890 to 1911 enrollment fluctuated between 350 (in 1896 when the A.M.A. was deepest in debt) and 500. Usually about half the students boarded at the school. By 1907 more students were able to pay in cash than formerly. Tuition was from fifty cents to $2 a month, depending upon the grade level. Board, which included a furnished room, light, and plain washing, rose only slightly from the early figure of $2 a week to $9.40 for a four-week month. An incidental term fee of fifty cents was charged all boarding students. Music was a relatively expensive course because of the student's need to rent instruments for practice. Besides money payments, a daily hour of service saved the school the cost of hiring the work done. Taking at face value assertions of the administration that students in the industrial department became skilled workers, they must have made some contribution to the construction of buildings, for which they were paid but five to eight cents an hour. Products from the school's farm and industrial department brought $400 on the commercial market during the biennium of 1889–91.

From the beginning of their schools in the post-Civil War years Negroes contributed to the education of their race. They paid in taxes and tuition. Their churches throughout the South donated thousands of dollars in an early experiment with the matching idea, which later became so popular. Assuring a constant flow of money from so many sources was a monumental task. The marvel of it all is that the A.M.A. and Tougaloo could do it as well as they did.

12

Public Relations During the Administrations of Pope and Woodworth

A MISSOURI NEWSPAPER CORRESPONDENT visiting Mississippi found it incredible that, in a state where the Negro was so totally a nonentity, Tougaloo was heartily commended by white Mississippians. Southern prejudice that usually ostracized a "nigger teacher" was rarely applied to the Tougaloo faculty. Visiting the school did not cause white Mississippians to lose caste; it was the thing to do. White men of the highest standing had served on the school's board of trustees. The discontinuance of state appropriations from 1877–79, resulting from a difference with American Missionary Association (A.M.A.) policy, was accompanied by no hostility toward the school. When the visiting committee replaced the function of state board members, the most respected white people served on it.

Woodworth thought the favorable attitude of the "best" whites could be explained by Tougaloo's emphasis on industrial education. While all A.M.A. colleges operated on the assumption that education must be of the mind, heart, and hand, Tougaloo coordinated the industrial and academic sides of learning more completely than most other schools. Around the turn of the century A.M.A. Secretary Beard was amused at the excitement created in northern schools over the value of industrial education—an idea accepted by A.M.A. schools, especially by Tougaloo, from their inception.

Priding itself on never neglecting the "talented tenth"—a

112

phrase used by W.E.B. DuBois—to whom the race must look for its leaders, Tougaloo gave even them thorough industrial training. One young man, I. S. Sanders, who must be described as part of that group, used his carpenter's training during summers to earn his next year's school expenses. Sometimes his precision work was not appreciated, as when he was criticized by a contractor for wasting time "feeling" a joint. Advanced to the position of a finish carpenter, his painstaking work was valued. Equally proficient at metal work, this student helped to make the gate at Tougaloo's entrance.

The need of the state for black teachers and the quality of teachers whom Tougaloo produced predisposed the state to want good relations with Tougaloo. The superintendent of schools in an adjoining county, a member of the Tougaloo board of trustees, remarked on the moral influence of Tougaloo teachers in his county. Col. J. L. Power, editor of the *Clarion*, publicly repeated this sentiment at Tougaloo's commencement.

Commencements constituted an important means of promoting good relations. Events leading up to graduation extended over several days. These included meetings of the Sunday School Union and the Temperance Society, lectures, sermons, plays, special music, and exhibits of the year's academic and industrial work.

Commencement was a gala time for all. Parents of the graduates, who sometimes traveled as many as two hundred miles, welcomed Tougaloo's inexpensive bed and board. Alumni converged on the campus from long distances to meet former classmates; in 1881 one young man traveled thirty miles on foot. That same year two came from Tennessee to be married at their alma mater during the commencement festivities. The limited capacity of regular trains was augmented by excursion cars to bring people from within a radius of a hundred miles. Others, carrying large lunch baskets, came by horse- and mule-drawn vehicles, which they hitched at an early hour to the trees on the edge of the campus. Some from Jackson took the evening train to hear the choir perform the works of the great composers. By the end of the century the popularity of these concerts necessitated a special performance to accommodate the Jackson guests. Hundreds of Negroes from miles around, having no connection with Tougaloo but catching the spirit of the occasion, picnicked in the shade of the trees on the Tougaloo side of the Illinois Central station. Invited guests had to walk around or through this happy throng.

During the festive days preceding commencement, the campus assumed the appearance of a fair. Tables displayed examples of tinning, carpentry, shoe repairing, iron work, and sewn articles. Lunch foods prepared by the students were sold at stands. Strawberries from the school's new plants made a hit in 1878 and persuaded many farmers to plant their own acres from Tougaloo's berry runners. Mechanics visited the industrial shops. Colonel Power remarked that Strieby Hall, Ballard Hall, Ballard Shops, and Berkshire Cottage—practically every nail of which had been driven by students—were the best industrial exhibits. Farmers were entranced by the blooded cattle, swine, and sheep. Many, taking to heart Tougaloo's slogan, "A poor man cannot afford a poor cow," made arrangements to use Tougaloo's animals to improve their own breeds. Less dramatic, but equally important, were the exhibits of student essays, mathematical problems, drawing, drafting, and other exercises.

Before Woodworth Chapel was built, the commencement exercises were staged in the shade of the moss-tasseled oaks, weather permitting. A platform was surrounded by improvised seats which never fully accommodated the audience of possibly a thousand persons. On occasions of rain, the attendance was less but still too great to crowd into the Washington Hall Chapel, resorted to in 1879, or Ayrshire Hall in 1881.

On commencement day students gave an impressive accounting of their achievements. At the conclusion of oral examinations, the privilege extended the guests to cross-examine the students proved to the admiring audience that their knowledge was not superficial. While every senior had written an acceptable essay, only the top ranking boy and girl of the high normal, normal, and grammar schools were honored with the privilege of declaiming their essays. Beginning in

1901 (with the first college graduating class) the two top college graduates declaimed their essays also.

Specially invited guests, whose names always read like a Who's Who of Mississippi, almost vied with one another in their praise of the school's performance. Colonel Power, referring to one oration entitled "Whitewash," declared there was no whitewashing done at Tougaloo—it was genuine stuff. Admitting he was once prejudiced against education for Negroes, he confessed that Tougaloo had changed his opinion. He assured the school that the white people were then convinced of the need of education for all, white and black. At his seventeenth commencement he expressed regret that, because the new (1890) state constitution prohibited appropriations to a sectarian or nonfree school, the state could no longer aid Tougaloo financially.

Student orations impressed an educator by their lack of a Negro accent. With his eyes shut, he said, he would have believed the speakers were white—accent, thought, expression were white. Dr. Charles B. Galloway, then editor of a Methodist publication known as the *Southern Christian Advocate*, commended the school on the original, direct, practical, commonsense way in which essays and orations were presented without any "grandiloquent gush." Thirteen years later he paid eloquent tribute to the noble character of the teachers who had come from their northern homes. Another of Jackson's leading citizens said, "Take back to your northern churches our acknowledgment of their generosity, and tell them of our appreciation of the work they are doing here."

A Jackson correspondent wrote for the New Orleans *Times-Democrat* that all who attended were loud in their praise. "See this work, Major," said one white gentleman to another, pointing to a neat class exercise. "Do you see that neat writing? And do you know that was done by a little darkey from one of the *cabins. . . ?* It is wonderful." Gen. A. J. Smith, State Superintendent of Education, commended Pope on the class examinations. Especially in mathematics the students surpassed his expectation. He was also surprised that the institution had such good discipline. Colonel Preston, a later state superintendent of education, declared Tougaloo had shown what could be done with Negroes, while Professor J. R. Dobyne, superintendent of the state school for the deaf stated, "You have the growing sympathy and respect of the best people of the state." A leading banker in the state, Major Millsaps, for whom a Jackson Methodist college is named, assured the audience that the best intelligence of the state was heartily in sympathy with the work of educating the Negro. Judge Brame spoke of the whites' desire to accord justice and opportunity to the colored.

One might well ask if there were a relationship between the Mississippi Negro's political nonentity and Tougaloo's acceptance noted by the Missouri correspondent. Seldom did Tougaloo's administrators cross social or political swords with the white power structure. Neither Pope nor Woodworth attempted to mix socially with the white community. Young Negro men were taught they could do little to protect their women from the white man's lust other than to respect black women themselves. The school and the A.M.A. usually stood aloof from politics and sometimes acquiesced in them.

Secretary Strieby, while acknowledging the wisdom of the amendments enfranchising the freedmen, saw nothing to be gained from a partisan enforcement of them. The use of force, he believed, would only renew old bitterness and bring but a temporary victory. Better to educate the Negro to be an intelligent and responsible citizen. This would give him a permanent victory. "If every colored voter could be accompanied to the polls by a file of soldiers armed with musket, his ballot would represent the musket and not the man." But if the Negro "becomes a property owner, and takes an intelligent interest in the welfare of the community, and if he acquires a character that challenges respect, he will need no soldiers to guard him at the polls and his vote will represent the man and not the musket."

Strieby contributed to the popularization of the deception that Reconstruction had been a colossal failure. It would be a disservice to the Negro, he thought, again to give him political power before he was educated to use it. During Reconstruction his "reckless rascality" squandered the public funds to the "ruin of the state" and the "disgrace" of the nation. President Pope subscribed to the same fallacies. The carpetbag regime, he held, but put the South in "turmoil."

Later historians, including Negroes who were among the first to search dusty documents for actual facts, gave a different view of the period of Reconstruction. They found that no state legislature was ever controlled by blacks. Negroes were in a majority only in the lower House of the South Carolina legislature. Mississippi had sixteen black members in its House in 1876 and five in the Senate; six in the House and none in the Senate in 1890. The revisionist historians further found that money recklessly spent benefited whites more than Negroes; that money involved in southern scandals was minor compared to what was squandered by the Tweed Gang, the Whisky Ring, and other notorious northern operators during the Grant Administration or the money embezzled and wasted immediately before and after Reconstruction in Mississippi. As for carpetbaggers (a term of derision used to describe Northerners who came south after the Civil War), they were found to be good and bad in about the same proportion as the usual run of politicians. Tougaloo was, in fact, indebted to numerous carpetbaggers, among them Allen P. Huggins and Gov. Adelbert Ames.

After a Tougaloo student publication printed an article unflattering to whites, Pope acted to pacify the irate Jackson *Clarion*. He promised to examine future material that went into the student paper. Alarmed that their rights were being whittled away and their representation in government diminished, students clamored for political action. Pope told them they should fit themselves for intelligent citizenship, stay out of politics, and accept the Jim Crow situation as one not to be helped by "bad spirit." He urged them to accept what they could not remedy. Pope's advice appears little different from that of Henry Baldwin, Jr., a northern man sent to the South to operate an efficient railroad, who admonished the Negro to "avoid social questions, leave politics alone; be patient; live moral lives; live simply, learn to work and to work intelligently." A few students resented Pope's attitude and left Tougaloo rather than submit to his policies.

A man of Woodworth's intelligence and reading must have followed the newspapers of the state, which openly reported that the basic reason for rewriting the constitution in 1890 was to disfranchise the black man. The Jackson *Clarion-Ledger's* editor wrote that Mississippians did not object to the Negro's voting "on account of ignorance but on account of color." His paper quoted with approval the statement: "If every colored man in Mississippi were a graduate of Yale College the two races would remain just as widely separated as they are now in all political and social matters." This editor was none other than Tougaloo's most ardent admirer and friend, Colonel Power.

Though A.M.A. officials by then were decrying the discussion of Negro rights which they believed were not open to debate, and though Senator Lodge's Federal Election Bill in Congress attempted to end the fraud which frequently nullified the Fifteenth Amendment in Mississippi and other southern states, Woodworth used his pen to extol the Mississippi constitution of 1890. Because it required that every voter must be able to read any section of the state constitution or "be able to understand the same when read to him, or give a reasonable interpretation thereof," Woodworth thought it said in effect, "You can vote if you can read." This, he predicted, would stimulate the Negro to get an education, and Tougaloo would no doubt be compelled to expand. Perhaps Woodworth could not find it in his heart to believe his fellow whites would not live up to the promise implied in the new constitution that those who were educated could vote.

But the Negroes soon learned that the general understanding at the constitutional convention that registrars would pass illiterate whites but not illiterate blacks meant, in practice, a limitation on all blacks—both literate and illiterate. No amount of knowledge, not even a sophisticated explanation made by a college graduate of the most profound clause in the constitution, would qualify a Negro to vote if the registrar did not want him to qualify.

The "best" white people of Mississippi could well afford to support Tougaloo University. So long as it acquiesced in the social and political arrangements of the state, they had nothing to lose and everything to gain by being magnanimous. In the summers the great lumber mills of Mississippi and Louisiana called for all the students Tougaloo could give them. The school sent out excellent school teachers, scientific farmers, good workmen, and moral homemakers. None of these was a threat to white Mississippians.

Before anyone sits in judgment on Tougaloo's policy let it be remembered that Pope and Woodworth lived in an era when most of the nation's best universities refused to enroll blacks and taught social Darwinism (survival of the fittest) and white superiority as theories of social science. Pope and Woodworth, however, held steadfastly to the belief that God had given this downtrodden black race the same potential as the white race. If Pope and Woodworth acquiesced in the political and social structure of the region, they did so that they might buy time in which to educate the Negro. Within their limited means, they did this well. The time was approaching when an educated people would not be denied.

13

Campus Expansion

In 1913 Woodrow Wilson entered the White House, and William Trumbull Holmes entered the mansion at Tougaloo College—on April Fool's Day, as he was wont to recall. President Holmes, in his late forties, limping slightly from a tubercular hip, ascended the long stairs in the center of the mansion's entry hall. His wife of but a few years, burdened with excess weight and a chronic knee difficulty, clung to the mahogany rails for support as she accompanied her husband to the second floor rooms which would be their home for the next twenty years.

President Holmes came to Tougaloo well equipped for his assignments. He held two degrees, an A.B. from Oberlin and a B.D. from Hartford Theological Seminary. Successful pastorates in the East and Midwest gave him a host of friends on whom he might call in the interest of the college. And, as one of the faculty members phrased it, he was able to speak the language of money.

Four years after Holmes took office the United States declared war on the Central Powers. The long arm of the draft reached into every corner of the nation taking some blacks off plantations for the first time in their lives. Tougaloo assumed its share of the war effort. Of the fifty-four stars on its service flag four turned to gold. After Negro organizations persuaded the government to provide an officers' training camp for Negroes, several Tougaloo men received commissions.

120

White as well as black speakers appeared on the platform of Woodworth Chapel to encourage students to support the Red Cross, buy war stamps and liberty bonds, and save food. The speaker who made the greatest impression on the students was George Washington Carver, who demonstrated new uses for common plants which would release food products in short supply for war needs. The sweet potato could be used for bread. Tuskegee, Carver said, saved twelve dollars a day on its bread by using sweet potatoes which the school raised. Thereafter the baker at Tougaloo made sweet potato bread and the students pronounced it good. Dr. Carver also demonstrated how "milk" could be extracted from the soybean. Subsequently the students learned with pride that this distinguished Negro scientist had been accorded high honor and respect by a congressional committee for his discoveries. Some high government officials declared Dr. Carver's products a boon to Herbert Hoover's effort to save wheat and sugar for use of the allied armies. Carver was one of the talented tenth. How fortunate for the nation that his education had not ended with an industrial skill!

For the first time Tougaloo had a president who would spend much of his time raising funds and encouraging foundations to take an interest in the program at Tougaloo. Every winter Mrs. Holmes packed her husband's "heavies" to keep him warm as he limped his way about the North in search of dollars. His system was to speak in a church on Sunday morning and take a collection. During the week he called on individuals whom he had met the previous Sunday to present personally the needs of Tougaloo College. Back at Tougaloo, using two fingers (he never had a secretary) he pecked out "thank-you" letters on his typewriter. Small gifts were as promptly and graciously acknowledged as large ones. Most letters were a full page in length and told something of the work which the donor's gift would forward or some human interest story about a student. Each year he wrote follow-up letters suggesting to the donor that he might want to renew his subscription.

Holmes overlooked no opportunity to keep Tougaloo in the minds of northern friends. He frequently sent articles to the

American Missionary. Before the Christmas season he offered
through this journal Spanish moss for Christmas decorations
to any who requested it. The moss "used in light festoons hang-
ing from chandeliers or against dark backgrounds of Christmas
greens" was most effective, he wrote. One pound would serve a
parlor, three a small church, ten a large church. Tougaloo sent
the moss without charge, asking only that every church accepting it inform its membership that this Christmas greeting
came from Tougaloo College, an A.M.A. institution in Mississippi for advanced Negro education. It was hoped, he wrote,
that the membership would also be told that $155 would en-
able Tougaloo College to give one Negro a year of tuition,
board, room, heat, light, laundry, books, and incidental fees.

In June 1923, President Holmes asked the General Education Board, created in 1901 to administer gifts from private
donors of whom the Rockefeller family was the largest, for a
grant of $50,000. The money would be used for an auditorium
and classroom building. Representatives of the General Education Board visited Tougaloo College, examined its enrollment, faculty, sources of income, and property. Later visitors
from the same foundation reported that Tougaloo's buildings
were neatly kept and most of them in good repair. The greatest
need was for a new classroom building to replace Strieby Hall,
which had been torn down in 1917 as no longer safe. As a consequence classes were held in scattered rooms about the campus. The visitors added that the teaching which they saw at
Tougaloo was distinctly above average. They recommended a
$25,000 grant to be matched by the school for a one-story brick
building. Students and faculty alike rejoiced when President
Holmes announced the grant, the largest ever offered up to that
time by the General Education Board to a Negro school in Mississippi.

The Executive Committee of Tougaloo College and the
A.M.A. decided on a three-year campaign for an enlargement
fund of $140,000. In addition to the auditorium and classroom
building, the enlargement fund would provide $35,000 for a
boys' dormitory and $30,000 for current expenses to prevent
incurring a debt during the three-year campaign. The balance

was to cover the expenses of moving Ballard Hall down the hill to make room for the new auditorium and classroom building, of cement sidewalks and graveled roads on campus, of enlarging the water facilities and electric light plant and of an adequate sewer system—the lack of which had limited the installation of modern plumbing.

One of the sources of money which Holmes had his eye on was the Rosenwald Fund, established in 1917. Julius Rosenwald of Sears, Roebuck and Company used the major portion of his $22,000,000 fund to encourage the building of southern state elementary schools for Negroes. It being a policy of Rosenwald to give only the last dollars necessary for a project, Holmes waited until he was within $1,400 of raising the $25,000 needed to obtain an equal amount from the General Education Board. Then Holmes urged Rosenwald to consider the dependency on well-trained teachers of the many Rosenwald schools dotted over the state of Mississippi. One third of Tougaloo's living graduates were principals, teachers, or matrons of schools. Holmes quoted the state supervisor of Negro rural schools, Bura Hilbun, as saying that Tougaloo trained Negro teachers at lower cost than any other institution. William C. Graves, secretary to Rosenwald who personally passed on every grant, wrote in April that Mr. Rosenwald considered it a privilege to contribute $1,000 to Tougaloo College.

When it was learned that the new building would cost $70,000 rather than the anticipated $50,000, the General Education Board promised $10,000 more, contingent again on Tougaloo's matching the amount. At a special meeting of the board of trustees called in April 1925, Holmes reported that the fund was completed.

The architect, E. J. Hull, attempted to circumvent the problem of Mississippi's shifting soil, which had caused the ruin of some of the school's best buildings, by designing a structure of one story with low walls and a strong foundation. However, despite his precautions, the foundation fell victim to the soil as had all other buildings before it. Some years later, its stabilization cost about $56,000.

The one-story feature proved a misnomer, for the slope of

the land made basement rooms above ground possible under the two north wings. The building was designed in the form of an H with open corridors and two courtyards. The design was considered economical for construction, efficient for school purposes, and architecturally appropriate for open southern country.

The laying of the cornerstones was an important feature of the 1926 commencement. Nelson M. Willis, A.B., '14, spoke of Cyrus Hamlin whom he had known in the hey-day of the dean's influence. The cornerstone of the auditorium (the crossbar of the H) was laid in his memory. Mrs. Estelle Rials Nash, '07, who as a student had been close to Mrs. Woodworth for whom the library was to be named, spoke of her as the stone for it was laid in the southeast wing.

The building, ready for occupancy at the opening of school in the fall of 1926, was dedicated in December. Jackson Davis of the General Education Board, Dr. James H. Dillard of the Slater Fund, the Episcopal bishop, Theodore D. Bratton, who was president of the Tougaloo board of trustees, Tougaloo alumni—including Professors Isaiah S. Sanders, Lewis L. Romans, and Hartwell T. Tanner, all of Alcorn College—honored the occasion with their presence and their remarks. Three men were given special recognition for their work on the new building: Dean Henry W. Cobb, whose ideas and close supervision made the building educationally efficient; E. J. Hull, the architect, who contributed his skill; and Robert B. Ricketts, a Jackson member of the board of trustees, who served as chairman of the building committee.

Those present enjoyed several surprise announcements. The Jackson Tougaloo Club gave an added contribution of one hundred dollars, which when combined with five dollars previously given, was exactly the price of thirty auditorium chairs. The secretary of the A.M.A., Fred Brownlee, announced that the trustees had voted to name the entire building Holmes Hall. President Holmes had no hint of this development. The service concluded with the stirring Negro national hymn by James Weldon Johnson and his brother Rosamond.

Plans for the use of the auditorium expanded midway during construction to include accommodations for physical education classes and socials. This change meant the auditorium floor had to be level. Unfortunately the change in the structure interfered with the acoustics, which were always "dreadful." The Paul Robeson Dramatic Club often preferred to use the study hall of Ballard though its seating capacity was limited to 113. Some performances were held outdoors despite Mississippi's unpredictable weather. The flat floor disappointed those who had expected a good auditorium with a sloping floor. Nor was the physical education department satisfied. Agitation soon began for a properly designed and well-equipped building to meet the needs of that department.

Holmes Hall was only the beginning of the building program. Added to the former list of needs were a girls' dormitory, laundry and equipment, three teachers' residences for families, an addition to the dining hall, and a practice housekeeping bungalow at a total cost of $100,000. Again the General Education Board came to Tougaloo's assistance with a commitment of $33,333.34, payable if Tougaloo raised $66,666.66 before February 1, 1930.

One month after the General Education Board's offer and on the eve of the dedication of Holmes Hall, the school's jubilant spirit was sorely tested when the school hospital caught fire. Men and boys fought it with fire extinguishers and water. In their excitement some boys threw their bowls and pitchers of water on the fire, doing little to put out the fire but breaking much of the dining room crockery. Others, more levelheaded, cut holes in the roof to pour water on the fire below, until they discovered they were creating a draft which caused the fire to burn hotter. Finally the hospital was abandoned. Most stood watching the "pretty fire," but some young men redirected their efforts toward saving Ballard Hall next to the hospital. To protect them from heat, those working on its roof were drenched in water by students manning the hoses.

All thoughts of building expansion were pushed aside in the interest of a new hospital, which cost $16,000. Added to insurance collected on the old hospital was $6,000 from the sale of Mt. Hermon Seminary and an appropriation from the A.M.A.

Individuals and clubs, the Jackson Tougaloo Club being one, furnished the wards. A jeweler in Chicago who was an alumnus of Tougaloo made the memorial plate for a ward furnished by a Massachusetts lady. The A.M.A. appropriated $12,000 to endow the building. This was the first building to be endowed at Tougaloo College.

The new hospital was named for Sarah A. Dickey whose framed picture occupied a central place on the platform during the dedication ceremony and later hung in the entrance of the building. President Holmes briefly related how Miss Dickey, orphaned at an early age, struggled to get an education. After receiving her diploma from Mt. Holyoke Female Seminary, dated 1869 and also on display, she started Mt. Hermon Seminary for Negro girls. She gave the remainder of her life to the school. Dr. Silas Polk, a Tougaloo alumnus, spoke of various Tougalooians who were practicing in some branch of the medical profession. Dr. Underwood of the state board of health, with which Tougaloo cooperated in its nursing and first aid course, spoke of Tougaloo's contribution to Mississippi in the area of health. Climaxing the dedication service, every voice was lifted for the Negro national hymn, a song which was becoming traditional for high moments.

With the hospital rebuilt, Holmes resumed work on the $100,000 building program. Encouragement came from the Nashville agent of the Rosenwald Fund who recommended Tougaloo College as one of the outstanding institutions of its kind in the South. "There is no sham about this College. It is turning out some well trained teachers." Three weeks later he penned a postscript to a letter: "I do feel that this is a most worthy college and in great need of expansion to keep pace with advancing college standards."

Holmes based his request for another contribution from the Rosenwald Fund on the needs of blacks in Mississippi. "Populated by more Negroes than New Hampshire and Vermont have inhabitants, Mississippi has no standard College and no standard publicly supported Normal School for training Negro teachers." He continued to say that with fewer than 6,000 teachers for 464,000 educable Negro children, the number of teachers should be doubled. The need was the more urgent, he wrote, because of the increasing number of Rosen-wald schools. It was to help staff these schools that Tougaloo sought to enlarge. After much correspondence and delay, in part because of the Mississippi River flood of 1927 which caused Rosenwald to fear that the supplemental requirement could not be met, $8,000 was granted Tougaloo. When the supplemental funds were almost within grasp, the A.M.A. decided to appropriate an extra $25,000 to build a larger boys' dormitory than originally planned. Thus the goal was surpassed.

Altogether Holmes's fund-raising achievements increased the value of the campus's physical plant by approximately a quarter of a million dollars. Early in his administration he had built two of seven residences he eventually provided for faculty families and a brick building for single teachers. In 1929 the girls taking practice housekeeping moved from Berkshire Cottage into a fine home of their own. Old Galloway was replaced in 1930 by a modern dormitory for men which retained the name Galloway Hall. Beard Hall was completely renovated. The new laundry boasted the latest electrically operated equipment. Electrification of the entire campus made this possible. Sewers were improved so that more modern plumbing might be installed. Natural gas and a new water system served the campus.

The farm superintendent directed construction of a drainage system for the campus. Its puddles eliminated, the lawn took on new life. Campus roads were no longer washed out with each hard rain. To avoid washouts and pools of water, campus travelers had created a road that resembled a corkscrew. The farm superintendent laid a rock bed for a road that more nearly approximated the axiom that the shortest distance between two points is a straight line. While the Asa Turners, friends from the North, were mainly responsible for replacing the boardwalks with cement, students helped in the project. Even the Daniel Hand primary children gave a program under the auspices of the Parent-Teachers Association. With the admission charge a dime, the total was $22.60, which they contributed to the walk fund.

College buildings and campus had only one reason for be-ing—the education of students. Tougaloo still maintained that education for the Negro must not be *either* industrial *or* academic but *both* industrial *and* academic. With the aid of twenty-two fulltime workers, practical courses in stock breeding, agriculture, and green garden cultivation were taught.

The problem of making the farm pay financially continued to plague the school. The farm superintendent explained to the administration, when he took the position, that the plantation could pay its way only if the produce used by the school were credited to the farm operation at market value. A conflict of interest arose, however, when the dining hall matron wanted her department to make a showing of economy. The arbiter be-tween the two departments was the school treasurer—hus-band of the dining hall matron. After six years of failing to get a credit balance on the books, the farm superintendent left. Riley Alexander Hamilton, a Tougaloo graduate with a B.S. from Iowa State Agricultural College, became farm superintendent.

Holmes often said that when he came to Tougaloo Univer-sity in 1913 it was a manual training high school with a small college addendum. When he left it was a grade B college with a high school as a feeder. Gradually the South and the nation came to understand that a college education was necessary even for industrial education. Dr. Wallace Buttrick, president of the General Education Board, was fond of illustrating this point with a dialog he once had with President Theodore Roosevelt. Said the President, "I believe in Negro education, but I think eight grades enough." Buttrick reacted, "However, you'll admit that teachers of the eighth grade should have had at least a high school preparation." "Yes, I suppose so," Roosevelt conceded. Buttrick pushed further: "And . . . you'll admit that teachers in the high school should have had a col-lege preparation." "By Jove," exclaimed the President, "you're right! There's no end to this thing, is there?"

14

From Mission School to Accredited College

MANUAL TRAINING AT TOUGALOO assumed less importance as the emphasis shifted to the liberal arts. Most of Tougaloo's students were serious in their desire to fit themselves for life, but they worked under the handicap of a barren background. Those in the boarding school, by then sixth grade and above, were less prepared than were the day students who, living nearby, had attended Daniel Hand. However, the school had more opportunity to influence boarding students who were under its supervision twenty-four hours each day.

Teaching the lower grades at Tougaloo was often a cultural shock to a new teacher from an ivy league school of the North. Written English was poor, and a southern accent added to poor spoken English sometimes hampered communication between a Yankee teacher and her pupils. Edith Knight, a white mathematics teacher, stood before a sea of black faces on her first day and to get their attention started with rapid calculations. Not always understanding a child's answer—which might have been correct—she passed on to the next child for an answer. Such a buzz of resentment arose in the room that Miss Knight called, "Quiet, please!" The buzzing continued until finally she understood one who was saying, "The new teacher says she wants us to be quiet!"

When Lillian Voorhees became chairman of the English department, she and Nellie Augur revamped the program. Three days a week the students studied English or American

129

literature, one day written composition, and one day oral English. Because there was no other place in the curriculum for current events, they were used as the basis of the oral English. Club subscriptions to the *Literary Digest* and the *Scholastic* served as texts. Rotating each week, a chairman presided while students presented their reports, which were followed by questions and discussion. Miss Voorhees wrote up one current events lesson plan based on the *Literary Digest* and received a twenty-five dollar award which she almost threw away, thinking the envelope contained an advertisement.

Letters, being a form of written English in which students would need proficiency all their lives, received special attention. A well written letter might make the difference between getting and not getting a job. The structure, grammar, substance, penmanship, folding, and addressing of a letter were taught in detail. Teachers encouraged students to write home. Writing to their families frequently alleviated the homesickness which overcame many of those away from home for the first time. It also gave purpose to the lessons in letter writing.

English teachers required each student to read at least one book a month. But a problem for this program for awhile was the library. The books, at best too few, were not freely available. Mrs. Holmes, because of her experience as a church librarian, was in charge of the school library. Being stout and still having trouble with her knees, she had difficulty with the stairs between her second story apartment and the library on the first floor of the mansion. Thus the books sent to the school by friends remained inaccessible in boxes, awaiting her sorting and cataloging. Fearful that the books would be lost, Mrs. Holmes held tight control of the key. With the library locked except for Sunday afternoons, students had trouble getting their books for the monthly reports. Eventually Mrs. Holmes was persuaded to allow two of the English teachers to have keys. This arrangement continued until Woodworth Library was opened in Holmes Hall with a fulltime librarian.

The Round Robin Book Club had a two-fold purpose: to encourage the young men who went north for summer work to read and to help them save money. Working as porters on

Pullman cars, they were often stranded in big cities between runs with money in their pockets and nothing to do. Under such circumstances they easily succumbed to the lure of gambling and lost their money before returning to school in the fall. One of the English teachers gave each young man a book from her Book-of-the-Month collection and extracted from him a promise that he would pass it to the next person on the list when he finished it.

The English teachers encouraged creative writing. After Miss Voorhees left Tougaloo she coedited *The Brown Thrush*, an anthology of poems written by students at Tougaloo and Talladega colleges. A concomitant value of the publication was the raising of Tougaloo's prestige in the eyes of the Talladegans, who tended to look down their cultural noses at their country cousins in Mississippi.

The *Tougaloo Flyer*, a mimeographed publication, was sponsored to stimulate and reward good writing and to give the Business English class a business project. Candidates for the various offices of the *Flyer* were nominated on the basis of good scholarship and general qualifications for leadership. Officers elected at large were an editor in chief from the college department and an editor from each grade, a business and an advertising manager. At first very crude, the *Flyer* consisted of about eight pages held together with common pins. As student experience and advertisements increased the paper took on more sophistication.

Clubs reinforced classroom learning. One of the most prominent organizations was the Cheeseman Literary Society for young men. In it men learned parliamentary procedure and were given practice in making short speeches and quick rebuttals. Rudiments of a political campaign were grasped. Within the club an election was a "stupendous affair." For several weeks candidates made stump speeches around the campus. On the night of the vote Tougaloo's president, teachers, and students were invited to hear the final speeches of each candidate. The two leading candidates for each office were in the final run-off. Everything was done as nearly like a big political campaign as possible. The morning after the final election, the winners marched into the dining hall to the cheers of the students. "My but we felt good," recalled one Cheeseman. Inauguration day was the grand finale. On a Saturday afternoon the boys would select the most decrepit animal in the barn—mule, horse, or cow. Bearing the worst saddle available and decorated with a wreath, the animal was led to await the coming of the Cheeseman's new president. When he appeared, he was dressed in an evening suit, pleated shirt, standing collar, black tie, and a stove pipe hat nearly two feet high. "My but he'd be stepping!" His fellow Cheesemen lifted him into the saddle and led him about campus for a triumphal march to the front door of the mansion where the school's president would be waiting to give a short speech. The girls, boys, teachers—everybody—cheered.

Aside from the benefits the Cheeseman Society offered its members and the hilarity it gave the campus, it and the Willard Club for young women made a significant contribution to Tougaloo's cultural life. Assemblies sponsored by these two organizations featured a wide variety of literary offerings. Typical were a scene from *Romeo and Juliet*, Act III of *Julius Caesar*, a Dickens Evening, or a debate on a serious subject such as the Boer War or government control of corporations. Usually the programs included some musical numbers also.

The Paul Robeson Dramatic Club, organized in 1925, invited to membership any college, eleventh- or twelfth-grade student who was interested in dramatics and had a satisfactory academic average. Alumni who had shown an interest in dramatics when attending the school could be elected to honorary membership. The club aimed to appreciate and produce some of the best plays, to study, write and produce Negro folklore, and to gain experience in coaching for later service in community drama.

For students who cherished ambitions to write, there was Scribia, a club formed with the encouragement of the Rev. Jonathan H. Brooks, himself a poet. Several catalogs listed among the requirements for admission a rejection slip from some regularly published magazine or paper. When this "slip" was discovered, the catalog was corrected to read *acceptance or* rejection slip. At the fortnightly meetings students read and discussed their own short stories, verses, or articles. The club worked to bring the Harlem Renaissance to the Tougaloo campus. Considering Countee Cullen its godfather, it sponsored his visit as well as those of other prominent Negro writers of the twenties and thirties, among them Langston Hughes and James Weldon Johnson.

Other clubs continued or sprang to life as need appeared. College students who expected to teach organized a chapter of Alpha Sigma. The Phillis Wheatley Club was to girls of the grammar grades what Scribia was to older students. Musical groups enjoyed a perennial popularity. Most prominent among them were the glee club, orchestra, and choir. The two Ys had a long life and strong influence. Among the young men the Athletic Association was always popular.

A.M.A. colleges held out longer than most Negro mission schools against the "black power" advocates of the late nineteenth and early twentieth centuries who wanted blacks in policymaking positions. Tougaloo, like its sister colleges, had employed Negroes, usually graduates of A.M.A. schools, in the primary grades or in the industrial departments. Not until the late twenties under Secretary Fred Brownlee and his black assistant, Dr. W. A. Daniel, did the A.M.A. embark on a conscious policy of placing Negroes in the administration and on the college faculty.

Lionel B. Fraser was one of those who came to Tougaloo under this new stress on black faculty. From the Virgin Islands, he had earned his bachelor's degree at A.M.A.'s Hampton Institute and his master's degree at Harvard. Fraser had been in New York during the years of the Harlem Renaissance, a movement which imbued Negroes with pride and a determination to improve the lot of their race. On his return to the Islands where he intended either to enter politics or to teach, Fraser found the United States Navy in control. Disliking this situation, he accepted Dr. Daniel's offer of a position at Tougaloo. From 1929 until 1939 he directed practice teaching and was principal of Daniel Hand and the secondary school which together included grades one through twelve. When

Dean Henry W. Cobb retired, Fraser became academic dean of Tougaloo College.

The influx of Negroes on the faculty brought some changes in the school program. Though most of the black teachers had been trained in A.M.A. schools and were dedicated to the ideals of service, integrity, and spiritual values, they thought of themselves as Young Turks. They had definite ideas regarding changes which should be made in the school. Most interesting in light of events in the 1960s was the introduction of courses in Negro history and Negro literature. Another innovation was the accelerated program for eleventh grade students who made a better score on the college entrance examination than the average freshman. Those students were allowed to skip the twelfth grade, which was thought to be a year of marking time in most Negro high schools of that period. This program saved for college many able students who might otherwise have become discouraged with education. The highest average for the first semester of 1956–57 was made by an accelerated student.

Course offerings were multiplied. Whereas the catalog of 1926–27 offered three science courses—general chemistry, general biology, and physics—ten years later the catalog listed four different courses in the chemistry department, seven in the biology department, and twice the earlier number of physics courses.

Negro secondary schools and colleges operated outside the pale of the Southern Association of Colleges and Secondary Schools until 1928. When twelve hundred members of its predecessor, the Southern Education Association, met in Houston in 1911, a speaker who proposed that the Association should cooperate with Negro schools was looked upon as a radical. His supporting arguments—that the Negro was essentially a human being who could be educated, that professional education of Negro teachers was needed, and that education of Negro youth should be compulsory—went largely ignored. Members reflected the view of most white Southerners that blacks should be educated for the benefit of whites. They preferred that Negro schools concentrate on agriculture, stock and poultry raising, and domestic arts. But to control contagious diseases, black children *should* be taught hygiene and sanitation.

In 1913 Negro educators formed their own Association of Colleges for Negro Youth, later known as the Association of Colleges and Secondary Schools for Negroes. Encouraged by the General Education Board, this organization acted as an accrediting agency parallel to the Southern Association of Colleges and Secondary Schools (for whites). In 1928 a committee made up of both associations undertook to rate the Negro colleges as Class A or Class B. This rating led to a decline in the worthless diploma mills which had contributed to the disrepute of Negro higher education.

The early 1930s brought accreditation to Tougaloo College. In 1931 the Association of Colleges and Secondary Schools fully accredited Tougaloo's high school, making it the first Negro school in Mississippi to receive this standing. Thereafter, a diploma from Tougaloo High School admitted a student to any standard college which enrolled Negroes and which required no entrance examination. Because state policy was to approve any school accredited by the Southern Association of Colleges and Secondary Schools, Tougaloo High School was doubly accredited in 1931.

Although Tougaloo University had changed its name in 1916 to Tougaloo College, implying more limited goals, the college had difficulty qualifying for accreditation by the Southern Association. Its library, the academic degrees of its teachers, and its endowments fell short of the standards set by the Association. All these matters required money. The library was improved with the help of the Rosenwald Fund, which made three separate $250 grants between 1929 and 1931, each dependent upon Tougaloo's matching it with $500. Both the Rosenwald Fund and the General Education Board granted scholarships to various members of the faculty for upgrading their degrees. President Holmes convinced the Southern Association that the financial backing of the A.M.A. over the years was equivalent to a sizable endowment. Thus Tougaloo College received a Class B rating from the Southern Association of Colleges and Secondary Schools. With this recognition,

Tougaloo College's graduates were eligible to enroll in the graduate school of any institution requiring the bachelor's degree—except those with racial barriers.

State accreditation, automatically received with that of the regional Association, brought specific advantages to Tougaloo students who went into teaching. Tougaloo College graduates who had taken eighteen semester hours of education courses were given, without examination, a professional teacher's license valid for life. Those who completed two full years of college work with twelve semester hours in education were granted, without examination, a teacher's license of highest grade, good for two years.

Holmes believed in consistent enforcement of rules and regulations affecting students. At the beginning of the school year the home economics class examined each girl's uniform to see if it needed adjustment. A matron stood at the door to check the girls as they left the dormitory in the morning. If a skirt appeared shorter than the prescribed inches from the floor, the matron measured it then and there. In the interest of democracy no silk stockings were allowed. Matrons were charged with inspection of every girl's hosiery. Lillian Voorhees, a teacher who doubled as matron for the girls on her floor, confessed to insubordination in this regard. She refused to lift a girl's skirt to examine her stockings.

During evening study hours the girls were required to leave their doors open so that their activities might be visible to the hall monitor. Any girl caught writing a letter or reading a magazine during the study period received a proper sentence.

To avoid the possibility of poisoning from food sent through the mails, students were not allowed to receive food from home. If any nonperishable food arrived, it was returned, postage C.O.D. Anything perishable was used by the dining hall or given to some family on the school's plantation. Parents sometimes tried to conceal their child's favorite food inside a shoe or a pocket. One ingenious matron kept a Persian cat that sniffed all incoming packages. The cat invariably showed extraordinary interest in boxes that contained food.

Taking food out of the dining room was prohibited to prevent attraction of bugs and rodents to dormitory rooms. Some students found a perverse pleasure in sneaking out snacks. One, Mahala Irvin Smith, in later years wondered why she risked trouble over so trivial a matter. She always ate the food immediately and could just as well have eaten it in the dining room. Like stolen fruit, it tasted better outside.

Card playing and dancing were not allowed, but some contrived to do both. With a confederate to warn the cardplayers of an approaching authority, face cards were concealed while the players became very intent on a game of rook. Racing from the dining room in the evenings, the girls managed a few minutes of dancing in the music room at Beard Hall before their confederate gave the signal of danger. Not for some months did the girls learn that the president's mansion window gave him a grandstand view of their activity.

A few taboos were relaxed during Holmes's administration. Lillian Voorhees from Mt. Holyoke and her mother, the matron at Beard Hall, taught the popular dance steps to those girls who wanted to learn. There was no thought of dancing with boys. Though Tougaloo was the first coeducational institution in Mississippi, white or black, to permit social dancing—bringing some criticism from supporting northern churches—that was still further off in the school's life. William H. Lanier, Normal '81 and past president of Alcorn College, stormed in one day to remove his daughter from Tougaloo College because she had learned to dance. Mrs. Voorhees, mother of the "team of culprits," startled Mr. Lanier with, "We didn't teach *your* daughter to dance. She already knew how." He asked where she had learned. "That is for you to know," was the only reply given him. In the mid-twenties, tobacco, once forbidden entirely, was allowed off campus except for the younger boys. The catalog of 1932–33 failed to mention tobacco. By the 1930s students could look forward to Sunday with added pleasure. More consideration was given to the biblical admonition that the Sabbath was made for man. Although the school's policy did not yet permit social functions on Sundays, the Executive Committee voted to allow an Easter egg hunt in 1930 for the campus children.

President Holmes often patroled the grounds around midnight to discourage any wrongdoing. One night he spied a young man cautiously descending a ladder from a girl's dormitory room. The next morning he took the two of them to the courthouse, procured a license, and married them. Then the newlyweds were permanently dismissed from school to enjoy, presumably, a long honeymoon.

With the lure a good prank always has for boys, the administration had occasion to make numerous decisions. The boys' study hall never ceased to stimulate the imaginations of otherwise studious lads. One warm night with the windows open and spring fever in the air, the June bugs flew in and tumbled invitingly on the desks under the naked bulbs suspended from the ceiling. Some boys had thoughtfully provided threads. The June bugs took off like sky writers, which of course demanded attention from many of the sixty to seventy boys in the room. One inventive lad tied two June bugs together with a three-inch thread. The prize stunts occurred when a new teacher informed the boys on his first night that he was on to any little trick they might attempt. His education began promptly, and a few weeks later a more experienced teacher found his study hour duty doubled. Several young men accomplished the feat of placing Mr. Donald's buggy on the church roof. Another time some boys tied a calf to the rope which rang the church bell. Many had their nocturnal dreams interrupted before the cause of the erratic peals of the bell was discovered. The discipline committee expelled the leader of this prank. Though some forty of his classmates signed a petition for leniency, the verdict held.

Intoxicants were still "verboten." A few boys spiked the punch one night at a party. With an exaggerated solicitude for one of their most upright and beloved teachers, the students kept his glass full. Then they rocked with amusement at his tipsy behavior. Though the story of the incident had a long life and never failed to give the students a laugh, there is no record that anyone was severely punished for this prank. Not so fortunate was a young man on another occasion. Having appeared on campus the night before commencement with the odor of liquor on his breath, he was not allowed to graduate. He went to his grave years later minus his degree but not without a few bitter thoughts.

Student discipline sometimes involved more serious offenses. One young man, described as a "holy terror," had a penchant for carrying knives. Later, as a professional man and highly respected citizen, he sent his own sons to a school where one of his favorite, but most strict, teachers was then on the staff. Perhaps no better example could illustrate the success of Tougaloo in molding young lives.

Teachers were not encouraged to fraternize with the students. Reluctantly, Edith Knight was given permission to take a class on a picnic in the school's woods after its performance of *As You Like It*. Some days later she was called into the dean's office and shown pictures of a few of her students—boys and girls, cheek to cheek. Evidently some students had engaged her in conversation while others busied themselves with photography. The pictures proved to the administration that this young graduate of Mt. Holyoke in her first year of teaching was too naive to be entrusted with the supervision of students on a picnic—at best a dubious form of class activity.

Despite the heavy school load carried by most teachers, they found time for pleasure according to individual taste. Tennis, hikes, horseback rides, bird walks, flower cultivation, and carriage rides constituted a few of their interests. After Mr. and Mrs. Voorhees arrived at Tougaloo in a new Ford (1921)— the first automobile on campus—auto rides were another form of recreation for teachers. Miss Voorhees made a collection of Victrola records which she shared with students on weekends. Even hardworking men who came from neighboring farms to attend the pig and calf clubs asked to hear her records at their meetings. Rehearsals for amusing faculty programs, such as "Mrs. Jarley's Wax Works," gave fun to teachers and were often hilariously received by students.

Though two teachers apparently found enjoyment in not speaking to each other over a period of years, the relationship among faculty members was usually congenial. The jokesters, of whom President Holmes was perhaps the greatest, enlivened school life with their good natured banter. A very proper music teacher never heard the last of a note to Dr. Holmes which she hastily signed, "Love, Abbie." When a young lady from the North whose education had not included the mysteries of farm life asked what a steer was, she was told, "A eunuch." "What is a eunuch?" the young teacher persisted. "Read your Bible," came the amused retort. Thereafter her innocence caused much merriment.

President and Mrs. Holmes made every member of the faculty feel welcome in their mansion home, replete with tokens and pictures from abroad and choice books. They often gave receptions for the faculty, but more cherished were the informal occasions involving smaller groups where President Holmes frequently read aloud to his guests.

A critical illness brought a sudden end to Holmes's administration. For a while confined to his bed on the second floor of the mansion, he was removed by ambulance to a hotel in Jackson until he was able to travel to New York, where he and Mrs. Holmes spent the remainder of their lives. Holmes never lost his interest in Tougaloo College. After his recovery he wrote letters from his New York apartment, soliciting funds for the school. His term of twenty full years marked the transition of Tougaloo University, a mission school with a heavy stress on industrial education, to a modern, accredited college faced in the direction of a liberal arts school.

15

To the Utilities Revolution

IT IS DOUBTFUL THAT ANY ADEQUATE PAEAN has ever been written to celebrate the advent of modern utilities. Because Tougaloo University was in the country, it was deprived of city lights, water, and gas. When modern utilities were obtained in the more prosperous years of the 1920s, life at the school changed significantly.

During those early years when Tougaloo lacked modern conveniences and was concurrently plagued with a shortage of money, student work was an absolute necessity. Under the Protestant work ethic, student labor was considered not only a way of satisfying material needs, but, more important, it was thought essential for the development of character.

Ideally, and usually in practice, the work performed by students was a part of the instructional program. Their jobs rotated so they might learn different tasks. From the start each student was required to work one hour a day as a part of his tuition. This system evidently broke down for awhile, as Pope spoke of reviving it in 1878. The *Tougaloo Enterprise* (May 24, 1884) argued that it would have been more economical to use experienced workers. The claim might have been true had students been able to pay full tuition so that workers could be paid. Few could. Anyway, carefully supervised student work gave boys and girls the opportunity to "learn by doing" the normal tasks of the home. They also learned businesslike habits which would stand them in good stead were they either

141

to go into business or work for others. Economy, system, and punctuality were stressed as necessary to all work.

Those who could not pay even the modest tuition and board, which ranged roughly between ten dollars a month in the nineteenth century and twenty-seven a month in the 1930s, were given work aid in varying amounts depending upon the need. Work aid was seldom allowed until the student had proved himself worthy. No student was supposed to be admitted without sufficient cash to pay his first month's expenses.

In a few cases students who had no cash whatever were admitted as fulltime workers with the opportunity of attending night school. These signed a contract in which they agreed to work an average of ten hours a day for a full year. For their labor they received room, board, and tuition for night school. They also built up some credit to be applied in another year to their school expenses. Under exceptional circumstances they might receive some cash credit toward their future schooling. If a student were discharged for misconduct or failure to perform his duties properly, all board, room, and tuition credits were forfeited. If he left of his own accord, he also forfeited two-thirds of any cash credit he had accumulated. No day workers were retained who did not do good work and show an "honest purpose."

The number of day workers varied. In the 1920s there were about eight day girls—or adopted girls, as some called them. Each day girl was assigned to a faculty or staff member. A few of these supervisors gave their day girls money to attend a movie now and then. Because no money passed in either direction, the girls could do nothing that required a cash outlay without someone's aid. The male counterparts of day girls were known as farmboys. Their numbers were greater.

In the early days of the school an adequate water supply was a perennial problem. Nutting attempted to meet this need with more cisterns, one of which was not bricked for several years because of the financial straits of the A.M.A. Fortunately, the Pearl River ran within five miles of Tougaloo. When drought caused severe water shortage, student help drove a team and wagon to the river and returned with barrels of water.

Molasses Lake was another source of school water. The strange name has some quaint explanations. Its dark, murky water gave the appearance of molasses. Or, when the Union armies came, the mansion's molasses was dumped in the lake to keep the men in blue from benefiting from either the molasses or the water. Probably as plausible an explanation as any is that the lake was surrounded by sugar cane. When community volunteers cleaned the lake they were paid in molasses which the university made from the cane. All considerations of name aside, the lake served the school well. Its waters were pumped periodically into the school tank.

On the upper story of the mansion was a rectangular lead tank about three and a half feet high, two and a half feet wide, and seven and a half feet long. During antebellum days the tank was filled by slaves who carried water up the two flights of stairs. Under the school's administration the tank was probably served by a pump as was Ladies' Hall and later Strieby Hall. Ladies' Hall had bathrooms with hot and cold water. S.C. Osborn, superintendent in the 1870s, purchased a force pump and two hundred feet of hose to conduct water from the cisterns at the mansion to a cistern at Ladies' Hall. In 1875 he bought an Eclipse Wind Engine which he mounted on a tower fifty-five feet high, to pump water from four large cisterns to a reservoir on the third floor. From there water descended to the kitchen range where it was heated and carried through a hydraulic boiler to various rooms on the first and second floors. For Strieby Hall water was pumped to a tank on a platform partially supported by a gum tree. From that height it was piped to every floor in the building. The second floor boasted a bath for the young men.

With all this advance in plumbing, it comes as a surprise that Pope Cottage (1885), Ballard Hall (1886), Daniel Hand Primary School (1892), Beard Hall (1898), and Old Galloway Hall (1907) had little or no plumbing. (This may have been because of a shortage of water.) Teachers and staff members lived in three of these buildings. Each day students supplied them with a pitcher of water, carried out waste water, and dumped the contents of chamber pots in the outhouses nearby. Beard Hall had water piped into the hallways. Under each spigot was a drip pan. Overflowing pans and splashed water caused the floor boards to rot. Mrs. Voorhees, sometime after 1921 when she assumed the duties of matron at Beard Hall, persuaded the administration to put drain sinks under the faucets. This improvement saved the floors from further deterioration and eliminated the need for the working girls to go outdoors to dispose of the dirty water used in cleaning.

The Voorhees family solicited funds from their northern friends and relatives to meet in part the expense of installing a bathroom in their apartment on the first floor of Beard Hall. Mr. Voorhees personally helped to dig the sewer line to serve the bath facilities. The bathroom was shared with Miss Voorhees and another teacher who roomed directly upstairs.

For the convenience of the girls, whose welfare was ever uppermost in her thoughts, Mrs. Voorhees persisted in a campaign to get showers installed in the basement of Beard Hall. Sometime later a bath tub was set up in the same basement. Another tub was placed in the building for faculty use. These tubs, with no provision for intake or outlet of water, had to be filled by buckets and emptied in the same fashion. The rooms were unheated. A student would probably have given high priority to cleanliness if he took a bath in the winter under such circumstances.

Outhouses continued in use largely because of the water and sewage problem connected with modern toilets. These privies were smack up against Bible Hall and sometimes too close to other buildings.

Lack of modern plumbing facilities exacerbated the laundry problems. Operating evidently on the old adage that cleanliness is next to godliness, the school from the start assumed responsibility for the washing of all personal clothing as well as school linens. Each student was allowed a certain number of carefully marked pieces to be laundered each week. If a student had a penchant for more frequent changes—which might well be the case in the humid warm days of spring and fall—or if the student soiled more than the allowed number of pieces in doing an extra dirty chore, he or she might chance a few extras in the laundry bag. The efficient girls in the laundry usually stuffed any extras back in the student's laundry bag to be counted in the next week's wash allowance.

What happened to the engine-driven washing machine which President Nutting devised is difficult to say, but during the forepart of the 1900s students again bent over tubs to scrub clothes on a washboard. The laundry operations had at least moved from an outside shop with no equipment other than the washing machine, and later from the basement where the rats were prone to cut to shreds the freshly starched clothes stored in drawers. A new laundry house was built and equipped with a row of wooden tubs, hand wringers, a hand operated mangle, irons which were heated on the wood stove, ironing boards, and clotheslines—outside for use in good weather, upstairs for inclement days.

The laundry was one of the hardest assignments a girl could draw; and, in the judgment of the administration, an extra hour or two of service in it was suitable punishment for an infraction of a rule. Yet the laundry was not without its compensations, and often girls asked to work there. It offered more freedom for chatting and mild hilarity. On cold days the steam from washing and the heat from the stove were pleasant.

For over half a century the school depended on wood as its chief source of heat. The plantation woods were presumably inexhaustible, but D. I. Miner, farm superintendent in the 1880s, believed the school should buy wood when it was offered at a good price. Though he planted young trees to replenish the forests where trees had been cut, he feared the supply would run out before the new crop was ready. In the early years the mansion's fourteen fireplaces had made an inordinate incursion on the supply of wood.

Many young men performed their hour of required work in chopping, hauling, and cording wood for storage in a shed and in moving it, when needed, from the shed to the bins beside the individual stoves. One student in each class had the task of stoking the stove before the next class arrived.

There were times when the storing of wood was neglected. In 1874 Claflin was caught at the beginning of his assignment without enough wood to see the school through the heavy rains which fell in flood proportions immediately upon his arrival. G. Stanley Pope complained that hardly a stick of wood had been laid by before he came in 1877. Chips and old limbs had to be gathered to start the green wood, and then it took "about half the wood to get the other half fairly to turning." Gathering chips was almost an obsession with Darling, who filled one room of the mansion with bags of them. He evidently lost interest when his contract was not renewed; otherwise there would have been some for Pope's use.

Few buildings were adequately heated. The early dormitories had stoves in the hallways but not in the rooms. Miner hoped for kerosene stoves to heat individual rooms, but the A.M.A. withheld permission upon learning their use would invalidate the school's insurance. Miner later installed furnaces in the two dormitories, Ladies' Hall and Washington Hall—both of which were subsequently destroyed by fire. When Pope built the barracks he placed a stove in one room which the boys could use for study. Boys from Old Galloway Hall studied on the second floor of Ballard Hall where there were two stoves. At times some boy, weary of the tedium of Latin or English grammar, overstoked a stove. Then he would peel a bit of rubber from his heel and drop it on the almost red-hot surface. If the proctor were on his toes, the culprit was not allowed to go to the window for a whiff of fresh air. The girls, faring better than the boys, had no need for a central study room; they had central heat. For their comfort they were indebted to the young men who kept the furnace at Beard Hall stoked from early morning to late at night. Faculty members were assured a warm room. Those whose dormitory lacked modern heating facilities enjoyed the luxury of remaining snugly in bed until a student had a fire crackling in the wood stove and water heating for morning ablutions.

A school no less than an army runs on its stomach. An essential for food at Tougaloo was indicated in the title of the first lesson in the cooking course—"Making and care of a fire." Great honor is due those women and students who cooked for the large Tougaloo family on wood stoves that often parboiled the cooks along with the victuals. Day girls, remaining all summer, canned literally thousands of half-gallon jars of fruits and vegetables. These had to be preserved when brought in from the farm, regardless of what the thermometer registered.

While student labor compensated for the inadequate water supply, limited plumbing, and inefficient wood fuel, it also compensated for the lack of electricity. With no electric bells, the bellboy acquired great importance. He carried a watch, given him by the school, that was the envy of all other boys. According to its accurate time, he sounded the bell for every important event of the day. At exactly six o'clock in the morning he woke the campus with the bell's clear peal. His bell convened and dismissed classes. This duty necessitated his being a few minutes late to each class and leaving a little before the class ended, a privilege that added to his prestige. One bellboy, when called upon for a recitation near the end of the hour, said only, "It is time to ring the bell," and walked out. Probably no one was ever more literally "saved by the bell."

All lighting on the campus and in the buildings was done by kerosene lamps. Those on the grounds hung from posts along the boardwalks. A student lit them in the evening and snuffed them out in the morning at set hours. This was his hour's duty for each day. I. S. Sanders recalls with what pride he trimmed the wicks and polished the lamp chimneys in the dining room. Satisfaction in the gleaming chimneys and the even glow cast by his properly trimmed wicks was reward enough. Dramatic plays put on in Ballard study hall were staged entirely by the light of kerosene lamps which sometimes cast eerie shadows across the scenes.

In the hands of impetuous or emotional students these kerosene lamps were hazardous. One night several boys in the study hall gathered about the dictionary, which rested on a stand with its own special kerosene lamp. Suddenly two of the boys reared in anger. One grabbed a chair which he was about to hurl at the other. Not to be outdone, the other picked up the lamp to throw at his antagonist. At this point the proctor, a slight young woman of not more than a hundred pounds, shouted, STOP! The young men were shocked into replacing their weapons. One explained his anger as the natural response to being called a name so vile he could not repeat it to a lady. The "lady" meted out punishment to all the boys who were simply idling at the dictionary rather than using it for the purpose intended by Webster.

Another near disaster occurred when a student used kerosene in an attempt at revenge against her roommate for some offense. She spent the day carrying her own clothes up to her trunk in the attic of Beard Hall where by some inexplicable logic she thought them safe. In the evening, just before marching to the dining hall, this disgruntled girl threw a lighted match on her roommate's clothes, which she had piled in a heap on the floor and covered with kerosene. The Voorhees family, a bit delayed in going to the dining hall, saw a tongue of fire leap out a first floor window. Mr. Voorhees ran for the fire extinguisher and succeeded in preventing much damage to the building. Some fellow students recalled then that when the hospital burned shortly before, this girl had exclaimed, "What a pretty fire! I'd like to make a pretty fire like that." She was expelled as unsafe to have on the grounds.

Every institution has a potential fire hazard, but Tougaloo's dependence upon wood stoves and kerosene lamps increased the danger. Frequent incidents might have had serious consequences except for the quick thinking of a student or faculty member. A student, for example, was rushing to the dining hall when he accidentally brushed against the lamp, knocking it to the floor where it started a small conflagration. He pulled off his coat and, wrapping the lamp in it, carried the fire outdoors. Three times the school was not so fortunate. Fires leveled Washington Hall in 1881, Ladies' Hall in 1897, and the old hospital building in 1926.

With all the time-consuming inconvenience of outmoded utilities and the fire hazard involved, one can readily understand the excitement on campus when President Holmes announced a campaign for funds to purchase a Delco system. In 1922, after two years of soliciting through hundreds of letters and several trips to the North $1,510 was collected—enough to wire the church, the mansion, and several other buildings. Wiring for Old Galloway Hall and Beard Hall was left to the

Book reviews, story telling for children of the community, and displays made the library an interesting center of the college.

Class of 1893

Class of 1908

Class of 1928

Class of 1961

An unusual sight: snow at the mansion

Over the years Tougaloo has hosted many prominent guests. Here, Pres.
Beittel and others are in the receiving line for Dr. Ralph Bunche who spoke
on the occasion of U. N. Day.

Mrs. Thelma Sanders '46, receiving an "Alumnus of the Year" award here, was named to the Tougaloo College Board of Trustees (1969).

President and Mrs. Beittel chat with students during freshman orientation week.

The new science building, Kincheloe Hall, was built in 1959 on the site of the old laundry building.

Warren Hall (1962), dedicated in honor of Dr. Harold C. Warren, President of Tougaloo College 1947-55, houses dining facilities, recreational facilities, college store, and snack bar; air conditioned.

Dr. Robert Smith (Jackson-Tougaloo Club) receiving an award

Commencement Day, 1961

Joyce Ladner

Tougaloo College was well known for its interest in civil rights.

students to finance. A contest developed between the boys and girls to see which could first raise $200. Two painted thermometers, ten feet tall, were placed on each side of the walk in front of the mansion. Beginning with their red bulbs each thermometer was marked with degrees of 0 to 200. When the boys collected a dollar, red paint sent the Galloway thermometer up a degree. In the same manner were Beard Hall's collections registered. Both sides were elated when a check came from a northern man in appreciation of the care given him when he had been taken ill while visiting Tougaloo College. His check, divided between the two halls, sent both thermometers above the 100 mark. A boys' group gave dramatic plays; girls put on cooked food sales. Near the end of the contest the boys' drama troupe slipped away quietly to give its plays in nearby communities. Boys on campus, having heard by the grapevine that the girls were secretly scurrying around to raise their final $15, made their own collection before the actors returned. The result was that on the same day, April 11, 1922, both groups sent their thermometers soaring above the 200 degrees.

More letters and more trips to the North were necessary before Holmes could announce at commencement in 1923 the official closing of the campaign for electricity. He extended his thanks to the students and alumni who had contributed a total of $1,500 and told them again that his most effective argument with potential donors was that blacks did what they could to help themselves.

The school purchased a 20-horsepower Fairbanks-Morse Type Y special electric engine, one 12½-kilowatt electricity generator, one 10-kilowatt generator, the machinery for installing all these into one system, and the fixtures needed. Charles Bentley, Superintendent of Industries, having learned electrical installation the previous spring, saved Tougaloo the expense of contracting the installation. He did the work while carrying on his regular duties as a teacher and as supervisor of general repairs. This electrical system operated until 1928 when the Mississippi Power and Light Company extended its service to the college.

Electricity ushered in a new era for Tougaloo. The electric

light system was linked up with the water system. Water was drawn from the deep-well and deposited in a new cement cistern from which it was forced into a pressure tank which gave a steady flow. In 1929 a new laundry was built and equipped with the latest electrically operated machines. Gas replaced Tougaloo's dependence upon wood. Plumbing was installed in buildings erected in the 1920s, and some of the older buildings were remodeled to include running water and toilet facilities.

A technological revolution had eliminated many of the jobs that students had formerly performed as a means of helping themselves through school. Catalogs in the 1920s reflect the diminishing need for student help. Regarding the daily hour of work originally considered necessary for the development of character and home skills, the 1925–26 catalog said, "If for any reason this labor is not performed it must be settled for in cash." With a raise in school costs effective in 1927–28, a "student may perform one hour of work-aid labor per day," for which he was to be allowed $3.30 a month. The hour's work by that time had become "work-aid," the connotation being that it was for those who could not afford full payment. According to the 1928 catalog board and tuition cost $188.75 a year or, after deduction for one hour a day of "work-aid," $159. No mention of a daily work hour was made in the catalog for 1930–31.

Lost forever was the tradition that a student, regardless of his financial ability, should give an hour a day of service to his school. That service was done by electricity, plumbing, and gas. Furnaces fueled with gas eliminated the wood chopper, sawyer, corder, carrier, and stoker. Piped water, drains, and inside toilets ended the need to haul water, fill pitchers, carry out used water, and empty chamber pots. Electric bells summoned students to classes. Electric lights obviated the need of chimney polishing, wick trimming, and lamplighting. The pipe organ filled the chapel with melodious sound without a boy pumping behind the scene. Washboards gave way to electrically operated washers, and ironing was made simpler with electric irons.

The decade of the twenties saw unprecedented prosperity. More students could find money to pay school expenses than formerly. Prosperity was fickle, however, and the thirties would see students clamoring for work aid. But the hour a day of service as an integral part of tuition and an aid to building character was a thing of the past.

16

Depression and War

No institution exists in a vacuum. Like a person, it is often buffeted by external forces over which it has little or no control. Thus, four years after the beginning of Holmes's administration, World War I took priority over plans Holmes had made for Tougaloo College. Ironically, four years before his administration ended, the school began to reel from the impact of the crash on Wall Street. Only by diligent fund raising, cooperation of the General Education Board and the American Missionary Association, retrenchment in program, and reductions in salaries did Holmes keep the school's finances solvent.

Negroes felt the woes of hard times before other elements of the population did. As common workers they were first to be fired. Before any organized help came to their rescue, those fortunate enough to have jobs often shared their wages even with remote kinsmen and friends.

The depression gave birth to the New Deal, which was not an unmitigated blessing to the black population. Often government experiments in adjusting the economy worked hardship on them. When the National Industrial Recovery Act (NIRA) made higher wages mandatory, whites were hired instead of Negroes. The Agricultural Adjustment Administration (AAA), in giving cash benefits to farmers for removing land from cultivation, made many sharecroppers and tenant farmers, both black and white, expendable.

152

Some of the other alphabetical combinations were of more benefit to Negroes. From the Farm Security Administration (FSA, 1937) farmers rented land or borrowed to purchase their own acreages. Included in the FSA was an educational program which taught methods of production, marketing, bookkeeping, home management, and preparation of nutritious meals. A government survey indicated that during the first year of FSA operation more than ten thousand children in Mississippi were enabled to attend school as a result of FSA assistance and were more receptive to learning because of improved diets. FSA's field agent addressed an assembly at Tougaloo College to inform the students of benefits available to their people. Because of the nondiscriminatory policies of FSA's director, Will W. Alexander, the FSA was under constant attack from its enemies. By 1942 they succeeded in so sharply cutting FSA appropriations, never more than a fifth of the amount given the AAA, that its program was drastically curtailed. The National Youth Administration (NYA) aided the college more directly by paying students for work done at the school. The total aid to Tougaloo students was only about $2,000 over a period of five years.

Holmes's retirement in 1933 because of ill health left the college without a president at a time when it had little to offer a new man. A temporary solution was the extension of Charles B. Austin's duties to cover Tougaloo College as well as Straight University where he was president. The two hundred miles between New Orleans and Tougaloo were spanned by the Illinois Central, which Austin could board at eleven o'clock at night and arrive for an early breakfast the following morning at the other point. Austin probably traveled on a railroad pass as did his successor, Judson L. Cross.

Though Austin was a capable and energetic man, his inability to assume all the duties Holmes had performed necessarily increased the work load of other staff members at the same time that they were given successive salary cuts. One on whom extra work fell heavily was Jonathan Henderson Brooks. As pastor of a Baptist church in Kosciusko, Brooks had put himself through school, receiving his B.A. from Tougaloo in

1930. Upon graduation he was appointed assistant to the president, with a small depression salary. To augment his income he continued his pastoral work in Kosciusko on weekends. After Holmes's retirement, Brooks's increased duties demanded his full time. Resignation from his pastorate ended a close relationship with people he valued highly and also decreased his income by approximately four hundred dollars a year. Already on three occasions his salary at Tougaloo had been reduced. Struggling against a health problem (later diagnosed as tuberculosis) he drew heavily on sheer willpower to care for the needs of his wife, baby, dependent mother, and the college.

One of Brooks's assignments as assistant to the president was recruitment. Until the depression little had been consciously done to attract students to the school. Thomas Chase had earlier observed that Tougaloo should be judged only on the quality of its work, as it would be undesirable to "bring together a large crowd of these ignorant, degraded, rude children." President Pope had argued that a good catalog picture of Tougaloo's buildings was of more influence "with the ignorant people whose children we want here than a great many good speeches."

Aside from the catalog, Tougaloo had relied heavily upon its students to advertise the school as they spread out through the state on teaching assignments. In this capacity William H. Lanier was one of the most successful. Concerned for young people in his region, he held promotional meetings for parents of his pupils at Forest, where he first taught. Tramping into the backwoods on weekends, he encouraged parents to send their boys and girls to Tougaloo where they might have opportunities beyond anything they had ever dreamed. As director of a singing group he noticed one young lady, Amy Fulton, who always rushed in late for practice. Learning that she had been bound out to a white family, he arranged for her release and self-support at Tougaloo. Amy Fulton proved a good student, but before finishing the normal course she married a Tougaloo graduate. She lived an active and useful life well into her nineties. Like Lanier, many others teaching throughout the state were alert for promising students whom they could encourage to attend Tougaloo.

With the onslaught of the depression such low-keyed recruitment was insufficient, and enrollment dropped precipitously. A letter enclosing a fact sheet was sent to former Tougaloo students teaching in the state. They were urged to learn the facts by heart, talk Tougaloo, distribute literature, and send names and addresses to the Rev. Jonathan H. Brooks, who would then get in touch with prospective students.

College enrollment dropped less than that of the high school during the first few years of the depression. Backed by an "ardent slaving mother" or even a whole family who cut the home budget to a minimum, students having reached college level managed somehow to continue. The college helped many by allowing them to become indebted to the institution. To absorb these debts, faculty and students were urged to make every possible economy for the institution: turn off lights when not needed, reduce fuel consumption, and seek ways to minimize school costs.

Earnest students could look to the school for assistance in various other ways. While work aid was limited, most boarding students were able to earn from three to twelve dollars a month. The maximum for a freshman was six. Loan funds built up over the years by generous donors tided some over emergencies. Students who qualified as being in the upper twenty-five percent of their class or who could maintain a two-point average might win one of the scholarships offered by permanent scholarship funds or by the school. Among the scholarships and loan funds were those made by or in memory of Mary Helen Scott, Hattie M. Strong, Mrs. Lucius Eastman, and Dr. Augustus F. Beard. Numerous other scholarships were established in subsequent years.

The depression was no respecter of persons. Usually Tougaloo could do little more than acknowledge the numerous applications for teaching positions and wish the applicants well. Among them was the wife of the dean of Alcorn who, after twelve years in the president's office at Alcorn, was thrown out of employment along with her husband. Both were Tougaloo graduates. At the other end of the educational scale, an almost illiterate man asked for work to put shoes on his children's "bear" feet and to keep them in school.

With the cold of winter more feared than the heat of summer, Tougaloo's clothing shop became a necessity for many during the lean days of the 1930s. Friends from the North, beginning with Beals's arrival in 1869, regularly sorted, cleaned, packed, and shipped boxes of used clothing to Tougaloo. After first caring for emergency cases on or off campus, officials displayed the clothes in one of the industrial shops which students dubbed The Emporium—the name of a fashionable department store in Jackson. With the price at a minimum, students or members of the community could purchase clothing, thus preserving pride and independence. Low as prices were, especially during the depression, clothing sales brought the school a steady income of several hundred dollars annually. Whenever the supply fell off, the school sent an SOS letter to its friends, who never failed to respond.

The Rev. Judson L. Cross was made president of Tougaloo College in 1935. He had done eight years of promotional work with the American Missionary Association. Cross was largely responsible for the high morale of the school during those years of abnormal financial distress. When enrollment dropped, decreasing need for a full faculty, some teachers' positions were saved for them by fellowships from foundations to which Cross tirelessly made applications. The fellowships were also of benefit to the school in another way: when faculty members returned they held advanced degrees.

A fellowship from the Edward W. Hazen Foundation given to Mr. and Mrs. Brooks met a significant need. A small amount of only one hundred dollars a year, it was used as a supplement by Brooks in person-to-person relationships with students to help them find an "adequate Christian philosophy of life." If a student were discouraged and depressed, a meal at the Brooks home might help him snap back; a short trip, or attendance at a particular conference, might broaden a student's outlook. Brooks was invited to call upon his ingenuity in using the money to the best advantage of students. While he did not have

to account for every cent, his report on use of the money determined whether or not the fellowship would be renewed.

School spirit and morale were enhanced by the football
team. Under the leadership of W. H. (Duke) Williams the team
won conference championship for three successive years, giving the school permanent possession of a silver cup. Added to
this honor was the exciting news that one of Tougaloo's players
had been elected to the "All American Negro Team" by the St.
Louis *Argus*.

In much the same manner as heathens used to make human
offerings to appease the gods, the modern world periodically
offers its human sacrifice. The depression ended only with
sacrifice of the flower of the nation's young manhood. Tougaloo
felt the impact of World War II even before Pearl Harbor. While
the year 1940–41 opened with a greater enrollment than ever
before, composition of the student body was uneven. The absence of about sixty men serving in the armed forces left a pre-
ponderance of women in the college department. Reflecting
wartime prosperity, more children enrolled in primary and
secondary schools. An additional teacher had to be found to
care for Daniel Hand students.

School activities were modified to meet the exigencies of
war. After autumn of 1942, intercollegiate football gave way to
intramural sports in both high school and college. Emphasis in
physical education programs centered on physical fitness. Activities recommended by the army—calisthenics, marching,
running, climbing, and obstacle races—were added to regular
courses in physical education.

The annual High School Rally, begun a few years before
Pearl Harbor, was discontinued. With gasoline and food
rationed, gathering eight hundred or more students together
from high schools throughout the state was no longer feasible.
Since the High School Rally had become one of the most successful means of recruitment, a faculty committee was appointed to devise other means of making Tougaloo's offerings
known to potential students.

The building of a girls' dormitory at a cost of $75,000 had
been planned to celebrate Tougaloo's seventy-fifth anniver-

sary, but it had to wait until the war was over. With Beard Hall condemned for its obsolete equipment and falling brick, the girls moved into Galloway Hall. Since most college men were in the services, this arrangement was made at a minimum of inconvenience. Throughout the war period, money was raised; and when the dormitory, named for President Cross, was built in 1947, funds on hand were sufficient even to cover increased costs. The A.M.A. Division of Home Boards gave $25,000; the Missions Council voted to give special priority to the girls' dormitory at Tougaloo College; the Women's Home Missionary Union of the Congregational Churches of Massachusetts gave $25,000. Tougaloo students and faculty gave over $1,000. (The total was $118,000 besides the furnishings.) Congregational women and other friends sent linens, blankets, pillows, and small rugs. This activity represented only an increase in tempo, since Tougaloo's northern and western friends had annually cared for such needs. The school made a practice of sending lists of items needed for various buildings. Cross asked that whenever possible bedspreads be sent in pairs for the girls' dormitory, because those who shared rooms preferred their beds alike.

A new bus was greatly needed, but because of government priority on all automotive equipment it was unattainable. While $900 lay in the A.M.A. office as a deposit, the school managed with the old bus given to the school in 1939 by alumni and on which upkeep was increasingly costly. Not until 1949 did Tougaloo get a new bus, again provided by the alumni.

Such wartime inconveniences were taken in stride as a part of the price of victory, and Tougaloo was glad to cooperate with the government whenever possible. School and community members worked together on a committee to direct the local United Community Chest and War Fund Drive and again for the Red Cross War Funds campaign. The home economics department directed the planting and care of victory gardens. Members of the school's staff assisted persons in the community who needed help in filling out questionnaires concerning selective service, deferments, allotments, and rationing. Informative and inspirational patriotic assemblies were held, with service flags proudly displayed.

To dramatize Negro youth support of the war effort, Negro colleges were encouraged to sponsor a Freedom War Bond Rally during the week of both Abraham Lincoln's and Frederick Douglass's birthdays in 1943. During that period every Negro student was urged to buy a war stamp or, where possible, a bond. At the close of the week the President of the United States was asked to greet the Negro youth of the nation on a national radio hook-up. It was hoped such a dramatization might crystallize a more favorable public opinion toward Negroes.

On several occasions Cross requested the government to give consideration to the special needs of the college. The calling up of J. Orville Moseley, director of music, was a heavy blow to the school's entire program. Cross wrote Moseley's draft board asking that he be deferred until the end of the 1941–42 school year. Not only was he director of the choir, but he also supervised music for the college and for the secondary and elementary departments, a total of 442 students. Music was an integral part of the commencement program and required the services of a competent director. Many of the public schools were dependent for their music upon teachers whom Tougaloo sent out annually. Having searched four years for the right person to fill this important position, Cross urged upon the draft board consideration that Moseley's talent and service were needed to maintain and raise civilian morale. His appeal was denied.

The Work Projects Administration (WPA), having turned its attention from depression to war needs, wrote Tougaloo asking for scrap metals and rubber, to be used in the manufacture of shells, tanks, guns, planes, and other war equipment. The letter indicated that a WPA truck might arrive at a time that would conflict with commencement activities. Cross assured the state administrator of the school's desire to cooperate but asked that the truck not come until after "Tuesday of next week." Scrap on the school grounds would have to be collected by the school truck, which would be needed to transport students' trunks to the railroad depot in Jackson. Also, in the midst of commencement activities, no one could be spared to collect and sort scrap before the following Tuesday.

The government, in need of 16mm sound projectors for the army, asked if it might purchase Tougaloo's projector. Cross responded with a reiteration of the school's wish to cooperate. However, to release the projector he would have to obtain approval from the board of trustees, especially as the projector was a gift to the college by a friend in the North who made the gift conditional on Tougaloo's using it for the benefit of the community. Because transportation to Jackson was difficult and because the segregated theaters there offered only inferior facilities for Negroes, loss of the school's projector would deprive the entire community of moving pictures. Tougaloo used its projector to give weekly showings in the college auditorium for black citizens of the area—which helped to keep up their morale—and as a visual aid in classes. Thus, Cross wrote that he hoped enough favorable responses would be received without depriving Tougaloo College and its community of the benefits afforded them by this projector.

The United States Office of Education requested that for the war period college academic courses be telescoped into three years. To comply a summer school was necessary. Tougaloo's previous experience with a summer school (1935–36) had been a financial liability. To prevent another such loss, a small group of faculty members organized a cooperative summer school. All financial, social, and academic responsibilities devolved upon this committee, chaired by Coach "Duke" Williams. Lionel B. Fraser, dean of the college, was also dean of the summer school. Home economics instructors operated a cafeteria, and the librarian managed a bookstore. An agreement signed with the school administrators delineated responsibilities of the school and of the summer school committee. Participating faculty members agreed to divide any profit at the conclusion of the session. This proved to be sixty dollars a person during the first year. In addition to contributing to the war effort by speeding up the process of education, this venture helped teachers of Mississippi become more proficient and upgrade their credentials. After three years of the cooperative plan, summer sessions were offered by the college. Those forced to leave college before completing their work could earn their B.A. degrees through summer work.

Financing a private Negro college during wartime was difficult. Many northern colleges operated on income from endowments, but the combined endowments of all Negro colleges were less than those of many single institutions. President Patterson of Tuskegee Institute suggested a united campaign for private Negro colleges. They might thereby stabilize and financially strengthen institutions still vital as a source of leadership in education and improvement in race relations. After three conferences, twenty-five schools organized the United Negro College Fund. Only four-year accredited Negro colleges independent of any tax support were eligible to join. Cross had some misgivings. "It is one of those campaigns about which you feel that you take a risk in going in but you cannot afford to stay out."

First public announcement of the United Negro College Fund (UNCF) was made in March 1944, when Walter Hoving, an outstanding merchant of New York City, agreed to serve as chairman. Participating colleges sent to the UNCF staff more than ten thousand names of prospective contributors. Plans for the initial campaign centered in fourteen cities selected on the basis of trustee and alumni distribution, location of former and current donors to the various colleges, and experience in other national fund raising campaigns. All college presidents were expected to accept speaking engagements as assigned by UNCF headquarters during the months of the campaign, and no member college could solicit for its own school during that time.

Tougaloo's alumni were already committed to a five-year campaign for its Living Endowment Fund. UNCF agreed that the amount raised by them for the Living Endowment during the period of the UNCF drive could be credited to Tougaloo's share of the amount finally raised by the United Drive. "It will simply mean that that amount will be deducted from the total amount which Tougaloo receives from the United Drive."

UNCF set minimal standards for its member colleges. Faculty salaries had to have some relationship to cost of living if colleges were to secure and retain good teachers. The Fund sponsored the Cooperative Intercollegiate Examination for high school seniors seeking college admission.

President Cross's reluctance to join UNCF proved ill-founded. From the beginning Tougaloo has been able to depend upon this source for about eight percent of its operating costs, besides large sums from the Fund's drives for capital improvements. Membership in the UNCF was also a good recommendation for funds from philanthropists, many of whom considered it the most efficient organization of its kind in the United States.

Both world wars effected some changes in Tougaloo's curriculum. Negroes found opportunities to work in offices during World War I. Students, eager to break out of the confines of the few professions traditionally open to those of their race, clamored for training to prepare them for the business world. Popularity of commercial courses continued; and in the decade of the thirties, the college included business courses in the department of economics. In 1946 a department of secretarial studies was added to the college curriculum but was discontinued in 1952. With the administration intent on making Tougaloo a liberal arts college, commercial courses received no more than passing interest.

World War II led to a popular demand for engineers. Tougaloo cooperated with Lafayette College in a Three-Two Program. A student could take the broadening courses in humanities and social sciences as well as some pre-engineering courses during his first three years and specialize in a branch of engineering at Lafayette College during the next two years. After satisfactory completion of the five-year course, he received a bachelor's degree from each institution. Only superior students whose grade averages were B or better were eligible for this plan, and only students with better than average financial backing could attend Lafayette in Pennsylvania where costs were double those at Tougaloo. Others could major in pre-engineering at a northern graduate school. Even if a student ended his college education with the bachelor's degree, a pre-engineering major was a good basis for many vocations.

With the war nearing an end the faculty edition of the *Tougaloo News* in January 1945 was devoted to a discussion of adjustments to meet the needs of returning servicemen. The consensus was that emphasis on liberal arts should continue. This broad program had enabled most of Tougaloo's men who served in the armed forces to become officers, and it was surely the best basis for peace. In the fall of 1946 men restored the numerical balance on campus. A "red letter day" which symbolized the men's return was October 12, 1946, the day of the first football game since 1942.

17

Racial Climate

UNDOUBTEDLY THE MOST PERSISTENT IMPACT from any external force was the racial climate in which Tougaloo College operated. With Congress having lost interest in enforcing the Civil War amendments, Tougaloo kept quite generally to itself, concentrating on the task of education and discouraging students from creating trouble over their political, social, or economic deprivation. Often the college boasted of its good relations with white Southerners, but those relations seldom penetrated beyond a superficial courtesy.

In 1896 the Supreme Court had agreed to the principle of "separate but equal" where the races were concerned. Mississippi's schools, like those in other southern states, followed the principle of separation while conveniently forgetting its corollary, equality. In the early days when children began their education in the first grade at Tougaloo, those who continued through normal school were prepared for advanced work. With development of state schools, Tougaloo raised its entrance grade for boarders. Then Daniel Hand and the grammar school accepted only those living within commuting distance. Increasingly as students from state Negro schools entered college they were found deficient in preparation. By every test given, most Tougaloo College freshmen scored in "Below Average" or "Poor" categories. Tougaloo had to add tutors to help freshmen in English, mathematics, and science.

Unless Negro children were so superior that they could

164

learn at less cost to the public than white children, those scores were to be anticipated. While the state distributed money for education to the counties on the basis of numbers of educable children, it made no requirement that Negro children get their proportion. Consequently the average distribution in counties was for many years roughly ten dollars per white child to one dollar per Negro child, with the disparity running as high as forty to one in Bolivar County. Under such circumstances, classes were large in black schools. In 1940 ninety-two percent of Mississippi Negro boys and girls of high school age were not in school. Because of the state's delay in providing high school education for its Negro teenagers, Tougaloo maintained its secondary school until 1957.

The disparity between white and black was just as pronounced among teachers. At a time when the state still had more Negro children than white, there were ten thousand white teachers and fewer than six thousand Negro teachers. During the 1940s only ten percent of Negro teachers were college graduates, and many had less than a high school education. Their salaries were kept at significantly lower levels than those of white teachers. In 1953 a special investigating committee of the Mississippi legislature sharply criticized counties which failed to give Negro teachers money that the state appropriated to equalize salaries.

A Tougaloo graduate, Gladys Noel Bates, sued the state for salaries for Negro teachers equal to those received by white teachers doing the same grade of work. She lost both her suit and her position. The National Association for the Advancement of Colored People (NAACP) had prepared for this eventuality with a reserve from which to pay Mrs. Bates's salary until she could get other employment. Tougaloo's chaplain, William A. Bender, and Al Johnson, son of a Tougaloo man who founded Prentiss Institute, obtained the money each month from an out-of-state bank where it had been deposited for safekeeping. Mrs. Bates eventually was employed by the Mississippi Teachers Association (black) as its executive secretary.

I. S. Sanders (Tougaloo, '10), principal of the school where Mrs. Bates's husband taught, refused his superior's request that he leave Bates's name off the list of persons he recommended for renewal of contracts. He insisted that Bates's work had been entirely satisfactory. Bates's contract was not renewed, but Sanders had not lowered his colors.

Later the legislature committed the state to "equal pay for equal work," driven to it, Helen Griffith thought, by its need to make the doctrine of "separate but equal" look plausible.

Just as lack of financial support for Negro education meant a shortage of schools, large classes, poorly qualified teachers, and less pay for all Negro teachers, it also meant inadequate school buildings and equipment for Negro schools in the rural areas. When Stella Molette was loaned by Tougaloo to the state for three years (1937–40) to teach and direct student teachers in an experimental thirteenth grade program at Meridian, she was asked if she prepared students for school houses with holes large enough to throw a cat through. She answered that she told them of holes she had seen large enough to throw a dog through.

Mrs. Molette encouraged her teacher trainees to use their imagination and initiative to improve the cheerless schools. One young man built swings and made a see-saw of logs cut from nearby woods. Another student-teacher interested his pupils and their families in planting grass, shrubs, and cedars about the school. A young lady student-teacher used some of her small earnings (about twenty-five dollars a month) to install panes in her school's windows. This so impressed a white man in the community that he paid to have the entire building reroofed.

Finding a home in which to live was a problem for country teachers. Few Negro rural homes had more than two rooms, but families tried to give their best accommodations to the teacher. One young lady reported that she woke one morning to find the lower half of her quilts covered with snow. Mrs. Molette suggested to the student-teachers that they might want to spend a little of their salary left them after paying board and other necessities to add to the comfort of the home in which they stayed. "Put a patch on the roof even if it is only a piece of a box. Buy a small rug, or hang a burlap curtain at the door of the privy to give a little privacy." Sometimes the students could thus inspire the homes to continue making improvements.

At the same time that the state was shortchanging the Negro's education it attempted to interfere with effective education done by private agencies. In 1916 House Bill 489 sought to make it "unlawful for any person to serve as a teacher in a school attended by pupils of a different race than that of the teacher." One of Tougaloo's trustees, Bishop Theodore Bratton, used his influence to defeat that bill.

Unlike some southern states, Mississippi had no specific law which prohibited black and white students from attending the same classes. Its constitution of 1890, however, was explicit in stating that "separate schools shall be maintained for children of the white and colored races." Though technically this provision might have applied to public schools only, no one ever challenged it. Dean Henry W. Cobb's daughter, known on the Tougaloo campus as "The Little Ph.D.," attended a Jackson school. Most children of Tougaloo's white faculty members attended a school at Madison.

As long as Tougaloo conformed to southern racial decorum off campus and curried favor among leading whites of the state, it had a minimum of difficulty. With the coming of President Holmes in 1913, however, a slightly more affirmative stand was taken. When Thelma Lowe, a Tougaloo music major who continued her studies at Oberlin College, was delivering strawberries from her parents' farm during her summer vacation, she was stopped by a policeman. Asked a question, she answered with a simple Yes. He slapped her for forgetting her southern manners after being in the North. Learning of the incident, Holmes reached for the telephone to protest the policeman's conduct. The officer who heard his complaint criticized Tougaloo College for failure to teach the "niggers" to speak correctly and to show respect to whites with a proper "Yessir" or "Nosir."

Holmes, while protesting specific injustices, was not aggressive in trying to change southern mores or laws. A light complexioned young teacher, new at Tougaloo, was refused a seat in the colored car by the train conductor who did not recognize her as a Negro. Rather than make an issue of the matter, she rode in the white car from Jackson to Tougaloo. When Holmes met her train and saw her alight from the white car, he criticized her sharply. Probably he was thinking of her own safety, but as the story spread among the Negro faculty it was interpreted that he felt she should "keep her place."

White state and county officials who dealt with Tougaloo College usually had warm personal feelings toward the school. They did not hesitate to treat its personnel with dignity and a show of equality so long as no other whites were around. Courtesy titles were freely used by the state superintendent of schools, Mr. Easom, unless he was accompanied by a white woman. A county superintendent who had always addressed a certain Tougaloo teacher as "Mrs." lapsed into use of her first name when he met her at an interracial curriculum conference. There he even asked her to move from her seat beside two friendly white women from Mississippi State College. He clarified his position in his opening remarks, saying that while he believed in equality he also believed in segregation.

Race prejudice was easier for Negroes to accept off campus where it was an acknowledged part of southern life than on campus where A.M.A.'s policy of racial equality was presumed to prevail. One light Negro teacher who arrived at the school late at night was warmly greeted by a seasoned white teacher. The next morning the new teacher, hatless and in the bright light of day rather than in the flickering light of the kerosene lamp, was sure that the friendly warmth of the previous evening had vanished. She never ceased to believe that recognition of her race made the difference. A white Jackson minister's excellent sermon given in Woodworth Chapel was spoiled for some teachers when his wife hesitated to sit next to a Negro in the dining room. Young women students of light coloring, taking their cue from the dominant element of society, tended to sit together in church, pointedly excluding their darker sisters. Some believed that skin pigmentation determined which club a student would be invited to join.

Enduring little insults, large inconveniences, and actual

abuse would have been intolerable except for the saving grace of humor. Mr. Easom, who frequently visited the campus, would never remain for a meal. The faculty enjoyed setting up situations that would almost necessitate his eating with them, but he cleverly wormed his way out with one excuse or another. When a faculty member, whose white ancestors had practically erased any discernible Negroid feature, and an obviously Negro teacher went to Jackson to shop at one of the better stores, they would mischievously separate until a clerk extended the light teacher the courtesy of fitting her with shoes or a dress in the white section. Then the darker companion would walk in and casually ask if she were finding what she wanted. Their amusement came in watching the consternation and embarrassment revealed in the clerk's face. Mrs. Davis, principal of Tougaloo High School, was always taken for white in any new situation. When the conductor on the train tried to separate her from her companions, she breezily insisted, "I know where I belong." Once when an educational conference went all out to integrate the participants, Mrs. Molette was given a seat next to Mrs. Davis, whom the usher evidently thought to be white. Miss Voorhees, in taking two students north with her one summer, arranged with the conductor for the girls to ride on the segregated coach until they crossed the Mason-Dixon line, at which time the girls should join her. This they did in the middle of the night amidst the stares of the white passengers of Miss Voorhees's car.

In the North where no segregation laws existed, custom precluded integration almost as effectively. Miss Voorhees and Olivia Hunter, first a student then a music teacher at Tougaloo who was like an adopted member of the Voorhees family, were riding home one night after attending a concert in New York. They sat opposite some Mt. Holyoke students who were making exaggerated lip movements as they whispered to each other on the curious combination—not being sure whether Miss Hunter was actually a Negro. Miss Voorhees and Miss Hunter mimicked the girls' facial contortions as they mouthed the words affirming their racial identities with sly glances at the embarrassed girls.

One of the most frustrating aspects of racial discrimination was its uncertainty. Tougaloo faculty members enjoyed the Jackson Musical Association's programs until there was trouble over the seating at *Porgy and Bess*. With the house oversold, those from Tougaloo were asked to relinquish their seats. After that, the entire faculty forewent the concerts. When the dean, a Negro, went to see a white Jackson lawyer who was a trustee of the college, on a matter of business, he was asked inside, offered a seat, and served a cool drink. This was a surprise. Some who knew the trustee well regarded his hospitality as in keeping with his character; others who knew him equally well were not so sure.

While no single incident related above may seem important in itself, collectively they give an inkling of the kind of tight-rope walking in which Negroes and to some extent Caucasians who were associated with Negroes necessarily engaged. Tougaloo's history cannot be understood unless this racial climate is known.

Negro colleges in the South provided opportunity for interracial contacts where blacks and whites were otherwise isolated. Tougaloo, one of the most prominent colleges in this role, was fortunate in the proximity of Millsaps College, a white Methodist school more eager than most to reach across the divide to join hands and hearts.

Cooperation between Tougaloo and Millsaps had not occurred suddenly. In the early twenties some Millsaps boys, reacting to a rumor that someone had been killed, joined a crowd which took out after a Negro. The faster he ran the more determined the crowd was to lynch him. Fortunately the lynching was averted. The irony of the incident lay in the boys' asking their Bible professor to give them an excused absence from class. Their professor, understanding practical application of biblical teaching better than his students, refused. Earlier, when the same Bible instructor was himself a student at Millsaps, he and his classmates had slight awareness of Tougaloo students. On a dull Sunday afternoon some of the fellows might stroll the several miles down the railroad track to exchange a few words with some Tougaloo men at the gate, but the Millsaps boys were more curious than friendly.

When Mabel Cobb, wife of the dean at Tougaloo, taught modern languages at Millsaps, a more solid relationship developed—though Mrs. Cobb was white. Professor George E. Rice of Tougaloo took students to the observatory at Millsaps. Sociology classes from the two schools cooperated in a survey of the main Negro residential section in Jackson. Each school invited guest speakers from the other school. The Millsaps YWCA gave an assembly program on a religious theme at Tougaloo, after which the visitors were shown the campus. One Millsaps teacher acknowledged that the hand of Tougaloo's chaplain was the first Negro hand he had ever shaken. Both schools were obviously seeking ways to broaden communication and understanding.

For this purpose the Intercollegiate Council was organized and made a sustained effort to develop understanding between students of the two races throughout the South. All high schools and colleges in the Jackson area were invited to form a local chapter. Of the white schools only Millsaps could be depended upon for more than lip service. A Millsaps student was elected president of the first local Intercollegiate Council chapter.

The Ys were closely interlocked with the Intercollegiate Council; and through acquaintances made in the Council, exchange Y programs between Millsaps and Tougaloo were planned. In 1935 four students from Millsaps, Raymond McClinton, Caxton Doggett, Lucien Malone, and Robert Ezell, came to a Tougaloo YMCA meeting where, amidst a spirit of friendship and goodwill, they discussed how Christian organizations on campus might be made more effective. Though the Intercollegiate Council grew in size, its membership was always predominantly Negro. By 1953 Tougaloo members were numerous enough to require the school bus to transport them to and from meetings.

An additional opportunity for interracial experiences derived from the Social Science Forums directed by Dr. Ernst

Borinski. With the help of Foundation funds, provocative speakers knowledgeable in their subjects were brought to Tougaloo for evening talks once every three or four weeks. Invitations were always extended to white persons of the Jackson community who might be expected to respond favorably. A discussion period following the formal presentation gave an opportunity for interchange of ideas across racial lines. Discussions continued in small interracial groups when refreshments were served. These forums offered Jacksonians, provincial by reason of geography and population count, an opportunity to hear speakers who could be found at no other place in Jackson. Students from Millsaps, who were too timid to go to Tougaloo ordinarily, went to hear Einstein's manager or William Kunstler. Dr. Borinski was himself an attraction to Millsaps students. From Germany, he embodied a cosmopolitan spirit unusual in Mississippi. After the Brown decision of 1954 when relationships between Millsaps and Tougaloo became almost sub rosa, white students came to Tougaloo ostensibly to test their German against Dr. Borinski's fluency. This excuse had a particularly plausible ring for those who aspired to Fulbright scholarships.

Race relations in Mississippi polarized and hardened with organization of the White Citizens Council and other white supremacist groups, but a few at Millsaps and Tougaloo tried to keep the channels of communication open. The Christian Council at Millsaps sponsored a series of forums to present both sides of several issues uppermost in the minds of college students. On the race issue the Christian Council chose Dr. Borinski to present the case for integration and John Satterfield, a prominent white lawyer in Jackson, for segregation. Borinski referred in his talk to the unchristian nature of segregation. Newspaper publicity given Borinski was so unfavorable that two days later when the chairman of the Millsaps sociology department was scheduled to moderate a panel at Tougaloo, other members of the panel from Millsaps did not appear. About thirty Millsaps students came, however, and the discussion was more spirited than usual. Jackson newspapers accused Millsaps students of expressing heresies at the integrated meeting: That differences between the races were superficial and easily disappeared when persons of one race came to know persons of the other; that many whites knew nothing about Negroes except what cheap politicians told them. One young man was quoted as saying he had to come. "There comes a time when you can't compromise." Another from Millsaps said he came because he felt his academic freedom was threatened by the publicity. "Someone is trying to take away my right to learn from whom I want to. I resent it."

The White Citizens Council published an open letter challenging President Finger of Millsaps to tell where the college and every member of the faculty stood on the question of segregation. Finger replied that he was answerable directly only to the Millsaps board of trustees. He added that he joined with the entire Christian church in pledging "devotion to preserving a climate where freedom may prosper and where intimidation, fear and bondage are doomed." The board of trustees responded that neither segregation nor integration was an issue at Millsaps, that segregation continued to be the policy of Millsaps College, and that the board affirmed its faith in the integrity of the administration and faculty.

The Mississippi legislature took up the cause. "This white professor at a Negro college has been making some pretty brave statements," harangued a representative. He referred, the *Clarion-Ledger* elaborated, to Borinski's saying that the Negro wants "to ride the bus in the seat he chooses, go to the schools which are best, and go to the shows where the best movies are shown." After the Senate and the House unanimously adopted a resolution to investigate the means, methods, and "ultimate objectives in this state" of the National Association for the Advancement of Colored People (NAACP), Representative Morrow urged that Borinski, reported by the *Jackson Daily News* to be a member of the NAACP, be included in the investigation.

Tom Ethridge of the *Clarion-Ledger* used his column "Mississippi Notebook" (Feb. 5, 1958) to attack one of Tougaloo's trustees, the Rev. Mrs. Wyker, for a message written by her which the National Council of Churches urged read from every pulpit on Race Relations Sunday.

Tougaloo's role as an interracial meeting ground for visitors from out of state caused less commotion. When the Pomfret Preparatory School in Connecticut planned a student seminar in Africa, the financial sponsor insisted that the participating students first learn something about Negroes in the United States. The Tougaloo campus was chosen as the base for an experience with black people and conditions under which they lived in a southern community.

Samuel C. Kincheloe was then president of Tougaloo College (1956–60). Dr. Kincheloe earned his M.A. and Ph.D. at the University of Chicago and was a member of the Chicago Theological Seminary before coming to Tougaloo. An authority in sociology and religion, he arranged for visits with administrators of industry and with members of Millsaps College, and for field trips to cotton plantations of the delta and to antebellum homes of Natchez. A daily seminar was held, where the Pomfret group could talk with a counselor from one of the Negro high schools, hear lectures on the history of Mississippi and the sociology of race, or discuss with George Owens (who became president of the college in 1965) the problems of growing up in Mississippi. Mr. and Mrs. Charles B. Arzeni, members of Tougaloo's faculty who had lived in Africa, told of their experiences. Informal conversations between students of the two schools and recreational activities, including ball games and dancing, rounded out the ten-day experience. At the conclusion of their African seminar, Pomfret students reported to Kincheloe that they considered their experiences in Mississippi the most outstanding part of their entire trip.

18

Racial Discrimination in High Places

BECAUSE NO SCHOOL COULD AFFORD to bite the hand that fed it or that might be persuaded to feed it, educational foundations had a significant influence on Negro colleges. Industrial magnates of the late nineteenth and early twentieth centuries justified their phenomenal success by the theory of social Darwinism. They were not interested in a crusade for racial equality as were the early religious societies which sponsored the freedmen's schools. In the late nineteenth century only those Negro colleges which provided industrial education and normal schools and which discouraged Negro participation in politics could hope for grants from Slater, Daniel Hand, or Peabody funds. Although Peabody's instructions in 1867 specified that funds should be distributed without regard to race, a ratio of payments was adopted by the Peabody trustees in 1871 giving Negro schools two-thirds as much as white schools—and this at a time when black and white public school teachers in Mississippi received identical salaries. Trustees of the Peabody Fund, confident that southern states would maintain equal systems of education, urged Congress not to pass the civil rights bill pending in 1873, and they also advocated that Negroes work against it.

By the twentieth century big business ceased to be viewed by the public as a class virtue or poverty as a personal vice. In the Sherman Anti-trust Act of 1890, government had taken cognizance of evils which had grown up with monopolies, and

175

muckrakers were labeling large corporations unscrupulous. Labor conflicts threatened industrial peace and seriously tarnished the image of the new industrial class. Philanthropy in the South offered an opportunity for business to regain public confidence without digressing from the principle of rugged individualism. Southerners could be helped to help themselves, thereby increasing labor value where wages were low and opening markets for northern manufactured products.

Philanthropy, which had subtly helped to perpetuate segregation before 1900, through the kind of education encouraged, became more overt in its racial attitudes in the twentieth century. Officials felt that schools not following a policy of separating the races were likely to become unstable and inefficient in using foundation funds. Consequently philanthropists preferred to give aid in states which provided for racially separate schools. With equipment, inadequate from the start, worn out by the turn of the century and with diminished support from denominational societies, Negro schools were largely dependent upon the new philanthropy.

Tougaloo as an American Missionary Association college was in a more favorable position. A.M.A. interest continued longer and more steadily than that of other religious and benevolent organizations. But even the A.M.A. could not underwrite the increasingly high cost of its schools. It, too, depended to a considerable degree upon educational foundations. Mississippi observed the necessary qualification for philanthropic aid, with its rigid separation of the races in schools. Tougaloo was expected not to rock the boat by protesting state inequities in disruptive ways.

Tougaloo received money from many foundations, among which were Slater, General Education Board, Hazen, Phelps-Stokes, Danforth, Field, Ford, Rosenwald, Carnegie, and Whitney. (Tougaloo received money from several other foundations in the 1960s and 1970s.) Grants from foundations for capital improvement on the campus helped to build Daniel Hand Primary School, Holmes Hall, Brownlee Recreational Center, Kincheloe Science Hall, and Warren Student Union. Grants also improved the library and provided fellowships for faculty and students to do graduate work.

Anticipation of the 1954 Supreme Court decision in the Brown case increased racial tensions throughout the deep South. White leaders in Mississippi who had never been friendly toward liberal education for Negroes openly vowed that they would "get" Tougaloo. Action taken in the December 1951 meeting of the Southern Association of Colleges and Secondary Schools to discontinue A and B ratings of Negro colleges and to accredit them on the same basis as white colleges offered an opportunity to carry out the threat against Tougaloo. Local members of the Association's committee on Negro colleges failed to inform Tougaloo of the changes in standards until notification was received that the school's approved rating would terminate in August 1952 because of four deficiencies.

Harold C. Warren, a graduate of Princeton and a Presbyterian minister with a doctorate from the University of Pittsburgh, was Tougaloo's president at this time (1947–55). He phoned the Southern Association's secretary to ask why his recent letter had not mentioned the new requirements and named the specific areas in which Tougaloo was deficient. The secretary replied, "Well, you know, when I wrote you it was around Christmas time and I guess I was pretty busy." When A.M.A. Secretary Phillip M. Widenhouse called in person, the same secretary started the conversation by expostulating, "Well, that's the college that has both Nigras and whites on the faculty." After Warren and Widenhouse showed that A.M.A. support was equivalent to an endowment in excess of the required amount and that Tougaloo was spending a sufficient sum on its library, the Southern Association conceded an error had been made on those two counts. Deficiencies pertaining to salaries and faculty degrees were undeniable, however, and immediate steps were taken to correct them.

The problem of low faculty salaries had defied solution for some years. In 1939 Tougaloo's salaries were next to the lowest among Negro colleges with an A or B rating. A significant ad-

vance was made in 1944 when, with the help of the United
Negro College Fund, a bonus amounting to a total of $8,000
was given. President Cross then applied to the General Education Board for $10,000 to be spread over a three-year period to
enable the college gradually to absorb the increases as a permanent policy. The request was denied. Teachers grew restive
and petitioned the A.M.A. for an improved salary scale which
would put the school in a competitive position. After investigation by the A.M.A. another bonus was given. But salaries were
not brought into full compliance with standards of the Southern Association of Colleges and Secondary Schools until after
the announcement of Tougaloo's loss of accreditation. As an
emergency measure the A.M.A. appropriated money to bring
salaries up to the minimum requirements for the remainder of
the year. This move gave the college time to streamline its curriculum—in part by eliminating the departments of home
economics and secretarial studies—and make the salary adjustment permanent. Missionary teachers who served for a pit-
tance as in Tougaloo's past were no longer in vogue. They were,
in fact, an embarrassment for both the college and the regional
accrediting agency.[1]

With help from the A.M.A. Tougaloo began recruiting faculty members who had higher degrees. President Warren's
feverish and unrelenting efforts rounded up a faculty in which
over half held doctorates, though several were from Millsaps
College and served on a part-time basis. Thereafter no teacher
held less than a master's degree or its equivalent.

Though the Southern Association of Colleges and Secondary Schools had grudgingly admitted that the library met
minimum requirements, the college took a fresh look at its
holdings prior to the anticipated visit of the accrediting committee. Tougaloo had always had what passed for a library, but
its real beginning is accredited to Ellen Upson Woodworth, an

---

1. The 1953 salary schedule: professors, $3,900–5,400; associate profes-
sors, $3,400–4,400; assistant professors, $3,200–3,800; instructors, $3,000–
3,500. There were no instructors on the faculty at that time. Sherrod, Special
Study, Tougaloo Files.

English teacher and the wife of President Woodworth. Books which she assembled were piled flat on high wooden shelves built along the walls in the room to the right of the entrance to the mansion. Books came from northern friends, but, as before, too many were obsolete before their donors parted with them. Mrs. Holmes, wife of the next president, having had some experience in a church library, arranged the books by subject. Though she, upon advice of teachers, discarded many books (to be used to kindle fires and later to fill an old cistern), the library collection expanded until it overflowed into the next room. To charge a book a student wrote his name in a register alongside the book's title. With the building of Holmes Hall in 1926, the southeast wing was dedicated as the Ellen Upson Woodworth Library, and a fulltime librarian was employed to make the best use of the five thousand books. The Rosenwald Fund in supplementing A.M.A.'s and Tougaloo's book allowance exacted the requirement that titles should conform to a basic list formulated at Hampton Institute. By 1947 Mrs. Lucius Eastman's generosity, added to that of the Carnegie Foundation, the General Education Board, and the Tougaloo Alumni Association, brought the library into full compliance for a Class A rating of the college.

When Brownlee Gymnasium was completed, the library was moved into the section of Holmes Hall formerly used as an auditorium-gymnasium. It was equipped with modern furniture, including tables and chairs to accommodate over a hundred persons in the reading-reference room. The auditorium platform, furnished with easy chairs, reading lamps, tables, and magazine racks, was converted into a display lounge. Opening off the lounge was a room for children's literature. The southwest wing of Holmes Hall, together with the adjoining corridor, was equipped with steel shelves for stacks, and space was allowed for a workroom. Good lighting was installed throughout. In 1948 the entire facility was christened the Eva Hills Eastman Library. In 1954 Tougaloo conferred upon Mrs. Eastman the honorary degree of Doctor of Letters.

For the dedication of Eastman Library, paperback books were used in a central display. Afterward they were sold at cost to students. Paperbacks proved so popular that the library began stocking them to sell over the same counter where books were checked out for loans. (Later the bookstore assumed this function.)

L. Zenobia Coleman, the young librarian who held a master's degree from Columbia University and whose efficiency deeply impressed a local white doctor at the inauguration of President Warren, constantly sought ways to make the library attractive and useful to the students. Through slogans such as "Read a book a week," displays of new books, open stacks, and library teas featuring book reviews, she and her staff called attention to the importance of books. A few students caught a glimmer of the library's practical value. One, for example, rushed in, thumbed through the almanac, and left confident that he had the facts to win an argument. Another astounded his classmates by his knowledge of the latest dance steps. Only the librarian knew his secret after she discovered him in a secluded part of the stack section with an issue of *Theater Arts* in his hand, practicing the steps described in the magazine.

To be doubly certain that the accreditation committee would find no grounds for complaint in the library, obsolete books were removed and new books ordered. They came in so fast and in such numbers that the books were shelved after accession, classification, and preparation for use. When the visiting committee departed, leaving behind words of praise for the library, permanent catalog cards were typed and filed.

President Warren distributed frequent bulletins to faculty and students to keep them informed as to the reasons for loss of accreditation and the progress toward regaining it. The visiting committee later praised both students and faculty for being so knowledgeable about the school. Only one class graduated before the school was reestablished as fully approved by the Southern Association of Colleges and Secondary Schools in the autumn of 1953—this time by the same standards and the same examining commission as for white schools. Psychologically, however, the Southern Association of Colleges and Secondary Schools was still unready to make no distinction between black and white schools. Though standards for qualification were the same, the Association conferred upon Negro schools the rating of "approved" while white schools were "accredited."

Nevertheless Tougaloo was jubilant over the winning of approved status. It was the only Negro college in Mississippi to hold membership with the Southern Association of Colleges and Secondary Schools. The dean felt a great celebration was in order, but President Warren insisted on a dignified acceptance, saying the school had only regained something of which it had been robbed. He personally found satisfaction in foiling the efforts of whites who had always been antagonistic toward Tougaloo.

In the process of obtaining approved status with the Association, Tougaloo's reputation was enhanced, and it became widely known as a college of quality with its teachers holding a larger percentage of doctorates than the faculty of any college in Mississippi, black or white. The freshman class, which had dropped to a low figure in 1952, increased in 1953 to the highest in Tougaloo's history and in 1954 numbered almost half of the school's enrollment.

One unfortunate concomitant of the whole episode was that, in bringing all existing buildings up to standard for the visiting committee, United Negro College Fund money marked for capital improvements had to be used for repairs. New buildings were thereby delayed, a disappointment to all.

While Tougaloo was in the final stages of resolving its crisis over accreditation, trustees of Southern Christian Institute, a junior college sponsored by the Disciples of Christ, suggested a merger of the two schools. The same hostile forces which tried to undermine Tougaloo had succeeded in closing Southern Christian Institute.

This school, located near Edwards about forty miles west of Tougaloo, had been chartered in 1875, and to it went the $10,000 which President Pope had hoped to get for Tougaloo in 1878. The school's history paralleled that of Tougaloo in its struggle to combat prejudice, ignorance, and disease (yellow fever and malaria, worse in the delta) with inadequate resources in money and leadership. Southern Christian Institute, with its 1,200 acres of rich delta land, continued its stress on vocational education. Students could earn their entire school expenses working in fields, blacksmith shop, dairy, saw mill, school offices, or faculty homes.

After World War II, preference of Negro youth for free and improved public schools, and state harassment of the institute made continuance of the school impractical. The trustees felt that by combining its resources with those of another college of similar aims a strong school might be formed to serve the black population better than two weaker ones. Several colleges considered by the trustees of Southern Christian Institute would have made use of the farm assets. Tougaloo had recently eschewed vocational training in favor of a strictly liberal arts program. But the Institute had other resources attractive to Tougaloo—namely endowments—and Tougaloo's religious orientation found favor with Southern Christian Institute. It was agreed that one of the first items of study would be that of implementing a strong department of religion. The United Church Missionary Society designated $200,000 as the Tougaloo Southern Christian Scholarship Fund. The Society also agreed to contribute its "Promotional Receipts" which were expected to be around $20,000 a year.

After preliminary negotiations the terms of merger were agreed upon. Though the merger under the name of Tougaloo Southern Christian College was not completed before the Southern Association of Colleges and Secondary Schools gave Tougaloo approved status, the anticipation of the endowments and financial aid strengthened Tougaloo's stance before the accrediting committee.

The Southern Christian Institute campus later was used for a community service and conference center under the names of Mt. Beulah or the Delta Ministry. More recently it was sold to the United Presbyterian Church, U.S.A.

Tougaloo's President Warren felt that the attempts to cripple if not actually to destroy the two schools had proved a blessing in disguise, but a Jackson lawyer and trustee of Tougaloo Southern Christian College took a less optimistic view. Success in accreditation and in merging the two schools had brought Tougaloo into the public eye. He foresaw that, with the forming of prosegregationist groups, Tougaloo would be drawn into the controversy. It would "take the best efforts of all people concerned with the good of the college to come through this situation without harm," he predicted.

The Civil Rights generation of the sixties sometimes is critical of its predecessors for not demanding their constitutional rights, forgetting that each generation has had its frontier. For the freedmen and their sons it was necessary to obtain the rudiments of education and social amenities of a free people. With practically no background for either, that work required some years. Then the frontier moved into areas of responsibility. Some national Negro leaders constituting what might be termed a "black power movement" of the late nineteenth century insisted on more black teachers in Negro colleges. Those colleges sponsored by denominations with large constituencies of southern Negroes, such as the Baptists and Methodists, were first to submit to this pressure and to place Negroes in teaching—even in policymaking—positions.

James M. McPherson, reading a paper at the 1968 annual meeting of the American Historical Society, reasoned that with few Negroes in the Congregational Church, the A.M.A. until the late twenties was not pressed so hard by black leaders. In the thirties A.M.A. Secretary Fred Brownlee listened sympathetically to complaints of black people within the A.M.A. who felt they should be given policymaking roles. Reviewing the relationship of the A.M.A. to the Negroes, Brownlee realized that in the beginning the situation had been comparable to that of infants and parents. It had been easy to see only the dependence of the Negro and the devotion of the missionary. The dominant race held a religious conviction that it must, in the name of Jesus, give to the poor ignorant dark people "who also are the children of God" the blessings and benefits of white civilization and white religion. So much could be done *for* the Negro that few thought to work *with* him.

Though the missionaries ate, worked, played, and worshiped with blacks, there had been a general and perhaps unconscious attitude of racial separateness. In the 1920s a veteran white teacher at Tougaloo advised a new teacher to limit recognition of a coworker whom she might meet in Jackson to a polite nod. Another white teacher told a student who continued working at his desk when she entered the room that a "polite white boy" would have stood. Another told a faculty member it was too bad that so able and interesting a man as he was "colored."

With eighty percent black illiterates on the statistical table having been reversed to eighty percent literates, Secretary Brownlee thought the Negro who wrote to ask him why a black man was not considered for the presidency at Talladega College in Alabama had a point. If after more than sixty years of A.M.A. colleges none was qualified, it was prima facie evidence that the A.M.A. had failed. But, in Brownlee's judgment, the A.M.A. had not failed; many Negroes were qualified to fill administrative positions when the Association was ready to accept a man of color as an equal.

Tougaloo did not get a black president until 1965, but the frontier was gradually extended in other ways. In the thirties Negroes were placed in policymaking positions. Jonathan H. Brooks was assistant to the president, as was William Bender, his successor, who came to Tougaloo as a day worker in 1907 and later studied at Moody Bible Institute. Lionel B. Fraser became academic dean in 1939. With President Cross in poor health and President Warren often absent in search of funds, operation of the school was left largely in Fraser's hands. A scholar and an able administrator, Fraser worked to improve academic standards. Students who went to graduate schools during his deanship are said to have been thoroughly prepared.

With the return of GIs who had experienced personal freedom, Tougaloo's paternalistic policies came under student scrutiny. Dean Fraser was criticized for his strict enforcement of college rules for student behavior. Of slight stature, he did not hesitate to reprimand a big GI who forgot that smoking was limited to a particular room. When an excited teacher stood before a chapel assembly waving an empty liquor bottle he claimed to have found on the campus, many students found his performance hilarious. Some teachers were unsympathetic with the rule against the use of all intoxicants and refused to cooperate in its enforcement. Students on choir tours understood from their director that an occasional transgression would receive no notice so long as their conduct brought no embarrassment to the school. Students pushed against the rules limiting the organizations they could form on campus. President Warren lent his support to the demand for Greek letter societies. But a local chapter of NAACP did not meet with approval until later, though William Bender was a prominent state leader in that organization.

Other forms of paternalism were undermined by students and some faculty members—even administrators. Though fraternization between students and faculty was against school policy, it occurred both covertly and overtly, resulting in several marriages between faculty or staff and students. Racial attitudes were reexamined when a courtship developed between two faculty members of different races. Though the A.M.A. had always espoused the concept of equality, the Tougaloo administration could not lightly accept an interracial marriage, which Mississippi law prohibited. Unheedful of advice generously given by the administration, Chester Slocum and Frances Walker married and thereby brought to light a sharp division among faculty and students over the issue of miscegenation. The bride and groom had to leave Tougaloo.

All these frontiers were to be rolled back before students were equipped to attack the southern way of life, a bastion which most believed impregnable. Until they had the education to comprehend their constitutional rights, until they had broken through the racial barriers that existed within the school, until they had gained more control over their personal lives and had the right to organize for freedom, students were not prepared to move into the civil rights frontier.

In the thirties and forties while most Tougalooians were yet concerned with little more than annoying rules and racial attitudes which they thought did not quite measure up, some few were fighting a lonely and dangerous battle out in the real world against adamant forces of racial injustice. Since most of these were alumni, positive influences may have been at work during their undergraduate years. No doubt one such influence was Lulu Johnson's American history classes where the traditional interpretation of slavery and Reconstruction was challenged. Students studying Arthur Schlesinger, Sr.'s work stood a little taller as they learned of the constructive acts of southern governments in which their forefathers had a part. The Rev. William Bender, both a graduate and a faculty member, joined a fledgling group which was the nucleus for the first NAACP chapter in Mississippi. At a time when to be associated with the NAACP in any way was to court trouble, a handful of men met in unusual places and seldom in the same place twice in succession—at the corner of Farish and Amite, in the colored waiting room of the Illinois Central, and once in the sickroom of the Rev. M. C. Collins.

Weak as this small, furtive group was, it may have prevented a lynching. When a Negro was accused of killing a white man, the group called Walter White, executive secretary of the NAACP. He obtained cooperation from the President of the United States, who brought influence to bear on the governor of Mississippi. The accused was quietly escorted from his jail cell to a train bound out of state.

While Bender was president of the state NAACP it enrolled the fifty members needed for a state charter. Action was focused on getting out the vote. Bender, accompanying two students, Napoleon and Earl Lewis, to the Madison courthouse to register, was met by the sheriff who threatened to shoot if any of the three crossed a designated line. Rather than risk the students' lives, Bender retreated. But the young men were not defeated. They were to be heard from again—most dramatically in testimony against a senator. Napoleon Lewis, Bender, and other Tougaloo alumni were among those who testified against the seating of Sen. Theodore Bilbo in 1946. They and other witnesses established that Bilbo had won election by fraud, intimidation, and violence. The Senate tabled the question of seating Bilbo when it learned that he was dying of cancer. His death followed several months later.

In these and many other less dramatic ways, courageous black pioneers—far ahead of the crowd—were blazing the trail some years before students were ready to make a bold strike for their rights.

19

Outreach

TOUGALOO BEGAN DURING THE THIRTIES a conscious attempt to close the usual gap between town and gown. A Boy Scout troop was sponsored by Daniel Hand Parent-Teachers Association, and 4-H Clubs were sponsored by the secondary division of the school. Farmers and their wives were encouraged to form an organization on campus to promote programs at which state and county demonstration agents spoke and social activities were enjoyed. To stimulate interest in home improvement Daniel Hand sponsored a fair in the fall of each year with exhibits of home garden produce, cooking, canning, and sewing. For a while pre-Thanksgiving dinners in Daniel Hand School brought faculty and neighbors together in good fellowship.

Lionel B. Fraser, having made a comprehensive study of the community, proposed an arrangement with Madison and Hinds counties whereby students in the immediate Tougaloo vicinity might be absorbed by Daniel Hand Primary School. The plan was adopted, with Madison and Hinds counties paying the salaries of three teachers for a six-month period. Children who lived in the public school districts affected by this arrangement attended Daniel Hand without cost to them for six months— the usual school term for Negroes. If they completed the year, their parents paid for the months not allowed by the counties' school systems. Tougaloo hoped to reduce the number of over-aged students by improving the quality of education for more elementary children.

The home economics department devised several plans to bring Tougaloo into a closer relationship with the community. High school home economics students cooperated with the Daniel Hand P.T.A. to conduct a cafeteria for the elementary children. Parents who came to Tougaloo to cultivate corn, okra, butter beans, tomatoes, and snap beans, and to can garden and meat products for use in the winter earned hot lunches for their children during the school year. College and high school students gained permission from a local family to use its home in a kitchen improvement program. Only discarded and inexpensive materials were used. The home economics department and the Daniel Hand P.T.A. conducted semimonthly sewing and mending circles for women of the community.

Tougaloo's department of education adopted certain local public schools, where students observed and helped in the classrooms. Sometimes an entire class made an observation trip. After such a visit the teacher led a discussion on the problems of administering a one-teacher rural school of six or seven grades. Some students accompanied the Jeanes Teacher[1] of Madison County as she visited rural schools. Classes in education also visited larger schools in Jackson to compare procedures and advantages between urban and rural schools. With financial help from the Phelps-Stokes Fund, Tougaloo cooperated with Rogers High School in Canton. Members of the Tougaloo faculty met with the high school teachers to work out ways to improve instruction.

Tougaloo had always been generous with its water supply. When the new well was drilled to a depth of more than six hundred feet and an immense tank constructed far above the roof of any college building (a challenge to the more daring college boys to write their names on it), neighbors preferred to get their drinking water from it rather than from their shallow wells or cypress cisterns of rainwater collected from their roofs. Some in the school wished to give the community further help with its water problem, by developing a community system with safe and plentiful supply. They felt the college's re-

---

1. Anna T. Jeanes, a Quaker, left a fund to pay salaries of supervising teachers for colored public schools in the rural South.

sponsibility to its community and to its students who boarded in nearby homes.

Madison County, with a population of thirty-eight thousand, of whom thirty thousand were Negroes, had but one public health nurse until 1939, when another was added. The need among Negroes was significant not only because of their larger numbers but also because of the greater incidence of illness among them. Of thirteen diseases listed by Madison County in 1940, the death rate of Negroes was higher in all but heart disease, cancer, and diphtheria. While public health services were expanded in 1939 for the white population to include preschool clinics and school health programs, black children were only immunized to prevent the spread of communicable diseases. Tougaloo College could do relatively little for those thirty thousand Negroes of Madison County; but beginning with its own students, it worked outward.

National Negro Health Week in each April called attention to the deplorable conditions among Negroes and to the need for public services to examine and instruct them in healthful practices. Tougaloo usually observed the week by inviting public health officers, physicians, and dentists to speak at daily assemblies. Each year the school nurse, with help from a local physician and a dentist, featured some phase of health practice and preventive medicine. In 1935 Dr. A. H. McCoy, a Tougaloo graduate, and Dr. L. A. Smith gave a thorough examination, including inspection of teeth, to ninety-five Daniel Hand children, and all were immunized against typhoid. In 1936 the emphasis was on complete chest examinations and x-rays by the clinician of Mississippi State Sanitorium and on free orthopedic surgery where needed.

Elizabeth Williams, the school nurse, and one of the matrons visited community homes in 1935, preliminary to starting a community health campaign. Mrs. Williams planned a prenatal clinic and a preschool health center to immunize children between eighteen months and six years against typhoid, scarlet fever, diphtheria, and smallpox, and to test them for tuberculosis. Such an ambitious program was obviously beyond satisfactory implementation by Tougaloo during

the depression years, but a start was made with the cooperation of the Daniel Hand P.T.A., the midwives clubs, and the
churches.

Tougaloo's outreach was extended when the health department of Madison County began working with the school.
With Tougaloo's infirmary used as a clinical center for sharecroppers and tenant farmers of the community, the school approached the social service center which the A.M.A. earlier
contemplated for all its institutions. Many Tougaloo students
received first-aid and nursing experience under guidance of
Mrs. Williams and the county nurse. In 1938 over three
hundred persons were vaccinated for smallpox and typhoid,
and more than a hundred were immunized against diphtheria.
Thirty-six were given tuberculin tests, and eight received free
chest x-rays. These children were transported to the college
infirmary by trucks and cars.

Calls made in the community by Tougaloo's nurse sometimes uncovered economic needs more severe than medical
needs. A partially blind old man and his wife, practically helpless from sunstrokes, were found living in a dark, damp, cold
store building with a leaky roof. Even that shelter was about to
be taken from them because they had been unable to meet the
taxes demanded by the owner as rent. Their only financial aid
had been their old-age pension of three dollars—later increased to five—a month. Though Tougaloo could not care for
all needy families in the shadow of the school, it responded to
this emergency. President Cross paid for bedding and food that
students took to the old couple. Members of the school's YMCA
cut and delivered a truckload of wood, and the home economics classes occasionally prepared food for them. When one of
Tougaloo's staff offered his small country house to the couple,
the Y boys repaired the house; and the home economics class
cleaned and furnished it to make the old people comfortable.
Usually cases of dire need discovered by the nurse were referred to the appropriate public health authority. Often the
desperate need was the result of a fire. Fires, then as today,
were common among the poor because of inadequate heating
devices. Attempting to keep warm, people overstoked defective

woodstoves. The result was quick tragedy, and families counted themselves fortunate if no lives were lost. The Ys often had benefit socials to help a family which had been burned out.

When a large building in the Negro section of Natchez was gutted by fire in 1940, with a loss of more than two hundred lives, Tougaloo College released its registered nurse, Mrs. E. F. Scott, to work with the Red Cross. This was the first all-Negro disaster in the history of the Red Cross and the first time it had used Negro nurses. Of the ten nurses serving under its administration, the three Negro nurses were assigned to supervise burials. On her first day of service, Mrs. Scott officiated at forty-three funerals—twenty-five at the Catholic cemetery and eighteen at the colored cemetery. Her duties included making certain the graves were of prescribed depth and ready in time for a steady succession of burials. Her work was made more difficult by those who fainted at gravesides—sixty-eight on the first day—who required her attention. The burials completed, Mrs. Scott was assigned to home visits. Some, she found, had developed pneumonia; they were sent to Charity Hospital, where three of the white Red Cross nurses were caring for the fire victims. Usually her home visits required checking temperatures, dressings, and food supply and the administration of tetanus antitoxin. The fine work of Mrs. Scott won many friends for Tougaloo, and the Red Cross expressed its appreciation to President Cross.

Tougaloo attempted to teach health principles by example, but inspectors from both Madison and Hinds counties were critical of some health hazards found on the campus. An open cistern, ditches, ponds and potholes were cited as potential breeding places for mosquitoes. Privies at Daniel Hand School, located below a crest of land where gravity hindered rather than helped, were condemned in 1935 as unsanitary. They were still unacceptable five years later. The A.M.A. looked upon Hand School as a temporary arrangement until the counties took over elementary education. Under these circumstances the inspectors recommended the construction of cinder or brick pits to replace the septic tank overflow from various buildings. The barnyard was criticized for not being well drained.

But Tougaloo was praised for its cleanliness. The boys' dormitory and the hospital were in "excellent condition"; the girls' dormitory was "very sanitary"; the dining room and kitchen were "in a very high state of cleanliness"; the model home was "very clean"; and the "sanitation of the administration building was unquestioned." The reports summarized the general condition of the college as very good, and the cooperation given the inspectors led them to request special government labor to do work necessary for mosquito control.

Tougaloo's church was open to membership from the community, and the school's chaplain administered to the spiritual needs of those who sought his help. When an avowed atheist well known for his blasphemy died, his daughter came to the chaplain saying her father had made the family promise to keep his body, in death as he had kept it in life, out of the church. But the distraught young lady said that "wicked " as her father had been, the family could not bury him "like a dog." So she asked the chaplain to conduct a funeral service in the college church while her father's body lay in the hearse outside. Thus, to comfort his sorrowing family and to reveal once again Tougaloo's concern for its community, the man had a Christian funeral with many in attendance to commend him to God for the good in him that he often hid under a show of disbelief.

Tougaloo's choir introduced the college to many people in Mississippi and throughout the nation. Choir tours were usually annual events, though long sojourns were infrequent because of the prohibitive cost. In the late fifties one tour took the choir to New England and New York; another to the Midwest. Directors from the tenure of Mrs. Cyrus Hamlin through that of Ariel M. Lovelace were highly competent, and under their leadership the choir won many friends and high respect for the college.

Most gratifying has been the willingness of graduates to help others. It has been common practice for an older child of a family, after completing his own college work, to apply a generous share of his earnings to the education of a younger brother or sister. Alumni chapters carry on this concern for education of others in a more organized manner. Tougaloo clubs throughout the nation look to the Jackson chapter as the national office. During the general exodus of black people to the North after World War I Mississippi clubs were reduced from eight to just the one in Jackson. The Chicago club has always had the largest membership—about five hundred—among which may be found a large percentage of professional persons. The financial support of this one chapter has been of inestimable value to the college.

Alumni clubs have sponsored projects for Tougaloo. Typical of the help which the National Alumni Association has given was a bus with a seating capacity of thirty. Painted in the college colors, red and blue, and inscribed on each side with the name of Tougaloo College, this bus helped to maintain the enrollment of Jackson students. One project of the Los Angeles Alumni Club was a student loan fund named for W. A. Bender in appreciation of his "tremendous efforts" through the years to attract and keep new students.

Concomitant advantages have accrued to alumni clubs and their communities when they undertook projects to aid the school. Working together has kept alive the spirit of Tougaloo, and money raising programs have enriched the cultural life of the communities. A recital by Roland Hayes would have been a momentous occasion for Jackson even if it had not raised over five hundred dollars for the bus presented to Tougaloo in 1939. The inspirational address given by George N. White, A.M.A. secretary (brother of NAACP secretary Walter White), at Chicago's Good Shepherd Congregational Church was a special event for those of the Windy City.

Another gratifying aspect of the graduates is their willingness to share honors. The greatness of the school lies in its faculty and staff, as many are quick to say. One recalled that just to see a certain teacher walk across the campus was an inspiration, as his very life embodied all that he taught in the classroom. To know teachers willing to give their skills, time, and money far beyond what was required impressed others. One graduate reported that he finally dissuaded a teacher in her desire to finance a student through graduate school. He pointed out to her that, while her earning days would shortly end, the student had years ahead of him and could use the first of them to earn money to further his own education. Some staff members were quick to give credit to the American Missionary Association, an organization which "has done more for my people than any other." By implication credit should be given all who, through their contributions, made the A.M.A. a viable organization. The American Missionary Association and Tougaloo's faculty, staff, alumni, and students, with the help of many friends, have worked together throughout the years, putting up with one another's foibles, persisting always toward the goal of full opportunity for every man and woman regardless of color. Herein is the source of Tougaloo's success.

20

Beittel and Civil Rights

DR. ADAM DANIEL BEITTEL ACCEPTED the invitation of Tougaloo Southern Christian College's board of trustees to become the school's president as of September 1, 1960. It was a difficult decision for Dr. Beittel and his wife, Ruth. After a distinguished career as both dean and teacher in two Quaker colleges, president of Talladega College, and dean of the chapel and professor of religion at Beloit College in Wisconsin, Dr. Beittel looked forward to a sabbatical in the Middle East and retirement in four years. To leave Beloit for troubled Mississippi did not make sense. Only the assurance of the board that he could continue until age seventy (with his option to continue after sixty-five on a yearly basis) persuaded him and his wife to sell their home overlooking the Rock River, to give up the sabbatical, and to assume the responsibilities at Tougaloo.

As with previous presidents, most of Dr. Beittel's time was absorbed by the normal duties of administration. But a few figures attest to his success in the financial aspect of administration. The school's assets increased from $1,648,423.35 in 1960 to $2,730,421.03 in 1964. The operational deficit of $34,982.67 in 1961 was erased, and by 1964 there was a surplus of $15,486.41. Foundation grants increased. Among the new grants received were those from the Merrill Trust, Fund for the Advancement of Education, Field Foundation, Cummins Engine Foundation, Carnegie Corporation, and Alfred Harcourt Foundation. Also the United Negro College Fund sent its first

196

distribution from the Capital Funds Campaign, which amounted to $200,060 for Tougaloo.

The physical plant was improved. Warren Hall, which serves as a cafeteria and student union, was completed. A home for the president, with bedrooms adequate to house visitors, was built.

Academic standards of the school improved proportionately. There was a steady increase in the number of Tougaloo graduates who entered graduate schools. Several programs, such as those of the National Science Foundation, and the prefreshman summer course, were brought to the campus. Some grants sent students and faculty to other institutions for special summer courses. An exchange program between Tougaloo and some northern schools was promoted. Willie Anderson did so well at Ripon College in Wisconsin that he was given a scholarship to continue his work at Ripon. There were white exchange students and others, like Joan Trumpauer, who came to enroll as regular students. Steve Rutledge held the office of student body president in his senior year. Both he and Joan graduated from Tougaloo—the first white graduates from the college. (Luella Miner, daughter of the farm superintendent, graduated from the normal school before the college program was started.)

Tougaloo and Brown University joined in a cooperative program. Under this arrangement faculty and student exchanges were encouraged. A fifth year at Brown was designed for Tougaloo graduates who needed a firmer grounding in subject matter or broader experience before entering graduate schools. Brown was also helpful in encouraging foundations to make grants to Tougaloo.

Dr. Beittel was active in organizations which could strengthen the college indirectly. He served on the Mississippi Advisory Committee to the U. S. Commission on Civil Rights, was a director on the board for the Southern Regional Council, secretary of the United Negro College Fund, and vice president of the Association of Colleges and Schools for Negroes.

Impressive as were these achievements, Dr. Beittel would be remembered more for his support of civil rights. He worked to revive the defunct Human Relations Council; and when no one dared take the office of president, he added it to his duties.

The local white citizenry looked with some apprehension on Dr. Beittel's work. In September 1961, just one year to the day after his arrival at Tougaloo, he was invited to appear on the Jackson television station WLBT to be questioned by a panel of journalists. The first question was "Are you a member of the NAACP?" In 1961 most white Mississippians equated the NAACP with the Communist Party. Dr. Beittel answered that technically he was not a member but that he subscribed to its literature.

Many of the panel's questions dealt with Tougaloo's role as host for visiting groups of mixed races, a policy so controversial that the only white Mississippian on Tougaloo's board of trustees resigned in protest. Dr. Beittel freely acknowledged that two interracial groups of distinguished churchmen had enjoyed Tougaloo's hospitality. Unfortunately some of each group were arrested before leaving Jackson. Regarding the Freedom Riders who were housed on the school's campus, Beittel said the college "simply provided hospitality to human beings who needed a place to sleep."

In leading up to the library study-in attempted by Tougaloo's NAACP chapter (whose adviser was Chaplain Mangram) and which resulted in the use of dogs against civil rights activists for the first time by the Mississippi police, a panelist asked if Tougaloo's library were inadequate for student needs. Dr. Beittel went directly to the heart of the panel's concern, saying, "I don't think the students came to the Jackson city library primarily for books." He added that they felt the injustice of being refused use of a public facility and that they had the support of Tougaloo's faculty, administration and board of trustees. Dr. Beittel said he had not been in on the planning of the sit-in but that as soon as he learned students were in jail he got them out on bail. Asked if he would expel the students should they be found guilty in the up-coming trial, he answered, "There is a difference between going to jail for stealing something and going to jail for a conviction. I should respect [the students] for being willing to pay the price for what they believe to be right." Actually the school never expelled anyone for civil rights activities. Conversely, Tougaloo enrolled some students who had been expelled from other schools for engaging in movement activities.

Dr. Beittel was then asked if he thought it right to oppose community customs and rules. He answered, "All customs and rules should be abided by when they are consistent with our highest ideals," but "when people pay taxes to support an institution" they should be able to "participate in the benefits." He had never heard of Negroes being exempted from taxes, he continued, because they could not use the facilities provided by those taxes.

"Will you discourage off-campus activities in the future?" a panelist asked. "No, I don't think so," came the answer. Then he said that students might be discouraged indirectly because the college would not excuse anybody from class or give grades for sitting-in. When a panelist asked if Dr. Beittel realized that a continuation of Tougaloo's controversial activities would bring trouble, he countered that he doubted education could occur without some controversy but that no trouble was necessary. If the authorities had ignored the students at the library there would have been no trouble had they sat there and read for three hours.

Until the spring of 1964 foreigners, even of dark complexion, were served in Jackson restaurants. But three incidents during the week of Indian Prime Minister Jawaharlal Nehru's death ended this tolerance for a time. Jerrodean Davis, a Tougaloo student, Dr. Savithri Chattopadhyay, a visiting Brahman Indian professor, and a white faculty member went to Morrison's downtown cafeteria where, to their great surprise, they were served. Police did nothing beyond keeping watch through the large windows. The next day when word came of Nehru's death, Dr. Savithri and Mr. Dennis Strete, also an Indian, were stricken with grief. They drove to Jackson to send a cablegram. On their way back to the college they stopped at Morrison's other cafeteria on the outskirts of the city and were refused service. Dr. Savithri demanded an explanation and was told by the manager that on the day before three women, one a white and one an Indian dressed in a sari, were served at the downtown cafeteria because no one knew for sure whether the third was a Negro or another Indian. Since then it had been learned that she was a Negro. As a result Morrison's two cafeterias had orders not to serve any Indians.

On the following day, Dr. and Mrs. Beittel, at the request of the U.S. Department of State, met Dr. Ram Manohar Lohia and his traveling companion at the airport. Dr. Lohia was a member of the Indian parliament and head of the Socialist Party in that country. Returning from the airport, the Beittels took their guests to a Morrison's cafeteria and were stunned when they were refused service.

Dr. Lohia was a pacifist in the tradition of Gandhi. He insisted on returning the next day for lunch, not as a representative of India but as an Indian citizen. To do less would not show concern for the treatment of local blacks, he believed. He informed the manager at Morrison's, the police, and the press of his intention. Dressed in a white robe and sandals, he walked to the door of the cafeteria. There he was met by the manager, who informed him that his business was not wanted, that he was on private property, and that he was being asked to leave.

Dr. Lohia replied, "I tell you with the greatest humility I am not leaving." Then the police arrested him and led him across the street to a paddywagon. Dr. Lohia talked with the police about the meaning of justice for some twenty minutes, after which he was released.

Each of the three incidents was independent of the other. Mr. Strete, who took Dr. Savithri to Morrison's after sending the cable, knew nothing of the incident at the downtown Morrison's; Dr. Beittel knew nothing of either of the two previous episodes. Yet it would have been hard to convince Morrison's that the three incidents were not planned, each bringing into the act persons of greater prestige than those of the day before.

Of more concern to the business community than Tougaloo's hosting of out-of-state mixed groups, the library sit-in, or the incidents at Morrison's cafeterias, was the boycott of a few carefully selected downtown Jackson stores in protest against their discriminatory practices. Beginning in December of

1962, a group of students and faculty which often met at the home of Professor John Salter (commonly referred to as Salter's Coffee House) joined the Mississippi NAACP and others in encouraging persons to buy elsewhere. Some Jackson businesses were eventually forced to close because of the financial squeeze. Yet none was willing to change its discriminatory practices.

In an attempt to keep the pressure on the businessmen, several persons, including Professor Salter, and two students, Memphis Norman and Anne Moody (later the author of *Coming of Age in Mississippi*), took seats at Woolworth's segregated lunch counter; they were refused service. Enraged bystanders squirted them with mustard and catsup and emptied salt and pepper shakers and sugar bowls on them. Norman was thrown to the floor and kicked; all the others were beaten. Dr. Beittel, having been phoned by Edwin King, the college chaplain, contacted police and Woolworth's management (local and national) to ask them to stop the mob action. Finally a company supervisor closed the store, and the mob dispersed. Dr. Beittel helped take the injured persons from the lunch counter to his car. During this episode the president of the student body, Eddie O'Neil, and two women from Tougaloo, Jeannette King (sociology instructor) and Margrit Garner (community worker), were jailed for picketing nearby with signs saying JACKSON NEEDS A BI-RACIAL COMMITTEE.

In the fall of 1963 the Tougaloo Movement, under the leadership of two students, Joyce Ladner (black) and Joan Trumpauer (white), decided to concentrate on two areas—live entertainment and white churches. Leaders of society and government as well as persons who considered themselves moderates, could be confronted in both areas. If moderates could see segregation enforced in all its ugly aspects, they might be persuaded to work for peaceful integration, especially in the public schools, which would soon be under court order to desegregate.

A student, Austin Moore, was made chairman of a Cultural and Artistic Agitation Committee. This committee focused first on Millsaps College, where a ferment of dissatisfaction was already at work. Many at Millsaps were embarrassed that police and dogs had been used to prevent Tougaloo students from sharing in the college's cultural programs. Through negotiations, led by Dr. Beittel and the Tougaloo chaplain, the Cultural Committee and Millsaps reached an agreement to open events held in the Christian Center auditorium. The first occasion was carefully planned. Several blacks from Tougaloo sat in the middle of the auditorium while white students from Tougaloo sat at either end, and sympathetic Millsaps students occupied the rows immediately in front and behind. This arrangement precluded any local whites being seated next to a black. No difficulties were encountered, and cultural events at Millsaps were steadily made more available to blacks, though not without hardships for the administration and financial officers.

The Royal Philharmonic Orchestra from London was scheduled to give the first concert of the 1963–64 series sponsored by the Jackson Community Concert Association. Though whites at Tougaloo had purchased season's tickets, use of them by any blacks would certainly result in arrest. Therefore, the Committee appealed to the Orchestra to insist that the concert either be open to all or cancelled. When it refused, Dr. Elizabeth Sewell, a British citizen and a visiting professor at Tougaloo, made a personal telephone call to the director, Sir Malcolm Sargent. He stated that Mississippi's racial problems were not his responsibility.

Cancellation failing, the Committee chose to send representatives to the concert. An Englishman, Nicholas Bosanquet, who was visiting Jackson at the time to assist SNCC in voter registration, and Robert Honeysucker, a Tougaloo music major, presented their tickets at the door of the concert hall. They made it to the foyer before the police moved in. Then, just as Sir Malcolm raised his baton to begin the "Star-Spangled Banner," a walkie-talkie voice crackled through the auditorium, "Yeah, a colored man and a white one, but we got them and will take them right to jail." The two were released the next morning on bonds of five hundred dollars each.

This seeming failure had some positive facets. There was no physical violence; the British Embassy intervened to get the charges dropped, and the *Manchester Guardian* gave the incident a wide publicity which made other artists hesitate to subject themselves to the same embarrassment.

When the ticket salesperson for the "Original Hootenanny U.S.A.," sponsored by three white colleges, refused to sell a ticket to a black student, the Cultural Committee met the folk singers at the airport. The performers were sympathetic. They tried to have the auditorium opened to blacks as well as whites. Unsuccessful in this, they cancelled their performance at a loss of $2,500 and gave a free concert at Tougaloo College while some 1,500 frustrated ticketholders stood in line at the city auditorium to get refunds.

One week in February 1964 was later described as a "Protest Festival." Climaxing weeks of correspondence with the Tougaloo students, television's "Bonanza" artists, Hoss, Little Joe, and Ben Cartwright canceled their scheduled appearance. That same week while white Jackson was still nursing its injured pride and urging people to go to church on Sunday nights rather than watch "Bonanza," two "Beverly Hillbillies" sent word that they would not perform as replacements for the "Bonanza" troupe. The following day, after 5,000 people had waited forty minutes to hear the white jazz trumpet player Al Hirt from New Orleans, a man walked onto the stage and read a telegram from the Tougaloo students. In it the students requested Al Hirt to cancel because the performance would "serve the purpose of perpetuating the vicious system of segregation in Jackson." Mr. Hirt would not be there. An angry crowd left, many of them vowing they would "get" Tougaloo. A radio announcer stated he would never again play an Al Hirt record.

Other artists canceled as a result of the Cultural Committee's efforts. The *New York Times* publicized the work of the Committee, and it seemed the fight was practically won; but there were still troubles ahead.

"Holiday on Ice" refused to cancel. An exchange student, Eli Hochstedler (white) bought two tickets, giving one to Marion Gillon (black). When asked to leave the hall they refused and were arrested. Because of a prior arrangement for bail

made with Charles Evers of the NAACP the students anticipated little time in jail, but the promised bail money did not
arrive. Eli and Marion were clapped in segregated cells. The
jailer asked Eli to button his collar before he entered his cell.
Later it was learned the buttoned collar signaled to the in-
mates that he was the race mixer. The white prisoners then
knew they could beat up this race mixer with impunity. When
the two were released after almost a week, Marion was overcome with relief, for during his detainment he had been told Eli
had died from the beatings given him. Fortunately Eli was
alive, though so terribly bruised as to be scarcely recognized.
(The movement understood that students could not remain in
jail as did fulltime movement workers. Students had to ar-
range for bail as soon as possible so they could carry on with
their studies. Particularly important was bail in this case, as it
was near time for exams.)

After the "Hootenanny," sponsored by students of three
white colleges, canceled and performed at Tougaloo, the
Tougaloo students gained the cooperation of some students
from five schools, two of which were black, to plan an integrated folk music concert. Joan Baez agreed to do the show at
the Tougaloo campus. On the night of the performance Woodworth Chapel was filled with the most integrated audience of
its entire history. The evening ended with refreshments in the
student union and finally with many lingering in groups to
talk, sing, and dream.

The Civil Rights Act was passed during the summer of
1964, and the next year Tougaloo College was included among
the sponsors of the cultural programs in Jackson. One final
ironical touch was enjoyed by white Jackson and caused
amusement on the campus. Ed and Jeannette King, faculty
members, had their money for tickets returned. These two native white Mississippians, having defied the customs of the
state, were beyond the pale.

Churches proved more difficult to integrate than cultural
events. Under the American system of separation of church and
state, even the passage of the Civil Rights Act could not force
churches to open their doors. Few attempts were made to at-

tend white churches before the summer of 1963 when local Jackson citizens and students in an ecumenical work camp at Tougaloo (sponsored by the National Council of Churches) tried to worship in white churches. The Catholic and Episcopal churches accepted them. The Lutheran church was irregular in its policy. Other Protestant churches followed the NEVER line of the White Citizens Council, an organization formed in 1956 to prevent integration.

After the fall school term opened someone made almost weekly attempts to attend white churches. Most efforts were channeled through the school's chaplain, the Rev. Edwin King. A white native Methodist Mississippian, King was denied membership in the Mississippi Methodist Conference (white) because of his liberal racial views. He was then accepted as the only white ministerial member of the Mississippi Methodist Conference (black) at the invitation of Bishop Charles Golden.

The procedure for confronting the churches called for small racially mixed groups to walk toward the church until they were stopped by a cadre of ushers—referred to by students as the "bouncing committee." The visitors, who were often both black and white ministers from outside the state, in company with a black student, would engage the churchmen in dialog, asking such questions as how they could reconcile an exclusionary policy with Christian doctrine. When the "ushers" refused to talk, the visitors might open their New Testaments and silently read until the police arrived to take them to jail in the paddywagon.

John Garner, a physicist at Tougaloo College, and Margrit Garner were active members of Galloway Memorial Methodist Church. On October 20, 1963, Garner took two ministers from out of state and a black student, Joyce Ladner, to Sunday School. All four were arrested on charges of trespassing and disturbing a worship service.

During the same month three young women students, Bette Poole and Ida Hannah (both black) and Julie Zaugg (a white exchange student from Illinois) went to Capitol Street Methodist Church in Jackson. After some conversation on the church steps with the ushers, they were given three minutes to leave. As they were walking away the police arrested them. The girls were held in jail incommunicado until the next afternoon when they were allowed to call their attorney.

Obtaining bail money for those arrested was an increasing problem. Visitors took care of their own bail, sometimes with the help of their churches back home. The church of Garner's parents paid his bail. Most unforgivable in the eyes of Jackson's white church people was the payment of bail by the Washington-based Women's Division of the Board of Missions of the Methodist Church. The campus movement secured services of out-of-state attorneys William Kunstler, Arthur Kinoy, and others who, together with the local black lawyer, R. Jess Brown, defended the "trespassers."

Not all activities ended in arrest; some even had elements of humor. On one occasion a white faculty member who was also a member of Galloway Methodist Church dressed up in her best finery and without consulting anyone went to church to welcome the visiting men she knew would be on the church steps. She broke through the ring of ushers who surrounded the black and the white ministers, extended a gloved hand, and said, "Welcome to our church. I hope you enjoy the service." Leaving the startled group, she escaped to the balcony where she removed her feathered hat and mink stole. Out of the corner of her eye she saw two men enter the balcony and look the worshipers over carefully before leaving. The Jackson newspapers carried the story, saying an "unidentified white lady" welcomed the visitors. When the men were released from jail a week later, one of them said the timing was perfect, as the ushers were at that moment explaining that everyone in the church was of the same mind; all endorsed the policy of "whites only." Of course, this was an overstatement; a few members were unhappy with the exclusionary policy.

When L. Zenobia Coleman, librarian, asked Clarice Campbell (white) of the faculty to join in a birthday dinner for the assistant librarian, Julia Bender, the teacher said she would be happy to do so but had promised to attend the annual conference at her church at 7:30. She asked the two librarians to go with her after the dinner. The birthday lady demurred, saying she had never gone where she was not wanted and did not propose to court trouble on her sixty-fifth birthday. The teacher assured her there would be no trouble, as this was the bishop's meeting and he had insisted it be open to all.

Following a good meal at Morrison's cafeteria, by then in compliance with the Civil Rights Act of 1964, the three women went to the church, climbed the many steps and were in the foyer before they were accosted by one of the Sunday ushers. Addressing the white woman by name, he said, "You know better than to bring these two women." With that he took the arm of the member and the arm of one of her black guests and fairly shoved them out the door. The other guest scuttled down the steps as fast as she could. The white church member turned on her heel and found the associate pastor on the front row of the crowded church. Breathlessly, she told him that she and her guests had been physically ejected from the church. He followed her to the foyer and, finding the man responsible, asked him if he were an usher. "No," he replied, "but I am an usher on Sundays, and I know the policy of this church." The minister explained that this was the bishop's meeting and the bishop had stipulated that it must be open to all. Men gathered around and asked the woman what should be done. She suggested that the Sunday usher might apologize to the two black women. "Students who are rebuffed readily bounce back, but these women are crushed. They were reluctant to come in the first place." When the Sunday usher refused, the minister offered to make the apology. The two librarians were found standing by the locked car. The minister invited them to return, saying there had been a misunderstanding. The women thanked him but said the feeling of some had been made obvious and they had no desire to go where not wanted. The minister ended his conversation with them, saying there were many ways of serving the Lord and they had chosen one good way to serve him that evening. The two women thought it an experience they would not want to repeat but that in hindsight it could be viewed with amusement and even satisfaction because they had further cracked the walls of segregation in the house of God.

Another book would be required to cover all the church related episodes, but one story is unique. Cleveland Page, a black
music instructor at Tougaloo, had applied for graduate work at
a northern university. He was asked to submit a tape record-
ing of his pipe organ playing. A white member of the Tougaloo
faculty (also a member of Galloway Memorial Methodist
Church) obtained permission from her pastor, Dr. W. J. Cunningham, for Mr. Page to use the church's pipe organ on a day
when no meetings would be in session. Mr. Page was apprehensive and insisted that two other church members should be
present. The church organist agreed to be there long enough to
introduce Mr. Page to the organ, and Mrs. Paul Arrington, a
leader in the local and national Methodist Church, agreed to
remain. Mr. Page was understandably tense, not knowing what
might happen should unsympathetic persons learn of his presence in the church. An unknown man at one time rattled the
front doors trying to get in; all that could be seen from inside
was his hat. Afterward Mr. Page described his thoughts as he
was playing: Would a Citizens Council member learn of this?
Or a KKK member? A shot in the back perhaps? If so, he
thought what a dramatic ending he could make with one last
minor chord as he fell forward on the keys. A faculty member
wrote Mr. Page this poem:

> *Pièce d'Occasion*
> FOR CLEVE PAGE
>
> Someone has begun to play
> In the church at Galloway.
> Organ music, proud and fine,
> Echoes round the sacred shrine.
> Who is playing? That is Cleve.
> Wow! whoever gave *him* leave?
> For within this hallowed spot,
> Some may play and some may not—
> (Axiom that would seem dippy
> Anywhere but Mississippi).
> In the haunts of Methodism,
> Cleve, defying separatism,
> Adumbrates a cataclysm.

Busy with baroque arpeggi,
He is feeling slightly edgy.
That requires no understanding:
Bach's sufficiently demanding—
But, his back to aisle and pew,
Cleve has other things in view,
Thoughts to make the stoutest quiver:
Bang! a bullet in the liver.
Contemplating being shot
Makes one's playing go to pot.
Do the skimming fingers falter?
(Who's that lurking by the altar?)
Classic fugue-dom and toccata-dom
Do not normally lead to martyrdom;
Are White Citizens familiar
With the fate of Saint Cecilia?
Anyway, in Jackson town
Everything is upside down:
That the righteous cause may win,
Christians do their brothers in,
To protect with gun and knife
Mississippi's Way of Life
Any Protestant church pillar
Could conceal a ruthless killer.
Facing premature Nirvana,
Cleve thinks Papua or Ghana
Might know more of *vox humana*.

As he's playing, Cleve, meanwhile,
Plans to die in splendid style.
If dispatched to meet the Lord,
He will strike a monstrous chord.
Seventh, maybe, and diminished
For his Symphony Unfinished?
Pathos far as it will go,
Pianissimissimo?
Tune the bellows! final wheeze,
Then fall forward on the keys?
No! if he must choose his fate,
Cleve decides to play it straight:
Surely nothing could be finer

Than expire in C Sharp Minor.
Having taken which decision,
Exorcised the grisly vision,
He concludes in deft precision.

Let the anticlimax fall:
Nothing happened after all.
We are rather glad, dear friend,
It was fugue's, not journey's end.
Remains to say, in love and rage,
May better worlds your gifts engage—
Long life and happiness, Cleve Page!

—Elizabeth Sewell

With the passage of the Civil Rights Act of 1964 it was imperative that blacks use their regained rights. These same rights had been theirs during Radical Reconstruction after the Civil War but had been lost in part because they were not used. Of course, to have used them might have meant personal tragedy of the worst kind. It could mean tragedy to use the rights in 1964, also, but that chance had to be taken or the rights would again be shelved.

Students and faculty members patronized restaurants and motels in small racially mixed groups. In November of 1964 a student, Altamese Rutledge, president of the History Club, went with two history professors, Joe Herzenberg and Clarice Campbell, to the Southern Historical Association meeting at Little Rock. En route they stopped for the night at a motel in Indianola, birth town of the White Citizens Council. Though Ms. Rutledge did not go in when the rooms were engaged, the desk clerk probably recognized her as a black when he peered out the window to note who was in the car. But the next morning all faces in the coffee shop froze when the three entered. The manager quickly ushered the three outside. He was aghast when he learned that they had stayed in his motel overnight.

The three drove on to Greenville, considered one of the most enlightened towns in Mississippi. Because the Holiday Inns in Jackson had complied with the new Civil Rights Act no difficulty was anticipated when the group entered the restaurant at the Holiday Inn in Greenville. After the three had waited for some time at a table, the manager came to them and, with an ingratiating smile, said, "We are not serving you." Herzenberg said, "You are aware that you are violating the Civil Rights Act?" The woman left the table without further comment.

From there the three went to the Downtowner—a beautiful new motel also in Greenville. After a time the hostess went to the racially mixed table to say, "We will serve *her*," indicating the black student, "but we will not serve *you*," indicating the two white faculty members. When the manager was asked for an explanation, he said it was against their policy to serve mixed groups. Because the three were already late for the meeting in Little Rock, they separated and used three tables so as not to divide on a racial line. Oddly, the patrons of the restaurant showed little concern for the presence of a black.

In the spring of 1965 a white faculty member drove four Tougaloo students to the University of Mississippi to discuss with officials the possibility of their enrollment in the fall. At that time only two blacks were attending Ole Miss; one, Cleveland Donald, had taken his freshman year at Tougaloo.

When darkness and rain overtook the group at Grenada, an attempt was made to stay overnight at a motel. Two rooms were engaged by the faculty member. As the students were getting the suitcases out of the car a frantic voice from the office insisted that they come back. The clerk wanted to return the check and retrieve the keys. He said he should have been told there were "colored" in the party. After some discussion with the manager in which the faculty adviser tried to make a number of points, the manager pleaded, "I'm sure all that is true, but I have to depend on Mississippi for business and the motel would be ruined, possibly bombed, if it accepted your group."

By that time a group of men and boys had gathered outside. They were later described to the U.S. Justice Department as "white trash, trouble makers, and known bootleggers, some of whom had done time in the state penitentiary." A sheriff was on guard as well as two city policemen in their car. The adviser of the students asked the police if they would escort the Tougaloo car at least to the city limits as she feared the mob which surrounded them. The police called headquarters and were told to take the city attorney with them.

When the attorney came, the adviser asked his name—a procedure the FBI had suggested she always follow. Testily, he answered, "What difference does my name make to you?" She quickly replied, "None, really. Would you please escort us to the new interstate highway going north?" Both parties got in their cars. Then the attorney got out of his car, came to the Tougaloo car, and said, "Ma'am, I don't mind if you know my name. It's Dye." Southern men find it very difficult to be rude to a white lady. Mr. Dye evidently didn't want his rudeness weighing on his conscience.

With the murder of the three civil rights workers the summer before still vividly in mind, the law officers were taking no chance on Mississippi's image being further tarnished. Outside the town of Grenada a highway patrol car assumed the task of escorting the Tougaloo car. As each county line was approached, another patrol car was waiting to take over. When Oxford, the seat of the University, was reached, the adviser thanked the last patrolmen, saying "Where but in Mississippi could one get protection like this!" The driver snorted, "Lady, I don't know what you mean by protection, but you are the worst driver I ever followed."

Potential or actual violence was a frequent companion of many at Tougaloo during the early 1960s. Cars occupied by men unknown to the school sometimes raced through the campus with guns ablaze. Reporting the license numbers to authorities brought no response. Faculty homes at the extreme west end of the campus were shot at often from cars driving down the county road. When a white faculty member, Bill Hutchinson, was driving his wife, his baby, and a white student to church, men in several cars maneuvered him to the side of the road and blocked the road in front and behind. A heavy pipe wielded by one of the men against the hood of Hutchinson's car did some damage, but by a dramatic gunning of the car Hutchinson made his way around the blockade. Once safely in

Tougaloo College pre-freshmen of 1964

Teams of two students each were funded to give tutorial help to under-achievers in the community during the early difficult days of school desegre-gation.

In 1973 the new L. Zenobia Coleman Library was dedicated.

Presenting tickets to the Governor for the Opera/South production of "Othello" presented April 17, 1974 are, from left to right: President J. Louis Stokes, Utica Junior College; Governor William L. Waller; President John A. Peoples, Jr., Jackson State University; President George A. Owens, Tougaloo College.

Ground-breaking for new dormitories 1969

One of two dormitories built under the Master Plan

President Owens, Vice-President Branch, and Chaplain King greeted Robert
Kennedy in 1967.

A faculty home near the highway was bombed—part of a wave of racist terror
in the state.

Ronald Schnell not only paints and teaches art but brings outstanding art
exhibits to the campus; he is constantly looking for important works to add
to the college's permanent collection.

Walter B. Lewis, '53, as alumni banquet speaker in 1968 then employed by the U. S. Commission on Civil Rights.

Mr. I. S. Sanders receiving honorary degree from Tougaloo College during commencement of 1967 (Dean Huffer reads as President Owens and Mr. Dockins listen.)

The inauguration of President George Owens

Dr. Van S. Allen '50
President of National Alumni Association
Executive Director of TACTICS

Dr. Walter Washington '48
President Alcorn State University

Mrs. Thelma Sanders '46
Owner of Sanders' Boutique

Dr. Edgar Smith '55
Provost University of Massachusetts, Amhe

Mrs. Edith B. Rice '66
Alumni Executive Secretary
Tougaloo College National Alumni Association

Mr. H. M. Thompson '36
M. W. Stringer Grand Lodge,
F & AM, PHA

Representative Corneal A. Davis '17
Assistant Majority Leader
Illinois House of Representatives

Mr. Walter Turnbull '66
Tenor, Lake George Opera

Mr. Joffery Whisenton '55 (left)
Special Assistant to the Secretary of
Housing, Education and Welfare
Dr. George Johnson '50 (right)
Vice President of Student Affairs
Jackson State University

Mr. Leroy Jackson '37
Past President Tougaloo College
National Alumni Association
Teacher in California Public Schools

Dr. A. Strickland '51
Professor of History, University of Michigan

Ms. Anne Moody '64
Author of *Coming of Age in Mississippi*
Photo credit: Jack Schrier

Mrs. Julia Bender always has a cheerful word for everyone who checks books out of the library.

Dr. H. Pfautz from Brown University at a Social Science Forum at Tougaloo

the church, he called the campus security officer to alert any who might be planning to leave the campus. Dr. Beittel and others went to the church to escort the Hutchinsons home.

One night after a civil rights meeting in Canton, seventeen miles to the north of Tougaloo, a car of faculty members and students was chased by four cars of white men and forced to the side of the road. The men talked within hearing of the Tougaloo people about what should be done with them. Finally, Ed King was able to make the men understand that the driver, a Pakistani, was a foreigner, and any harm done to him would bring down the wrath of the U.S. government.

Crosses were sometimes burned at the Tougaloo campus gate. Telephone calls with obscene messages, threats, or just heavy breathing were made to the King home in particular. At the height of the threats, Tougaloo men students, armed only with whistles, organized a night patrol. On a few nights some students guarded the campus with guns—a fact kept secret from the faculty and administration but surely known to police and other whites.

When democratic and constitutional machinery for the airing of grievances is not open to the people, they have several choices: submission, violence, or nonviolent protest. The Tougaloo movement, heavily influenced by Chaplain King, was committed to a nonviolent protest in the spirit of Gandhi, Martin Luther King, Jr., and the Student Nonviolent Coordinating Committee (SNCC).

The murder of Medgar Evers, Executive Secretary of the Mississippi NAACP, might be considered the nadir of Mississippi blacks' hope for justice under law. Their leader had been slain in his own carport as he returned from a mass rally. At 5:30 the next morning, June 8, 1963, Ed King, John Salter, a sociology professor, and Stephen Rutledge, student body president, woke those at President's Beittel's home to tell him of the tragedy. Out of the ashes of defeat and despair, the blacks and their sympathizers answered the White Citizens Council slogan of NEVER with slogans of their own, ONE MAN, ONE VOTE, and FREEDOM NOW.

The Mississippi Freedom Vote was developed by SNCC and

led by Robert Moses as a means of organizing blacks and demonstrating to the nation that if blacks were allowed to vote, the election results would be quite different. Students from Tougaloo joined SNCC, CORE, NAACP, and SCLC under the united banner of COFO in a mock election during the fall of 1963, time of the state elections. Dr. Aaron Henry, the black president of the Mississippi NAACP, also chairman of COFO, and Ed King, the white chaplain at Tougaloo, were selected as candidates for governor and lieutenant governor. Those few blacks who were registered were advised to write in these two names on their official ballots. Others were asked to vote unofficially the Freedom Ballot, to register their wishes.

Cardboard ballot boxes were placed in the student union at Tougaloo and in black service stations, stores, and churches. Some students joined other civil rights workers in distributing and collecting these votes, often going disguised as field hands onto cotton plantations. There were some arrests with high bail exacted. The white opposition sometimes chased the workers, shot at them, and formed mobs to block them. Some ballot boxes were confiscated by the police. But eighty to ninety thousand people, including some of the most oppressed workers, succeeded in casting their unofficial ballots. Aaron Henry and Ed King received over ninety-nine percent of the mock election votes. The victory rally at the Masonic Temple in Jackson gave black Mississippians new pride and faith in what could be done when they united. On a practical plane the organization for this Freedom Vote was invaluable for future victories.

The Mississippi Freedom Democratic Party, led by Fannie Lou Hamer (whom Tougaloo later granted an honorary degree of Doctor of Humanities), Aaron Henry, and Ed King, went to Atlantic City to contest the seating of the regular Mississippi Democratic delegates. They argued before the convention that the regular delegates should be disqualified because about forty percent of the citizens of voting age had not been allowed to participate in choosing the delegates.

At the request of President Johnson and the Justice Department, a team of FBI special agents infiltrated the Freedom delegation and worked to thwart its effectiveness. The Democratic Convention refused to recognize the challengers, but it offered as a compromise to seat Henry and King as delegates at large. They refused, believing it just another attempt to buy off the leaders of a protest. After the convention, FBI Director J. Edgar Hoover gave a special commendation to Cartha DeLoach, the agent who supervised the infiltration of the Freedom Democrats, for sparing President Johnson embarrassment.

The state of Mississippi looked for legal ways to curtail these activities stemming from Tougaloo College, referred to by many whites as a nest of Communists and rabblerousers. An examination of the school's charter revealed a forgotten clause limiting the value of the school's physical plant to $500,000. Buildings and grounds by then being far in excess of that amount, the legislature drew up a bill to revoke the charter. However, with letters of protest coming to the state from colleges and universities outside Mississippi, the bill was allowed to die in committee.

Another bill was introduced. It provided for the separation of state accreditation from regional accreditation by the Southern Association of Colleges and Schools. If this bill became law the state could deny Tougaloo College state accreditation and make it impossible for the school's graduates to teach in Mississippi. Fortunately the bill was modified, and, though enacted, gave little more than an emotional satisfaction to the detractors of Tougaloo.

In June 1963, an injunction was issued against "The Trustees of Tougaloo University," A. D. Beittel, NAACP, CORE and others. All these were enjoined against "engaging in, sponsoring, inciting or encouraging demonstrations" including kneel-ins at churches. This injunction was appealed, and it too came to nought.

Despite all the harassment, the school continued to function as an educational institution; and, with the cooperation of Brown University, foundation money was coming to the college in unprecedented amounts. The board of trustees seemingly supported President Beittel. Because the future looked

brighter, the announcement in the spring of 1964 by the board
of trustees that Dr. Beittel would be leaving as of September
came as a shock.

A press release authorized by the board of trustees stated
that Dr. Beittel would retire, but gave no adequate reason.
People conjectured various explanations: the president must
have a serious illness; he is weary of facing the Citizens Council, the politicians, and other racists; or the board of trustees is
yielding to political pressure. Hardest to answer were those
students who begged him to reconsider and friends of the college who feared that Tougaloo was finally surrendering to intimidation.

Three Mississippi religious leaders, Reverend Bernard Law
(Catholic), Reverend Duncan M. Gray, Jr. (Episcopal), and
Rabbi Perry E. Nussbaum wrote the board of trustees of Tougaloo College, saying in part: "The undersigned are members
of the Board of Directors of the Mississippi Council on Human
Relations, one of us is its current President, all of us have pursued the cause of social justice for many years and in considerable degree." (Reverends Law and Gray have since become
bishops.)

The leaders said Dr. Beittel and his wife "brought into
focus, for members of both races, the salient challenges" of the
area. The letter continued:

Under his forthright guidance on the Tougaloo campus, the College at
long last has become a beacon light, as well as a goal, for the fulfillment of the principles so necessary for Mississippi. His leadership as
President, his unhesitating expressions of courageous insight into our
problems on the campus and in public, his display of moral integrity
without regard to personal cost, his dignity, if you please, all of these
qualities have redounded to the credit of the Congregational-
Christian Churches who sponsor Tougaloo, as they have been a profound source of strength for others.

We, of course, will not presume to intrude in the particular academic
and administrative areas which are your concern as members of
Tougaloo's Board of Trustees. We do take the liberty of emphasizing
that a change in the Presidency at this juncture will so complicate

current critical issues about Tougaloo and race relations that the advances of the past few years will be seriously endangered. The reaction of the enemies of Tougaloo has already been made obvious in the press: Dr. Beittel's leaving is a victory for them and the first step in the control which must be exercised by the racists of Mississippi on the campus. Tougaloo is finally surrendering to intimidation.

The board asked Dr. Beittel to announce his voluntary retirement, but he chose not to be a part of the deception. He would not have left his former post at Beloit College for a mere four years at Tougaloo. He had the board's written assent to his remaining until age seventy. In short he was not retiring of his own free will, yet he could not openly oppose the board at so critical a time for the college. The board asked George Owens, the school's business manager, to be acting president as of September 1, 1964.

In 1967 the Mississippi State Sovereignty Commission claimed a major role in the dismissal of Beittel. Members of the Sovereignty Commission asserted that they met privately with three of the college trustees in New York a few days before Beittel was dismissed and told the board members that Mississippi and Tougaloo College were on a collision course but that "the crisis might be avoided if Dr. Beittel were dismissed and a new president appointed who was more concerned with education than agitation" (Report on Mississippi State Sovereignty Commission [1964–1967] made to the governor in January 1967, p. 7). Now that the crisis of the sixties is past, Dr. Beittel readily asserts that he did not voluntarily resign. The trustees' motives in dismissing him are still unclear. After leaving Tougaloo College Dr. Beittel remained for five years in Jackson as director of the American Friends Service Committee's work in Mississippi and neighboring states.

21

Rounding out the Century

THOSE MEMBERS OF THE board of trustees who were persuaded that Tougaloo needed a younger man at the helm expected to bring to the college a scholarly and distinguished person to be the new president. Several such persons did come to Tougaloo to make their own appraisals of the position offered.

Overlooked by those confident board members was the Mississippi setting in which the school had to operate. Segregation of the races was still rigid with the Citizens Council distributing NEVER buttons, the police arresting any who tried to break through the racial barriers, and the city of Jackson refusing to consider a bi-racial committee. Public schools in Jackson were under court order to integrate. Anticipating such court action, the state legislature had repealed its compulsory school attendance law in 1956 to obviate the necessity of any white child's having to sit in a classroom with a black. Private academies were burgeoning in Jackson as elsewhere in the state for those whites who opposed desegregation and could stretch their budgets to include the expense of educating their children.

The "younger man" whom the board wanted as a replacement for Beittel was likely to have children of school age. His failure to see any advantage in giving up a position he had for the vagaries of Mississippi was understandable.

After a year of looking for a new president, a member of the

218

board came to Tougaloo to announce that in the board's search far afield it suddenly realized that it was overlooking the talent at Tougaloo's doorstep. Acting President George Owens, the board member asserted, had the qualifications sought. In addition, he was thoroughly familiar with Tougaloo, his alma mater, where he had earned his bachelor's degree in economics. He had been Tougaloo's business manager under two presidents and for the past year had served well as acting president.

Impressive as these qualifications were, Tougaloo's first black president was felt to be disadvantaged in some ways. He lacked an earned doctorate though several institutions would soon bestow honorary degrees upon him. His master's degree from Columbia University in business administration and his limited experience as a junior executive at Saks 34th in New York, while unusual for a black man in the mid-twentieth century, did not appear to qualify him to administer a liberal arts college. While he was acknowledged to be a competent business manager, first at Talladega College then at Tougaloo, these positions hardly gave him the broad background expected in a college president. Some alumni and friends of the college even feared that a black president might find it difficult to establish rapport with influential whites. He might have difficulty in raising money and pressing for the school's needs before state officials.

If President Owens was concerned over any of these matters, he gave no evidence of it. Rather, he entered the presidency with high hopes and aspirations, many of which he was to fulfill.

Three important themes stand out as President Owens guided the school through the last six years of its first century: campus development and financial problems; academic excellence and postgraduate placement; and intellectual and ideological ferment. Often these themes overlap.

Tougaloo's physical plant has seldom been entirely commendable. It has usually had a few good buildings, which it features in catalogs. One alumna admits she had been influenced in her choice of schools by the pictures of Kincheloe and Warren halls. When she was confronted with numbers of old buildings, the shock was too great for her. She threw herself on her bed and sobbed that she wanted to go home. In another case, a father who had brought his son to enroll as a freshman called a professor aside and indicated that he was distressed by such old buildings. Fortunately Tougaloo had other attractions, but there was no denying that it needed new buildings.

During the administration of President Owens several faculty houses and apartments were built. To relieve the crowding in the dormitories, temporary annexes were constructed at both Galloway and Judson Cross dormitories.

In early 1965 the Cummins Engine Foundation of Indiana contributed $75,000 to Tougaloo for the development of a master building plan. Drawn up by the architectural firm of Gunnar, Birkets and Associates, the plan was unveiled in April of 1966. Its nontraditional style came as a surprise—if not shock—to the audience gathered for the occasion. The plan projected the replacement of all existing buildings except Warren and Kincheloe halls with structures which the architects said were designed to integrate the three functional activities of a campus—living, learning, and recreation. The estimated cost for the new construction was between fifteen and twenty million dollars. The bulk of this amount would come from foundation grants and government loans.

Three buildings were erected under the master plan. The library, a beautiful and functional structure, has been widely acclaimed. It is named for L. Zenobia Coleman, Tougaloo's librarian for thirty-four years. The other two buildings are dormitories constructed on high pillars in accordance with the master plan. The space under the dormitories was designed for parking, but the land has never been leveled and prepared for cars. The women's dormitory is named for Jennie Renner, a member of the Renner family who contributed $100,000 toward its cost. Several explanations have been offered those who have expressed disappointment over the dormitories. The radical changes in the physical plant contemplated by the master plan require years to develop. In the meantime some buildings may give no sense of fitting in with the old. They appear out of another world. Also, the plan's aesthetic success depends on the razing of old buildings. First to meet opposition to its demolition was the old mansion, which has come to symbolize Tougaloo much as the Lyceum building symbolizes Ole Miss. To retain the mansion, the location of the library deviated from the master plan.

Students have clamored for more recreational opportunities. In 1972 President Owens said that, while the addition of tennis courts had been a help, no doubt student enrollment would increase if the college could have a gymnasium-recreational facility replete with swimming pool. But the financial problems have so far precluded the fulfillment of this need.

On becoming president, Owens took immediate steps to increase the college income. In 1965 A. A. Branch, academic dean since 1952, was made vice president, with one of his chief functions that of finding funds for the campus buildings and various academic programs. Mr. Branch encouraged the faculty to write proposals for grants to finance projects which would increase their division's effectiveness. Outside funding from grants thus received enabled the college to offer enrichment programs.

The prefreshman program, begun under Dr. Beittel's administration, continued, with a generous Ford Foundation grant, to give talented high school graduates summer courses in reading, composition, mathematics, and study skills. From another grant a course in science was continued during summers for high school students.

During the spring of 1966 the college was awarded a grant of $117,025 from the Office of Economic Opportunity to conduct an Upward Bound program. Re-funded in every subsequent year, this program targets low income secondary students to stimulate interest in advanced learning.

Outside funding also led to the college's sponsorship of several other services. A Head Start program was operated in four Mississippi counties, although many civil rights veterans were disappointed when Tougaloo turned down a request to sponsor the statewide Child Development Group of Mississippi

222   The View from Tougaloo

(CDGM); after Tougaloo's refusal, Mary Holmes College agreed to host that program.

A cooperative education program gave students opportunities for on-the-job training in business and industry while earning pay and credits. Other cooperative programs with industries and educational agencies provided students with incomes from summer work which advanced their career goals more than chopping cotton or waiting tables had in the past. A Supplementary Training program, formerly offered the Choctaws by the University of Southern Mississippi, was transferred by the government to Tougaloo with its accompanying grant. Tutorial programs were funded which allowed teams of two students each to go into the homes of underachievers in the lower school grades. Underachievers in secondary schools received help at a campus center, not only in their school lessons but also in leadership. Help for public school children was especially needed during those years because of the integration of formerly segregated schools.

A quite different service was provided by a grant for "Opera South," awarded to Jackson State, Tougaloo, and Utica Junior colleges. These funds enabled students of these three schools to appear in operas. Tougaloo was not in a financial position to continue with this project; but it did have a part in getting it started, and Jackson State University has continued it.

Indispensable to the survival of the college was the general educational act of 1965. Title III funds have been received annually since the initial award in 1967. They have also been used in the Tougaloo-Brown University cooperative relationship to enable faculty to do more research and to provide student and faculty exchanges, curricular innovations, and fund-raising workshops. These funds have also made it possible for some students to take a junior or fifth year at Brown and for others to study in Africa or France.

A grant of $232,834 was awarded Tougaloo in 1968 to secure National Teaching Fellows, to assist in the cooperative arrangement with Brown University, and to aid the Office of Career Planning and Placement directed by Vice President Branch. Working out of a mobile building given Tougaloo by the College Placement Bureau, Inc. in Pennsylvania, Branch urged students to take every test that might open a way to a career. Recruiters from major universities and national businesses were invited to visit the campus and talk with students at the Career Center. On Career Days alumni explained their work to students and emphasized the strengths they would need to achieve success. Aided by other faculty members, also, students were placed in careers for which they were best adapted—some of them not previously available to blacks. Dr. Borinski placed many graduates, including the first black social workers for the state of Mississippi.

The college established a Development Office in 1966 to work for an increase in endowment. Transfer to Tougaloo of title to all land and properties held by the American Missionary Association boosted the school's permanent funds considerably. The Development Office sought contributions and financial support from many sources, including alumni. President Owens often says, perhaps a bit facetiously, that he wants Tougaloo graduates "to get good and rich" so they can contribute to their alma mater. "I don't want to have to go to the Ford Foundation all the time."

It was disheartening, after all the attention given to improving the financial situation, to end the century with "significant current and capital debts." In his report to the trustees in 1972 on rounding out the first century of Tougaloo's history, President Owens suggested that stabilizing the financial situation through debt reduction and increased endowment should be one of the priorities for the seventies.

Deficient as school finances were, Owens could still point out that Tougaloo is a great economic asset to Mississippi as well as a cultural and educational asset. The financial impact of Tougaloo's annual budget of several million dollars ($5,115,000 in 1976–77) upon metropolitan Jackson has probably done as much as anything to improve the college's relationship with the local community and state.

A college's physical plant and finances are important only as they contribute to the education of students. Success in this regard may be judged in part by the school's graduates.

Thirty-five percent of the class of 1966 entered graduate school, thirty-six percent took teaching positions, and fourteen percent acquired employment in business, industry and government. Nearly all the graduate students received fellowships, scholarships or assistantships from their schools. Among the first black applicants to—and graduates from—the University of Mississippi Medical Center were Tougalooians. As many as forty Tougaloo graduates have been enrolled in medical schools during a single year.

Jumping ahead to take a look at the first decade of the second century, we find over half the senior class of 1977 was accepted for graduate professional work and eight persons for medicine and dentistry. Tacked to trees and buildings on the campus were large, handmade posters congratulating each student as he or she was accepted in a graduate school. The posting was a spontaneous act on the part of friends of those accepted. At the Awards Assembly in March, students applauded as enthusiastically when a name was called for having a four point average as they would had a great athlete's name been given.

That the student body should hold scholarship in such high esteem gave a great sense of satisfaction to President Owens, a man who settles for nothing less than a thorough academic preparation for Tougaloo's graduates. A story told by Ken Lawrence of Jackson illustrates this point. After Judge George Crockett gave the keynote speech at Tougaloo's criminal justice symposium in February of 1977, Lawrence told Owens that he had been in Detroit at the time of the shoot-out to which Crockett had referred. In the aftermath the police had arrested everybody who had attended the Republic of New Africa gathering in the New Bethel Church and held them without charge. Judge Crockett got out of bed at midnight to convene recorder's court to issue writs of habeas corpus and release everyone arrested. Lawrence remarked to Owens that it was a shame Mississippi didn't have a Judge Crockett in August of 1971 when a similar event occurred at Republic of New Africa headquarters in Jackson, resulting in three persons now serving life sentences in Parchman. Owens agreed but pointed out another aspect. He said that Judge Crockett was able to release the New Bethel victims and survive public criticism because he knew the law. "Many students believe they can short-cut the process and don't understand that without acquiring the fullest possible education they won't be able to perform properly when the time arises."

Faculty research also speaks well for the educational quality of the school. Of particular interest was the publication of a high school text, *Mississippi: Conflict and Change*, in 1974. This book was edited by Dr. James W. Loewen of Tougaloo and Dr. Charles Sallis of Millsaps who drew on the research of other faculty members and of some students. *Mississippi: Conflict and Change* recognizes the contributions of blacks, women, and ethnic minorities to the state's history. The book has been acclaimed by scholars, teachers, and reviewers across the country and was awarded the Southern Regional Council's Lillian Smith Award. Unfortunately, the Mississippi State Textbook Purchasing Board chose not to accept the book as one of five from which public schools may choose their text. Instead, the only text for Mississippi history in high schools which can be used at state expense is John Bettersworth's, giving him a virtual monopoly. The Textbook Board faulted *Mississippi: Conflict and Change* for its account of slavery and Reconstruction (based on modern scholarship), the picture of a lynching, and the treatment of the civil rights movement. Loewen and Sallis are contesting the decision of the board in court.

Tougaloo continued its role as a haven, a virtual oasis, in a land hot and fuming with public policies designed to thwart full participation in a free society. Its campus was the safest place to hold meetings of the Mississippi Council on Human Relations. The Mississippi chapter of the American Civil Liberties Union was organized there in 1969.

President Owens is quoted in the November 1973 issue of *Encore* as saying, "We are proud ... that here a student can hear it all. He is in close proximity to conservative and segregationist views. At the same time, all kinds of black ideology are brought on campus for the student to examine."

It is true that speakers of many persuasions were allowed use of the podium in Woodworth Chapel during the 1960s and early 1970s. Among them were Ralph Bunche and Pauline Frederick, who spoke on the United Nations—a "subversive organization" in the eyes of most white Jacksonians of those years; Rep. Julian Bond, SNCC leader whom the Georgia legislature refused to seat until the U.S. Supreme Court gave the order; Norman Thomas of the Socialist Party; Tapson A. Mawere of the Zimbabwe (Rhodesia) African National Union; Gerry Condon, who deserted from the Green Berets to become an antiwar leader; Herbert Aptheker, historian and member of the Communist Party; Sallye B. Davis who spoke at a time when her daughter Angela was facing trial; and Stokely Carmichael, leader of SNCC. Others included Fannie Lou Hamer, James Baldwin, Roy Wilkins, Robert Kennedy, Medgar and Charles Evers, besides the usual academic scholars.

Not only were students permitted to hear these various views; they were also given freedom to express their own ideas. In 1967 at least six student mimeographed papers were published more or less regularly and freely circulated on campus.

Except for *The Occasional Ripple*, which dealt with information on campus activities, dissatisfactions were more newsworthy than the usual good things which were going on all the while. The complaints of several papers dealt with matters as mundane as room inspection and co-ed visitations to those as important as black liberation and the Vietnam war.

The Student Voice had its beginning in the early 1960s and served as an organ for the student government. It spoke out clearly during the turbulent era of the civil rights movement. *Harambee* represents the student body today though in a rather moderate tone as compared to its militant stance in the late 1960s. Then it lashed out against the predominance of whites on the board of trustees, the faculty, and as division chairpersons. It claimed the whites had systematically brainwashed incoming freshmen to believe that blacks could not perform well as campus leaders. *Harambee* decried in its issue of April 18, 1969, that only after ninety-six years did Tougaloo get a black president.

Alpha Speaks questioned the Brown-Tougaloo relationship, feeling that students at Tougaloo were but "Brown babies," and the editors wondered if Dr. Beittel's dismissal (never satisfactorily explained) might have been linked to Brown's embarrassment over an association with a school deeply involved in the movement for social change.

The Nitty Gritty, organ of the Political Action Committee (PAC) chaired by Howard Spencer, was one of the most militant of the student papers. It continually called for organized efforts to get out the vote, to educate the surrounding black communities on their heritage, and to campaign for black candidates running for political offices. *The Nitty Gritty* rang with slogans of Black Pride, Black Power, and antiwar arguments. "Hell no, we won't go!" summed up the feeling.

PAC, like Martin Luther King, Jr., linked the cause of black liberation with that of the antiwar protests. When Dow Chemical tried to recruit students, PAC took a firm stand in *The Nitty Gritty*. It described one of Dow's products, napalm, and insisted "WE CANNOT FALL INTO THE TRAP OF HELPING THESE CRIMINALS."

PAC was not alone in the protest against the war in Vietnam. The history department showed films, and antiwar demonstrations in Jackson were carried out with the cooperation of other community groups.

Tougaloo embraced the civil rights struggle at every turn. Students and faculty examined issues and events constantly and reacted as they thought appropriate.

James Meredith's close brush with death in 1966 as he started his march through Mississippi brought national leaders to the state to continue the march. Meeting with opposition all the way, often denied the use of facilities for cleaning up, forced to move out of Canton by the police who sprayed them with tear gas, the marchers looked forward to their arrival at Tougaloo, where they expected a strong welcome. Even there they were disappointed to have only minimal access to facilities, but they were invited to camp out on the campus, where a spirited rally was held with Dr. Martin Luther King, Jr. the featured speaker. The next day 20,000 marchers descended upon the state capitol in Jackson, where Stokely Carmichael electrified the nation with his Black Power speech.

In May, 1967, a student demonstration developed against the city police, who questioned a driver of a speeding car which turned into the Jackson State College campus twelve miles southwest of Tougaloo. One thing led to another; and the next day Benjamin Brown, 22, not a student but a civil rights worker, was shot and killed. The demonstration evolved into a protest march. A number of Tougaloo students, having joined the demonstration, were trapped in Jackson by a 10:00 P.M. curfew ordered by Mayor Allen Thompson. Students Bennie Thompson, Richard Moman, and Constance Slaughter, president of the Tougaloo Student Association, drove back to Tougaloo, removed the college bus without authorization (which they had earlier been denied), and returned to Jackson to pick up the students. The business manager filed disciplinary charges against Slaughter and Thompson. Students, who were infuriated because the Student Disciplinary Committee was bypassed in favor of the Disciplinary Review Committee made up of faculty, administrators, and students, led in a demonstration. The campus gates were closed, and the students conducted a rally on the president's lawn. For a while communications between the administration and students came to an impasse. As student frustrations soared, several windows were broken, including a large one at Warren Hall. Damage was done to some of the cars on campus. There were rumors that the campus would be fire-bombed. Some urged the president to call the sheriff, but he resisted the pressure.

The bombing did not materialize. In the end, with the encouragement of Branch, Borinski, and Chaplain King, a compromise was reached; the case would be heard by the Student Judiciary Committee subject to review by the Judiciary Review Committee. The verdict was that Slaughter would be denied participation in her commencement exercises; her diploma would be mailed to her. Thompson was placed on social probation for two semesters.

It is of interest to note here that all three Tougaloo students at the hub of the protest have achieved success in their chosen careers. Thompson was elected alderman in the town of Bolton, then mayor in 1973. Moman is a partner in a thriving real estate business. Slaughter practices law in her home town, Forest; she directed the Southern Legal Rights Association; recently she became the first black woman judge in Mississippi when she was temporarily appointed to the family court bench in Scott County.

Violence, harassment, and vandalism from the community were frequent. The home of a new faculty member, located near the county road, was bombed. Though the Klan was suspected, no arrests were made. Police harassment became so pervasive that PAC circulated a petition, gathering some six hundred signatures of students, faculty and administrators. The petition called for a halt to police beatings, unlawful arrests, illegal car searches, cutting of male students' hair prior to their appearance before a woman judge, use of the term "boy" for black males and demands that blacks answer "Yes, sir" rather than a simple "Yes." The petition was presented to Gov. John Bell Williams by the student body president and others.

During the 1960s and the 1970s, the Jackson FBI office took great interest in campus activities because "Tougaloo College has been a staging area for civil rights and militant Negro activities in Mississippi."

When FBI Director J. Edgar Hoover began the Counter-Intelligence Program (Cointelpro) against groups and individuals in March of 1968, the Jackson office listed the Tougaloo College Political Action Committee among its potential targets to "disrupt, discredit, or neutralize." The reason was stated in a memorandum dated April 4, 1968:

The Tougaloo College PAC activities have, in the recent past pertained to the sponsoring of on campus out-of-state militant Negro speakers, voter registration drives, and African culture seminars and lectures. Additionally, the group has vocally condemned various publicized injustices to the civil rights of Negroes in Mississippi.

The following month "A Jackson source provided the identities of all members of this student group. A large number of these members were interviewed during the summer of 1968 while they were home on summer vacation." The author of the Jackson memo concluded that these interviews had an "upsetting effect" resulting in decreased activity by PAC members.

In January of 1969, Hoover authorized the Jackson and Atlanta FBI offices to write and send an anonymous letter to SNCC in Atlanta implying that someone in the PAC was a police informer. The letter read:

What's going on?—just heard NAME DELETED last summer sold list of PAC people to local honkies for 250 cash—that dude used $ to finance trip to Europe, white chicks & all—believe it baby!

Soul Brother

Next the Jackson FBI office proposed a plan to discredit the college itself by leaking derogatory information to a newspaper. Hoover vetoed this plan, asking his agents to concentrate on PAC, "since Tougaloo College, per se, is not a counterintelligence target." In response, the Jackson office asked for and received permission to send an anonymous threatening letter to Muhammad Kenyatta, a political activist. When Kenyatta subsequently left the state, the FBI concluded that "a black extremist has been cut off from his usual contacts and area of operation by counterintelligence technique."

In May of 1969, after a year of these activities, the FBI decided that its harassment campaign had successfully crippled the group.

The Jackson Division has been concentrating with informant coverage and other counterintelligence measures on the Tougaloo College Political Action Committee (PAC), a SNCC affiliate at Tougaloo, Miss. In the past several weeks, in large part due to these efforts, PAC has had a significant decrease in activities, membership and popularity on the TC campus. Informants say that PAC has reached its lowest level since its beginning a few years earlier on the campus.

After that the FBI became more selective in its concern with activities at Tougaloo. When Detroit Judge George W. Crockett, Jr. was scheduled as Tougaloo's centennial speaker in October of 1969, the FBI helped a *Jackson Daily News* writer with an editorial attacking the college and Judge Crockett. Similarly, when a group called the Black Unity Coordinating Committee (BUCC) announced that it would hold a meeting at Tougaloo in February of 1971, information furnished by the FBI appeared in a *Daily News* column by its editor, Jimmy Ward, attacking the BUCC. The meeting was subsequently cancelled, and the Jackson FBI office attributed the cancellation to the article.

On the evening of April 4, 1968, Tougaloo's choir was performing in New York's Carnegie Hall with Duke Ellington's orchestra when the announcement was made that Martin Luther King, Jr. had been shot and killed in Memphis. A wave of disbelief and acute anguish swept through the vast hall. The show had to go on, but the music seemed to cry out in an expression of the grief which permeated the entire hall.

When the students returned from their spring vacation, the school commemorated Dr. King's life in several planned activities. A memorial service was held under the direction of Chaplain Hickman Johnson. Professor Lou Holloway's recitation of King's "Mountain Top" speech was a touching highlight of the service. Two days of seminars based on Dr. King's book *Where Do We Go from Here?* were held. Rallies, talks, and films focused on the civil rights movement for three days.

Most Jackson public schools held some kind of an observance of the tragic death of King, but Madison County schools were prohibited from doing so. Madison students walked southward down highway 51 toward Jackson en masse, not knowing exactly what they would do. Confronted by highway patrolmen, the students turned and approached Tougaloo's campus. President Owens met them and invited them onto the campus, assuring the patrolmen that he would be responsible for them.

Chaplain Johnson conducted a special memorial service for King with the high school students in attendance. Because it had begun to rain during the service, President Owens sent the Madison students to their homes in Tougaloo's bus.

Thirty Tougaloo students, chosen by drawing names from a hat, attended Dr. King's funeral. After all possible had been done to assuage grief, students went back to their studies in what was perhaps the best tribute to a man who placed high priority on education for freedom.

Tougaloo's students were not unlike other blacks and many whites who foresaw a bleak future for blacks. In retrospect it seemed that the murder of Medgar Evers in 1963 was but the beginning of a sinister plan to eliminate black leaders. Dr. King's death was seen as a part of the unfolding design.

In their frustration the students struck at the school. Many objected to the social science seminar texts, which they claimed were written from a white frame of reference. They boycotted classes in a demand for more black professors and courses in black history. Eventually a department of Afro-American studies, directed by Professor James Poole, was added to the curriculum.

At the height of black awareness in 1969, Tougaloo students promoted a Black Spring Weekend on campus, which they publicized throughout the city of Jackson. Some of the meetings were closed to whites with quasi-official sanction. Three white faculty members, John Garner, Larry and Claire Morse, decided to register their protest by presenting themselves at the door of Woodworth Chapel for one of the closed meetings. They were met with hostility and asked to leave. One young person slapped Garner, knocking his glasses off. As he later started to return to his home, he was kicked on the inside of his right thigh. Stumbling down the chapel steps, he saw several raised, clenched fists amidst shouts of "Black Power." Someone struck him in the mouth, causing his teeth to cut the inside of his lower lip. Dr. Robert Smith, the school's physician, took Garner to his office to administer first aid and suture the lip. Claire Morse was also struck. Some of the persons standing by were particularly shocked to see a woman treated in this fashion. Though it was claimed that the abuse of Garner and Dr.

Morse was the work of persons from off campus, some students
with whom Garner had worked and suffered in the movement
looked on and made no attempt to stop the assaults.

Not all students—probably no more than a small minority—approved the violence. When the few regular occupants
of Beard Hall left to spend the next night elsewhere, a white
visitor who was doing research was left alone in the hall. Henry
Briggs stopped by to assure her that she would be safe. Several
men students had volunteered to guard Beard Hall. John
Dittmer, the academic dean, and others sat out the night on a
porch, having heard rumors of anticipated violence. President
Owens moved about all night talking in his usual calm manner
to any persons he met, thereby alleviating fears. Morning
dawned without any more campus disturbances.

Later, evaluations of the weekend were mixed. Some
thought the school had compromised its principles in allowing
some meetings to be racially exclusive. A greater number apparently felt that the violence which had occurred caused students to re-think their positions and to come out for nonviolent
techniques in their work for social change. Unlike 1967, when
the administration was quite rigid in dealing with student dis-
senters, President Owens maintained a flexible attitude, which
enabled him to take advantage of any options. Many have declared it was his finest hour.

During all these turbulent events the school carried on with
its traditional activities. Both queens and candidates for *Who's
Who in American Colleges* were elected. Basketball games were
won and lost with the Tsudas[1] and their dog Bonnie rooting at
every home game and giving the players sukiyaki dinners in
their small apartment. Outstanding art exhibits on loan from
various museums continued to be displayed by Professor
Ronald Schnell, and the choir made its usual tours. Students,
having deliberately chosen what was probably as demanding a

---

1. Mr. Takeshi Tsuda of Japanese descent left California during World War
II rather than be sent to a relocation camp. Mrs. Ora Tsuda, a Caucasian, followed him soon after. He was the chief accountant at Tougaloo and she the
head matron for eight years.

school as any in the state, continued their studies. For most, life went on as expected in a college.

On Saturday, May 24, 1969, Tougaloo College Alumni celebrated the school's one hundredth anniversary at the Heidelberg Hotel. Lerone Bennett, Jr., senior editor of *Ebony* and a native son of Mississippi, was the banquet speaker. This nationally coordinated fund-raising event began a series of events which extended into 1970. The music department conducted a series of Centennial music concerts throughout the 1969–70 school year. A ground-breaking ceremony for the new dormitories was held on October 11, 1969, during the Centennial Founders' Day Weekend. The Tougaloo College State Centennial Committee presented Congresswoman Shirley Chisholm on November 22, 1969 at the College Park Auditorium in Jackson.

The Centennial celebration was centered around the theme, "One Hundred Years of Continuing Commitment—College and Community." During January, Dr. John Monro, director of freshman studies at Miles College in Birmingham and a trustee of Tougaloo, spoke on the relationships possible between the college and the community. Mrs. Fannie Lou Hamer of Ruleville led a discussion later in the month on "The College and Its Relationship to Community Organization." An art festival, consisting of artists, dancers, jazz concerts, plays, and art exhibits, was held during April. The Centennial observance culminated with the Tougaloo alumni Centennial banquet and the first commencement of the second century.

The celebration of Tougaloo's Centennial occurred during the administration of its first black president—a president whose hallmark is his sense of mission for graduating students who are prepared to take their part in the mainstream of American life where they can fill policymaking positions. He wants blacks to be in on the decision-making process rather than always on the receiving end.

Now that public schools are open to all ethnic groups, twice as many blacks are enrolled in white institutions as in black. But many of these drop out. President Owens says, " . . . we wouldn't have let them sink. The pressures at these schools for black students to be black 24 hours was a bit ridiculous. . . . On a black campus you don't have to be super-black."

A disproportionate number of black leaders have come up through black colleges—Thurgood Marshall, Martin Luther King, Jr., and Stokely Carmichael, to name but a few. President Owens says, "I think the people who believe and nurture the theory that black colleges are on the wane may have a grand design to weaken us. We have the church and our black colleges. An individual can't do much; you've got to have groups and institutions."

This need for black schools was seen by Tougaloo's founders, though the school has run through several cycles of emphases since then. While at first admittedly and purposely following a white paternalistic pattern, during the thirties, at the insistence of blacks influenced by the Harlem Renaissance, the administration transferred more policymaking positions to blacks. Lionel Fraser's work symbolizes this change. With the GI Bill bringing more mature and experienced students to the campus, the in loco parentis role of the school was modified.

Throughout these various emphases the "Tougaloo Family," as the college was wont to call itself, worked together for the advantage of students and community. The unconscious "benevolent" racism which had occasionally surfaced earlier was superseded by a close partnership between the races. This was symbolized in the sixties by Tougaloo faculty and students, black and white, going to jail together (assigned to segregated cells), when they engaged in nonviolent direct action which threatened the white power structure.

The injection of the concept of Black Power, symbolized by the Black Spring Weekend of 1969, was an aberration for Tougaloo. White members of the school tried to take it in stride: some because they saw no other way; others because they felt that until blacks became conscious of their power potential they could never negotiate with the white power which controlled their lives. The Black Power movement with its many elements of hostility toward whites, and with a willingness to resort to violence if necessary, was short-lived and took a more pragmatic turn during the early seventies. Students again looked to education for power and concentrated more on their studies. President Owens continued in his belief that, to exercise power, blacks must get into policymaking positions; this he thought could best be done with education inferior to none. Symbolizing this emphasis is the number of today's career-oriented graduate students.

Tougaloo started as an offspring of the American Missionary Association, whose members covenanted with one another and with their "colored brethren" that they would not obey any law that "contravened the higher law of their maker." This brought the A.M.A. into direct conflict with the United States government over such laws as the Fugitive Slave Act. After the Civil War the A.M.A. felt education of the freedmen a fitting way to repent of America's long oppression of the Negroes. In this work it was assisted by the very government whose laws it, and other abolitionists, had previously opposed and violated. The A.M.A. then found itself in the mainstream of American life. Though it never lost sight of the need for education of blacks, there were times when its comfortable position in the mainstream led to a softening of its voice where basic rights were concerned. It took no strong stand regarding enforcement of the Fourteenth or Fifteenth Amendments during the late 1800s and early 1900s.

However, to the credit of Tougaloo and its sponsors, when the crunch came in the 1950s and the 1960s, the school stood firmly on the original promises of the A.M.A. It rededicated itself to the "removal of caste," to "speak the truth in love," and to "refuse compromise on the issue of slavery" (by then illegal but with vestiges of economic and political slavery remaining), so that today Tougaloo College is as much honored for its leadership in the area of human rights as for its scholarship.

Tougaloo has always been faced with problems and the first years of the second century have shown no let up in difficulties ranging from inadequate financing to the vehement controversy when the administration decided to bring ROTC to Tougaloo. When President Owens called the Madison County sheriff to the campus to quell a student protest, resulting in the arrest of the student body president, Richard Porter, many wished Mr. Owens had used less extreme measures as he had in earlier times of turmoil. But Tougaloo's greatness is in surmounting problems and differences while continuing to carry on a solid program of education. The future augurs well for the school.

The future of the state in which Tougaloo operates also augurs well. Gone is the "NEVER" policy of the past. The desire now is for compliance with United States government requirements so that Mississippi may get its full share of public funds. Politicians court the black vote.

During the heat of the struggle for full citizenship rights for blacks, a popular saying of whites was that laws can never change attitudes; that love can not be legislated. Those doomsayers were wrong. Laws can and did break down the wall of segregation. When people began to know one another as equals, a respect for one another developed. Love and attitudes may not respond directly to legislation, but laws can dictate a setting in which changes of attitudes, and sometimes even love, can grow.

One would like to think that Tougaloo College—where blacks and whites met on equal terms, even before the government concerned itself with the legal niceties—had a part in preparing Mississippi to enter the mainstream of American life. If this be so, the state owes much to Tougaloo College.

Has Tougaloo Made a Difference?

THE MEASURE OF A COLLEGE can best be determined by the quality of its product—its graduates. A college's history is more than that of buildings, finances, faculty and administrators; its people are most important. The raison d'etre for Tougaloo College was and is to educate men and women for service to their community. The school must be evaluated in light of the accomplishments of the men and women who entered and exited through her portals of learning. A vital chapter in the history of Tougaloo College is the story of the persistence of excellence by its alumni in a society that discouraged black achievement and denied equality of opportunity.

The result of the ongoing struggle to achieve and to excel probably exceeds even the greatest expectations of the college's founders. They planned better than they knew. Tougaloo College graduates have changed the quality of life in America and have advanced the common good. Since the first graduating classes, their names have cropped up in virtually every walk of life, especially as more doors opened to minority groups. They are employed throughout the United States and in several other countries, with an increasing number pursuing their careers today in Mississippi and in other parts of the South.

Many Tougaloo graduates are well known in their chosen fields of endeavor. Some, such as Anne Moody, whose book revealed to the world the reality of oppression in Mississippi, are even more widely known and admired. In every major area of

238

human activity—government, politics, law, social service, education, health care, science, art, music and literature— Tougaloo's influence is felt.

A catalog of the achievements of Tougaloo's alumni would be a book. A few examples are listed here. Other outstanding Tougaloo graduates are included in the appendix. The names are for the most part those of men and women whose usefulness to the college began in their student days and continued long after graduation.

Tougaloo has provided the state of Mississippi and the nation a good number of experienced teachers at the elementary, secondary and post-secondary levels. Illustrative is the impact the alumni are making presently upon the city of Jackson. Tougaloo is providing the Jackson Public Schools with forty elementary teachers and two elementary school principals (Mr. Cleo McGee, '49 and Mrs. Jether W. Brown, '50); twenty-one junior high school teachers and one junior high school principal (Mr. Lonnie King, '61); nineteen senior high teachers and a senior high school principal (Mr. Emmitt Hayes, '48) and an assistant principal (Dr. George M. Vincent, '56, Ed.D., Administration, University of Colorado). The number of principals in Mississippi who are graduates of Tougaloo is significant in light of the diminishing number of black principals resulting from the lack of fair play after desegregation of the public schools.

During earlier years, Tougaloo graduates provided important leadership for Jackson Public Schools. Outstanding among these was Dr. I. S. Sanders, '10, who after serving as dean at Alcorn was principal of Lanier High School for thirty years.

Four schools in Jackson are named after Tougaloo graduates, attesting to the strength of their contribution to public education and to their character: Lanier High School in honor of W. H. Lanier, '81, Sam Brinkley Junior High School in honor of Sam Brinkley, '96, G. N. Smith Elementary School in honor of Golden Nathaniel Smith, '03, and Dawson Elementary School in honor of Georgia Beatrice Dawson, '54.

In other communities across the state of Mississippi,

schools and educational buildings bear the names of Tougaloo graduates who distinguished themselves as teachers, principals, and citizens. The Walter Washington Administration Building at Utica affirms Dr. Washington's role in advancing Utica Junior College and public education in general. In the sixties the black citizens of Carthage honored O. E. Jordan, '51, for his efforts as principal by affixing his name to the new high school. After desegregation, the school was renamed.

Other principals in Mississippi are Ray Brooks, '50, at Nugent Center in Bolivar County, Ambrose T. Williams, '47, at O'Bannon High School in Greenville, Howard Sanders, '61, at Hollandale. Sanders succeeded his father, T. R. Sanders, '33, as principal.

Elsewhere in the nation, Tougalooians are educational leaders: Dr. Lawyer Chapman, '57, is assistant superintendent of district three of the Philadelphia (Pennsylvania) Public Schools. Dr. Joffre T. Whisenton, '55, was, during the Ford administration, special assistant for educational policy to the secretary of the Department of Health, Education and Welfare, while on leave from the Southern Association of Colleges and Schools in Atlanta. A staunch supporter of Tougaloo and the cause of black colleges, Dr. Whisenton is a member of the college's board of trustees.

Few Tougalooians have been as loyal to the college over an extended period of recent years as Dr. Van S. Allen, '50 (Ph.D., public health, University of North Carolina). Dr. Allen, prior to becoming executive director of TACTICS in the nation's capital, taught biology at Bennett College in Greensboro, North Carolina. For a number of terms he has been a member of the National Alumni Board and chairman of the Annual Alumni Giving Fund. He is a trustee of the college.

A good percentage of the talented high school graduates in the state flocked to Tougaloo during the middle forties. The GI Bill provided financial impetus for World War II veterans, and a liberal work aid and scholarship program attracted others who desired to acquire the best Negro liberal arts education in the state. Graduates of the various classes during that time and subsequent decades were destined to provide the needed educational and professional leadership for each succeeding decade. To date, at least seventy-five graduates of the college have earned academic doctorates and are staffing colleges, universities, hospitals, industries and various agencies.

Tougaloo graduates have distinguished themselves as employees at both historically black and predominantly white colleges and universities across America. Within the state of Mississippi Tougaloo graduates are employed on the staff and faculty of all the black colleges and universities. At Mississippi Valley State University, Dr. Nathaniel Boclair, '49 (Ed.D. mathematics education, Rutgers University) is professor of education and director of graduate students. Dr. Zelma T. Howard, '40 (Ph.D., English, Howard University) is professor of English at MVSU, and is the author of *The Rhetoric of Eudora Welty's Short Stories*. Dr. Robbye Robinson Henderson, '60 (Ph.D., educational leadership, Southern Illinois University) is a member of the education faculty at MVSU.

Vital to the successful growth of Jackson State University, the fourth largest of the state's eight universities, are some twenty-two graduates of Tougaloo. Nine of these are holders of doctorates, four are department heads, one is a vice president, two are deans and others are on the faculty.

Dr. Annie J. Cistrunk, '49 (Ph.D., Florida State University) is head of the English department. Dr. Sinclair Lewis, '52 (Ed.D., University of Kentucky) is head of the department of guidance and counseling. Dr. Jesse C. Lewis, '53 (Ph.D., Syracuse University) is professor of mathematics; Chairman, Division of Natural Sciences; Head of the Department of Computer Science and Director of the Computer Center. Dr. George A. Johnson, '50 (Ed.D., Mississippi State University) is Vice President for Student Affairs. Dr. Oscar Allan Rogers, Jr., '50 (Ed.D., University of Arkansas) is Dean of the Graduate School, and Dr. Beatrice Mosley, '49 (Ed.D., University of Southern Mississippi) is dean of the School of Education.

The list of teachers includes: Dr. Lena Myers, '58 (Ph.D., Michigan State University) in sociology; Dr. Beatrice Buckner, '63 (Ed.D., Rutgers University) in English; Mildred J. Brackett, '61, in English; Samuel C. Jordan, '63, in mathematics; Henry

Calvin Frazier, '62 (Ph.D., Southern Illinois University) in general science; Princess Beasley Jones, '45, in English; Rose Portis, '43, in English; Patricia McGill, '63, in economics; Inez R. Morris, '51, in English; and Leroy Terry Smith, '48, in social science education.

H. M. Thompson, '36, is Mississippi Grand Master of Prince Hall Free and Accepted Masons. He has culminated a distinguished career of public service locally, nationally and overseas.

Few Americans have achieved so much as Dr. Walter Washington, '48, who is President of Alcorn A & M State University. Among the first blacks to receive a doctoral degree from the University of Southern Mississippi, Dr. Washington is the immediate past national president of Alpha Phi Alpha Fraternity. A sociology major at Tougaloo and president of the Student Government Association, he has applied his leadership skills through the years to many aspects of education. He has been a high school teacher, a principal and a junior college president. He was an early promoter of the United Negro College Fund, the National Tougaloo Alumni Association, and the Southern Association of Colleges and Schools. Dr. Washington is in demand nationally as a speaker and consultant on social issues and personnel administration. President Washington's wife, Carolyn Washington, '48, holds a doctorate from the University of Southern Mississippi. She is professor of sociology and social science at Alcorn State University.

A member of the class of '59, Dr. Eugene DeLoatch (Ph.D., engineering), is associate professor of engineering and chairman of the electrical engineering department at Howard University. Dr. DeLoatch holds a dual engineering degree from Tougaloo and Lafayette, and earned the master's degree in electrical engineering from Brooklyn Polytechnic Institute.

The chairman of the chemistry department at Alabama A & M University is Dr. Richard A. Evans, '59 (Ph.D., organic chemistry, Louisiana State University). Thelma Bradford, '42, is a long-time mathematics instructor at North Carolina A & T University.

Dr. Henry J. Young, '67 (Ph.D., religion and philosophy,

Hartford Seminary Foundation) is assistant professor of philosophy and theology at Interdenominational Theological Seminary in Atlanta, where he also edits the Center's journal.

Dr. Vernon Henderson, '51 (Ph.D., biology, University of Oregon) is professor of biology at Grambling State University, Louisiana.

Dr. Alvin J. McNeil, '41 (Ed.D., University of Denver, Colorado) is professor of education at Texas Southern University and coordinator of the doctor of education program.

Dr. Rosentene Purnell, '54 (Ph.D., English, University of Oklahoma) was chairman of the English department, Fisk University, director of interdisciplinary and freshman programs, and coordinator of the humanities division at Fisk University. Dr. Purnell was a visiting scholar at Princeton University in 1974 and a visiting professor at Rutgers University.

A class of '56 graduate of Tougaloo, Dr. Zadie Whisenton (Ed.D., elementary education, University of Alabama) was associate professor of elementary education at Norfolk State College, Norfolk, Virginia.

Dr. Carrie C. Robinson, '31 (Ph.D., library science, University of Illinois) is a librarian at Alabama State University in Montgomery, Alabama.

Dr. Naomi J. Townsend, '38 (Ph.D., English, University of Pittsburgh) is academic dean at Tougaloo College. Dean Townsend has had a distinguished career as a teacher and counselor at Tougaloo.

The late Henry E. Briggs, '47, epitomizes the ideal Tougaloo collegian who was employed at the college. He served Tougaloo in many capacities until his untimely death in 1973. He enrolled at Tougaloo in 1939 and graduated in 1947 after a tour of duty in the army. Athletic, gentle and greatly admired throughout his life, he was employed in 1950 at the college as an instructor in the department of health and physical education. Later he took on the additional duty of director of public relations, and in 1969 he became assistant to President Owens. He was also the national executive secretary of the Tougaloo Alumni Association.

Representatives of alumni on the faculty at Tougaloo are

244   *The View from Tougaloo*

Naomi J. Townsend, academic dean and professor of English; Ruth B. Johnson, assistant professor of English; Lou E. Holloway, associate professor of history; K. C. Morrison, assistant professor of political science; Jeannetta C. Roach, head librarian; and Dr. London J. Thompson, assistant professor of education.

Among the early pioneers who integrated predominantly white universities as fulltime professors are the following persons:

Dr. Sammie Blakney, '50 (Ph.D., mathematics, University of Illinois), who is professor of mathematics and chairman of the mathematics department at the University of Toledo, Toledo, Ohio.

Dr. Edgar Smith, '55 (Ph.D., biochemistry, Purdue University) is provost of the University of Massachusetts at Worchester and associate dean of the school of medicine. A former trustee of Tougaloo, Dr. Smith is on the Southern Educational Foundation Board and chairman of the board of trustees of Morehouse College.

Dr. Vandon E. White, '55 (Ph.D., biochemistry, Purdue University) is Dean of the School of Allied Health Services at Florida International University.

Dr. Benjamin Shepherd, '61 (Ph.D., biology, Kansas University) is department head and assistant professor of zoology at Southern Illinois University, Carbondale.

Dr. Daniel Offiong, '69, who earned the Ph.D. in sociology from Purdue University, is assistant professor of African Studies at West Georgia College at Carrollton, Georgia. Also holding a doctorate in sociology is Joyce Ladner Carrington, '64, who graduated from George Washington University. An associate professor of sociology at Hunter College in New York, Dr. Carrington is a writer, lecturer and civil rights activist who delivered the commencement address at Tougaloo in 1973.

The coordinator of elementary education at St. Louis University in Missouri is Dr. Savannah M. Miller, who earned the doctorate there in 1972. Dr. Opaline Simmons Denhamn, '52, also received her Ph.D. degree in education at St. Louis University.

Dr. Tommie A. Samkange, '53 (Ph.D., psychology, Indiana

University) is head tutor and lecturer, Afro-American Studies Department, Harvard University.

Dr. Slayton A. Evans, '65 (Ph.D., chemistry, Case Western Reserve) is assistant professor of chemistry at the University of North Carolina.

Dr. Arvarh Strickland, '51 (Ph.D., history, University of Illinois) is professor of history and special assistant to the chancellor at the University of Missouri at Columbia. Dr. Strickland has authored several works in history and was commissioned by the state of Illinois to write a portion of the state's sesquicentennial history.

Dr. Charles Pickett, '59 (Ph.D., physics, University of Southern Mississippi) is on the mathematics and science staff at Mississippi State University.

Quite early in the college's history the alumni began to make significant contributions in the area of health services. Foremost of these graduates was Dr. Robert W. Harrison, Sr. who was born on April 2, 1888 in Vicksburg. He attended Tougaloo College and was graduated from Meharry Medical College as a doctor of dental surgery. Dr. Harrison practiced dentistry at Natchez, where he pioneered in organized dentistry among blacks. Through his direct influence a number of talented high school graduates were directed to Tougaloo and other colleges. He was a president of the dental section of the National Medical Association and was a trustee of Tougaloo College. His son, Dr. Robert W. Harrison, Jr., '37, graduated in dentistry from Northwestern University in 1941, breaking the trend of Tougaloo College graduates to enter Meharry and Howard Medical Schools. With the opening of opportunities for blacks at other medical schools, Tougalooians entered those schools. Dr. Robert W. Harrison III, '61, the grandson of Dr. Harrison, Sr., followed his father and graduated from Northwestern Medical School, '66, in endocrinology and is now employed at Vanderbilt University School of Medicine.

Dr. James Lawrence Lowry, '37, received the doctor of medicine degree from Meharry and studied at the University of Michigan, Michigan State University, Syracuse University, Cook County Hospital in Chicago and Homer G. Phillips Hospital in St. Louis. Dr. Lowry was a captain in the United States

Army Medical Corps and Medical Director of the Mound Bayou Community Hospital during his distinguished career.

The following chart shows some of the known graduates who earned their degrees at Meharry Medical College and Howard Medical School.

TABLE 1　Tougaloo College Graduates who Received M.D. Degrees from Meharry Medical College

Physician	Graduation	Residence	Specialty	Year M.D. Received
M. S. Love	1924	Gulfport, MS		
James Lawrence Lowry	1937			
Henry J. Williams	1939	Corpus Christi, TX		1950
Emile Coleridge Nash	1939	Washington, D.C.	Gastroenterology	1943
Eddie Lee Clark, Jr.	1940	Philadelphia, PA		1944
Velma W. Davis	1941	Berkeley, CA	General Practice	1951
Ernest Braddock	1942	Washington, DC		
Earl Shaw	1942	New York, NY		1945
James W. Vines, Jr.	1946	San Bernardino, CA	Psychiatry	1957
Ernest Hodge	1950	Winston-Salem, NC		1956
Felton Pilate	1950	Los Angeles, CA		1956
David Ross, Jr.	1950	Gary, IN	Pediatrics	1955
Matthew Page	1952	Greenville, MS	Family Practice	1956
Joseph Jones, Jr.	1952	Canton, MS	General Practice	1958
Douglas Parris	1952	Chicago, IL	Obstetrics/Gynecology	
Col. Willard L. Johnson	1953	Tinker, OK	Pediatrics	1959
Martin L. Beard	1953	Flint, MI	General Surgery	1960
Felix Liddell	1953	Detroit, MI		
Ernest L. White, Jr.	1954	Durham, NC	Surgery	1958
Aaron Shirley	1955	Jackson, MS	Family Practice	1959
Lawrence D. Seymour	1957	Memphis, TN	Pediatrics	
James R. Todd, Jr.	1963	Natchez, MS	General Surgery	1973
Frank McCune	1964	Nashville, TN	Surgery	1973
Will E. Moorehead	1964	San Francisco, CA	Orthopedic Surg.	1969
Charles K. Jones	1964	Philadelphia, PA		1972

TABLE 1 (CONTINUED)

Charles E. Quinn	1964	Kansas City, MO	Obstetrics/Gynecology	1969
Sammie L. Pulliam	1966	Nashville, TN		1971
Lawrence Sutton	1971			1975
Ruthven N. Sampath	1972			1976

TABLE 2   Tougaloo College Graduates who Received
M.D. Degrees from Howard University

Physician	Gradua-tion	Residence	Specialty	Year M.D. Received
Albert B. Britton	1943	Jackson, MS	General Practice	1947
Avery C. Topps	1948	West Point, MS		1954
Benjamin Vines	1948	Claremont, CA		1954
Charles Washington	1950	Pasadena, CA	General Practice	
Gage Johnson	1950	Detroit, MI		1955
Theodore R. Brooks, Jr.	1951	Greenbelt, MD		1973
Henry B. Smith	1957	Baltimore, MD	Pathology	1961
Robert Smith	1957	Jackson, MS	General Practice	1961

Three of the most prominent physicians and graduates of the college, practicing in Jackson, are Albert Bazaar Britton, '43, Robert Smith, '57 and Aaron Shirley, '55. Dr. Britton graduated from Howard Medical School in 1947, served in the Army Medical Corps and was decorated with the Bronze Star. Active in promoting professional medicine and medical care for all ages, Dr. Britton has received national acclaim.

Dr. Robert Smith, also a graduate of Howard University Medical School, was active in the civil rights movement during the 1960s. A founder of the Medical Committee for Human Rights, he coauthored the Neighborhood Health Center concept of health care delivery and has been active in initiating several Neighborhood Health Centers in the state. Since the early 1960s Dr. Smith has directed the Tougaloo College Health Services, has worked with the Tougaloo Pre-Health Club, and was awarded an honorary degree by the college. Currently Director of the Mississippi Family Health Center in Jackson, he was among a group of physicians who visited the People's Republic of China by invitation of the Chinese Medical Association.

Dr. Aaron Shirley, a graduate of Meharry Medical School, specialized in pediatrics at the University of Mississippi Medical Center. He is director and pediatrician of the Jackson-Hinds Comprehensive Health Center. An active civil rights advocate, Dr. Shirley is also a national authority on health care delivery to the poor. Utilizing federal appropriations he pioneered in providing adequate health facilities for low income people of the country.

Among the medical doctors who were graduated from Meharry in the forties are Dr. Eddie Clark, '40, of Philadelphia, Pennsylvania; Dr. Earl Shaw, '42, of New York City; and Dr. Ernest Braddock, '42, of Washington, D.C.

The 1950s saw a record number of Tougaloo graduates entering medical school and subsequently receiving the M.D. degree. To Meharry went Dr. David Ross, '50, in pediatrics; Dr. Ernest Hodge, '50; Dr. James W. Vines, Jr., '46, in psychiatry; Dr. Ernest L. White, '54, surgery; Dr. Henry J. Williams, '39; Dr. Velma W. Davis, '41, general practice; Martin L. Beard, '53, general surgery, and Col. Willard L. Johnson, '53, pediatrics.

Similarly, to Howard went Dr. Charles Washington, '50, general practice; Dr. Albert B. Britton, '43, general practice; Dr. Theodore R. Brooks, '51, general practice; Dr. Henry B. Smith, '57, pathology; Dr. Robert Smith, '57, general practice; Dr. Avery C. Topps, '48, general practice; Dr. Benjamin Vines, '48, general practice, and Dr. Gage Johnson, '50.

During the sixties and seventies the Tougaloo pre-med graduates gained entry at other medical schools: Malcolm Taylor, '69, John Farmer, '70, Jerome Carroll, '69, and Juniper Trice, '68, received their M.D. degrees from Tufts Medical College. Peggy Johnson Well, '70, and Dan Smith, '70, were graduated from the University of Mississippi Medical Center. Richard Adams, '70, completed his work at Marquette Medical School in 1974.

Concurrently during the decades from the forties through the mid-seventies, a host of graduates received their dental training at Meharry, Howard and Tufts. Some of the graduates who studied dentistry at Meharry are doctors William H. Allen, '38, prosthodontics and former dean of the dental school at Meharry; Clarence B. Clark, '48; Fred Fielder, '56, operative dentistry and assistant dean, supervisor of the dental clinic at Meharry; A. E. Jagbandhansingh, '56; Mavis N. Jones; Theodore C. Jones, '62, orthodentistry (Tufts, post-doctoral work, '74); Royal Jordan, '55; Dindial Mahabri, '63; Eugene Mason, Jr., '38; Leon Nash, '34; Phillip R. Norman, '55; Willie G. O'Reilly, '52; Barbara Sias, '69.

Howard University Dental School graduates include doctors Benjamin Bullock, '48; Ardee Johnson, '49; Leroy Lucas, '50, clinical instructor, pedodontic dentistry, University of the Pacific; Newman C. Taylor, '36; Jermiah Taylor; Terrell A. Waters, '58, dental surgeon; Dr. DeWitt Webster, '56.

In health related fields can be found: Dr. Robert E. Bates, '50, of Gary, Indiana, graduate from the Illinois College of Pediatrics. LaHarry Norman, '51, completed pharmacy at Xavier University of New Orleans and operates Norman's Pharmacy in Chicago. Dr. Roland H. Powell, '54, a graduate of Tuskegee Institute of Veterinary Medicine, operates a thriving animal clinic in Jackson.

Representative of a sizable number of Tougaloo graduates of the 1960s who have received master's degrees in social work is Gwen Nero Loper, '52, employed at the Veterans Administration. Mrs. Loper was appointed by Gov. William Waller to the Mississippi State Board of Mental Health in 1975. She was the first black woman to serve on a state board.

Governor Waller also appointed Dr. Robert Harrison, Jr., '37, to the Board of Trustees of Institutions of Higher Learning. Dr. Harrison is also the first black person to serve on this important board, which oversees the state's eight universities and other research institutions.

As expected, especially since blacks won their rights in the courts as well as in the streets, Tougalooians sought legal training. Practicing both alone and in firms in principal cities across the nation, they hold degrees from some of the nation's most prestigious law schools.

Early alumni who are lawyers include Carl T. Robinson, '35, of Chicago. Walter B. Lewis of Washington is a faculty member of the Cornell School of Law and Public Administration. George Moore, '41, of Cleveland Heights, Ohio is assistant chief attorney for the Veterans Administration. Jesse J. Johnson, '39, of Hampton, Virginia is a retired lieutenant colonel and a federal housing referral officer. Ivory B. Shelton of Chicago received the J.D. degree from the John Marshall School of Law in 1950. He is affiliated with the Cook County Department of Psychiatry. James L. Howard, '40, of New York City is also a CPA.

Eddie M. Cole of Toledo, Ohio received the J.D. degree from the University of Illinois in 1971. The dean of the lawyers who are Tougaloo alumni is Judge Henry Heading of Detroit. Louis Mehlinger, who lived in Washington, D.C. and earned his law degree at Howard University School of Law, was graduated from the Tougaloo High School in 1905.

Taking their degrees at Howard University School of Law were Tougaloo alumni James L. Harris of Chicago; Roosevelt Robinson, Jr., '51, of Los Angeles, a past president of the National Tougaloo Alumni Association; Henry C. Wilkerson, '48, of Los Angeles; Eddie Hunter, a past president of the National Tougaloo Alumni Association; James Milton Abram, '61, of Jackson; Roscoe Foreman, '63, of Chicago; and Jack H. Young, Jr., now a city judge in Jackson, Mississippi. Until recently Howard University was the only law school available for southern blacks.

Willie L. Bailey, '69, a 1972 graduate of the National Law Center of George Washington University, provides rural legal services for the citizens of North Mississippi. Also providing legal services in the state are Edward Blackmon, '71, a 1973 graduate of George Washington University, and Attorney Nausead Stewart, '53, a 1970 graduate of the University of Mississippi Law School.

Among the list of women graduates who are making a contribution to the practice of law is Mary Scott Knoll, '63, a

1973 graduate of Rutgers, providing legal aid in San Diego, California. Patricia Murray, '69, a 1974 J.D. graduate from Georgetown University School of Law, is a member of the New York based firm of Whitman and Ransons. Geraldine Hines, '68, resides in Massachusetts and is a 1971 law school graduate of the University of Wisconsin at Madison. Margaret Burnham, '68, received the J.D. degree from the University of Pennsylvania.

Other noted attorneys include James L. Campbell, '68, a 1974 graduate of Southern University School of Law; Solomon Osborne, '70, a 1973 J.D. graduate of the University of Arizona; Norris J. Thomas, Jr., '67, a 1971 graduate of the University of Michigan; Theodore Lawyer, '67, a 1973 graduate of the Columbia School of Law. Attorney Lawrence Guyot, '63, a 1972 graduate of Rutgers University Law School, was a leader of the Mississippi Freedom Democratic Party in the mid-sixties. Melvin Jennings, '62, and Alfred Rhodes, '65, received the J.D. degree from the Jackson School of Law and M.S. in Ed. from Jackson State University. Jennings practices in Jackson and is active in politics, and Rhodes has a solid record of involvement and service in poverty and civil rights programs in Hinds and Yazoo counties.

Edward R. Dyson, Jr., '72, and Johnny L. Williams, '73, received their law degrees from the University of Iowa; Frankie Walton White, '66, and Constance Slaughter, '67, earned their law degrees from the University of Mississippi; Lenal Anderson, '68, earned his law degree from Columbia University. Reuben V. Anderson, '64, graduated from the University of Mississippi Law School in 1967 and is now a county judge in Hinds County, Mississippi.

Tougaloo has made distinct contributions to the cultural life of the nation. Her graduates have taken with them from the college humanitarian ideas and ideals. They are enriching their lives and those of others with presentations in art, dramatics and music. Dr. Ben E. Bailey, chairman of the music department, speaks with pride of the music majors who are instructing and entertaining. Dora J. Wilson, '66, is assistant professor of music at California State University, Long Beach.

Robert Honeysucker, '64, concert and operatic baritone and former Tougaloo College Choir director and voice teacher, is Administrative Director of the Community Music Center in Boston. His master of music degree in performance is from Miami University. Eddie Jones, '73, also holds a master of music degree from Miami, where he is director of the gospel choir. A particularly outstanding and talented voice graduate from Tougaloo is Walter Turnbull, '66, concert and operatic tenor. He earned the master of music degree from Manhattan School of Music. He has performed in several operas, including one with Opera South. Florence Russell, '71, vocal instructor at Rust College, earned the master of music degree in performance from Miami. Dr. Bobby G. Cooper, '61 (Ed.D. in Administration, University of Colorado) is director of music at Utica Junior College. Dr. Rosa P. Welch, '22, of Denver is a world renowned teacher and a soloist, and she is a former member of the Tougaloo College board of trustees.

Dr. Aaron Boddie of New York is both a U.S. post office clerk and an actor-model. He is a member of the Screen Actors Guild and the Negro Actors Guild of America. He has made appearances on national television in a leading soap opera and has played in over sixty-eight major movies.

Whereas the number of graduates of the college entering the Christian ministry in the past has been small there are indications that this is changing. To list a few: Rev. Richard Jones, '60, Charles A. Thurman, '69, and Ricks Anderson, '70, received master of divinity degrees from Colgate Rochester Divinity School. The Rev. Mr. Jones is pastor of the New Hope Baptist Church in Braddock, Pennsylvania. Dr. Eddie O'Neal, '63, is professor of pastoral theology at Andover Newton. Rev. Tommy Elias Harris, '59, of Port Gibson is a minister of the Christian Church, and Rev. Eddie McBride of Vicksburg has an established record in political reform. O. A. Rogers, Jr., '50, earned a S.T.B. degree from Harvard Divinity School in 1953. For the past fifteen years he has served as pastor of Asbury United Methodist Church of Bolton and Kingsley Chapel of Edwards.

During the period 1950–1970 when there was considerable

demand for professionally trained librarians, a number of persons took preliminary library courses at Tougaloo. As many as three dozen of these students subsequently earned degrees in library science programs in various parts of the United States.

Outstanding examples of Tougaloo graduates who earned the M.S.L. degrees are: Darlene Carter (Syracuse University), Sue Willa Wright Woodfork (University of Denver), Hazel Stamps Moore (Atlanta University), Norma Miller Poinsett (University of Illinois), Melvin McKinney Bowie (University of Illinois), Charlene Smith Cole (Syracuse University), Jeannetta C. Roach (Syracuse University), Evia Briggs Moore (University of Wisconsin), Verlean Delaney (Atlanta University), Robbye R. Henderson (Atlanta University), and Clara L. Bedenfield (Wayne State University).

Tougaloo alumni can be found also in the business world: H. Connell Ward is senior engineering specialist for GTE Sylvania in California; Edward Harris, Jr. is a supervisor with Campbell Soup in Sacramento; Thelma Sanders, '46, is a Jackson businesswoman, owner and manager of Sanders' Boutique, and a member of the Tougaloo College board of trustees; Myles B. Harris, '53, of Los Angeles is a research engineer employed by the Northrop Company; Leroy Ellis, '48, is a businessman in Westpoint, Fairfield, and Norwalk, Connecticut; James W. Coleman, '57 (Ph.D., microbiology, University of Louisville School of Medicine) is a senior associate at Joseph E. Seagram and Son, Inc. Dr. Arlington Finley, '70, is employed as an organic chemist at Dow Chemical Corporation in Midland, Michigan.

Nearly two dozen Tougalooians who have earned master of business administration degrees are engaged in a variety of business related activities. Attorney James Howard, '40, of New York, who is also a Certified Public Accountant, is Vice President of United Mutual Insurance Company and a member of the law firm of Mash, Howard and Company.

Calvin Brown, '64, Lenal Anderson, '68, and Willie Mayfield, '69, hold degrees from Harvard Business School. Attorney Anderson is assistant professor of finance at Central State University. Richard Anderson, '61, and Edward T. Lewis,

'69, are graduates of the M.B.A. Program at the University of Massachusetts. Edward T. Lewis is employed by Mobil Oil Company in Philadelphia, Pennsylvania. At Atlanta University, Richard L. Moman, '70, Josephine Neely, '72, and Samuel Rundles, '70, earned their M.B.A. degrees. Major Roosevelt Matthews, '62, earned his business degree at Golden State University, San Francisco. James McLaughlin, '62, graduated from the University of Missouri, Ernest Brandon, '72, from Indiana University, and David Ford, '68, from Columbia. President George A. Owens received an M.B.A. from Columbia in 1950.

The successful acquisition of M.B.A's at these outstanding schools of business attests to the excellence of the economics curriculum at Tougaloo College.

Tougaloo college graduates who have impacted politics include Bennie G. Thompson, '68, who was elected the first black mayor of Bolton, Mississippi. He is also administrative assistant to the director of Jackson-Hinds Comprehensive Health Center. Andrew D. Graffenreidt, '51, is in his second term as the first black city commissioner of Fort Lauderdale, Florida. The Hon. Corneal A. Davis, assistant majority leader in the Illinois House of Representatives, completed thirty-eight years as a member of that body.

The achievement of the alumni in the many and diverse academic fields and careers speaks well for the liberal arts curricula of the college. Much credit is due the relatively small classes and to the high caliber of students who choose to enroll in the tradition of the college. The students undoubtedly attend Tougaloo because of the assurance of obtaining the best available education by a multicultural, dedicated faculty teaching in the freest academic climate in the entire state.

The state of Mississippi and the nation would be poorer if it had not been for Tougaloo and its graduates. The lives of countless masses have been enriched beyond measure, and as long as the College survives it will continue to produce graduates who care about Mississippi and the quality of life for its people.

* This epilogue was drafted in 1976, therefore most of its factual material is limited to that date.

Bibliographical Essay

PRIMARILY THIS STUDY IS BASED ON letters, minutes, and reports found in the Amistad Research Center located on the Dillard University campus in New Orleans and the files in the L. Zenobia Coleman Library at Tougaloo College. Though the American Missionary Association (A.M.A.) began sending its records to Fisk University in Nashville, Tennessee, in 1943, their disorganized condition discouraged most scholars in their use until Dr. Clifton H. Johnson, director of the Amistad Research Center, recently catalogued them.

A.M.A. records pertaining to Tougaloo College cover the periods 1868–1870, 1873–1879, and 1939 to the present. The first break in continuity resulted from the Chicago fire which occurred during the time that Tougaloo University was reporting to Gen. C. H. Howard at the A.M.A. Chicago office. This loss explains the scant information available for Beals's administration. Records for the first eight years consist chiefly of letters and simple reports written by the school's personnel and by a few political leaders in Mississippi, addressed to the A.M.A. New York office. Letters from influential A.M.A. secretaries to faculty and staff at Tougaloo University were seldom preserved. Ironically, the office that was most faithful in maintaining its files is now disadvantaged, for the researcher has much material covering the first years from the viewpoint of Tougaloo workers but little giving that of the beleaguered secretaries. What is known of the secretaries' side of the story is

255

gleaned from occasional letters from one secretary to another. Material from the A.M.A. office covering 1939 to the present was released to the Amistad Research Center only in 1969. This material consists of reports made by presidents and deans, minutes of the board of trustees, and letters. What happened to A.M.A. records for the intervening years, 1879–1939, is a moot question.

Records at Tougaloo College represent largely the diligent efforts of L. Zenobia Coleman, Tougaloo's librarian for more than thirty years, and the present librarians, Jeannetta Roach and her assistant, Virgia Shedd. Miss Coleman collected old records while saving materials current during her tenure and filed them in fireproof cabinets given the library for that purpose by the student history club of the 1940s. Despite this precaution, many of Tougaloo's records were destroyed. The building which housed the late W. A. Bender's unfinished history and supporting papers was demolished by fire. Charles Austin, until his death in California, had been engaged in collecting material on Tougaloo's history to assist the Rev. Mr. Bender. This collection was inadvertently lost during settlement of his estate. Thus, the collection at the L. Zenobia Coleman Library is irregular in coverage. Unfortunately too, many short items in the files are unsigned, and some are undated.

Of Tougaloo's publications the most enduring has been the *Tougaloo News*, usually four to six pages in length. Started as the *Tougaloo Enterprise* in 1884, the paper's name was changed in 1885 to *Tougaloo Quarterly* to avoid confusion with Rust University's *Enterprise* which predates Tougaloo's. With need for a monthly paper in 1890 the paper's name was changed to *Tougaloo News*. Except for a few years after Tougaloo's merger with Southern Christian Institute, the name of *Tougaloo News* has continued to the present. After the turn of the century *Tougaloo News* reverted to quarterly issues with the spring publication serving as a catalog. Between 1940 and 1957 the January issue took the form of a small journal which published scholarly articles written by members of the faculty. Other Tougaloo publications came and went as needed. Alumni have at intervals sponsored a quarterly *Bulletin*; students published the *Flyer* in the 1920s, the *Informer* in the 1950s, the *Student Voice*, *Harambee*, and numerous other papers in the 1960s. *Tougaloo Tidings* was an exceptionally fine weekly news sheet put out by the administration from 1933 to 1937.

The *American Missionary*, a monthly publication of A.M.A., might be considered an official outlet for the secretaries' points of view, since they approved all material printed in it. However, its articles, written to encourage laymen to support the A.M.A. work, overlooked human frailties. At the very time when most of the staff and faculty at Tougaloo were resigning in protest against A.M.A. policies, the *American Missionary* carried a glowing account of work at the school. Nevertheless, the *American Missionary* offers a good picture of ideals toward which A.M.A. workers in office and field were striving and a broad scope of the Association's work. Its monthly account of monies received and the annual reports reprinted in the magazine give necessary data on business aspects of the Association.

There are few secondary works on Tougaloo College, but several books and articles touch on life at the school. Augustus Field Beard, *A Crusade of Brotherhood* (1909), and Fred L. Brownlee, *New Day Ascending* (1946), in giving the history of the American Missionary Association which each served as secretary, devoted a few pages to Tougaloo. Edward Mayes's *History of Education in Mississippi* (1899) was one of the earliest to pull together some facts about Tougaloo. Helen Griffith's *Dauntless in Mississippi* (1965) tells the life story of Sarah A. Dickey whose school in Clinton was always closely associated with Tougaloo. Dr. Griffith also wrote "The Rich Years of Retirement," *Mt. Holyoke Alumnae Quarterly*, 39 (Winter 1956), 142–144, in which she relates the peculiar problems faced by a Negro college and the happiness she found in her association with Tougaloo after retirement from Mt. Holyoke. Another former teacher at Tougaloo, Gilbert R. Gredler, took a more critical view in "Frank Look at Tougaloo," *Unitarian Christian Register*, 130 (June 1951), 22–25. Two other former Tougaloo teachers, August Meier and Chester Slocum, answered Gredler in the same journal with their article,

"Tougaloo College Revisited," 130 (Nov. 1951), 27–31. They pointed to achievements in face of great odds and claimed that some of Gredler's complaints such as an over-emphasis on social and athletic events could be more accurately charged to the white president. Ernst Borinski explained "The Social Science Laboratory at Tougaloo College" in the *Journal of Educational Sociology*, 22 (Dec. 1948), 276–286. David E. Guyton, from a prominent Mississippi family, was so impressed with Tougaloo College when representing his alma mater at President Cross's inauguration that he wrote "A Trip to Tougaloo College," *The Mississippi Woman's Magazine*, 24 (May-June 1948), 8–9. President Warren's alma mater ran a story in the *Princeton Alumni Weekly*, 52 (May 16, 1952), 19, entitled "Princeton College Presidents XI: Harold Collins Warren '12." Two articles refer to Tougaloo only as it is a part of the A.M.A. Richard B. Drake's "Freedmen's Aid Societies and Sectional Compromise," *Journal of Southern History*, 29 (May 1963), 175–186, indicates that the A.M.A. followed a policy of racial accommodation. On the other hand, Wesley A. Hotchkiss's "Congregationalists and Negro Education," *Journal of Negro Education*, 29 (Summer 1960), 289–298, claims that the A.M.A. deliberately freed itself from ecclesiastical control to avoid the influence of financial gifts from slaveholding church members and that throughout its history it acted upon the slogan "Equal brotherhood in the family of Christ."

Numerous secondary sources give a general picture of Negro education in the South. *The Northern Teacher in the South, 1862–1870* (1941) by Henry Lee Swint offers insight into the character and purposes of teachers who came South during and after the Civil War to teach freedmen. More can be accomplished for the black man's education by accommodation to white society than by defying it, according to Joseph Winthrop Holley in *You Can't Build a Chimney from the Top* (1948). *Along This Way* (1947), the autobiography of James Weldon Johnson, describes the author's experiences at the A.M.A.-sponsored Atlanta University, showing some parallels with Tougaloo, though Atlanta was better financed and staffed. Dwight O. W. Holmes's *The Evolution of the Negro College* (1930) is a standard work which is part of Teachers College, Columbia University's series on *Contributions to Education*. H. S. Ashmore's *The Negro and the Schools* (1954), Carter G. Woodson's *The Mis-Education of the Negro* (1933), Horace Mann Bond's *The Education of the Negro in the American Social Order* (1934), and Henry Allen Bullock's *A History of Negro Education in the South* (1967) are all critical of industrial, to the neglect of academic, emphasis and the influence of foundations in this regard. Louis R. Harlan in *Separate and Unequal: Public School Campaigns and Racism in The Southern Seaboard States, 1901–1915* (1958) asserts that philanthropic agencies surrendered to the idea of white supremacy. Swint also takes a cynical look at philanthropy in "Northern Interest in the Shoeless Southerner," *Journal of Southern History*, 16 (Nov. 1950), 457–471.

Of those whose writings center on philanthropic foundations, Joseph C. Kiger, "The Large Foundations in Southern Education," *Journal of Higher Education*, 27 (March 1956), 125–132, takes the more favorable view that foundations have raised the whole character of southern education and elevated Negro education incalculably. Other works sympathetic toward educational foundations include Will W. Alexander's *The Slater and Jeanes Funds: An Educator's Approach to a Difficult Social Problem* (1934); Benjamin Brawley's *Doctor Dillard of the Jeanes Fund* (1930); and Ullin W. Leavell's *Philanthropy in Negro Education, George Peabody College for Teachers Contributions to Education* (1930). Merle Curti and Roderick Nash deal with Peabody, Slater, Hand, Jeanes, and Rockefeller funds in *Philanthropy in the Shaping of American Higher Education* (1965).

For articles on Negro education the *Journal of Negro Education* is a prolific source. Three concerned with financing Negro colleges are D. O. W. Holmes's "The Negro College Faces the Depression," 2 (Jan. 1933), 16–25, in which the author sees consolidation as necessary; William J. Trent, Jr. explains the United Negro College Fund in "The Problems of Financing Private Negro Colleges," 18 (Spring 1949), 114–122; and Henry G. Badger studies the drop in student fees during the depression years in "Finances of Negro Colleges, 1929–1939," 9 (April 1940), 162–166. Charles H. Thompson's "The Critical Situation in Negro Higher and Professional Education," 15 (Fall 1946), 570–584, touches on finances also as he complains of the "brain drain" after World War II when southern Negro teachers were enticed by higher salaries to other regions.

Several books and articles are helpful in understanding the Freedmen's Bureau and its relationship to Tougaloo. John A. Carpenter's *Sword and Olive Branch* (1964) gives a sympathetic picture of the Bureau's director, who was influential in founding Tougaloo University. George R. Bentley concentrated more on the Bureau's work, in *A History of the Freedmen's Bureau* (1954). LaWanda and John Cox in "General O. O. Howard and the Misrepresented Bureau," *Journal of Southern History*, 19 (Nov. 1953), 427–456, took the position that criticism stemmed from Southerners' adamant stand against racial equality. Clifton Lloyd Ganus, Jr. wrote as his doctoral dissertation *The Freedmen's Bureau in Mississippi* (Tulane University, 1953), a copy of which may be found in the Mississippi Room of the library at the University of Mississippi.

An understanding of Mississippi's economic and political factors is needed as a background for Tougaloo College's development. Ross H. Moore's doctoral dissertation at Duke University, *Social and Economic Conditions in Mississippi during Reconstruction* (1937), is helpful. Vernon Lane Wharton's *The Negro in Mississippi 1865–1890*, first published in 1947, is well written with no obvious bias. James Wilford Garner's *Reconstruction in Mississippi* (1964) gives detailed information but reflects what Carl Becker might call the "climate of opinion." The book was written around the turn of the century when theories of white supremacy and social Darwinism were rampant. Careful and critical reading is required, since Garner sometimes explains in footnotes the improbability of what he writes in the text. The book also contains a number of contradictory statements. Nevertheless, it provides sources of information.

John R. Lynch, a Negro who, as a Mississippi legislator,

Speaker of the House, and member of Congress, was personally involved in the state's political life, wrote *The Facts of Reconstruction* (1913), a comprehensive, well-written account. *Adelbert Ames* (1964), written by his daughter, Blanche Ames Ames, is a carefully and extensively documented biography which avowedly was written to vindicate her father because of scurrilous attacks on his character by early historians who were unsympathetic with the idea of political rights for the Negro. The book gives an intimate view of the man on whom Huggins said the A.M.A. would be dependent for any favors. It also gives a good picture of the troublous years in Mississippi between 1869 and 1877.

For more recent years A. Wigfall Green's *The Man Bilbo* (1963) and Albert D. Kirwan's *Revolt of the Rednecks* (1951) give descriptions of Mississippi from the viewpoint of whites low down on the totem pole. The views of such people were usually anti-Negro. William Alexander Percy's *Lanterns on the Levee* (1941) reveals the paternalistic attitude of the "aristocrats" toward the Negro. All three books testify to corruption in Mississippi politics and wide disparity in economic advantages. *The Journal of Mississippi History* is a source of information about many aspects of the state's history.

John and Margrit Garner's mimeographed letters to family and friends give a contemporary account of life at Tougaloo during the 1960s as do the mimeographed letters of Clarice Campbell during the years 1963–1969. The Rev. Edwin King's "The Civil Rights Movement in Mississippi" (1970), written under a Field Foundation grant, is invaluable. Dr. W. J. Cunningham's manuscript of his experiences at Galloway Memorial Methodist Church gives another view of the efforts made by some at Tougaloo to integrate the church. Both of these manuscripts will be published at a later date.

The report of the Mississippi State Sovereignty Commission in 1967 claims "credit" for President Beittel's dismissal. This claim should be viewed in light of the purpose of the report, which was to persuade the legislature to refund the Commission. If the complete files of the Sovereignty Commission are ever made public, no doubt the historian will better understand the influence of the state of Mississippi on events at Tougaloo College during the decade of the sixties.

FBI files, obtained under the Freedom of Information Act, gave the viewpoint of motel and restaurant owners whose business establishments some Tougalooians had attempted to integrate. These files also gave some startling facts on what might be termed "spies and lies" in regard to Tougaloo personnel. When more FBI files are opened, a greater understanding of the problems faced by Tougaloo College in the decade of the 1960s will likely be possible.

The Jackson newspapers, *The Clarion-Ledger* and *Jackson Daily News*, gave an inordinate amount of space to Tougaloo during the late fifties and the sixties, as they did to all civil rights activities. Letters to the editors filled pages rather than columns. These letters make fascinating reading and reflect the emotional and racial climate in which Tougaloo was forced to operate during those years.

The *New York Times* and newspapers around the country frequently carried articles on Tougaloo, particularly during the 1960s. Letters and reports found in various administrative offices at Tougaloo were helpful. The *Congressional Record* contains an incredible account of the hearings on the Ku Klux Klan after the Civil War. "Profile of Tougaloo," *Encore* (Nov. 1973), included in the *Congressional Record* at the request of Sen. Edward Kennedy, gives information highly favorable toward Tougaloo.

While this book has a minimum of footnotes, anyone interested in detailed documentation may consult the Ph.D. dissertation, "History of Tougaloo College," by Clarice T. Campbell, 1970, in the libraries at the University of Mississippi, Tougaloo College, and Rust College. The dissertation may also be ordered from University Microfilms, Ann Arbor, Michigan. *Mississippi: The View from Tougaloo*, a revision of this dissertation, parallels it enough to enable one to locate documentation for chapters I–XIX. FBI files, letters, reports, and student papers in the L. Z. Coleman Library at Tougaloo College give documentation for chapters XX–XXI, which cover the administration of President Beittel and the first years of President Owens' administration. Surveys of alumni conducted by the Tougaloo Alumni Office are largely the authority for "Has Tougaloo Made a Difference?". Such periodic surveys form the basis of articles appearing in the *Tougaloo News*.

Herman Blake
President
1984-1987

Charles Baldwin
Interim President
1987-1988

Adib Shakir
President
1988-1994

Edgar Smith
Acting President
1994-1995

Joe A. Lee
President
1995-2001

James H. Wyche
Acting President
2001-present

22

The Changing of the Guard
1984-2001

WHEN GEORGE OWENS announced his retirement in 1984, an era in the history of the presidency at Tougaloo had come to an end. It was true that the appointment of Owens in 1964 was a new step for the college in that he was the first black president, but with his retirement the character of the presidency would change. Owens had come in as Tougaloo president during a period of great turmoil, both in state and nation. The Viet Nam war had reached a critical stage; the Civil Rights Movement had made some gains toward social justice; campuses throughout the nations became scenes of agitation, demonstration and controversies. Tougaloo had been the center of some of the disturbance within the state, not so much from student activism but because it was considered to be the haven for those who battled for social justice. George Owens had been able to keep a steady hand on the school, yet he did antagonize some because his approach to these matters was considered conservative by some. Nevertheless, he was able to preserve the integrity of the institution and to keep it alive despite misgivings about its viability. A new day was dawning, however, and a new direction had to be taken.

Colleges in 1984 were entirely different from those in 1964 and with this change of the institution itself came the change in the character of the person who would lead it. This was particularly true of the Historically Black Colleges and Universities. The majority of historically black colleges were founded after the civil war with the primary

265

mission to train the freedmen to become literate and to become teachers. Throughout their histories, these institutions faced a multitude of problems, spanning from opposition from the white power structure to the constant struggle to obtain adequate resources to survive. There were continuous calls for their closure from educators throughout the country. Their critics maintained that black colleges were isolated from the mainstream of American education and that it was unwise to maintain the illusion that these colleges provided its students with what one called a college education. This storm of criticism became even more strident following *Brown vs. Board of Education*. The argument was that the black college was no longer needed now that integration was the law of the land. Black students could pursue their dreams at the college of their choice.

This did not develop in the many decades since the decision was handed down. The need for the black college was still there. Changes had to be made, but the end result was the same. Black colleges tended to be inclusive rather than exclusive, accepting those students who were rejected elsewhere. This is important when one considers the poor standards of secondary schools and the strength of support programs at these institutions. Black colleges maintained a strong sense of mission and an obligation to the larger community. Integration was beneficial in some circumstances, but the black community still struggled to maintain itself. Black colleges afforded its students the opportunity to develop and become leaders. This was old tradition throughout the twentieth century there were few black leaders in all fields who had not had some contact with the black colleges and universities.

As a whole these colleges entered into a period of growth during the late 1980s. In 1965 there were approximately 250,000 black students attending colleges in the United States, and half of these attending historically black colleges, the rest were spread throughout the many mainly white universities across the country. In 1977 there were approximately 1,000,00 black students attending college with approximately 20% attending black colleges and the other 80% attending the predominantly white colleges. Some of the growth came as a result of students recognizing the need to continue with their education if they were to play a significant role in society. Some growth was the result of a larger proportion of black students choosing black institutions over their white counterpart. Although the figures showed that the greater percentage of black students was entering the predominantly white universities, the historically black schools were responsible for a greater percentage of those who graduated.

The burden that had been placed on these institutions was more than some could bear. Some with little resources collapsed under the growth of the student populations and the demands that they brought with them. Others were forced to alter their mission and to change their whole outlook. Still others continued even with limited resources. Many sought innovative ways to improve their financial conditions through aggressive leadership. The most dramatic change in the HBCU was in the character of the person who would lead them. Many colleges throughout the country recognized that the college president was not an educator alone. The demands of the institutions themselves forced college-governing authorities to look for the Renaissance man or woman.

TOUGALOO AND THE CHANGING ENVIRONMENT

Since the end of World War II the mission of Tougaloo College has gradually been changing. The change has reflected some of these changes that have taken place in the "outside world." A greater emphasis had to be placed on the preparation for careers and the ability to function in a multi-ethnic society. Although Tougaloo had been established primarily as a teacher training college, there had been a gradual change in direction throughout the sixties and seventies. Students became interested in other careers, and the faculty became more interested in developing a curriculum where blacks and other minorities were underrepresented. The effects of the College's historical involvement in the civil rights movement were felt in all phases of the college life. The emphasis in the mission of the College had always been on freedom and openness, but the experiences of the sixties and the changing world around the College forced its leaders to rethink its role. The educational program had to emphasize a program that took the students away from the narrow confines of the South in general and Mississippi in particular to the wider world.

By 1984 the College was 2.5 million dollars in debt and many of its buildings were in disrepair. Tougaloo however had to keep pace with other institutions in order to survive. A strange paradox had developed in that greater opportunities were presenting themselves in Mississippi for college students and their graduates. The emphasis on the technology raised the cost of education considerably with the needs to purchase equipment, remodel the aging plant and hire qualified faculty and staff added to the growing expense. Many of the students found the financial cost too great. With the changes in opportunities, some students were seeking placement in colleges and universities that could meet their needs both educationally and financially. These opportunities were available at many different colleges and universities, both black and white throughout the country. Ironically, some of these changes in the state were a direct by-product of the civil right struggle that had been close to the College's heart. This was a serious situation since small colleges with little endowment depended on student enrollment to meet their expenses.

Determining the focus of managing these changes and setting a new course for these colleges had become the responsibility of the Chief Executive Officer and the management team. The choice of a CEO could mean the success or death of struggling colleges. Even though some candidates for the presidencies were distinguished educators with innovative ideas in the field, this would not be enough in the changing environment. Presidents, above all, had to be a more than adequate fundraisers. This is particularly true for small colleges like Tougaloo with small endowments. There was the continuing struggle to raise the funds to meet the needs of the educational program, repair the infrastructure, meet the changes brought about a changing world, maintain a salary structure that would please, attract, and maintain an adequate faculty and staff, and plan for the future of the institution. In addition to being an educator and leader, Tougaloo's new president had to be familiar with the corporate structure, a land manager, and a labor negotiator. In addition, the new president would have to be familiar with the new type of Tougaloo student that was evolving, the restlessness of the faculty searching for its own independence, the demands of an ever changing Board of Trustees, the concerns of the alumni, and the wishes of those who had been involved with the college in recent years.

THE BLAKE ADMINISTRATION / 1984-1987

In 1984 the Tougaloo Board of Trustees selected J. Herman Blake from California as its choice to succeed George Owens. Blake, a Mount Vernon New York native had been the Provost at Oakes College, a divi-

sion of the University of California at Santa Cruz. He had received a
doctorate in Sociology from the University of California at Berkley in
1973 and had spent much of his educational career in the California
area. He had, as well, studied at the Institute for Educational
Management at Harvard Graduate School of Business Administration.

Much of Blake's educational career and research background had
centered on the education of the nontraditional student. Oakes College
was founded in 1972 as a part of the University of California at Santa
Cruz and was an experimental college with a mission to provide a high
quality education for students from diverse backgrounds. It appeared,
however, to be more of a large program supported by a larger university,
rather than a four-year institution like Tougaloo. There were many such
"open universities" developing through out the country in response to
students cry for more relevant learning. Much of these programs' financing came from various grants developed by the chief administrative
officer and existed at the mercy of outside forces. This particular program, however, was innovative and pointed to a new direction in education. The question was whether Blake had the skills to bridge the gap
between an experimental institution and lead an institution as formal as
Tougaloo.

Blake's critics were quick to point out that the administration of an
experimental college would be different from that of a four-year institution like Tougaloo. There were many questions raised about his administrative ability, his knowledge of the Tougaloo legacy, and his general
attitude toward the South. His critics pointed out as well his lack of
involvement in many traditional academic pursuits, pointing out that
there were more viable candidates available. Although Blake appeared
to enjoy the support of the leadership on the Board of Trustees, there
was an uncomfortable opinion by others about his qualifications and his
commitment to the Tougaloo program.

His appointment as President of Tougaloo was truly a break with the
past. He was the first President who had no contact with the American
Missionary Association, the United Church of Christ, or any of the
affiliates that had been involved in the founding and development of
Tougaloo in the past. To many, both at Tougaloo and in the community, he was an outsider.

Blake was not discouraged by his critics nor the soaring debt and
falling enrollment at the College. He welcomed the challenge and in no
way characterized Tougaloo as a dying institution. He pledged as well to

strengthen Tougaloo's academic programs, upgrade college facilities, raise faculty salaries and bring the faculty into the school governing process. In April 1984, as he took over the helm, Blake helped to launch a 4.5 million-dollar fund raising drive and voiced hope that the college's deficit would be eliminated in the next fiscal year. In addition, Blake focused his attention on the college's decaying infrastructure, particularly the Holmes Hall classroom complex and Judson Cross and Renner Hall dormitories.

Blake continued his optimistic attitude throughout his first year in office, and his enthusiasm became infectious. Dr. Theodore C. Jones, president of the Tougaloo College Alumni Association, commented on the raised spirits at the institution and looked forward to an increased enrollment and financial viability. Indeed there were many successes during Blake's first year in office. A generous donation was made to the College by the actor Bill Cosby; the five year fund raising campaign exceeded expectations; enrollment increased from a low of 530 students in 1983-1984 to 612 in 1984-1985, with an expectation of an enrollment of 630 in 1985-1986 school year; and the faculty enjoyed an increased involvement in the decision making and governing of the College. The new president planned as well to increase the number of grants coming into the College. At his inauguration in 1985, he did not speak of the deficit or the crushing financial plight that faced Tougaloo, but instead focused on the goals and history of the College, and urged that all concerned would work together to continue the institution's outstanding legacy.

The inauguration was possibly the highpoint of the Blake administration. Standing problems were not being resolved and the faculty and some alumni were becoming increasingly restless. The continuing financial struggle of the College caused Blake and other officials to consider the sale of some of the College's land. In September 1985, Tougaloo officials requested a zoning change before the Madison County Planning and Zoning Commission. The request was to change the property from primarily residential and special use to commercial and industrial. The continuing use by the college for educational purposes could pay some of the mounting debts. Some alumni objected to the proposed sale. Karl Banks, a Madison County supervisor and a 1971 Tougaloo graduate, expressed concern that the administration was thinking of selling some of the land since this was the College's major asset. Blake emphasized that the whole project was an idea that was in the early planning stage, but something should be done quickly to bring the College to a firm financial footing.

BLAKE VS. THE FACULTY

It is difficult to pinpoint exactly where the controversy between President Blake and the faculty began. One could expect that in the transition from long time president Owens to the new administration there would be some ill feelings. That is to be expected in the change of administrations on any college campus. Owens held the respect and admiration of many on campus, yet Blake was cut from a different cloth. As well, in a major shake-up, Blake had dismissed three longtime administrative assistants. He insisted that the move had to be done in order to streamline the administration and to make it more effective in meeting the needs of the College

Dr. Ben Bailey, a longtime music professor and chairman of the humanities division since 1971, led the opposition to Blake. Bailey enjoyed the respect of the faculty and the academic community throughout the country. A humanistic scholar, Bailey was considered by many to be an authority on black music. He had continued in the tradition of developing the Tougaloo choir and had written several books on the history of music at Tougaloo. He was a close supporter of President Owens and devoted to academic excellence at the institution. Many on the faculty looked to Bailey for guidance and he had in many ways taken over the role as leader of the faculty. Throughout the academic year 1985-1986, Bailey waged a steady critical campaign against the President. His criticism of Blake came through letters, memoranda, and continual efforts to rally the faculty in opposition to the administration. He accused the President of making unilateral decisions about the academic program, personnel and other matters without consulting the faculty. Bailey felt that many decisions made by Blake—particularly when these decisions affected students and faculty—were contradictory to Blake's public statements that the faculty enjoyed a greater opportunity for governance under his administration.

In January 1986, Bailey publicly called for Blake's resignation, citing the following reasons: a serious concern about his spending policies; the high incidence of staff firings at Tougaloo without sufficient reasons; the need for closer contact between the faculty and the administration; a serious concern about the behavior of campus security; a serious concern about the cost of redecorating the President's home.

On the surface Bailey's call for the Blake's resignation appeared to be a tempest in a teapot. Blake immediately said that he had no plans to resign, and others rose to his defense and criticized Bailey's efforts. Much of the criticism centered on the recurring theme of Tougaloo's financial plight and the need to take innovative and decisive action to cure the College's ills. Asoka Srinivasan, the head of Tougaloo's biology department and the chairman of the faculty's steering committee stated that most of the faculty did not share Bailey's concern. Srinivasan pointed to Blake's continuing effort to create a quality educational program with limited resources. Robert Jones, Chairman of the Board of Trustees was even more vehement in denouncing Bailey's allegations, calling them a disservice to the community. Jones emphasized that Blake was indeed making changes, but he had not been hired to continue the old ways of operating the College.

Clearly, Blake enjoyed support in high places. The support did not, however, deter him from issuing a strongly worded rebuttal to the efforts by Bailey to unseat him. In a long letter to Robert Jones, Blake took issue with Bailey's attacks upon him and his staff. He particularly expressed concern about the criticism of his wife and members of his staff who had come with him from California. He expressed doubts that 25% of the faculty formed the opposition to his administration, and he implied that many on the faculty were concerned about the discord that had arisen among members of the faculty and the administration. More fundamentally, Blake questioned Dr. Bailey's positions on the organization of certain sectors of the College, the financial plight of the College and the dismissal of members of staff. Blake felt that he had to take some of the measures that he had taken in order to insure the survival of the College, for he had inherited "an institution with monstrous debt, run-down, inadequate facilities, great needs in equipment, and among the lowest faculty salaries in the nation."

Blake's written defense and the support from members of the Board of Trustees did not stem the criticism from the faculty. The criticism continued throughout 1986, with Bailey criticizing the president on every move he made. In May 1986, the Tougaloo faculty passed a resolution voting no confidence in Blake's administration. At that time a selected group of faculty members aired the grievances of the faculty before the full Board of Trustees, the full faculty and administration. The vote, the complaints, and the alienation of a significant group of the faculty did not change Blake's attitudes or his administrative style. He continued to make personnel changes at the College and Bailey insisted that these changes divided the College, affected the academic program and forced some of the senior faculty members to either retire or find positions at other institutions.

In 1987 the controversy between the faculty and the President came to a head. In its January 26 meeting the faculty council voted unanimously to give Blake and his administration a vote of no confidence. In its February meeting, the Board of Trustees debated as to whether it should give Blake a three-year renewal on its contract. Before the Board could vote on the three-year extension on his contract, President Blake submitted his resignation.

In his statement of resignation, Blake avoided any specific mention of the controversies that had engulfed the campus during his tenure. He admitted that changes "naturally creates some difficulties and misunderstandings." He felt that these changes would result in making Tougaloo a stronger place. In his announcement, Blake outlined his accomplishments since coming to Tougaloo: the reduction of debt with the sale of warrants it owned in the TV station WLBT in Jackson; balancing the budget through planning and conservation; the increase in enrollment; the repair to dormitories; and the refinancing of the College's land not directly adjacent to the campus. These were the challenges that Blake felt had to be met in order to insure financial stability for Tougaloo, and he felt that it was time for him to take on a new challenge.

The resignation was not a time for rejoicing or for weeping. Students were either suprised or apathetic. Though the Board of Trustees did not vote on the renewal of Blake's contract, there was some confusion among Board members. Some voiced concern about the relationship that Blake had with the faculty and the effect on the management of the college. Dr. Albert Britton of Jackson, a new trustee, felt that a majority of the trustees opposed giving Blake a new contract and surmised that when Blake heard of the Board's stance, he submitted his resignation, Robert Jones, chairman of the board, was quick to state that Britton's statements were "more imaginary than real." He denied that the position of the board had anything to do with Blake's resignation, and the resistance of the faculty to Blake did not sway them.

Whatever the situation, the resignation by President Blake showed the deep division within the College community, particularly within the faculty. Whether this could have been avoided is opened to question. When Blake became president in 1984, Tougaloo faced a financial crisis. He immediately called for improved enrollment, more fund raising, a balanced budget, and better management. If he were to reach these goals, then there had to be some substantive changes. He made these changes and caused a storm of criticism from the faculty. It is difficult to assess blame in this situation. The changes had to be made if the College were to survive, and the board said that Blake had met all of their expectations. Robert Jones praised the president for slashing 1.6 million dollars from a 3.6 million deficit.

J. Herman Blake felt that he was successful as President of Tougaloo College. His critics felt that he was a failure. It was possibly Blake's style, more than substantive changes in the administration of the college that raised the ire of the faculty. He altered the more fatherly approach of George Owens to students, replacing it with a more relaxed demeanor. He brought in administrators from California, at competitive salaries, and dismissed other administrators who were well liked and supported in the college community. He made academic decisions for Tougaloo students that he felt were best for the student body, yet he did not consult the faculty on these decisions. Blake did not "stick with the old ways" and the changes he made would change the direction of the College.

FACING THE NEW CENTURY

The short administration of J. Herman Blake ended quietly. The interim presidency of Charles Baldwin brought some peace to the campus, but in no way eliminated the problems that faced the institution. The new administration would face monumental challenges. A two million-dollar deficit clouded any plans of an incoming administration. Some renovations of the existing buildings had been made under Blake, but a lot of the physical plant was in disrepair. Some of the older historical buildings, such as Beard Hall and Woodworth Chapel, were in such disrepair that they were either condemned or judged unsafe for use. The new administration had to search for funds to maintain their legacy.

Academically the College was sound. The curriculum met the needs of the students. Tougaloo graduates continued to excel in their chosen professions and were being admitted to some of the more prestigious graduate and professional schools throughout the nation. There were, however, ominous signs even on the academic horizon. The demands of a growing society placed pressure on small colleges, and the expansion of technology forced them to invest in equipment and staff in order to prepare their students well. As well, the competition for freshmen grew more intense, as graduating high school seniors demanded better tools for this accelerated learning. Questions were being raised about the viability of the small black colleges and whether they would survive.

Problems with the faculty came to the public's attention. Previously these problems were in-house matters and there was an attempt to resolve them within the structure of the College. The missionary commitment that had been found at Tougaloo and other historically black colleges was eroding with the rise of black administrations and the opportunities for black educators to find employment elsewhere. Many of those hired to fill these positions did not share the allegiance to the college mission that had previously been present. Faculty members became impatient with the quality of students and the poor conditions present on campus. This impatience was viewed by some to have racial overtones. In his daily journal, Ernst Borinski had voiced concern that some white professors had lost the sense of commitment. He felt that one should examine all the variables present at the institution, accept changes made in the world around them, but keep in mind the commitment to the institution and the principles for which the institution stood.

The crucial issues that faced Tougaloo, as the search for a new president began, were immense and called for a person who had many different skills. The College needed a visionary who would direct the institution toward the new century both in the development of a unique educational program and in the construction of new facilities that could handle these programs. The College needed an administrator who could select a capable faculty and staff and ensure the maximum productivity from their efforts. The College needed a diplomat who would be able to form links with the community and others who were willing to help Tougaloo. Above all, The College needed someone who could raise substantial amounts of monies, for existing programs and new expenditures program.

THE SHAKIR ADMINISTRATION / 1988-1994

In January 1988 the Board of Trustees named Adib Akmal Shakir as the person to succeed Blake to the presidency of Tougaloo College. A native of Hampton, Virginia, Shakir came to Tougaloo after serving as the Vice President of Academic Affairs at Bethune-Cookman College in Daytona Beach, Fla. In his thirties, Shakir was a graduate of Morehouse College and received his doctorate from Florida State University in Tallahassee. He had served for five years at Bethune-Cookman first as a professor of psychology and then as the second highest official on campus. He brought to Tougaloo youth, the tradition of the black college, and the vision to change the fiscal makeup of the college as well as alter its academic directions.

Of all the challenges Abdid Shakir had to meet, one of the most daunting was to prepare the college for an evaluation visit by a team from the Southern Association for Schools and Colleges. The self-study, which preceded the visit, was already underway and the process gave Shakir an opportunity to look at the institution and to advance those changes that he deemed necessary to make Tougaloo more viable. The self-study became his talisman. In his inaugural address, Shakir laid down the gauntlet for students, faculty and administrators. He called for a renaissance on the campus. This renaissance would reflect on the traditions that had made Tougaloo an outstanding institution. It would energize all those who supported Tougaloo to work toward solutions of the many problems that plagued the campus. Finally, it would rededicate all segments of the Tougaloo family to making the College stronger. Reflecting, renewing, rededicating became the theme of the self-study for Tougaloo and the watchword for the Shakir administration.

SHAKIR AND ACADEMIA

Despite the many problems during the Blake administration, Tougaloo continually maintained a high academic standing. In many areas the academic performance of the College, considering its size and lack of resources, caught the eye of educators throughout the country. The institution had benefited from its close association with Brown University. Its science and math programs produced doctors and career scientists who were taking the lead in their profession. It had sent many candidates to prestigious law schools and other graduate programs throughout the state and nation. As it had done throughout its history, Tougaloo was in the forefront of developing black leaders throughout the nation. Among its other positives, the College was able to maintain this high level of academic accomplishments in part because it continued to attract some of the best minds from high schools throughout the nation. In 1989 the U. S. News and World Report had recognized the College's performance in this area in its fourth "America's Best College Survey." The journal acknowledged that the school should be noted for its stringent and highly selective requirements for admission.

The accolades given to the College made President Shakir even more determined to continue the tradition of academic excellence. He realized that the academic team he chose to direct this mandate had to reflect his concern determination. He chose as his Vice President for Academic Affairs, Bettye Parker-Smith, a Tougaloo graduate. Parker-Smith had been noted for her activism both in women's affairs and in the civil rights movement. She was above all dedicated to the continued academic growth of Tougaloo. She chose Mabel Henderson as her assistant. Henderson, too, was a graduate of Tougaloo and was committed as well to academic excellence. She aspired to maintain the standards that she had known when she was a student on the campus. These two set out to carry out the mission of the new administration—maintain high academic standards and prepare Tougaloo graduates for the coming century.

One of the first efforts on the part of the administration was to streamline the curriculum so that it would meet the needs of the student body and fit within the resources of the institution. After she took office, Parker-Smith immediately initiated a review of all courses. In the past, courses were created and allowed to exist even though the demand for them had faded. This could cause a demand on the College's finances since the structure of the course had to be maintained. Some of these courses were allowed to die after the review was completed. Others that were in the same situation, were popular, but had no funding were allowed to exist as a search was made for adequate funding. Gerontology, a social science course focusing on the maintenance of the aging, was a prime example. It had been started through Federal funding, but when this had ended, it became necessary to seek funding elsewhere so that the course could continue. Funding was found and the course continued.

Many areas in the academic world demanded close attention by the administration and faculty. One was that of writing. The faculty had resolved that all Tougaloo students should develop effective writing skills. Through support by the Andrew Mellon Foundation and other benefactors, a writing center was established for those students who had difficulty in developing adequate writing skills. The center later became known as the John Munro Writing Center, in honor of John Munro who had left his post as the Dean of Students at Harvard College to become an instructor in writing first at Miles College in Birmingham and later at Tougaloo. Munro dedicated much of his career outside of Harvard in developing models for writing to be used at black colleges.

In addition to the Munro Writing Center, the faculty dedicated itself to the principle of writing across the curriculum. Guided by Dr. Ben Bailey and supported by the Mellon Foundation, the efforts of this program were directed toward an emphasis on writing in every discipline. All professors were expected to have their students complete written assignments in the respective courses. Each department also required that its students take a writing intensive, upper-level course in the respective discipline. The total process of this continual experience in writing was to culminate with the completion of a major project within the discipline at the end of the senior year. The emphasis on writing was buttressed by the graduation requirement that a student pass an English/Writing Proficiency Examination.

Since their students have come from diverse and sometimes poor backgrounds, nearly all black colleges have had to maintain some form of remedial program. Tougaloo was no exception. These programs were meant not only to get its freshman students adjusted to college life but also to determine where there were deficiencies and move quickly to correct them. Tougaloo had maintained an *Invitation to Learning* program within the curriculum, but in the spring of 1988, this course was eliminated from the curriculum for lack of funding. In the spring of 1989 a new general education program was adopted. In addition to the regular courses that were a part of the general education program, a two-semester seminar named *Mission Involvement* was adopted. *Mission Involvement* was a required course that sought to give students a sense of shared destiny and acquaint them with the various forms of learning that they would encounter on a college campus and in life. In time all freshmen (named freshpersons by Parker-Smith and her associates) came under a freshman division that in time was elevated to a full academic division labeled the Comprehensive Academic Resources Division (CARD). The CARD faculty was not only responsible for advising freshpersons in class schedules, the selection of a major, and other academic matters but also in their progress in life adjustment. One of the high points of a Tougaloo freshperson's year was the ceremony aptly named "the rite of passage," as students showed their readiness to take on the responsibilities thrust upon them.

The College continued to increase or maintain the efforts to support students to adjust to the rigors of learning, both on and off campus. The college maintained a series of special programs whose principal mission was to provide academic support to all students who could encounter academic difficulties. The Student Support Program was devised to help students on campus; the Upward Bound Program had been in existence on campus since 1968 and was designed to provide motivation and training for those who wanted to continue their education beyond high school. Further assistance was given to the community through Education Talent Search, a program that provided information regarding a variety of post secondary educational opportunities, student financial assistance, and academic assistance for students in central Mississippi.

Tougaloo expanded its commitment to the community by insuring that its students would be involved in the community on some level. The College required its students after the 1992-1993 academic year to fulfill a community service requirement. This service was to be rendered after the sophomore year and could be performed in any agency that seeks to serve the social needs of the community. The emphasis by Tougaloo on community service was nothing new for Historically Black Colleges and Universities. Since their founding, service to the community has been a part of their foundation.

One issue that caused great concern among many was the call by some in the administration for a more Afrocentric view of the world. Dr. Shakir himself called for the inclusion of the Afrocentric view as opposed to the Eurocentric view, which had dominated the American educational horizon since the founding of the Republic. The controversy between Afrocentrism and Eurocentrism had been prevalent in many academic circles since the seventies. It may have had its formal beginning with the call for black power, started with the Meredith Freedom March of 1966. The controversy may have gained its impetus with the growth of theories that developed in many Black Studies programs found at many colleges—both black and white—throughout the nation. Many felt that the Afrocentric position would introduce a new form of separatism within the nation. Others felt that the whole concept lacked a historical foundation. The debate had its supporters on both sides, from all racial groups. At Tougaloo the support for Afrocentrism had the support of both Parker-Smith and Shakir. It was evident in parts of campus life-particularly in campus speakers, student garb, and even in the crowning of Miss Tougaloo in 1990; yet the concept did not totally invade the curriculum or maintain a foothold within the classroom. Some paid lip service to the concept, while others saw Afrocentrism as a part of the historical mission of the black college.

The controversy did not hamper the faculty from taking a multicultural initiative teaching, research, and writings and to upgrade their skills in the classroom. The faculty became involved with Jackson State University in the international program and in the Mississippi Consortium for International Development MCID. In addition, the faculty took the lead in developing a relationship with Guyana in South America. This was done through the Partners for the Americas Program. Through the Bush Faculty Development Grant, the faculty set out to hone their skills in a variety of areas that would influence their teaching in the 21st century. This was done through exploratory methods on campus and the development of faculty seminars through symposiums of Historically Black Colleges and Universities. Other foundations as well as the Bush Foundation aided the faculty in broadening their outlook. The PEW Foundation and the New York University Faculty Network were some of the valuable contributors in this area. Brown University continued in its efforts to give Tougaloo faculty the opportunity to strengthen their skills through summer learning experiences and semester involvement on the various campuses.

Through these many efforts, the Tougaloo faculty improved their ability to make changes and produce stellar students from "diamonds in the rough." One of the most exciting programs that developed stellar students was the Mellon Scholars program. Aided by the Andrew Mellon Foundation, students who displayed unique ability were designated as Mellon scholars. Jerry Ward, the Lawrence Durgin Professor, was one of the most ardent supporters of the program. He saw that it would give these students the opportunity for academic experiences that they did not have previously. They received close mentoring by faculty members, were asked to travel to various conferences throughout the nation, and required to produce original works. Dr. Stephen Wheelock, a former Mellon Scholar went from this experience, to gain his PhD from Brown University, to his appointment as an assistant professor of philosophy at Pittsburgh University. Wheelock was among many of the scholars who had an impact on the academic world.

The expansion of lecture programs and the development of the Humanities Festival further amplified the academic life of the college. Speakers and performers from around the world visited the campus to share their ideas, to demonstrate their talents, and debate controversial issues. The Humanities Festival became one of the highpoints of activities during the year and established the contact between Tougaloo and accomplished artists and craftsmen.

STRATEGIC PLANNING AND ECONOMIC INDEPENDENCE

Shakir felt, as many others who had taken over ailing institutions, that the key to survival had to be strategic planning. All areas of the College's life had to be structured in some manner. Each sector had to work toward its own particular goal, yet that goal had to be shared by the institution. The planning was to be coordinated and directed from a central office. The College was a business and had to be treated as such.

In order to develop control and accountability, Shakir developed what he called the Vice Presidential form of administration. This administrative model moved senior administrative officers up a level. Bettye Parker Smith maintained her ranking as the Vice President for Academic Affairs. The Dean of Students Dr. Larry Johnson, moved up as the Vice President for Student Affairs. The Business Manager, Ms Lillie Woods, moved up as the Vice President for Fiscal Affairs. The Director of Institutional Advancement, Delores Bolden-Stamps, moved up to become the Vice President for Institutional Advancement. Shakir maintained that these "promotions" were actually a step to streamline his administration. He saw it as an attempt to get the institution ready for the 21st century.

The development of this form of administration appeared to be an unnecessary increase in expenses. Some members of the faculty saw the development as an unusual growth of the administrative component of the campus at the expense of faculty salaries and faculty development. Shakir knew he had to hold down expenses, eliminate the deficit, and increase revenues. He found excessive expenditures, with a great deal of waste in various departments. He saw the new form of administration as a way to accomplish these ends. His plan was to manage closely the activities of the College and to hold people accountable. His early plans were to cut one faculty position from each division and to personally review every purchase requisition of $500 or more. As well, Shakir developed an aggressive program of recruitment. This program raised the enrollment from 650 in 1988-89 to over 1,100 for 1992-1993 academic year. The increase in enrollment helped to bring the College more money and reduce its deficit.

THE ECONOMIC DEVELOPMENT CORPORATION

An important step in stabilizing the financial affairs of the college had been made at the Board of Trustees' meeting in May 1989. At this meeting the Board voted to affirm its intention to explore the possibility of a wholly subsidiary Economic Development Corporation which would immediately absorb the debts of the College and pursue plans for land development. This independent corporation won local support as it was envisioned that the corporation would lease portions of land to businesses seeking to establish operations in the Tougaloo area. Not all of Tougaloo's land had been given over to the campus. A large section of the land was available for the tremendous growth that had been going on in the Jackson-Madison County communities. Early in 1991 the United Church of Christ released to Tougaloo through the Economic Development Corporation the title to the land, and this procedure enabled the administration to use the land in its pursuit to stabilize its financial position through debt retirement.

This was the procedure that was initiated by Lillie Woods. Woods proposed that certain parcels of the land should be used as collateral to pay off outstanding notes to certain of the major banks within the community. In addition to the activities of paying off the debt there were continuous activities to have some of the debt forgiven either by private agencies, like Brown University or some of the community banks like Deposit Guaranty (now the AmSouth Bank).

The banks welcomed the opportunity. For among other issues the banks wanted to participate in the development of this area. The planning was for Tougaloo to be a full partner with the business community in the development of this area. This could only be done with the help and sanction of the business community. Shakir felt strongly that Tougaloo could not survive without the support of the local business community, and he aimed to show them that he was serious about making corporations partners with the college.

There were other issues associated with the fiscal activities involved in this planning and the use of the land. The College cooperated fully in the development of the County Line Road project. This was a project that has been aimed at the restructuring of West County Line road in order to make the highway safer and more reliable to the noticeable increase in traffic. The business community had been behind the project since when it was completed it should have increased business in the surrounding area. In addition to the County Line Road Project, the Economic Development Corporation was looking for other developers to assist in its planning for the use of its land. The Corporation saw clearly that the growth of its influence in land development in the overall Tougaloo area, and it envisioned that in the future that the college would be the catalyst in the construction of a Southern Heritage and Arts Center.

The use of Tougaloo's land was not the only issue considered seriously by the EDC. It became the means whereby the College involved itself in many different aspects of the community. The administration restructured its endowment portfolio and moved the management of its funds to locally based financial institutions. The Tougaloo art collection became an important commodity in the task of planning for fiscal stability. In order to enhance Tougaloo's prestige, negotiations started in an effort to bring the United States Post office to a campus location. The administration through the EDC became actively involved in the Farish Street Restoration Project, an activity that enhanced its prestige with the community. Once the home of the assassinated Medgar Evers had

been turned over to Tougaloo, the EDC with the help of the state legislature became actively involved in developing the residence into a Civil
Rights Museum and managing the property as a private entity.

Despite the plans put forward by the Economic Development
Corporation, Shakir recognized that the College had to be placed on a
firm financial footing through aggressive fund raising. In 1991 he
launched a 25 million-dollar capital campaign for new construction,
faculty raises, and an expansion of the academic programs. This was to
be the most ambitious financial undertaking in the history of the school.
Despite objections from many who thought that the goal was too unre-
alistic for a school of the size of Tougaloo. Shakir would not be dissuaded, for he saw the eventual growth of the institution. He had many supporters throughout the nation. Issac Byrd, a 1973 graduate from the
College, and a highly successful lawyer in Jackson, promised to give as
much as he could in order to spur the effort toward the goals laid out by
the administration. Reuben Anderson, a 1967 graduate, and another
prominent Jackson lawyer and State Supreme Court Justice, echoed
Byrd's sentiments and announced during the Founder Day ceremonies
in 1991 that 10 million-dollars had already been pledged.

THE REBUILDING PROGRAM

President Shakir would consistently tell the story of his first visit to
the Tougaloo campus in 1988. At that time the infrastructure was in
such poor condition he debated whether it would be wise for him to
take the position as president. Very little had been done for some time
on the campus to preserve the older buildings or to build new ones. The
last new buildings prior to his arrival had been the library and dormitory complex constructed in 1971. Beard Hall the third oldest building on
campus was in such disrepair that it was declared unsafe for habitation
and was closed. The Yazoo clay that had caused Beard Hall to be unsafe
claimed Woodworth Chapel as well. The standing dormitories had been
consider eyesores since their construction in 1971 and were not the type
of structures that would be inviting to incoming students.

The initial stages of rebuilding the campus were embodied in the
planning process. An elaborate plan was outlined by Shakir and his
staff. It included the establishment of buildings, walkways, and over-
head canopies that flowed from the Zenobia Coleman Library. The cen-

terpiece was to be the Southern Arts and Cultural Center, a building dedicated to the study of the arts, literature, and culture of the South with an emphasis on the contributions of underrepresented ethnic groups. This was a plan for the future. More immediate were rebuilding needs that would keep the College viable. These changes would be brought about through a mixture of sound financial planning, community support, and a response to events in the community, state and nation.

One of the first major projects began in 1989 when Tougaloo joined forces with the United States Department of Labor and MINACT, Inc., a minority business firm in Jackson, MS. Their task was to renovate Judson Cross Hall, a women's dormitory that had been built in the 1940s and not seriously renovated since the 1960s. Students who were training in the Department of Labor's Job Corp program did the construction work. This was highly unusual since Job Corp students train and work only in their region. With MINACT providing supervision for the trainees, with Tougaloo buying the materials, and with the Department of Labor paying other outstanding bills through Federal grants, the Job Corp trainees came to Tougaloo from many different regions to participate in the project. This cooperative effort gave new life to an old building.

Revitalization and renovation took place in other buildings. Galloway Hall underwent extensive renovations in order to improve its foundation and to correct other problems. Galloway was a victim of the plague of Yazoo clay and the building had become unstable. Ballard Hall, the second oldest building present on campus, underwent extensive renovation so that it could continue its task of being the music and fine arts building on campus. Holmes Hall that had been renovated under the Blake administration underwent some changes to make room for extra office space under the expanded academic program.

The Mansion and Woodworth Chapel were in dire need of extensive restoration. The Mansion, the oldest building on campus, was enduring many problems, resulting from its age and overuse as the administrative center. In 1991 Manuel Lujan, the U. S. Interior Secretary, announced that the Mansion had been chosen by the Interior Department as one of the 11 projects from Historically Black Colleges to be renovated through the use of corporate funds and private donations. The proposal was to save some of the more historical buildings on black campuses. The Mansion had been on the National Register of Historical Places

since the 1970s but the college had not been able to raise the necessary
funds to begin the renovation project. James Curtis Smith, the Director
of the Economic Development Corporation estimated that the cost of
restoring the Mansion to its original glory would cost up to 5 million
dollars. The appropriations for the renovation were delayed in Federal
red tape, and it was not until 1993 that the U. S. Senate agreed to spend
10 million dollars on projects at the historically black colleges.

The problems with the Chapel were another story. While the
Mansion had architectural history in its favor, the Chapel did not. It
was a plain church built in 1901 like many of the other churches that
were built during that period. Woodworth Chapel, however, was considered by many to be the "soul of the college." Its restoration and
preservation were essential. Continuous appeals went out for the financing of its restoration. Goals were made and some were reached, architects were hired and consultants made recommendations for changes,
yet there was little movement toward the restoration of the structure.
Nature and the ever-present Yazoo clay served to damage it more so that
in 1991 it was closed.

On January 25, 1991 a fire broke out in the historic Berkshire
Cottage. This cottage had been built by students in 1884 and had been
used as a dormitory up until the late 50s. Within the hour the 97-year-
old structure had been nearly gutted by the flames. The near total
destruction of this historic site was a tragedy since it was one of the oldest buildings on campus and had been serving as offices for the TRIO
program. It fitted well within the old architecture of the college and it
was doubtful that the structure could be replaced in its original form. In
time the building was demolished and the Berkshire building was built.
This building—referred to, as a cottage as its predecessor had been-was
a one million-dollar replacement and was the first major construction
project on the campus in nearly twenty years. The " cottage" contained
classrooms and the humanities learning center. Two 50 room dormitory
wings flanked the learning center. In an unusual move, Shakir
announced that part of the expense of building the new construction
was to be borne by the sale of bricks from the foundation of the old
Berkshire cottage. Henry Drake, President of the Tougaloo Alumni
Association, welcomed the opportunity to buy a brick from the old residence. He remembered fondly that his wife had lived there as a student
at Tougaloo.

CIVIL RIGHTS REVISITED

The hostility present during the sixties and seventies had been replaced by a calmness which showed blacks and whites willing to accept the legal changes. School systems had been legally desegregated, and the predominantly white colleges and universities had been integrated. Hotels, restaurants, and other social gathering areas were integrated as well. Blacks were winning elections for many political offices throughout the state and in 1988 captured a seat in the U. S. House of Representatives–the first since Reconstruction.

TOUGALOO AND THE STATE SOVEREIGNTY COMMISSION

Since Tougaloo had been in the forefront of much of the civil rights activity in Mississippi, it was only natural that the College would become an integral part of the events that would take place in the late 80s and throughout the 90s. There were activities by former participants, analysis by writers and historians, films and documentaries, and continual conferences and reminisces. For Tougaloo the excursion into the history of the Civil Rights Movement in Mississippi actually started with the debate over the opening of the official papers of the State Sovereignty Commission. The papers would depict the role of this governmental agency to thwart the freedom of the people of Mississippi in general and black people and their sympathizers in particular. The papers would reveal many things, but one thing was clear—Tougaloo was one of the Sovereignty Commissions primary targets.

The Mississippi State Sovereignty Commission had its beginnings shortly after the *Brown vs. Board of Education* decision. This decision, which declared segregated education unconstitutional, could be considered the watershed of what would later be known as the civil rights revolution. In 1955 in Memphis, Tennessee, a meeting was held with prominent white politicians to plan what action was to be taken to forestall integration in the South. The plans to forestall integration in Mississippi focused mainly on intimidation, legal control, and resistance any efforts by the Federal government to interfere in the affairs of the state. Governor J. P. Coleman and the Mississippi Legislature created a commission that was to protect the sovereignty of Mississippi from all acts of encroachment by any person, group, or organization. This particularly applied to the Federal government. The commission had the power to investigate, subpoena, and imprison those who resisted its authority. The commission came into being as McCarthyism gripped the nation as a whole, and anyone who disputed the authority of the government was a communist or a communist sympathizer. In Mississippi this meant that anyone who favored integration or who spoke out against the rabid segregationists that controlled the state was either a communist or a fellow traveler.

The Commission paid scant attention to events at Tougaloo during the early years of its existence. The Mississippi hierarchy had never favored the College. State laws demanded rigid segregation of the races in all areas of life, and the College officials at times fretted over little racial issues on the campus that could attract the attention of legal authorities and bring grief to many on the campus. Until recently the campus was basically isolated from the larger community and few cared what transpired as long as the students abided by the status quo. Tougaloo had struggled with racial problems since it's founding, causing some administrations to acquiesce and develop a harmonious relationship with the community. It had tried in every way to abide by the standards of the South even though some of them clashed with the principles of the American Missionary Association.

In the 1950s, however, race relations in the state had deteriorated greatly. Rev. George W, Lee of Belzoni was slain for registering to vote and encouraging others to do likewise. Lamar Smith of Brookhaven was slain on the courthouse steps in that southern Mississippi town for daring to oppose an incumbent judge. No crime in Mississippi caught the attention of the nation more than the slaying of Emmett Till, the fifteen-year-old youngster from Chicago who was purported to have made advances to a white married woman. This crime gripped the nation and people saw Mississippi as an oppressive entity. Lynching, unlawful imprisonment, brutal beatings, and a general reign of terror reinforced this opinion. The Sovereignty Commission became one of the enforcement arms of this oppression.

In 1961 a group of Tougaloo students entered the Jackson Municipal Library-a building reserved for whites only-and began to do research. The demonstration was peaceful and the students were hurriedly rushed into police cars and placed in jail. Myrlie Evers-Williams was to later characterize this incident as the beginning of a new day for race relations in Mississippi. The shock of this student demonstration in Mississippi, the presence of integrated meetings at St. Andrews Church, and efforts by Ernst Borinski to bring Tougaloo students into contact with students from the all-white Millsaps was an affront to the governmental authority. They in turn caused the commission to look even closer to what was going on at the Tougaloo campus.

Following the demonstration by the Tougaloo Nine, things did not get better in the state. In May 1961 the state faced the continuos incursion of civil rights activists who entered the state to combat racism. In 1962 the Reverend R. L. T. Smith, a close friend of Tougaloo was encouraged to run for Congress against John Bell Williams, and James Meredith was admitted to the all-white University of Mississippi after an all night rioting. In 1963 Medgar Evers, the NAACP Field Secretary was assassinated; John F. Kennedy who had been detested by many white Mississippians was assassinated; and the Congress of Federated Organizations (COFO), a loose federation of Civil Rights Groups in Mississippi, sponsored a "Freedom Votes" campaign. Tougaloo was in the midst of and affected by many of these events that occurred in Mississippi. Personnel of the College either actively participated in them, provided haven for many of the demonstrators, or verbally supported the efforts to bring democracy to Mississippi. The papers of the Sovereignty Commission clearly show that the agency waged an intense campaign against the College.

The Commission's campaign against Tougaloo was meant to show that Communist had infiltrated the College and that its staff, students, and alumni were intent on destroying the state of Mississippi. Their primary focus appeared to be on faculty members, administrators, and others who spoke at the College; yet extensive files were kept on students and graduates who were actively engaged in civil rights activities throughout the state. Erle Johnston, a newspaperman from Forest County, MS was appointed the Director of the Commission in 1963. He considered himself to be a moderate when it came to racial matters, but he was a firm believer in a segregated society and the Southern way of life. In addition, he was an ardent fighter against what he considered to be a communist threat. For Johnston the point appeared to be clear that the campus had become a haven for Communist sympathizers who used the racial unrest to bolster their own causes. Every attempt possible was made to place societies that had communist links with specific individuals on or who visited the Tougaloo campus. He attempted to link some organizations, such as the Southern Conference Educational Fund, the Student Non-Violent Coordinating Committee, and the Southern Christian Leadership Conference directly and indirectly with Tougaloo.

In order to substantiate the claim that the College had been infiltrated by members of the Communist Party or/and their sympathizers, Johnston and his colleagues sought information from every source. They used an article from the Jackson Advocate, a black news publication, to accuse the Southern Conference Educational Fund of being a Communist front organization and using blacks for the advancement of the ideas of the Communist party. The Sovereignty Commission papers went on to show that many on the Tougaloo campus—including A. D. Beittel, the president—had close ties to the Southern Conference Educational Fund, Inc. and its predecessor, the Southern Conference for Human Welfare. In a lengthy memorandum to Allen Dulles, the Director of the Central Intelligence Agency, Erle Johnston described many of the organizations that he considered to have been infiltrated by Communists and a threat to domestic security. Among the organizations named he included Tougaloo and noted that Tougaloo College had become a college of agitation instead of a college of education.

The Commission maintained a daily log of activities that took place on the campus. Speakers such as Dr. Ralph Bunch and Martin Luther King Jr. were noted as being on campus and their remarks recorded for future analysis. Printed articles that criticized the segregated society of the South were analyzed and catalogued. The commission became interested in a work-study project that allowed some students to work for some of the "front organizations" while maintaining the student status. Lectures were monitored, and any criticisms by professors of the state or country were duly noted. Foreign visits by friends of Tougaloo—such as that of Clarice Collins Harvey to Ghana—became a part of the ledger material. A close note was made of the changes within the Tougaloo catalogue to detect any drift away from the staid conservative nature of things advocated by the Sovereignty Commission and its allies. This series of logs clearly showed that the Commission followed every movement on the campus and reported this to the administration and the legislature.

Students came under close scrutiny. Although many Tougaloo students were branded as being radical and out of control, some students were investigated more than others. Of the many students who appeared in the papers, Joyce and Doree Ladner, Colia Lidell, Anne Moody, and Hollis Watkins stand out because of the intensity which the officers of the Commission maintained their scrutiny in their daily logs. They spent two days in Hattiesburg investigating the background of the Ladner sisters. All they found was that their community held the two in high regard, were highly principled young ladies, and had graduated at the top of their high school class. Colia Lidell was heavily involved with the North Jackson NAACP Youth Group and her association with John Salters, whom she had approached to organize planned demonstrations. Anne Moody and Hollis Watkins became national figures because of their activism. Moody became the celebrated author of *Coming of Age In Mississippi*, a work that depicts her life in Mississippi as she fought against racial oppression. The story and work of Hollis Watkins lives on. He was never deterred by the Sovereignty Commission's efforts to break him, nor would he let anything stand in the way of his drive toward human and civil rights.

As for the faculty, Ernst Borinski, the prominent sociologist, was constantly investigated. His close association with the faculty at Millsaps, his frequent comments about the racism present in Mississippi, his insistence on holding interracial seminars both at Tougaloo and Millsaps and his Germanic Jewish background made him a prime target of the Commission. Rev. Edwin King, the Tougaloo Chaplain, and John Salters, a sociology professor at the college, came under very close scrutiny as well. King and Salters had been instrumental in organizing the young people as an active NAACP group. The Mississippi authorities sought to brand them as outside agitators. This was difficult to do for Edwin King, since he was born in Vicksburg, MS. He was considered as an anomaly and a traitor to his white heritage. John Salters was another matter.

In 1961 John R. Salters, a mixed Native American accepted a position as professor of sociology at Tougaloo. Salters did not come to Tougaloo to participate in the civil Rights Movement. He admitted that he had no basic commitment to the cause and was not particularly enthused about the College itself. He did consider Mississippi to be the most repressive racial complex in the United States and he was a social organizer. When some of the members of the North Jackson NAACP youth group asked him to organize their efforts to protest discrimination and racial oppression, he became a force in the movement. The organization that Salters spearheaded with others became known as the Jackson Movement. It was associated with the NAACP and had as its goal integration of many facilities and used as its primary weapon the boycott of local businesses. The group was only marginally successful in this endeavor, but the public nature of their demonstrations brought national publicity. One of the most celebrated pictures of the Civil Rights Movement shows Salters and two others from Tougaloo being harassed during a demonstration in 1963 at the Woolworth lunch counter.

Ed King, the former Tougaloo chaplain, fought hard to keep the Sovereignty Papers closed to the public. His resistance surprised many, even some who had worked with him diligently during the time of the movement. Rumors abounded as to why king was so adamant in trying to keep the papers closed. Many felt that he had participated as a spy with the Commission. This does not even seem logical. King had suffered personally for his activities, with even his life endangered with a near fatal automobile accident. As the case against the release of the Sovereignty papers neared its conclusion, King revealed more of his reasons for his opposition. He alluded to the viciousness of the Commission in its spying activities on innocent people and how that spying found its way into the final papers. He did not see the need to open old wounds, to damage people's lives, and to cause dissension, merely to titillate the public's curiosity. He was a man of principle who had taken a stand with his friends during turbulent times.

On January 27, 1995, Erle Johnston died. In his last years he had made every attempt to atone for his years as the Director of the Sovereignty Commission. In 1989 he had published *Mississippi Defiant Years, 1953-1973*. This work was a chronology of the efforts by the state to defy integration and to control its citizens—both black and white. The work gained widespread praise from those who had been involved in the struggle on both sides. In this writing, Johnston admitted many of the things that had been done to prevent blacks from attaining their full rights. He felt that these acts had been done to preserve the Southern way of life. Tougaloo had been featured in many different instances in this work, particularly the clash that Johnston had had with A. D. Beittel.

As a show of good faith and atonement for past deeds, Johnston came to Tougaloo to explain his attitude and the rationale for his actions. In return Shakir asked him and Constance Slaughter-Harvey to form a team to preserve the Civil Rights Papers. This was a unique ending for Johnston in that he and Slaughter-Harvey were natives of Forrest Mississippi. Slaughter-Harvey had gone to Tougaloo, became the first black female graduate from the University of Mississippi Law School and was an activist in all causes for human dignity. Erle Johnston had taken the route that he had taken because he believed strongly in the old Southern Culture.

THE CIVIL RIGHTS HOMECOMINGS

The administration actively pursued and structured some of the historical study of the college's involvement in the movement. A series of conferences were held from 1990 through 1994, and since Tougaloo had been the safe haven for the movement, it was natural that it should be the site for the conferences. In 1990 an anniversary conference was held to celebrate the organization of the Mississippi Freedom Democratic Party. Doree Ladner, a Tougaloo graduate spoke of the fears that the original participants had in 1965 in contesting the power of the Democratic Party in the South. In 1991 a Freedom Riders Commemorative Conference was held on campus. Featured speakers at that conference were Congressman John Lewis and James Farmer, both significant warriors in the struggle for human and civil rights.

In 1994 there was a Mississippi Freedom Summer Homecoming that brought together those that had participated in those events which changed the direction of the whole movement. Albert Gordon, a collector of African art and a former Freedom Rider, recalled his stay at Tougaloo in 1964. He had then been arrested for demonstrating. After spending time in jail, he said that he hurried to the Tougaloo campus where he found safety and solace. He felt that he could never forget the kindness shown to him by those on the campus. At the end of the conference he gave the College a sizeable collection of African art. He said that this was the least he could do for the kindness shown to him thirty years previously.

In 1991 an anniversary conference was held to recall the efforts of the Tougaloo Nine. Three of the Tougaloo Nine, Ethel Sawyer Aldophe,

James Bradford, and Meredith Coleman, recalled their experiences not only during the sit-in at the library but the ensuing controversies with the police. The remaining six, Alfred Lee Cook, Ameenah Omar, Janice Jackson, Albert Lawrence, Jeraldine Hollis, and Joseph Jackson sent messages of inspiration and hope to the campus. Meredith Coleman summed up the feelings of the group when he said that what they had done was done because it was within their rights as citizens of the city of Jackson.

Gladys Noel Bates, class of '44 was honored for her courage in suing the state of Mississippi in 1947 to get equal pay for black teachers. Bates and her husband were fired from their jobs and ostracized by the total community. They moved to Denver, Colorado where they continued their efforts toward equality and educational progress. In 1994 the Gladys Noel Bates club was formed in the Division of Education and she became a model for students who had chosen education for a profession.

Dr. Aaron Henry, one of the leaders of the Mississippi Freedom Democratic Party, longtime president of the NAACP, an advocate for racial equality in all areas of life within the state, was honored with an honorary doctorate from the College. Dr. Henry, a pharmacist by training, was determined to preserve the history of the movement during his lifetime and thus had all his personal and public papers placed in the Tougaloo College Archives. Henry was known to be very helpful in the establishment of the Southern Medical Committee for Human Rights, an organization started by Dr. Robert Smith—a Tougaloo graduate.

Constance Slaughter Harvey, one of Tougaloo's most distinguished graduates was honored for her part in the legal system of Mississippi. Harvey, who was not granted her diploma because of her activism during the crisis at Jackson State University in 1972, was the first black graduate from the University of Mississippi Law School. She went on to become the Assistant Secretary of State and an advocate for equal justice for women and minorities. Harvey was to become a College trustee and a firm supporter of the Rueben B. Anderson Law Society.

None of the civil rights stalwarts made as much an impression on the college as Myrlie Evers-Williams, the widow of the Medgar Evers, the slain NAACP leader. She had moved to California following the death of her husband, but had maintained a close contact with her family and friends in Mississippi. In the late 1980s Mrs. Evers-Williams launched a crusade to reopen the case against Byron Beckwith, her husband's alleged assassin. As she proceeded in this effort, friends and officials at Tougaloo supported Evers-Williams. Medgar Evers had been very closely involved with Tougaloo, John Salters and the NAACP Youth Group. They were two of the principal persons linked to the College that the Mississippi authorities sought to brand as outside agitators. Myrlie Evers –Williams sought to expose all the racism associated with the attacks and murder of Medgar Evers and succeeded in helping to bring Beckwith to trial and conviction. In 1993 she donated the Evers homestead to Tougaloo. The college on its part sought and gained the financial support from the Mississippi Legislature to convert the home into a museum.

These conferences and visits by distinguished warriors were good for Tougaloo and its student body. Throughout the nation and the world, writers, historians, film producers, and news analysts began to look at the College to gain some perspective on the social movement that had so changed the face of the nation during the sixties. Tougaloo students were enthused to see their College in the midst of media attention. They felt proud of the part that the College had played in these events.

SHAKIR LEAVES THE COLLEGE

In October 1994 Tougaloo College President, Abdid Shakir, announced that he was resigning the presidency to accept a post as an administrator with Cassidy and Associates, a high profile consulting firm. It had been rumored for some time that Shakir would leave the college. He had been very prominent in national affairs, and had been chosen as an advisor on Historically Black Colleges and Universities for President Bill Clinton. In his announcement that he was resigning, Shakir noted that the College had experienced a renaissance during his tenure and a bright future lay ahead. One of the trustees applauded the young president's accomplishments noting that he had turned the school around during a very crucial time in its history. Another trustee spoke of his being a tremendous asset to the school but that the school would survive and build on the foundation that he had built.

Shakir had many accomplishments during his tenure, one of the most important being that he had led the College into higher visibility on the national scene. Under his leadership, Tougaloo had developed a strategic planning process, renovated buildings, built a new living learning center, increased student enrollment, and increased faculty salaries. In

1992 the College received a $100,000 gift from the prestigious Knight Foundation in recognition of his outstanding leadership and energy in directing the college. It was evident to many that Shakir had rescued the College at a period when there was a crisis in leadership. The College was viable, but many problems lay ahead. Shakir's successor would face as many problems as he had when he took over the presidency.

THE LEE ADMINISTRATION / 1995-2001

In June 1995 the members of the Board of Trustees chose Dr. Joe Lee as the next president. Lee came to the presidency after serving as the Vice President for Academic Affairs/Provost at Talledega College. He had earned his Bachelor of Arts degree in general biology at Talledega. He went on to earn a masters and doctorate in educational administration at Miami University in Ohio. His resume emphasized skills in fund raising, public relations, alumni affairs, and student housing. Lee presented a picture of a man who was humble, empathetic and comfortable with people. The trustees expressed confidence in his ability, and Reuben Anderson summed up the feelings of the Board when he noted that Lee understood the mission of the College.

Lee demonstrated that he did understand Tougaloo's mission and background. He noted at his appointment that the Board of Trustees had some of the finest minds among black people in the country. He spoke highly of the College and the position it was in as he assumed the presidency. Lee had come from the AMA tradition, being a graduate of Talladega, one of Tougaloo's sister institutions. He proudly emphasized his rural roots, his days in Alabama cotton fields, and his struggles for human equality. He understood clearly the need to involve the community in the operation of the college and understood the role of black heritage in setting his direction. Dr. Edgar Smith, who had served as interim president, said of the appointment that he knew he was leaving Tougaloo in good hands.

LEE AND ACADMIA

When Joe Lee became President of Tougaloo, the College still maintained its high academic standing. Dr. Bettye Parker Smith had left in late 1994 and accepted a position as a consultant at a prestigious firm in Florida. Mabel Henderson, her assistant, had taken over temporarily as the Vice President for Academic Affairs. She prepared for the coming of the new president. Throughout her term as the Acting Vice President, Henderson emphasized the importance of adhering to Tougaloo's mission and upholding the academic standing that the College had forged in the past. When Lee was appointed, no decision had been made as to what direction he would take with regard to choosing a permanent Vice President. Henderson, herself was ambivalent about assuming the position. She confided to her friends that she had dreams about the future of her alma mater, but she yearned for retirement and time with her grandchildren. She worried too about the conflicts developing in the faculty along racial lines and the lack of commitment on the part of many of the faculty to the mission of the College. Her dreams for a greater Tougaloo were not to be realized by her. At the beginning of the 1995-1996 academic year, Mabel Henderson suffered an aneurysm while talking to the parents of new students. She died soon after.

The void left by Henderson's death was one that Lee never seemed to adequately fill during his tenure. For a time he delayed in making a choice, being content to rely on the advice of senior faculty members. Finally, he chose Dr. Lewis Jones of Minnesota as the Vice President for Academic Affairs/Provost. On the surface, Jones appeared to have all the credentials to lead the faculty. He was young and energetic, with some experience in administration. He was a scholar who saw learning as a salvation for society. He was attuned to the demands of the growth of technology on campuses and saw the need for Tougaloo to accelerate its efforts to advance in this area. For a period Jones enjoyed the confidence of the faculty and appeared to provide the leadership that the College needed to maintain its position in the academic world.

Jones, however, had great difficulty in communicating with people. He was not, as well, attuned to some of the cultural differences within the College as opposed to those he experienced in Minnesota. Jones wanted to move swiftly to correct some of the deficiencies that he had found in the academic area, particularly with regard to faculty credentials and development. His basic intention was to remove unapproved faculty members, some had been at the College for some time. These intentions were admirable, yet Jones' methods were tactless. This approach angered many, and when his unyielding attitude extended to other areas of the academic world, Joe Lee decided not to renew his contract. Without a permanent Vice President for Academic Affairs, Lee muddled through academic problems, being content to rely on interim personnel or depend on the council of deans.

The faculty in general paid little attention to the administrative problems as far as its own governance was concerned. Already badly splintered, and without effective leadership, the academic divisions drifted further into their own respective worlds. For its part, however, the faculty did make contributions in many different fields. Steve Rozman of the Social Science Division became known as an authority on international affairs as well as domestic politics. Rozman was the catalyst behind the Partners for the Americas Program on the Tougaloo campus, and was directly responsible for establishing close contacts among Tougaloo and many different agencies in Georgetown Guyana. He and Johnnie Mae Gilbert, of the Art Department, were responsible for bringing folk artists from Guyana to the campus. Gilbert had already established her reputation as a premier artist in Mississippi. Her shows generated widespread interest throughout the state, and her showing of the *Slave Narrative* brought her accolades from the art community.

Jerry Ward, the Lawrence Durgin professor, was very prolific in his scholarship. He served as the creator and editor of the anthology, *Trouble the Water*, a compilation of 250 years of African-American poetry. Ward served as well as the national leader in the study of the contributions of Richard Wright to world literature and was the major contributor to the *Richard Wright Circle*. For this effort he gained international acclaim within literary circles. One of Dr. Ward's greatest contributions was his participation as co-director in the Delta Oral History Project. This project which looked at the participation of grass roots people in the Delta during the Civil Rights Movement was one of the most important historical projects done in the State of Mississippi. Jerry Ward's contributions to the Humanities, the world of literature, and the academic world in general set the standard not only for the Tougaloo faculty but also for all professionals in the world of Higher Education.

LEE AND THE BUILDING PROGRAM

President Joe Lee made the improvement of buildings and ground his top priority when he assumed the presidency of Tougaloo. He explained that it was very important to maintain a good appearance in order to attract new students and benefactors and give the impression that the College was alive and well. He faced three major problems in this area. First, he had to complete the projects that had been in various stages under the previous administration. Second, there was the ever-continuing need for renovation and maintenance. Third, there was the pressing call for new facilities to meet the needs of a changing world and incoming students. Of the unfinished projects, the most pressing were the building of the George and Ruth Owens Health and Wellness Center, the renovation of the Mansion, and the renovation of Woodworth Chapel.

The George and Ruth Owens Health and Wellness Center was a project that had grown from a 6 million dollar Federal grant to establish a comprehensive health care center to service 17 counties in central Mississippi. The Center would contain offices, a gymnasium, health clinics, and would be the seat for studies on the health and wellness of black people from this region. The plans for the Center would as well change the facade of the campus. The row of faculty houses that had stood for many years and served as a home for married and single faculty members would be demolished to make way for parking facilities for the Center. The playing field, where Tougaloo teams of years gone by had played for the glory of Tougaloo, would be uprooted to make way for the major structure and its surrounding area. The most controversial change that would take place as a part of the entire project was the building of a new gate.

Many objected to the moving of the gate because of its historical symbolism. The gate was a part of Tougaloo's history. Tougaloo students had built it and for many of the alumni it was a symbol of safety. Constance Slaughter-Harvey voiced her concern. The gate represented to her the entrance to a safe haven, once she was inside of the gate away from the hostilities of the greater society that threatened her life and dignity. The gate was a symbol of courage and tolerance. Martin Luther King had come through the gate as he led the last leg of the Meredith March for Justice in 1966. Those who had struggled for social justice and those who had entered the gate for an education to end the stranglehold of poverty and ignorance had looked at the Tougaloo gate as the entrance to a new life. The concern about the moving of the gate was not really necessary. It had, since its initial construction by Tougaloo students represented an entrance to the sanctity of Tougaloo's campus, yet it had been moved before. The building of the new entrance, the final construction of the George and Ruth Owens Health and Wellness Center, and the mere clearing away of the brush and trees, which in a way hid Tougaloo from the rest of the world, was symbolic in its own fashion. It represented a new day for the College and reflected its new responsibilities to the community at large.

The success of the construction of the Health and Wellness Center Project was a great boon to the Lee administration. It appeared that the unfinished projects of the previous administration would be completed and many of the problems dealing with facilities would be resolved. The Congress had appropriated the money for the restoration of buildings for many black colleges, and the Mansion had been designated as one of those buildings. Although, the monies appropriated by the Congress may not have been sufficient to bear all of the costs, the administration felt that the difference could be made up through donations from alumni, friends, grant proposals and a grant from the United Negro College Fund. Announcements were made, architects were hired, tests were done on the area surrounding the Mansion, and an overall plan was discussed for relocation of administrative offices. The restoration of the building did not move forward during the Lee administration.

There may have been some concern in some quarters about the inability to meet these goals, but the concern was somewhat muted on the campus and in the community. This was not to be the same with regard to Woodworth Chapel. Intense pressure was brought on the administration to complete the task. Lucille Frazier, a 97-year-old graduate of Tougaloo voiced the concern shared by many of her friends and colleagues. She spoke of how she missed the Chapel services and how much the Chapel was a part of her life. There had been great publicity about the importance of the Chapel in the Civil Rights Movement and of the many dignitaries that had spoken there, yet the most important element was at times missed—the Chapel was the community church and was missed by many. Mrs. Frazier was like many others who wished that the Chapel would be restored so that she could worship there again before she died.

In 1999 the repair of the Chapel began in earnest. The U. S. Park Service made an award of $800,000 to the College for the restoration. In 1999 the cost of restoring the building was estimated to be $1.4 million, but nature had taken a terrible toll on the building. Contractors found the damage to be extensive, predicting that the cost may exceed the previous estimate. With the College facing a $600,000 debt to meet the initial estimate, there was general apprehension about moving ahead with the final stages of the restoration. Supporters were adamant that the project should proceed. Many benefactors had already pledged and given thousands over the years. John H. Bryan Jr., chairman and CEO of the Chicago based Sara Lee Corporation, and a native of Mississippi, had given $100,000 to the cause, yet his gift was one of those outstanding ones. There were many that had given what they could in order to see the project completed. Lee would leave the College before these two unfinished projects were completed. There was, however, still much to be done on campus.

Any planned progress in maintenance and restoration were interrupted by a series of accidents. In December 1997 a natural gas explosion heavily damaged Kinchloe Hall, the College's science building. The explosion came at a time when students had left the campus for the Christmas holidays and the staff was not present in the building. This in itself was a Godsend since the classrooms that were damaged were consistently used for small and large classes. Should the explosion have occurred at another time there would have been casualties. The resulting fire had gutted a new computer center and a 100-student classroom, and the explosion had knocked out bricks, broke windows and damaged the building's foundation. The incident was a great financial loss to the College since the chemistry laboratories had just been brought up to standards, the physics laboratory had been renovated and the lecture hall had been restored. President Lee did not know immediately whether he would fix the building or construct a new one, but Richard McGinnis, Dean of the Natural Sciences, was sure that a new structure would replace the destroyed parts of the building. McGinnis' predictions came true. Because of a dedicated effort on the part of friends and supporters a new structure was built in the place of the destroyed lecture hall, and the damage parts of the science building were prepared. Over a period of time, students were able to return to a familiar environment for their science and computer classes.

A severe thunderstorm brought down the massive oak tree that had stood on the campus since its founding. Eaten away by disease, it fell victim to the winds. Again the gods smiled on the College. The accident happened on the Good Friday following the explosion at Kinchloe.

Trailers had been placed in the areas near Kinchloe to be used as class-rooms. One of these trailers had been placed directly in the path of the falling oak, and had not students and faculty been away from the campus for the Good Friday-Easter holidays there would have been serious casulties. For some, the passing of the great oak was ominous since it had stood for so many years as a near guardian for the campus; but for others it was the end of the journey for the massive oak. The old had died; newer trees would take its place.

The rebuilding of Kinchloe was a success story for the College, a landmark was preserved. There were other landmarks that vanished from the campus and new ones appeared. Beard Hall was finally demolished. Every effort to rebuild the stately structure that had stood on campus since 1898 failed. The structure had become a hazard to pedestrians and thus was torn down. The old walks that had been a part of the Tougaloo landscape for decades became a hazard for many and were replaced. A new playing field was built on the north end of the campus—a gift from donors. The facade of the campus gradually changed as Lee worked diligently to make his building program a success. A new lighting system was put in Coleman Library allowing more light for study and reducing overall electrical costs. Ballard Hall underwent repairs in order to accommodate a growing theater program. Plans were being made to convert Brownlee Hall into a museum in order to find a place for the College's Art. Brownlee Hall's use as a gymnasium was no longer necessary since the newly erected George and Ruth Owens Wellness Center. A new dormitory was being built in order to improve the residential facilities for students and thus improve recruitment.

LEE AND FINANCE

Since its founding in 1869, Tougaloo has faced one financial crisis after another. Sometimes the situation has been so critical that it was doubtful the school would survive. At other times the monies were not adequate to meet all needs but enough to keep the College opened and functioning. Actually, Tougaloo's situation was no different from other small, poorly endowed colleges. Their existence had basically depended upon three components: student tuition and fees; government grants and contracts; and private gifts and grants.

President Lee and his administration clearly understood the process and they were organized to maximize the resources of the College as much as possible. There was no suffocating debt to stymie growth, and if the three basic components held firm, then the College could meet its goals. In addition, there was tremendous growth around Tougaloo. A small shopping center had been erected close to the campus property and other parcels of land surrounding the campus were being developed for motels, garages, and small restaurants. Lee pointed out how important these developments were for Tougaloo's advancement and financial security. He stated that it would be a grevious error if the College did not take advantage of the present growth circumstances. He had chosen Nayyer Hussain, a trained economist, as his Vice President for Fiscal Affairs and DeJoyce Morgan, a development officer from Texas, as his Vice President for Institutional Advancement. He continued the close relationship with the Economic Development Council as an essential component of economic growth. The prospects for the continued development that had occurred under the previous administration appeared bright.

Lee encountered some of the same financial problems that have continuously plagued small colleges. The first problem was that of student enrollment. From the 1996-1997 academic year through the 1998-1999 academic year there was a significant slump in student enrollment, dropping from 1019 students in 1995-1996 to 890 in 1998-1999. This of course meant a comparative fall in income from student tuition and fees. The shortfall could have possibly been handled if there had been an increase in government contracts and grants and an equally significant increase in private grants and gifts. There were, however, no critical increases in government grants and contracts or in private grants and gifts. This overall decline in revenue placed the College in a difficult position, with a deficit to be handled, projects that had been planned put on hold, and monies taken from one project to meet the financial needs of others.

In these circumstances there were widespread accusations. Many attributed the decline in enrollment to the continuous increase in student tuition and fees. Others pointed to the lack of technological advancement on the campus compared to that of other campuses of comparative size. Lee's critics pointed to what they conceived as his poor fund raising skills and the ineptness of the Vice President for development. A look outside of the campus pointed to lack of government funds for Historically Black Colleges and Universities that was attributed to the control of the Congress by Republicans and the difficulties of the President. Without a doubt there was some truth in all of this, but the crucial fact was that Joe Lee as President of the College failed to deal effectively with the budget crisis. As fiscal problems mounted he appeared to remain passive in making decisions as to make the necessary changes to handle these difficulties. There was an increase in bequest and memorials during the 1999-2000 academic year, yet they were at times restricted funds and could not be applied to the continuous running expenses of the College. The aggressive need to pursue grants from private foundations and corporations appeared to be lacking, and the contributions from these two entities fell almost 50% during this same period. The College appeared to be facing a return to the same financial difficulties that had plagued it since its founding.

There were some changes made in order to avoid another crisis and move the school ahead. At the beginning of year 2000, members of the Board of Trustees became more involved in the operation of the school. Issac Byrd and Dennis Sweet led the way with substantial contributions and pledges. Reuben Anderson continued his strong backing of the *Reuben Anderson Pre-Law Society* with continued involvement and financial support. Jane Hearn continued her involvement in the development of the Tougaloo Art Colony, but she became committed to the evolvement of an art museum in Brownlee Hall. Beverly Hogan, a former trustee and the first director of the Owens Health and Wellness Center, took over as the Vice President for Institutional Advancement. Hogan's appointment was meant to bring some improvement in national fund raising, the development of a vision for the College, and an acceleration in institutional development

Many former proposals were revised in order to thwart another financial crisis and to increase the revenue of the College. One was the use of the land. Tougaloo set aside 400 of the 500 acres of the campus for commercial development. The emphasis was again on the growth of the area around the campus. One proposal was to lease 160 acres for the construction of a hotel and golf course. The idea of the golf course had been proposed once as the College campaigned to be the site for the building of Jackson's telecommunication center. When Tougaloo lost this campaign, the ideas of developing the land languished. The entrepreneur who proposed this new plan had a spotty record in developing golf courses throughout the country, and it seemed that although an agreement had been signed, this would not bring immediate financial benefits to the college. Leroy Walker, the McDonald's Magnate in the Jackson area, and president of the Board of Trustees, appeared somewhat skeptical about the new plan.

Whatever changes were to be made in the financing of the College, something had to be done. The revamping of the infrastructure in order to accommodate the advances in technology was costing the College dearly. Strong criticism had been levied on the administration about its continued reliance on government grants. The Title III program had become a crutch on which the College had come to rely on for needs. Tougaloo was not alone in its reliance on Title III. Many Historically Black Colleges needed the program in order to keep current with changes that were being made in the academic world. Yet all too often these colleges sought Title III monies for one project only to use it for others, or for merely the survival of the institution. Tougaloo had not reached that point as yet, but it was becoming clearer that the school had to develop a program where it had to develop an income based on "hard currency" rather than the whims of others as "soft currency" grants inclined to do.

LEE LEAVES TOUGALOO

In February 2001, President Joe Lee announced that he would be leaving Tougaloo at the beginning of the 2001-2002 academic year. He expressed his love for the institution and his gratitude for having the opportunity to serve it as its leader. Lee assured his listeners that he was not being forced out of his position but had been anxious to search for new challenges in the field of higher education. He expressed his fondness for Mississippi, as well as for the professionals that he had met in the six years that he had been at Tougaloo.

Lee's announcement did not come as a total surprise to the community. For over a year there had been rumors that he would be leaving. These rumors were coupled with a general dissatisfaction with his leadership in the areas of academics and development. Members of the Board of Trustees had been evasive about publicly criticizing him, and in October 2000 they had granted Lee a renewed contract for an unstated period of time. After his announcement, some of the members of the Board expressed appreciation for his skills and were sure that he would be a success wherever he went. Leroy Walker announced that a search for a new president would begin immediately with the hope that the new president would be chosen by January of 2002.

Lee's leaving was not new among presidents in higher education. As he was stepping down, throughout the state of Mississippi the position at the helm of a number of colleges was changing. Being a college president was a very difficult position. Being a college president at a small college with limited resources was even more difficult. In his parting words, Lee noted the changes in the position. He saw the presidency as more of a CEO, demanding a person with many skills in order to be effective in the modern era. Those who were proficient in these skills could be effective as a school leader, those who did not possess them could not move the institution forward.

THE FUTURE

In September 2001, the Tougaloo College Board of Trustees named Dr. James H. Wyche, Assistant Provost at Brown University as the Interim President of Tougaloo. Wyche was known nationally as a competent administrator, educator and researcher. As a part of the Brown-Tougaloo exchange team he had for years been closely associated with the College. Upon his announcement, Wyche maintained that he would build on the accomplishments of President Lee and wanted to be seriously considered for the position as the permanent President of the College.

If Wyche were to get his wish and become the 13th President of Tougaloo, it would indeed be a good omen. His vision for the College joining with other major institutions in providing learning resources for blacks and other minorities was in line with the mission of the American Missionary Association. At the beginning of the twentieth century, the AMA saw its continuing mission to provide training for teachers- to teach the children of former slaves in order to create an educated population. In 2001 the State of Mississippi faced an ever-growing shortage of teachers, particularly black teachers for an undereducated population. Despite the many gains that it had made in developing students for other careers, many on the staff saw the ever-present need to accept the challenge placed on the College since 1869. Tougaloo planned again to train teachers for the State and Nation.

Letter from the Interim President

I AM HUMBLED BY THE OPPORTUNITY to lead this historic institution at this strategic period in its history and I feel privileged to share a few thoughts with you at such an early time in my new role at Tougaloo College. I am, however, eager to become more involved with the exciting adventure that I have had the opportunity to sometimes observe from afar. There is an excitement at Tougaloo like nowhere else. I have experienced it on a number of occasions when visiting the campus. Interestingly, I have sometimes been a part of that excitement, such as events associated with the Leadership Alliance in which our students and faculty have been active participants. Recently, we celebrated the Silver Anniversary Celebration of Tougaloo's MARC program which has had a profound impact on the number of African American research scholars over the past two decades. It was also my pleasure to participate in the Capacity Building Conference sponsored by the Jackson Heart Study, and of course, I have enjoyed participating in the Natural Science Colloquium.

There are just a few issues that I would like to point out at this time. First, let me extend congratulations on your reaccreditation. Thanks to the Board of Trustees, we are moving forward with the Presidential Search. In no uncertain terms, the College is making visible progress in the enhancement of its infrastructure and in the restoration projects that will further strengthen valuable campus resources. Tougaloo is pleased to welcome aboard the many new students who have begun the next leg of their educational development. We especially commend those freshmen who received Presidential Scholarships and other honors. We are also proud of those May graduates who are now furthering their education at prestigious institutions throughout the nation.

Tougaloo is approaching the celebration of its founding 132 years ago. We already know that we must build on the College's rich heritage, strengthen the capacity of our resources, and yes, define and begin fulfilling a bold future. I do not have to remind you that Tougaloo is a healthy, interesting and intimate college and we hope to remain that way. It's what helps define and retain our uniqueness. But we do have challenges...we must strengthen the endowment, increase and stabilize enrollment, and move forward with plans to restore, renovate and expand campus facilities. I am both challenged and encouraged by what I see at Tougaloo. It is truly a caring community. These qualities are what I believe enable this institution to focus on enhancing its academic programs. Faculty and staff commitment and strong alliances with alumni and friends have yielded programs of distinction and many accomplished graduates. The compelling intellectual and cultural environment has been evidenced in the progress you will read about in this issue and in the successes of all the great scholars, physicians, artists, teachers and other leaders who comprise alumni throughout this nation. That's why you are able to build such a distinguished Hall of Fame. Faculty and alumni must continue to reach back and help the rising generation of student scholars.

This is truly a season of remembering, rededication, and renewal. It is a time for recalling the vision of the illustrious Founders who established a sacred and consoling place here, to assist in the development of young people for full participation and constructive service in our world. We must remember at this time of celebration that all else we do here will not be remembered for long. What we do for our students, and what these young people go on to do in their lives will affect generations yet unborn.

Sincerely,
James H. Wyche

Epilogue II

Tougaloo Continues to Make a Difference

TOUGALOO COLLEGE CONTINUES to positively impact the life of Mississippi and the nation. What a difference two decades make: Her faculty and staff increasingly acquired a national reputation inspite of the periodic fluctuating fiscal and physical development and growth of available resources. The College maintains and fulfills Her mission as a premier liberal arts college by educating thousands of sons and daughters of families across the nation. Each year around sixty per-cent of the graduates enroll in graduate and professional schools. Their achievements provide a sense of intellectual happenings around the campus.

A significant program in the George and Ruth Owens Health and Wellness Center is the Tougaloo College Family and Community Violence Prevention Program (FCVP). The FCVP is a cooperative ven-ture of community-based partnerships including Walton Elementary, parents, higher education institutions, private enterprises/corporations, local civic and community-based organizations, law enforcement and government agencies. The Health & Wellness Center's mission is to pro-vide primary and preventive health services and educational services that address the environmental, behavioral and social well being of the community. Its services are targeted to 26 counties throughout central Mississippi and the Delta region.

Tougaloo's faculty, men and women of vision, continue to produce leaders in education, medicine, law, and community service.

309

Alumni listed in Tougaloo Annals as college and university presidents include:

Dr. Matthew Burks '51 – Arkansas Baptist College; Little Rock, AK

Dr. Bettye Ward-Fletcher '70– (Acting) Jackson State University; Jackson, MS

Dr. Joyce Ladner '64– Howard University; Washington, D.C.

Dr. George A. Owens '41 – Tougaloo College and LeMoyne Owens College; Memphis, TN

Dr. Oscar A. Rogers, Jr. '50– Arkansas Baptist College and Claflin College/University; Orangeburg, SC

Dr. Joann R. G. Boyd-Scotland '72– Denmark Technical College; Denmark, SC

Dr. Edgar E. Smith '55– (Acting) Tougaloo College

Dr. Walter Washington '48– Utica Junior College; Utica, MS and Alcorn State University; Lorman, MS

Dr. Joffre T. Whisenton – Southern University; Baton Rouge, LA

A number of graduates hold administrative and professional positions at colleges and universities. Some examples are Bettye Parker Smith '61, Provost at Dillard University. Dr. Eugene M. Deloatch '59 remains the long-time Dean of the School of Engineering at Morgan State University. Other representatives of educators and professionals are cited in the College's Hall of Fame (1992-2001), see Table 3.

Dr. Margarette D. C. Butler '64 earned the Ph.D. degree in Environmental Science from Jackson State University. She retired from the Jackson Public Schools. Butler is presently affiliated with the Jackson Branch of the American Federation of Teachers. She is also a lead abatement consultant and motivational speaker.

Dr. Jesse C. Lewis '53 is currently serving as Senior Scientist Emeritus, in the Research Participation Program at the National Science Foundation (NSF) in Arlington, VA. Prior to this position of honor and recognition, he was Program Director for the Centers of Research Excellence in Science and Technology at the NSF. He graduated from Tougaloo College High School, earned a B.S. degree in Mathematics from Tougaloo; M.S. degree in Mathematics Education and M.A. degree in Mathematics from the University of Illinois; and the Ph.D. in Numerical Analysis/Computer Science from Syracuse

University. Lewis was vice president for academic affairs at Norfolk State University. He is considered as the father of computer science in Mississippi in recognition of his pioneering work from his computer laboratory at Jackson State University.

Lewis's sister, Ethel L. Lewis Rogers '50, is also a graduate of Tougaloo College High School. In addition, she finished the College's Daniel Hand School as did hundreds of other elementary students. Ethel earned the M.S. in Science Education at the University of Washington, Seattle, WA; and the Specialist in Education degree from Jackson State University.

After graduating from Tougaloo, she served three years as an X-ray technician Wave in the US Navy.

Ethel retired from the Jackson Public Schools. As first lady of Arkansas Baptist College and Claflin College/University, she taught mathematics, science, and computer science, and established a nontraditional student program which enabled adults to earn college degrees.

The 1997 Alumni Directory of the College revealed substantial alumni representation in 52 principal career fields from accounting to utilities and volunteering. Thus in every walk of life can be found Tougaloo graduates contributing to the quality of community life.

The College remains a major producer of professional educators, which is the result of faculty members such as Dr. Corrine Anderson, the College's Acting Provost and former Dean of Education. Dr. James Coleman '61 champions athletic and health education at the College and throughout the region. The Superintendent of the largest school district in Mississippi is Dr. Jane Sargent '67.

Hall of Fame (Table 3)

In 1992 the Tougaloo College Hall of Fame was established to recognize supportive alumni who have distinguished themselves in their profession. A special ceremony is held each October as a part of the College's Annual Founders' Day Celebration.
The selected members of the Hall of Fame listed below reveal the level of contribution Tougaloo alumni is making throughout America.

Year of Induction

Art and Entertainment

1992

Mr. Robert Honeysucker '64 earned the Master of Music degree in Voice Performance from Miami University, Oxford, Ohio. A baritone opera singer, he has thrilled audiences and critics alike from Melbourne, Australia to Portland, Maine, with this voice and musicianship.

Mr. Walter Turnbull '66 cited as a "musical genius," has performed in more than fifteen operatic roles is the founder and director of the Boys Choir of Harlem.

Mr. Aaron F. Boddie, Jr. '42 earned a B.A. degree in Drama Theater from Queens College in Flushing, NY. He played parts in more than seventy feature films. He also played in every New York based soap operas except one. He is noted for theater, television, and movie training and performance.

Athletics

H. M. Thompson '36 earned the Master of Science degree from Atlanta University and the Master of Arts in Teaching from Cornell University. He was noted for his teaching of mathematics at the public school and college levels. His leadership involvement in Boy Scouting, Prince Hall Masonry, the Mississippi Teacher's Association, and Tougaloo College was noteworthy. He was inducted posthumously into the Tougaloo College Hall of Fame.

Mr. Leroy T. Smith '47 received the Master of Arts degree from Northwestern University. One of Mississippi's most accomplished coaches, Smith has been honored by having the newly erected sports complex at Lanier High School names for him.

1995

Captain Jerry Howard Lewis '62 earned the Master's degree in physical education from Tennessee State University. Lewis acquired the title of Captain in the U.S. Navy Reserve. He was a long time coach at Tougaloo. He sought to shape the individual character of his basketball players.

Robert Moreland '62 earned a Master's degree in physical education from Indiana University. He received national acclaim as the all-time winningest basketball coach in Texas Southern University history.

Business

Mr. Thomas R. Sanders '33 received the first Master's degree from Jackson State College. He is a renowned educator and true humanitarian who assisted homeless and handicapped citizens in Hollandale, MS. Sanders sponsored Sanders Estate, a subdivision designed for elderly people. His business achievements are legion.

Mrs. Thelma Sanders '46 was inducted into the Tougaloo College Hall of Fame posthumously. She initiated the highly successful Tougaloo College Thelma Sanders annual Christmas Dance. Sanders millinery and apparel shops were established in Jackson.

Rev. Eddie Irons '60 received the Master's degree in Educational Administration from Memphis State University. He also studied at Memphis Theological Seminary. Irions was a mathematics teacher and an administrator in the Memphis city schools, and was the founder and owner of V-8 Brake Service and Auto Sales.

1996

Mr. Percy Moss '59 earned the M.A. degree from Chicago state University and Governors State University. Moss has taught extensively about entrepreneurship and how to achieve an education which will enable one to be better able to gain employment. He developed Trey's Movers, Inc. to incorporate these ideas.

Dr. Frank C. Dickey '66 earned the Master's of Art degree in Guidance and Counseling at Trinity College in Washington, D.C. He took doctorate course work at Virginia Polytechnic Institute. Dickey is the owner and manager of Frank C. Dickey Catering Company in Washington.

314 The View From Tougaloo

Communication

Mrs. Czerny Stewart Neal '42 served thirty-six years with the Agency for International Development in Washington, D.C. She devoted considerable time to informing the College alumni about the Eagle Queen through the Telephone Committee.

1993

Mrs. Lucille Moman Fraser '25 received her entire education at Tougaloo College. She taught in the Jackson Public School and assisted in the L. Zenobia Coleman Library. She is the widow of Lionel B. Fraser, Sr.

Mrs. Charlene Smith Cole '54 received the M.S.L.S. degree in Library Science from Syracuse University. For 41 years, Cole has been a faithful and dedicated employee of Tougaloo College. She has empowered the Tougaloo College family through library technology and other forms of communication.

Community Service

Mrs. Gwendolyn Nero Loper '52 a Jackson, MS social work pioneer, received a Master's of Social Work degree from Howard University. Loper impacted professional social work throughout the state of Mississippi through her pioneering affiliation with the Mississippi Department of Public Welfare, the V. A. Hospital, and the School of Social Work at Jackson State University.

Mrs. Gladys Noel Bates '42 an early civil rights activist, resides in Denver, Colorado where she taught and was an administrator in the public schools. Bates is praised for her role as plaintiff in the Gladys Noel Bates vs. State of Mississippi Teacher Pay Equalization Suit.

Mrs. Annie Seaton Smith '45 received the Master of Science degree from Colorado State University. A life-long member of the Tougaloo Town Community and the College, she knows every citizen and has promoted the interest of every community agency and organization.

Mr. H. T. Drake '50 earned a Master of Science degree in Secondary Administration/Guidance Counseling from Indiana University. He was an organizer of the High School Activities Association for black high schools in Mississippi. His educational and political involvement is extensive.

Mr. Wilbert L. Smith '57 a Chicago community activist, earned the M.A. degree in Business Administration from Governors State University, University Park, IL. His outstanding achievements are in the area of public and community relations, and teaching mathematics and physics. He is a program planner and researcher at Cook County Hospital, Chicago, IL.

1998   **Mrs. Theester Allen Carter '52** earned the Master of Arts degree from the University of California, Beckley and the Master of Library Science in Library Science. She is active in Church work and the Tougaloo College National Alumni Association in Jackson. Carter established the Bruce C. Allen Student Loan Scholarship Fund.

1999   **Mr. Robert Donald,** Columbia South Carolina resident, is a graduate of Tougaloo College Daniel Hand School, and he attended Tougaloo Prep High School where he achieved Athlete of the Year. Donald is a strong supporter of the Tougaloo National Alumni Association. He organized the Donald family into a club to lend financial support to Tougaloo College.

1999   **Mrs. Carrie L. Davis '74** earned a Master's degree in Education from Northeastern University in Chicago. She is the owner of Carrie's Designer Fashions, a successful clothes boutique. In addition, she is an avid community leader and Headstart administrator in Chicago.

Education

1992   **Dr. Eugene M. DeLoatch '59** earned the Ph.D. in Bioengineering from the Polytechnic Institute of Brooklyn, NY. He serves as the first dean of the School of Engineering at Morgan State University in Baltimore, MD.

1993   **Dr. George A. Owens '41** earned the Master of Business Administration from Columbia University of New York. He was the first African American President of Tougaloo College. Since 1984, he has been President Emeritus of Tougaloo College.

1994   **Dr. Walter Washington '48** earned the Ph.D. from the University of Southern Mississippi in Hattisburg, MS. He was the President Emeritus of Alcorn State University.

1995

Dr. Arvarh E. Strickland '51 earned the Ph.D. degree in History at the University of Missouri at Columbia where he is a Professor of History Emeritus.

1996

Mrs. Barbara Thompson Hilliard '62 received the M.A. degree in English from Jackson State University. She improved English instruction in the Jackson Public Schools International Baccalaureate Program.

1996

Mrs. Ruby L. Jackson '60 earned the M.S. degree from Chicago state University in Elementary Education and Library Science. She is the reading coordinator at the Chicago Randolph Magnet School.

1997

Dr. James Coleman '61 earned the Ed.D. degree from the University of Mississippi in Health, Physical Education, and Recreation. He is the Director of Athletics and professor of Education at Tougaloo College.

1998

Dr. Matthew Burks '51 earned the Ed.D. degree from the University of Virginia in Educational Measurement. Retired chairman of the Education Department at Mississippi Valley State University, he is currently treasurer of Tougaloo College National Alumni Association.

1999

Mrs. Johnnie P. Hamilton '60 was inducted into the Tougaloo Hall of Fame posthumously. She earned the MS degree from Syracuse University, and was principal of Ben Franklin Middle School in Chantilly, VA.

2000

Dr. Joyce A. Ladner '64 earned Ph.D. degree from Washington University in St. Louis in Sociology. She was the first woman president of Howard University from 1994 to 1995. Presently she is a senior fellow in the Government Studies Program at the Brookings Institution.

Government and Law

1992

Rev. Honorable Corneal A. Davis '17 attended John Marshall School of Law and Moody Bible Institute. A distinguished lawyer and clergy, Davis served more than thirty years as a member of the Illinois General Assembly, and nearly a decade as a commissioner for the Board of Directors of the city of Chicago.

1993   **Rep. Bennie Thompson '68** received his Master's of Science degree in School Administration from Jackson State University. Claflin University awarded him the Doctor of Laws Honorary degree for his public service in Mississippi and the U.S. Congressional House of Representatives.

1994   **Attorney Edward Blackmon, Jr. '71** earned the Juris Doctorate degree from George Washington University Law School. He represents District 57 in Madison County, in the Mississippi House of Representatives. Blackmon is the senior partner with the law firm of Blackmon, Blackmon, and Evans.

1997   **Mrs. Sophie G. Jackson '39** For 18 years Jackson was the first postal clerk and later postmaster at the Tougaloo, MS post office.

1998   **Attorney William J. Rice '75** earned the Juris Doctorate degree from the Thurgood Marshall School of Law of Texas Southern University. Rice is a practicing attorney in Houston, Texas.

2000   **Attorney Constance Slaughter Harvey '67** earned the first law degree awarded an African American female at the University of Mississippi School of Law. A civil rights activist, she is honored with the Slaughter-Harvey Endowed Chair in Political Science/Pre-Law at Tougaloo College.

Medicine

1992   **Dr. Jessie L. Sherrod '71** received the Medical Doctorate degree from Harvard Medical School. Sherrod is a noted pediatrician specializing in infectious diseases and public health services administration in Los Angeles, California.

1993   **Dr. Robert Smith '57** received the Medical Doctorate from Meharry Medical College. He has impacted health services for African Americans throughout Mississippi. He has been the college campus physician and a civic leader in Jackson and statewide.

1994   **Dr. Aaron Shirley '55** a Mississippi medical pioneer, earned the Medical Doctorate from Meharry Medical College. He has "demonstrated unusual concern for the welfare of the citizens of Mississippi and the nation through his medical practice and his extensive involvement in a variety of health related programs and activities." As a result of his commitment, he received a Mac Arthur Fellowship Grant.

1995   **Dr. Theodore Jones '62** earned the Doctor of Dental Surgery from Howard University and a specialty in Orthodontics from Tufts University. He later earned the Master of Science in Teaching from Jackson State University. These experiences enabled him to provide pioneering leadership in the School of Dentistry at the University of Mississippi Medical Center.

1997   **Dr. Fred Charles Field '56** received the Doctor of Dental Surgery from Meharry Medical College. He also received the Master of Science degree in Operations Dentistry from the University of Michigan. A long time employee and administrator of Meharry, Field became dean of the school.

1998   **Dr. Doris Browne '64** earned her M.D. from Georgetown University School of Medicine, and the Master of Public Health from the University of California at Los Angeles. Browne is the Deputy for Medical Research and material Command in Fort Detrick, MD. She is a colonel in the U.S. Army Medical Corp.

2000   **Dr. Roy L. Irons '72** earned a Doctor of Dental Surgery degree from the University of Iowa College of Dentistry. He taught at the University of Mississippi School of Dentistry and served as a captain in the U.S. Navy.

Religion

1992   **Dr. Oscar Allan Rogers, Jr. '50** earned his S.T.B. and MAT degrees from Harvard University, one of the first Tougaloo College graduates to attend Harvard. He earned his Doctorate of Education from the University of Arkansas. He successfully combined service focused careers in pastoring churches and higher education administration. He is President Emeritus of Claflin University at Orangeburg, SC.

1993   **Rev. Effie Stamps Burford '48**, ordained into the Christian ministry, served as a missionary in Bangkok, Thailand for the Disciples of Christ denomination. She has served in almost every leadership role of the church. She retired from the Indianapolis Public School System after more than 30 years.

Science

1992

Mr. George W. Nauflett '59 is presently a senior research chemist in the synthesis and formulations branch of the Naval Ordinance Station, Indian Head, MD. His accomplishments as a research scientist are numerous.

1993

Dr. Edgar E. Smith '55 received his Ph.D. from Purdue University. Smith has held leaderships roles at several universities, Board of Trustees of Tougaloo College, and interim president of Tougaloo College.

1992

Mrs. Henriene Topps Martin '46 received the Master's degree from Howard University. Martin taught science at the elementary and junior high levels for 31 years. She received numerous appreciation awards for skill in teaching science in Washington, DC.

1996

Dr. Tophas Anderson, III '71 earned the M.S. degree and Ph.D. in applied mathematics/computer science from Brown University. His involvements as an engineer in industry and NASA's space station training are extensive.

2000

Dr. Sterling S. Thompson '67 earned the Doctorate in Food Science from the Michigan State University in the Department of Food Science and Human Nutrition. Thompson is Senior Manager, Microbiology and Services, at Hershey Foods Corporation in Harrisburg, PA.

Tougaloo College
Law School Graduates (Table 4)

Considerable credit for the betterment in the quality of life for Mississippians belongs to civil rights, political and social activists who received much of their spiritual motivation from Tougaloo. Many assisted in electing political leaders in towns and cities, thereby enabling Mississippi to rank at the top of the most state elected African-American officials in the nation: Congressman Bennie G. Thompson, who represents the second congressional district, is in his third term in the House of Representatives. He is also a trustee of the College. Representative of alumni who are mayors of towns or cities are Violet O. Brown Leggett '57, Gunnison, MS; and Norissa Norman '46, Mound Bayou, MS. Joining the rank of mayor is Dr. Mamie Locket '76, Hampton, VA.

Tougaloo has always been noted for the education of social and political leaders. The present leading, long-time Tougaloo professor of sociology is Dr. Stephen Rozman, Dean of Social Science Division. Graduates with political science and sociology degrees are contributing to society as judges, attorneys, and state legislation, other civil servants and just good citizens. Tougaloo graduates are known to practice law in at least 18 states. Attorney Charles Holmes is the inspirational professor for political campus activism. As director of pre-law program, he is noted for teaching his students love of the law and American freedom. He is vigrously counseling them to consider careers in aspects of law.

Listed in the College's annals as lawyers are listed below in Table 4.

Alumni who served in the Mississippi Legislature include Attorneys Edward Blackmon '71, Tomie Z. Green '73 (now a Circuit Judge), and Willie J. Perkins '75.

Name	Year	Law School	Address/Position
Abrams, James (Deceased)		Howard University	Jackson, MS/
Adams, Donovan D.	1996	Mississippi College	Jackson, MS/
Allen, Ms. Chynee	1996	University of Mississippi	Winona, MS /
Allen, Royce M.	1994	Mississippi College	Jackson, MS/
Allen, Shonda R.	1994	Michigan State	Lansing, MI/
Anderson, Rania	1997	University of Mississippi	Jackson, MS/
Anderson, Gwendolyn D.	1965	UT-Kent College	Chicago, IL/Atty., Anderson & Asso.
Anderson, Reuben V.	1964	University of Mississippi	Jackson, MS/Atty., Phelps, Dunbar, LLP
Bailey, Willie L.	1969	George Washington University	Greenville, MS/ Atty.,Bailey & Griffin, Miss. State Legislature

Barnes, Mandie Marie	1972	George Washington University	Seattle, WA/Atty.
Beard, Myrna L.	1981	Thomas Cooley Law School	Flint, MI/ Atty., Myrna L.Beard Law Ofc.
Bell, Ms. Angelina D.	1994	Univ of TX, Austin	Austin, TX/Law Clerk, Travis CountyDist. Attorney's Ofc.
Bennett, Patricia W.	1975	Mississippi College	Jackson, MS/ Professor, Miss. College
Blackmon, Edward	1971	George Washington University	Canton, MS/Atty., Blackmon & Blackmon
Blackmon, Kenneth Tyrone	1980	John Marshall Law School	Atlanta, GA/ Investigator, Marriott Corp.
Body, Catouche	1996	Mississippi College	Jackson, MS/
Bratton, Paheadra D.	1994	University of Mississippi	Jackson, MS/Staff, Miss. State Legislature
Byrd, Isaac	1973	Northwestern University	Jackson, MS/ Byrd and Associates
Carr, Oona	1993	University of Mississippi	Jackson, MS/ Analyst, Miss. State Legislature
Carr, Ms. Pamela	1992	University of Mississippi	Providence, RI/ Policy Analyst/ Lobbyist,Urban League
Carter, Ray Charles	1978	Thurgood Marshall Law School	Ridgeland, MS/ Atty., Law Ofc. Of Ray Charles Carter
Caruthers, Mrs. Beverly R.	1987	Thurgood Marshall Law School	Houston, TX/Atty., Law Ofc. Of Beverly R. Caruthers
Cole, Eddie M.	1944	University of Toledo	Toledo, OH/Atty. (Retired)
Davis, Morris C., Jr.	1967	University of Illinois	Springfield, IL/Atty.
Davis, Sherry L.	1973	University of Miami	Washington, DC/ Atty.
Dixon, Rodney		Mississippi College	Jackson, MS/
Dowd, Felicia	1997	Loyola University	Jackson, MS/
Drake, Derricka	1999	Drake Law School	
Dyson, E. Rudolph	1972	University of IA	Kingsville, TX/ Judge, Kingsville Municipal Court

Ekpo, Mweni U.	1995	Indiana University School of Law	Ft. Wayne, IN/ Assoc. Counsel, Lincoln Natl. Life Ins. Co.
Gibes, Robert	1976	University of Mississippi	Jackson, MS/ Bruini, Grantham, Crower & Hewes PLLC
Givens, Angela	1997	George Washington University	Detroit, MI/ Clerk, U.S. Court of Appeals
Goholar, Dwana	1998	University of Mississippi	Jackson, MS/
Goss, Tylvester	1983	University of Tennessee	Jackson, MS/ Atty., Davis, Goss & Williams.
Govan, Derwin B.	1988	University of Mississippi	Greenville, MS/ Staff Atty., Center of Constitutional Rights
Grandberry, John A.	1975	University of Wisconsin	Milwaukee, WI/ Staff Atty., Wisconsin Dept. of Work Force Devel.
Green Gloria J.	1975	University of Mississippi	Jackson, MS/ Special Asst. Atty. Gen. State of MS
Green, Reginald	1993	S.W. Texas Law College	Houston, TX/ Career Counselor, S.W. Texas Law School
Green, Tomie Z.	1973	Mississippi College	Jackson, MS/ Judge, Municipal Court
Grey, Angela	1996	University of Mississippi	Jackson, MS/
Griffin, Willie	1976	University of Mississippi	Greenville, MS/ Atty., Bailey & Griffin
Guyot, Lawrence	1963	Rutgers University	Washington, DC/ Politician, Washington, DC
Hairston, Kaaren M.	1970	UDC Law School	Jackson, MS/
Harrion, Reginald	1995	Mississippi College	
Harris, Greta		Mississippi College	Jackson, MS/
Harris, Gwendolyn	1985	Vanderbilt University	Huntsville, AL/ Patent Atty., Intergraph Corp
Harris, Mario D.	1993	Southern Law School	Clarksdale, MS/ Law Student

Harris, Sandra B.	1985	William Mitchell Law College	Jackson, MS/ Deputy, Hinds County Sheriff's Dept.
Harvey, Constance S.	1967	University of Mississippi	Forest, MS/
Holloway, Gwenzetta	1996	Mississippi College	Jackson, MS/
Holmes, Angela	1994	Loyola-N.O.	New Orleans, LA/
Huff, Petrina	1992	Tulane Law School	
Hutton, Dorissa	1997	Northern Illinois	Chicago, IL/
Hymes, Clark J.	1986	Howard University	Washington, DC/ Clark Jeffery Hymes Atty-at-Law
Jefferson, Carolyn C.		Loyola University-N.O.	New Orleans, LA/ Judge, Municipal Court
Johnson, Derrick T.	1993	SW Texas College of Law	Jackson, MS/ Pres., D. L. Johnson Consultants, LLC
Johnson, LTC Jesse J.	1939	American School Ext. Law	Hampton, VA/ Retired Military Writer
Johnson, Tarik	1998	University of Mississippi	Grenada, MS/
Jones, Frank C., III	1993	University of Mississippi	University, MS/ Graduate Student
Knott, Sanford E.	1986	University of Alabama	Jackson, MS/ Atty. Sanford Knott Assocs.
Langford, Walterine		University of Mississippi	Vicksburg, MS/ City Atty.
Mack, Greta D. Miss. State Legislature	1992	Mississippi College	Edwards, MS/ Staff,
Mangum, Thomas	1999	Mississippi College	
Martin, Precious Tyrone	1994	Univeristy of Mississippi	Jackson, MS/ Atty., Byrd & Assocs.
McPherson, Nicole	1995	University of Pittsburgh	Pittsburgh, PA/
Melton, Tesslyn	1994	Mississippi College	Jackson, MS/ Bruini, Grantham, Grower & Hewes PLLC
Monty, Robert A.		Mississippi College	Greenville, MS/ Partner, Court Network
Moore, George W.	1941	DePaul University	Fanwood, NJ/ Retired Supervisory Gen. Atty.
Myles, Linda M.	1978	New York University	New York, NY/

Nichols, George	1967	University of Mississippi	Canton, MS/ Atty-at-Law
Osborne, Solomon C.	1970	University of ILL-Campaign	Greenwood, MS/ Atty., Law Ofc. Of Solomon C. Osborne
Owens, The Hon. Denise S.	1976	George Washington University	Terry, MS/ Chancery Ct. Judge, 5th Judicial Dist., State of MS
Owens, CAPT LaRhonda R.	1992	University of DC Law School	Jackson, MS/ Atty-at-Law, JAGG
Peace-Jackson, Marva	1964	Georgetown University	Washington, DC/ Atty. Advisor, U.S. Dept. of Labor
Peaches, Sandra F.	1976	Georgetown University	Lanham, MD/ Dir.-Bus./Regulatory Affairs Prince George Cnty.
Perkins, Willie J.	1975	University of Mississippi	Greenwood, MS/ Lawyer, Miss. State Legislature
Powell, Thomas W., Sr.	1982	Washburn University-Topeka	Jackson, MS/ Legal Instr/Hinds Community College
Prince, Joyce Combest	1967	DePaul University	Chicago, IL/ Dir. Of Desegregation, Rockford Sch. Dist.
Rice, William J.	1972	Texas Southern University	Houston, TX/ Former Judge, Atty Rice & Assocs.
Richards, Bennie	1994	University of Mississippi	Jackson, MS/ Atty., Byrd & Associates
Richardson, Willie	1999	Mississippi College	
Rosenthall, John A.	1970	George Washington Univ.	Alexandria, VA/ Atty.
Ross, James			Jackson, MS/
Ross, Tamara L.	1994	Case Western Reserve Univ.	Chicago, IL/ Asst. State's Atty. Cook Cty. State Attorney's Ofc.
Saddler, Ms. Tammi S.	1993	Thurgood Marshall	Jackson, MS/
Sampson, Agela A.	1987	Mississippi College	Jackson, MS Atty., Robinson Law Office
Sanders, Mildred J.	1976	University of Mississippi	Coldwater, MS/

Smith, Robert S.	1993	St. Louis University	Jackson, MS/ Asst. Public Defender, Ofc. Of the Public Defender
Smith, Roy	1998	University of Mississippi	Canton, MS/ Blackmon & Blackmon
Stewart, Nausead L.	1953	University of Mississippi	Jackson, MS/ Retired Atty.
Sweet, Dennis C., III	1977	George Washington University	Jackson, MS/ Atty., Langston, Frazer, Sweet & Freese, PA
Taylor, Erika	1995	University of Mississippi	Washington, DC/ Arnold & Proctor
Taylor, Jessica D.	1994	Howard University	Washington, DC/ UNCF
Taylor, Mrs. Stephanie B.	1994	Harvard Law School	Greenville, MS/ Atty., Fulbright & Jaworski LLP
Teeuwissen, Pieter J.	1987	University of Minnesota	Jackson, MS/ Danks, Simon & Teeuwissen
Thames, Veda	1992	George Washington University	
Thomas, Norris J., Jr.	1967	University of Michigan	Detroit, MI/ Chief Deputy Defender, St.Appellate Defender's Ofc
Thompson, Carol	1994	University of Illinois	
West, George F.	1962	University of Mississippi	Natchez, MS/ Gen. Practice, George F. West, Jr. Atty-at-Law
Wheaton Bondurant, Freida	1975	Washington University	St. Louis, MO/ VP-Assoc. Gen. Counsel, Citicorp Mortgage Inc.
Whitley, Onetta S.	1982	Mississippi College	Jackson, MS/ Special Asst. for Atty. Gen.
Williams, Azonda W.	1992	University of Pittsburgh	Clerk, Chancery Court - Hinds County, MS
Wilson, Psonya C.	1996	University of Mississippi	Moss Point, MS

Tougaloo College Graduates Who Received Advanced Degrees in Health Related Fields (Table 5)

Cited in the annals are alumni who enrolled in advanced degree programs in health related fields are physicians and health related researchers listed in Table 5, a continuation of Table 2.

Minority Access to Research Careers Program
Dr. Bharati Mehrotra , Director of MARC, is the 2001 recipient of a National Commemorative Citation from President Bush as part of the Sixth Annual Presidential Awards for excellence in Science, Mathematics, and Engineering Mentoring.

1979-2001

Name	Date Graduated	Degree Completed
Kirk Stoval (**Deceased**)	May 1979	D.M.D., University of Pittsburgh
Bernice Jackson	May 1979	M.D. Harvard Med School
Carol Tanner	May 1980	M.D., University of FL
Angela (Moore) Beasley	May 1981	M.S., Hlt Care Adm. MS College
Linda (Clark) Slater	May 1981	R.Ph., Xavier University
Glenda Coleman	May 1982	M.D., Brown University
Norma Phillips	May 1982	M.S., Univ of Southern MS
Wayne Murray	May 1983	M.D., Brown University

Jennifer Scott	May 1983	M.S. Emory University
Michelle Abram	May 1984	M.D. Johns Hopkins University
Valee (Miller) Adams	May 1985	M.D. University of Iowa
Percy Anderson	May 1985	D.P.M., CA College of Podiatric
Richard Hairston	May 1985	M.D. Johns Hopkins University
Jacqueline Hampton	May 1985	M.A., Washington University M.D., UMMC, Internal Med
Marvette Brown	May 1985	M.D., New York Med College
Roger Huey	May 1986	M.D., UMMC, Internal Med
Sonya Lewis	May 1986	D.M.D., UMMC, Dentistry
Jimmie Clark	May 1987	M.D., Brown University
Loretta (Williams) Jackson	May 1987	M.D./Ph.D., UMMC, Emerg.
Emma Simmons	May 1987	M.D., Brown University
Rosie Starks	May 1987	R.Ph., Xavier University
Marcia Eley	May 1988	M.D., Brown University
Lenise Lynn	May 1988	D.M.D., Harvard University
Debra Washington	May 1988	M.S. University of Texas (Austin)
Dwight Coleman	May 1988	M.D., Brown University
Tanya Kelly	May 1988	Ph.D., University of AL
Angelia Watson	May 1988	Ph.D., Mississippi State University

Lavette Newell	May 1989	Ph.D., Mississippi State University
Robbye McNair	May 1990	M.D., Johns Hopkins University
Anthony Cambers	May 1990	M.D., UMMC, Family Medicine
Tanya Washington	May 1990	M.D., University Iowa
Stephanie Collier	May 1990	Ph.D., Mississippi State University
Stacie Tyler	May 1990	Ph.D., Mississippi State University
Danurus Williams	May 1991	M.D., UMMC
Paula Carr	May 1992	M.D., Brown University
Tammy McMillian	May 1992	M.D., UMMC
Angelia Reed	May 1992	M.S., Jackson State University
Clyde McMorris, Jr.	May 1992	M.D., Case Western Medical School
Teaster Baird, Jr.	May 1992	Ph.D., Duke University
Michelle Williams	May 1993	M.D., Brown University
Valerie Cohran	May 1993	M.D., Washington University
Marcus Ware	May 1993	M.D./Ph.D., Harvard University
Aretha Green	May 1993	M.D., Mississippi State University
Eddye Bullock	May 1994	M.D., Brown University
Jerrod Taylor	May 1994	M.D., Brown University

Karita Williams	May 1994	Ph.D. University of AL
Erick Falconer	May 1994	M.D. University of CA San Francisco
Ako Bradford	May 1994	M.D., University of Virginia
Undrea Walker	May 1995	Occupational Therapy Technician
Catherine Garner	May 1995	M.D., Brown University
Carolyn Cohran	May 1995	Ph.D., Washington University
Audray Harris	May 1995	Ph.D., University of AL
Timothy Beacham	May 1997	M.D., UMMC *
Lora Wilson	May 1997	Ph.D. Univ of CO*
Latasha Wright	May 1997	Ph.D., New York University *
Kentrell Liddell	May 1997	M.D., University of Iowa*
Ashalla Magee	May 1997	Ph.D., University of AL*
Shelia Rushing	May 1997	Ph.D., Louisiana State University *
Corey Wilder	May 1997	Ph.D., Univ. of FL*
Kendia Ward	May 1998	M.D., Syracuse, NY *
Valerie Jones	May 1998	D.M.D., UMMC*
Alethea Fletcher	May 1999	Ph.D., University of AL *
Kimberly Anderson	May 1999	M.D., UMMC *
Siddeegah Bilal	May 1999	M.P.H., University of Michigan *

Adisa Jones	May 1999	M.D., Brown University *
Sheikilya Lewis	May 1999	M.P.H., University of AL *
Monica Peeler	May 1999	M.D., University of Southern AL *
Jason Taylor	May 1999	M.D., Univ. of Missouri*
Ayanna Jenkins	May 2000	M.D., Boston University *
LaShonn McNair	May 2000	DVM, Cornell University*
Rosalind Ramsey	May 2000	M.D., Brown University *
LaTonya Washington	May 2000	M.D., University of TN*
LaFarra Young	May 2000	M.D., Boston University *
Tedric Campbell	May 2001	Ph.D., Florida State University**
Dennis Tanner	May 2001	M.D., Brown University **
Carlie Gaunty	May 2001	M.D., Brown University **
GaChavis Green	May 2001	Ph.D., Howard University**
LaTonya Ware	May 2001	D.M.D., Tennessee State University**

*currently enrolled
**pursuing degree

APPENDIX

Presidents of Tougaloo College

Rev. Ebenezer Tucker (Principal)	1869 – 1970
Mr. A.J. Steele (Principal)	1870 – 1873
Rev. J.K. Nutting (Principal/President)	1873 – 1875
Rev. L.A. Darling (Principal/President)	1875 – 1877
Rev. George S. Pope	1877 – 1887
Rev. Frank G. Woodworth	1887 – 1912
Rev. William T. Holmes	1913 – 1933
Mr. Charles B. Austin (Acting)	1933 – 1935
Rev. Judson L. Cross	1935 – 1945
Dean L. B. Fraser (Acting)	1945 – 1947
Dr. Harold C. Warren	1947 – 1955
Mr. A.A. Branch (Acting)	1955 – 1956
Dr. Samuel C. Kincheloe	1956 – 1960
Dr. A.D. Beittel	1960 – 1964
Dr. George A. Owens (Acting)	1964 – 1965
Dr. George A. Owens	1965 – 1984
Dr. Herman Blake	1984 – 1987
Dr. Charles A. Baldwin (Acting)	1987 – 1998
Dr. Adib A. Shakir	1988 – 1994
Dr. Edgar E. Smith (Acting)	1994 – 1995
Dr. Joe A. Lee	1995 – 2001
Dr. James H. Wyche (Acting)	2001 –

Recipients of Honorary Degrees From Tougaloo College

Year	Recipent	Degree
1949	Ludwig T. Larsen	Doctor of Divinity
1954	Eva Hills Eastman	Doctor of Humane Letters
1955	Harold C. Warren	Doctor of Divinity

331

1960	Samuel Kincheloe	Doctor of Humane Letters
1961	Emory Ross	Doctor of Humane Letters
1967	Irving J. Fair	Doctor of Humane Letters
	John Hope Franklin	Doctor of Humane Letters
	Isaiah S. Sanders	Doctor of Humane Letters
1969	Fannie Lou Hamer	Doctor of Humane Letters
1970	Charles Evers	Doctor of Laws
	Robert O. Wilder	Doctor of Laws
1971	A. Leon Higginbotham	Doctor of Laws
1972	Walter Washington	Doctor of Laws
	Vernon E. Jordan, Jr.	Doctor of Laws
1973	Gordon W. Sweet	Doctor of Laws
	William K. Fox	Doctor of Divinity
	B.B. King	Doctor of Humane Letters
1974	Robert A. Smith	Doctor of Humanities
1975	A.A. Branch	Doctor of Laws
	Lee E. Williams	Doctor of Laws
1976	Corneal A. Davis	Doctor of Laws
	Thomas A. Murphy	Doctor of Laws
1977	David C. Driskell	Doctor of Humane Letters
	Carl Strokes	Doctor of Laws
	Justine T. Priestley	Doctor of Humane Letters
	Merton P. Stoltz	Doctor of Laws
1978	Morris Berthelo Abram	Doctor of Humane Letters
	Margaret Walker Alexander	Doctor of Literature
	Ernest G. Green	Doctor of Laws
	Aaron E. Henry	Doctor of Humanities
	Donald Eugene Procknow	Doctor of Laws
1980	Balfour Brickner	
	H. Carl McCall	
	R.L.T. Smith, Sr.	
1981	Ernest T. Collins	
	Claiborne DeBarda Pell	
1982	Ralph P. Davidson	
	Henry J. Kirksey	
	Richard Mather Mapes	
	Fredrick O'Neal	

1983   Derrick A. Bell, Jr.
          Robert Walker Harrison, Jr.
          Jewell Jackson McCabe

1984   George Earle Owen
          Aaron Shirley
          Wesley A. Hotchkiss

1985   Carol Penney Guyer
          David L. Guyer
          Vincent Harding
          J. Herman Hines

1986   Charlayne Hunter-Gault
          Samuel Ripley Pierce, Jr.
          E.B. Robinson, Jr.

1987   Excy Edwards
          Everett C. Parker
          Randall Robinson
          Michael Espy

1988   Bonnie Guiton
          Emmett Paige, Jr.
          Howard Swearer
          Raymond Mabus, Jr.

1989   Walter Turnbull
          Landon Knight
          Annie Devine
          Herman Cain

1990   R. Jess Brown (*Posthumously*)   Doctor of Laws
          Audrey Forbes Manley
          Robert Edward "Ted" Turner

1991   Clinton Wilson
          William Greaves
          Bertram Lee, Sr.
          Roland W. Burris
          Ruby Dee
          Ossie Davie

1992   Cleopatra Davenport Thompson
          Jean Fairfax
          Unita Blackwell
          Eleanor Holmes Norton

1993   Rims Barber
          Dorothy Height

	John Monro	
	Alvin F. Poussaint	
1994	J. Carter Brown	
	Lois Mailou Jones	
	Jessie Bryant Mosley	
	Myrlie Beasley Evers	
	Ronald Schnell	Doctor of Humane Letters
1995	Kamau Brathwaite	
	Paule Burke Marshall	
	Marian Wright Edelman	
1996	Mabel J. Henderson (*Posthumously*)	
	Robert W. Jones	
	Louis Westerfield	
	Joyce A. Ladner	
1997	Willie L. Brown, Jr.	Doctor of Humane Letters
	M. Deborah Hyde	Doctor of Humane Letters
	Jeremiah Jerry O'Keefe	Doctor of Humane Letters
1998	Bernard J. Ebbers	Doctor of Humane Letters
	Robert P. Moses	Doctor of Humane Letters
	Bennie Gordon Thompson	Doctor of Humane Letters
1999	Clay E. Simpson, Jr.	Doctor of Science
	Bettye Ward Fletcher	Doctor of Law
2000	Robert L. Bernstein	
	J.L. Holloway	
	Charles J. Ogletree	
2001	Avery Franklin Brooks	Doctor of Humane Letters
	Catherine W. LeBlanc	Doctor of Humane Letters
	Danny Glover	Doctor of Humane Letters

PHYSICAL FACILITIES

ACADEMIC BUILDINGS

Ballard Hall
    Built in 1886
    Accommodates Department of Music and Dramatics.
Beard Hall
    Built in 1898
    Houses the office of Development and Public Relations and faculty offices.

Basement
    Accommodates Social Science, Education laboratories, Upward Bound Program
    and offices.
Berkshire Cottage
    Built in 1994
    Living and learning center.
Brownlee Gymnasium
    Built in 1947
    Is the college gymnasium
Coleman Library
    Built in 1972
    Provides individual study carrels, a listening room, a typing room, two conference
    rooms, faculty study, several lounges, the archives and a special collection room.
George and Ruth Owens Health and Wellness Center
    Built in 1998
Holmes Hall
    Built in 1926
    Houses admissions office, classrooms, Early Childhood Development, art
    classrooms, language laboratory and faculty offices.
Judson Academic Complex
    Built in 1965
    Houses six classrooms.
Jamerson
    Built 1918
    Houses student personnel offices, Career Placement Services and the chaplain's
    office.
Kincheloe Science
    Built in 1959
    Houses classes in biology, chemistry, electronics, physics, and mathematics. Major
    repairs and addition after gas explosion in 2000.
Mansion
    Built in 1848
    Houses administrative offices.
Woodworth Chapel
    Built in 1901
    Is the center of the religious life for the college and the surrounding community.
New Unnamed Women's Dormitory
    Built in 2001

BUILDINGS DESTROYED BY FIRE

Strieby Hall   Upson Shop   The Hospital
    Built 1881   Built 1898   Built 1889
    Burned 1929   Burned 1975   Burned 1926

Berkshire Cottage
  Built 1894
  Burned 1991

Washington Hall
  Burned 1881

DEMOLISHED BUILDINGS

Cottage 10 – 11
  Built 1946
  Demolished 1975

Old Chemistry Building
  Built 1946
  Demolished 1961

Daniel Hand School
  Built 1892
  Demolished 1960

Laundry
  Built 1929
  Demolished 1960

Dining Hall
  Built 1900
  Demolished 1963

Beard Hall
  Built 1878
  Demolished 2000

Physical Facilities (Continued)

Faculty Residential Buildings

Student Residential Buildings

Apartments No. 1, 2, 3
  Built (1, 2) 1964, (3) 1965
Cottage No. 1
  Built 1918
Cottage No. 2
  Built 1918
Cottage No. 3
  Built 1927
Cottage No. 4
  Built 1927
Cottage No. 5
  Built 1927
Cottage No. 6
  Built 1931
Cottage No. 7
  Built 1931
Cottage No. 8
  Built 1946
Cottage No. 9
  Built 1946

Galloway Hall
  Built 1930
Galloway Hall (annex A and B)
  Built 1966
Judson Crosss Hall
  Built 1947
Judson Cross (annex B and C)
  Built 1966
Renner Hall
  Built 72
Residence Hall B
  Built 1972

Service Buildings

Sarah Dickey Hall
  Built 1927
  Provides health services for all members
  of the Tougaloo College community.

Faculty Residential Buildings Continued	*Service Buildings Continued*

Cottage No. 12
  Built 1960
Cottage No. 13
  Built 1962
Cottage No. 14
  Built 1965
Cottage No. 15
  Built 1965
Dean's Cottage
  Built 1929
Pope Cottage
  Built 1885
President's Residence
  Built 1962

Warren Hall
  Built 1962
  Provides recreational opportunities for members of the college community, as well as being the center for campus scoial activities. The Tougaloo Art Gallery is also housed here.

Tougaloo College National Alumni Association

The Tougaloo College National Alumni Association has experience an effective tenure through four name changes: Tougaloo University, 1869; Tougaloo College, 1916; Tougaloo Southern Christian College, 1954; and returned to its original name, Tougaloo College in 1963. The Association was chartered in 1988. The Association has been guided through growing pains, financial problems and alumni interest. As a result of visionary leadership, the Association has helped to create a spirit in alumni that has helped to sustain and perpetuate Tougaloo College, which ranks as one of the top colleges in America. The Association's involvement with recruitment, fund raising, political action, image building and other vital supporting activities has been essential to the welfare and survival of our Alma Mater. The following individuals have served as president from 1905 through 2000:

Mr. Edward R. Garrett	1905 – 1907
Mr. C.S. Ledbetter	1907 – 1909
Rev. R.V. Simms	1909 – 1911
Mr. C.S. Ledbetter	1911 – 1915
Mr. P.G. Cooper	1915 – 1917
Rev. W.A. Bender	1917 – 1921
Mr. R.A. Hamilton	1921 – 1931
Mr. Jonathan Brooks	1931 – 1933
Mr. R.A. Hamilton	1933 – 1935
Mr. N.D. Taylor	1935 – 1937
Mrs. Doris Hall	1937 – 1939

Mr. T.R. Sanders	1939 – 1940
Dr. C.B. Christian	1940 – 1941
Dr. O.F. Smith	1941 – 1943
Dr. Naomi J. Townsend	1943 – 1945
Dr. C.B. Christian	1945 – 1947
Dr. Walther Washington	1947 – 1950
Dr. Gladys Noel Bates	1950 – 1953
Dr. George A. Owens (Tougaloo College)	1953 – 1955
Mr. George Lewis (Southern Christian Institute)	1955 – 1959
Mrs. Maggie Dunson	1959 – 1961
Mrs. Ruth B. Pendleton	1961 – 1963
Mrs. Annie Seaton Smith	1963 – 1965
Attorney Roosevelt Robinson, Jr.	1965 – 1967
Dr. Ernestine Holloway	1967 – 1969
Mr. Leroy Jackson	1969 – 1971
Attorney Eddie Hunter	1971 – 1974
Mr. Leroy Ellis	1976 – 1978
Dr. Van Allen	1978 – 1980
Dr. Euguene DeLoatch	1980 – 1982
Mr. Wilbert Smith	1982 – 1984
Dr. Theodore C. Jones	1984 – 1986
Dr. Roy L. Irons	1986 – 1988
Mr. H.T. Drake	1988 – 1991
Mrs. Barbara T. Hilliard	1991 – 1994
Attorney Willie Bailey	1994 – 1997
Mr. Thomas W. Gray	1997 – 2000
Mr. Stanley Weakley, Sr.	2000 – Present

Clarice Thompson Campbell,
Co-author of Mississippi:
The View From Tougaloo
with Rogers, Civil Rights and
Woman's Activist

Christoff Ian Rogers, Oscar Rogers '50,
and Ethel Lewis Rogers '50, Co-author of
Mississippi: The View From Tougaloo
with Campbell, President Emeritus Claflin
University

H.T. Drake '50, President
Emeritus National Alumni
Assocation of Tougaloo College

Dr. Jerry W. Ward '64, Lawrence
Durgin Professor of English

1st Row (seated L to R) Robert Wilder - Washington, D.C.; Hermand Bennette, Jr. - New Orleans, LA; Jane Hearne - Jackson, MS; Theodore Jones, D.D.S. - Jackson, MS; Barbara Preiskel, Esq. - New York, NY; Rueben Anderson, Esq. - Jackson, MS; Doris Browne - Washington, D.C.; Joe A. Lee, President; Howard Glenn, D.M.D. - Memphis, TN; Bernard Slaughter, Sr. - Chicago, IL

2nd Row (standing L to R) Joffre Whisenton, Ph.D. - Atlanta, GA; Stanley Weakley, Sr. - Houston, TX; Frederic Pryor, Ph.D. - Swathmore, PA; Isaac Byrd, Esq. - Jackson, MS; Edgar E. Smith, Ph.D. (Trustee Emeritus) - Jackson, MS; Robert W. Jones - New York, NY; William Meier - Cuyahoga Falls, OH; Harry Walker - Jackson, MS; John Foulkes, Sr. - Indianapolis, IN; Richard Hales - Jackson, MS; Wesley Prater, M.D., - Canton, MS

INDEX

INDEX TO CHAPTER 22

Graduates of Tougaloo College

CLASS OF 1879
J. Newton Granberry
Luella Miner
Pope F. Tevault

CLASS OF 1880
G. W. Jackson
R. W. Jackson
E. E. Sims
R. T. Sims
Chas. Taggett
Hartwell Tanner
Joseph Walton

CLASS OF 1881
William H. Lanier

CLASS OF 1882
Jerry M. Gill
Edward H. McLane
Allen L. Strong
Hettie Cunningham (Garrett)
Rosa McCutcheon (Jackson)
Nannie Tapley (Spann)

CLASS OF 1883
Frank B. Hood
Frank W. Sims
Wade H. Thomas
Joanna Jones (Russell)
Angie B. Williams

CLASS OF 1884
T. B. Buckner
Jessie Rhone
Matthew Stevens
Allen Ward

CLASS OF 1885
Allen Herbert
Henry Jones
Marion S. Jones
M. W. Whitt

CLASS OF 1886
James C. Brown
Henry A. Collier
Eaton H. Haynes
Owen W. James
Cornelia Levy
Millie Miller (Hemphill)
Lucy L. Page

CLASS OF 1887
Fannie Green
M. Delia Woods (Herbert)

CLASS OF 1892
Benjamin F. Fulton
Mary J. Gibson
Marion S. Jones
Sara J. Thomas (Land)
Rachel R. Trigg (Webb)

CLASS OF 1893
Rachel J. Pepper (Scott)
Florence E. Roberts (Jones)
Porter F. Roberts
Richard V. Sims
Annie T. Spraggins (Gray)

CLASS OF 1894
Eugene Collier
Rachel E. Collier
James Garrett
William Harris
James M. Jones
Sara Page
Mary Whitfield

CLASS OF 1895
Anna Dabney (Harris)
Hiram Johnson
Henry Nichols
Etta Vassar Stone

CLASS OF 1896
Samuel Brinkley
Eugene Collier
Mary Collier
Charles Cook
Anna Harris
Andrew Washington
Eugene Washington

CLASS OF 1897
Susie Anna Bass
Belle L. Blackburn (Hutcherson)
Andrew M. Brewer
Margaret A. E. Collier
Traverse S. Crawford
Elizabeth E. Dabney (Lanier)
Henrietta Dabney (Sims)
Hattie Dougherty
Jerry Madison Edwards
Edward Harris
Beulah Johnson
Nettie Elizabeth Johnson (Robinson)
Mary Catherine Parker (Nash)
R. V. Sims

CLASS OF 1898
Judge A. Cowan
Ella Davis
Minnie Lee Hardin
Sarah Ellen Harris (Fletcher)
Isaac P. Lucas
Minnie Cooper McAlpine (Pickens)
William G. O'Neal
Alice Edna Pepper (Harris)
Wirt Washington Sumlin

CLASS OF 1899
Daniel A. Carney
Silas W. Polk

CLASS OF 1900
Henrietta L. Bedgood
Parker G. Cooper
Norma Helena Grey
John B. Lee

CLASS OF 1901
Alexander Archibald
Celestia B. Archibald
Rosalia Burnes
Regina Crawford
Traverse S. Crawford (A.B.)
Nancy J. Flanders
Edward R. Garrett
George W. Griffin
Sarah Ellen Harris
James S. Wadlington

CLASS OF 1902
Judge A. Cowan (A.B.)
Ida Leon Crabbe
J. Madison Edwards
Luckie Roy Harris
Sarah Ellen Harris (A.B.)
William A. Harris
Halle Johnson
Clara Jency Lee
Minnie C. McAlpine (A.B.)
Josephine G. Miller
Preston Alexander Moman
Lela A. Roberts

Ada Alma Rush
Beatrice A. Turner
Missouri Drucele Wood

CLASS OF 1903
Erasmus T. Caston
Martin T. Hornsby
Selena C. Jackson
Cæsár S. Ledbetter
Lottie S. Lee
Willye Ethel Mollison
George G. Mosley
Silas A. Polk (A.B.)
Geneva L. Pugh
G. Nathaniel Smith
Henry C. Tate

CLASS OF 1904
Henrietta L. Bedgood (A.B.)
Parker G. Cooper (A.B.)
Leo J. Foster
Nancy Cortez Hardy
Charles A. Harris
Meade Hicks
Eugene Lawrence
John B. Lee (A.B.)
Sarah Jennings Lewis
Willye Ethel Mollison
Estelle E. Reid
Susie G. Roberts
Newman D. Taylor
James Thigpen
George Benjamin Williams
Leila Ernestine Wingate

CLASS OF 1905
Marcilite Estella Bennett
Annabel Clark
Edward Richard Garrett (A.B.)
Nina Beatrice Jones
Louise R. Mehlinger
Leonia L. Polk
Margaret A. E. Polk
Narcissa C. Tate

CLASS OF 1906
Julia B. Alfred
Emma L. Burke
Inda A. Crawford
John W. Edwards
Mary E. Harris
Samuel T. Kelley
Benjamin F. Ledbetter
Ori S. Mosley
Addie W. Pickel
Isaiah S. Sanders
Martha A. Simpson
Stance J. Trotter
Shepard F. Walker
Henry R. Williams

CLASS OF 1907
Geneva B. Bridgman
Rankin S. Brown
Lydia E. Carr
Cora B. Elliott
Lemuel L. Foster
Sarah E. Howard
Cæsar S. Ledbetter (A.B.)
Flossie V. Reid
Estelle L. Rials
Eva C. Roberts
Mabel L. Sims
Edward Trigg
Lewia P. Wade
Thomas Williams, Jr.

CLASS OF 1908
Etta A. Bemiss
William P. Foreman
Anna D. Foster
Leatha A. Graham
Katherine G. McBeth
Gertrude McKinnis
George C. Moseley (A.B.)
Almeda E. Sims
Newman D. Taylor (A.B.)

CLASS OF 1909

Chas. A. Garrett
Corean Irvin
Lydia W. Mollison
Odessa A. Moyse
Ollye M. Pickel
Eva C. Roberts
Idella B. Seals
Mabel L. Sims
Frances F. Taylor
Jesse J. Thorpe

CLASS OF 1910

William A. Bender
Arthur G. Brown
Lemuel E. Bynum
Mary E. Carter
Eliza D. Dinkins
Winfield B. Dudley
Samuel M. Griffin, Jr.
Riley A. Hamilton
Penninah S. Harlan
Annie E. Moman
Ernestine H. Mosley
Neubin E. Pope
Lewis L. Romans
Isaiah S. Sanders (A.B.)
Nelson M. Willis

CLASS OF 1911

Lynce C. Bowling
Ida Ailene Burns
Robertha Myrtle Carbo
Stella M. Dixon
William Harris Foster
Beatrice Hattie Frazier
Sarah Beatrice Howard
Evie Olenia Johnson
Ruth Neville MacAllister
Marie Antoinette MacBride
H. W. Marshall
Fannie McDaniel
Lardell McLaurin
James E. Mehlenger
Carrie Adella Mitchell

Welborne A. Mollison
Pansy M. Moseley
Josephine Ousley
Edward P. Pickel
Annie May Reid
Fannie M. Reid
Eva Cordelia Roberts (A.B.)
Eva A. Ross
Laura Adella Shipp
Frasier Andrew Vernon
Lewia P. Wade (A.B.)
Frederick Roscoe Whiteman
Crimea K. Wooley

CLASS OF 1912

Algene Byrd
Caesar B. Christian
Benjamin J. Farnandis
Mary Alberta Franklin
Ophelia C. Holmes
Alice E. Howard
Beulah Belle Mason
Nancy May
Susie Moman
Pauline Belle Murphy
Benjamin Ousley
Ola Minerva Raiford
Angie L. Robertson
Madelyn Vernona Shipp
Oscar S. Smith
Lela Belle Willis
Stampp Willis
Lilybel Ernestine Wilson

CLASS OF 1913

Cordelia J. Alfred
Maggie B. Cheatham
Suvelia Dunson
Harvey B. Ellis
Addie Fox
John F. Gray
Octavius G. Henderson
Emma A. Mason
Annie Mae McNeil
Ether Nola Miller

Lydia Wells Mollison (A.B.)
Hubert Moman
Wayne B. Mosley
Nicola Ousley
Robert Pickett
Christine Preston
Howard Amos Roberts
Edward L. Samples
Sallie A. Spencer
James Stallsworth
Bettie L. Tramiel
Gladys A. Wilson
Willa G. Woolfolk

CLASS OF 1914

William A. Bender (A.B.)
Sadie E. Bishop
John H. Boles
Arthur G. Brown (A.B.)
William Osmond Cain
Maude Ethel Cameron
Tennie Birdette Cameron
Ruth W. Christian
George Cromwell Cobb
Viola Olivia Crawford
Sallye Dawson
Beulah Olivia Duncan
Samuel M. Griffin, Jr. (A.B.)
Olivia Griffith
Riley A. Hamilton (A.B.)
Olive Anderson Johnson
Oda Anna Kirkland
Ernestine H. Mosley (A.B.)
Lela Elizabeth Patton
Amanda H. Richardson
Lewis L. Romans (A.B.)
Florence E. Russell
Bessie A. Scruggs
Arleaf Henry Semmes
Evangeline P. Walker
Bettie Mahala Williams
Nelson Morton Willis (A.B.)
Pompey James Winston
Mamie Rosina Wong

CLASS OF 1915

Lynce Crawford Bowling (A.B.)
Avenue Alicia Buckley
Effie Mae Edwards
Lurilene Blossom Gullage
Annie Bell Harris
India Anna Hill
Corinne Helen Jones
Grady Dewitt Kirkland
Sadie Jean Macallister
William Joseph Ousley
Beulah Virginia Polk
George Franklin Sanders
Mable E. Mildred Sanders
Frasier Andrew Vernon (A.B.)
Albert Levi Webster
Alma Glendower Williams
Olga Lucille Williams

CLASS OF 1916

Caesar Benjamin Christian (A.B.)
Katie Mae Dulaney
Rutherford Birchard Edwards
Minnie Lucinda Fisher
Israel James Holmes
Henry Mack Jones
Claracy B. Kimbrough
Ethel Annie Lee
Leonard McDaniel
Henrene Thelma McNeal
Minnie Cecil Meyer
Irvin Charles Mollison
Robert Lanier Moman
Sapolio Romancy Morris
Benjamin Leonidas Ousley (A.B.)
Rachel Cornelia Polk
Henry McNeill Reese
Bobbie Beatrix Scott
Gertrude Estelle Scott
Sadie J. Snowden
George Frank Taylor
Katie Mae Wilson
Annie Mae Woolfolk

CLASS OF 1917
Hattie Irabella Brown
Corinne Elida Petro Burrage
Lillian Constance Burrage
Viola Olivia Crawford (JR. TCHRS.' COLL.)
Ruby Rebecca Dancy
Robert Milton Dunnings
James Leo Finley
Disraeli Rudolph Henderson
Marguerite Olivia Grace Jones
Maude Amaryllis Jones
Clara Juanita King
Willye Alice Lemons
Pinkie Levy
Leona Macallister
Beula Alberta Marr (JR. TCHRS.' COLL.)
Irma Lue Moody
Pauline Belle Murphy (A.B.)
Pearl Lucile Myles
Lucile Nelson
Nicola Ousley (A.B.)
Julia Etta Patton
Mary Inez Roby
William James Rouser
Dorothy Lillian Louise Sims
Ola Lee Snowden
Odell Gladys Stone
Naomi Vivian Thomas
Tener Jessie Whiting
Elva Addie Willis

CLASS OF 1918
Lura Selma Christian
Eliza Williams Henrene Clemons
Otha George Beal Cobbins
Addie Johnnie Dorena Colter
Mamie Elizabeth Cox
Katie Mae Dulaney (JR. TCHRS.' COLL.)
Willye Pauline Goins
Augustus Greenwood
Augusta Marie Griggs
Missouri Luella Herbert

Victoria Marie Johnson
Lavinia Henrietta Miller
Mahala Elnora Mimms
Viola Esther Nelson
Annie Mae Olive
William Matthew Page
Edna Evangeline Ridgley
Minnie Elvirda Small
Marie Louise Spencer
Isaac Lucile Stallsworth
Bowman Macklin Thomas
Trilby Chamberlain Thomas

CLASS OF 1919
Mary Virginia Brock
Lille Mae Brooks
Lillian Leondra Burwell
Ollie Belle Caston
Zenobia Ernestine Christian
Mary Esther Coleman
Marguerite Beatrice Harvey
Rosa Lee Hill
Clemon Alma Martin
Ruby Helen Martin
Ethel Lucile Mims
Beatrice Ozella Nelson
Flora Myrtle Parrish
Hattie Bernice Patterson
Hugh Napoleon Sims
Paola Malinda Wallace
Henry Hudson Weathers
Leona Beatrice Webster
Eugenia Adelina Woods

CLASS OF 1920
William Almond Berry
Willye Thelma Brown
Albertine Janie Coleman
Eva Lydia Griffin
Bertha Marie Harvey
Marguerite Elizabeth Harvey
Alma Aileen Lewis
Celestine Rosalye Macallister
Annie Belle Marshall
Elizabeth Ernestine Moore

Louberta Moore
Clifton Frederick Nelson
Viola Esther Nelson (JR. TCHRS.'
    COLL.)
Henry Lewis Polk
Rachel Cornelia Polk (A.B.)
Bessie Mae Scott
Mary Bernice Williams
Pompey James Winston (A.B.)

CLASS OF 1921
Ethelbert Napoleon Anderson
Jeannette Carolyn Anderson
Bessie Estella Barnett
Bessie Alma Battley
Manuella Noella Beck
Mary Esther Coleman (JR. TCHRS.'
    COLL.)
Ella Christian Farish
Viola Lilly Golden
Milas Sloan Love
Shelly Luster
Ethel Lucile Mims (JR. TCHRS.' COLL.)
Ida Ardelle Nelson
Conrad Leslie Oakes
Laurence Franklin Packer
William McKinley Peterson
Fannie Powell
Emily Louise Preston
George Franklin Sanders (A.B.)
Myrtle Henrene Simpson
Eugenia Adeline Woods (JR. TCHRS.'
    COLL.)

CLASS OF 1922
Erthel Camille Ammons
Julia Rose Bell
Oscar Rayford Berry
Mildren Estelle Brumfield
Revelia Lee Coleman
Inez Williams Crawford
Emma Georgia Dillon
Thelma Lorean Effinger
John Alexander Gambrel
Harriet Elizabeth Garrett

Archie Wildon Hanford
Thomas Horton Harvey, Jr.
Robert Lee Huffman
Olivia Marie Hunter
Velma Florine Johnson
McKinley Mack
Charlotte Desiree Mosby
William Matthew Page (A.B.)
Malinda Calon Robinson
Henry Calvin Sturgies
Levi Marcellus Sturgies
James Lloyd Turner
Annie Louise Walker
Rosa Page Welch
Henry Lawyer Whisenton
Loraine Marie White
Lauretta Cecile Whitehead

CLASS OF 1923
Ephraim Alton Berry
Belle Washington Boyd
Bienville Brooks
Maggie Augusta Buckingham
Hattie Jane Coleman
Lillian Marie Dawson
Ethel Beatrix Digman
Gertrude Alice Farrell
Amber Louise Greene
Annie Henrietta Harris (A.B.)
Helen Constance Harris (A.B.)
Maggie Lucille Hayes
Marie Elizabeth Henderson
Mabel Hill
Mildred Willetta Humphrey
James Washington Hunter, Jr.
Eddie Mae Johnson
Hettye Mae Johnson
Audie Valentine Kirkland
Charles Sidney Lee
Lela Cornelia Lewis
Solomon Owens Martin
Elmer Ellsworth McConnell
Admiral Herbert McCoy
William Lloyd Tavis Miller
Ida Lucille Moman

Wilhelmina Ione Moman
Edward Adelbert Neal (A.B.)
Johnetta Arvenia Nelson
Anna Hall Polk
Curtis Smith
Ethel Lloyd Stone
Edgar Gilchrist Thomasson
Angella Flora White

CLASS OF 1924
Thomas Carl Almore
Erthel Camille Ammons (TCHRS.' COLL.)
Wyrlie Louise Beasley (TCHRS.' COLL.)
Malissa Erskenrine Bobo
Mildred Estelle Brumfield (TCHRS.' COLL.)
Thelma Theresa Clement
Georgia Beatrice Dawson
Ruby Alma Dawson
Iola Mae Donald
Mahala Ervin
Mary Beulah Earline Everett
Alphonso Frederick Finley
Laura Jane Gambrel
Rosa Lee Garnes
William Hilliard Greene
Commodore Hamblin
Alix Elmiria Hollins
Alma Albertha Huddleston
Freddie Miller Hunter
Mamie Clifford Johnson
Edward Jones
LeRoy Jones
Gibson Thomas Land
Mamie Lear Lucas
Theodore Roosevelt Martin
Ira Kalantha McCoy
Noah Columbus McNeil
B. Ettson Miller
Eva Trenna Nichols
Herbert Grayson Pickett
Sarah Fannye Pinkston
Henry Lewis Polk (A.B.)
Calvin Richardson

Edward Earle Richardson
Norwood Herbert Smith
Willie Mae Smith
Constantine Arvetta Tibbs
Pearl Malissia Weddington
Mary Ellis Wesley
Clotile Amelia White
Loraine Marie White (TCHRS.' COLL.)
Ethel Laller Wilson
Myrtle Catherine Wilson

CLASS OF 1925
Jeannette Carolyn Anderson (A.B.)
Priece Bedenfield
Helen Louise Brown
Lillian Gertrude Brown
Charles Thomas Butler
Charles Ervin
Gertrude Allice Farrell (TCHRS.' COLL.)
Rachel Chaucer Ferrill
LaFayette Garrett, Jr.
William Howard Gay
John M. Gibson (A.B.)
Fannie Alfretty Hall
Hyrtacena Jane Harris
Lurley Henderson
Elihu Root Hunter
Katherine Linette Jackson
Stephen Stanley Jackson
Eddie Mae Johnson (TCHRS.' COLL.)
Idelle Jones
Milas Sloan Love (A.B.)
George Martin
Agness Bratton Middleton
Alton Bismark Moman
Ida Lucile Moman (TCHRS.' COLL.)
Alice Atlanta Moore
Ethel Dorotha Patterson
William McKinley Peterson (A.B.)
Addie Ennels Preston
Alice Viola Robinson
Daniel Homer Stephens
Ruth Camille Stephens
Eric Hood Thomasson
Thelma Augusta Thompson

Louise Helen Trotter
Ruth Elizabeth Tucker
Elma Cynthia Turner
Madie Beatrice Whitfield
Mary Katherine Woods

CLASS OF 1926
Dorothy Roselyn Blue
Mary Eliza Boddy
Genevieve Brodnax (TCHRS.' COLL.)
Blanche Marion Cade
Thelma Theresa Clement (TCHRS.' COLL.)
Mattie Lee Coleman
Susie Elizabeth Cowan
Reginald DeVaughn (A.B.)
Wilhelmina Dunlap
Mahala Ervin (TCHRS.' COLL.)
Mary Beulah Earline Everett (TCHRS.' COLL.)
Leonidas Hartzell Gibbs
Wilhelmina Gore
Tyree Greenwood
Susie Anna Hartzog
Ruth Esther Harvey
Lewis Hill
Mildred Hill
James Hopkins
Olivia Marie Hunter (A.B.)
Fannie Bernice Johnson
Sadie Evans Johnson
Ira Kalantha McCoy (TCHRS.' COLL.)
Laura Delle McLaurin
Emmett James Marshall
Beulah Sophia Martin
Willie Celeste Michael
Margaret Virginia Middleton
Herdesena Dora Moman
Mary Moore
Maudie Mae Piguese
Anndell Pollock
Francis Green Robins
Pearl Isabelle Robinson
Elma Senthia Slaughter
Grace Lee Smith

Thomas Smith
Iva Helen Stephens
Sadie Eleanor Stewart (TCHRS.' COLL.)
Isaiah S. Sullivan
Theresa Bernice Tharp (A.B.)
Rose Theodosia Washington
Josie Beatrice Weddington
Susie Henrine Whisenton
Carrie Lutitia Wiggins
Melba Druciele Williams

CLASS OF 1927
Bertha Avril Berry
Bettie Bernice Bobo
Katie Ernestine Bradford
Hattie Bernice Caldwell
William Jolly Clark
Carrie Lee Coleman
Teddy Belle Davis
Frances Dier
Artemese Fleming (A.B.)
Flora Evangeline Grace
Amber Louise Greene (A.B.)
Hyrtacena Jane Harris (TCHRS.' COLL.)
Steve Macbeth Harris (A.B.)
William Moody Hayes
Lurley Lorene Henderson (TCHRS.' COLL.)
Martha George Hopkins (TCHRS.' COLL.)
Rhoda Mae Hopkins (TCHRS.' COLL.)
Irma Maudess Johnson (TCHRS.' COLL.)
Mary Lee Jones
Mollie Elizabeth Jones
Emily Elnora King
Alice Gloria Lee
Lucille Theresa Lee
Thelma Alice Maddox
Lawrence Courtney Moman
Richard Leroy Moore
Susie Lee Myles
Hugh Sidney Nash
Mary Virginia Nichols
Louise Bynetter Pendleton

Edwin Powell
Alice Viola Robinson
Thomas Roosevelt Sanders
Henrietta Louise Stevenson
Walter Jones Stewart
Eddie Verneise Swaggard
Thelma Augusta Thompson
Oma Mae Ethel Vaxter
Eugenia Vertenia Ward
Odessa Elizabeth Wesley
Willabe Beatrice Whitfield
Beatrice Williams
Gurline Callie Wilson
Hannah Rachel Woods

CLASS OF 1928
Archie Anderson
Bernice Bacon
Bennie Louise Brown
Vernanda Estella Cook
Ida Lee Davis
Stella Violet Douglass
Alva Juanita Griffin
Lillie Mae Hall
Mamie Sarah Harrison
Odess Edward Hicks
Mildred Hill
James Washington Hunter, Jr. (A.B.)
Charles Jarrett
Fannie Bernice Johnson
Sadie Evans Johnson
Stella Emma Johnson
Cornelius William King
Irdelle Victoria Love
Leon Sydney Love (A.B.)
Thelma Elois Lowe
Josephine McLaurin
Thelma Elizabeth Martin
Edna Allain Miller
Hazel Mae Dorris Moman
Herdesena Dora Moman
D. W. Moore
Alice Hope Morris (A.B.)
Arlena Littie Myers
Lemaud James Nash

Helen Matilda Nathaniel
Alexander Davidson Otis (A.B.)
Evelyn Marjorie Pendleton
Maudie Mae Piguese
Anndell Pollock
Edward Robert Qualls
Edward Earle Richardson (A.B.)
Mary Eliza Rockingham
Norwood Herbert Smith (A.B.)
Eula Clifford Stephens
Iva Helen Stephens
Hattie Lorene Stewart
Lucy Caroline Tappan
Levi Woodward Walker
Rose Theodosia Washington
Elvira Earline Watson
Josie Beatrice Weddington
Henry Lawyer Whisenton (A.B.)
Carrie Lutitia Wiggins
Larla Ardell Womack
Lillian Bobbary Wright

CLASS OF 1929
Julia Odessa Barnes
Priece Bedenfield (A.B.)
Homie Evelyn Blackburn
Minnie Louise Blalocke
Ida Mae Buckley
Rosa Caldwell
Alma Carter
Virginia Lee Chrismon
Eva Lydia Crawford
Vivian Crawford
Geneva Viola Davis
Josie Lee Davis
William Howard Gay (A.B.)
Susetta Eloise Gibson
William Hilliard Greene (A.B.)
Mamie Louise Griffin
Elnora Beatrice Harris
Jessie Geneva Harris
Katherine Linette Jackson (A.B.)
Idelle Jones (A.B.)
Leandrew Jones
Leora Louise Jones

Lillie Heloise Lee
William Lucas
Hattie Monroe McGrue
Alton Bismark Moman (A.B.)
Ethel Iola Moore
Gather Lee Fordie Myers
Mary Magdalene Myers
Marie Elizabeth New
Tahmer Deen Olive
Herbert Grayson Pickett (A.B.)
Alberda Polk
Margaret Amelia Powell
Sherman Powell
Emola Elizabeth Rials
Rebecca Virginia Robinson
Frank Taylor Simpson (A.B.)
Gladys Cornelia Sims
Katie Eugenia Sims
Naomi Ruth Sims
Alverson Joel Smith
John Mildred Smith
Millie Dolores Smith
Theodore Roosevelt Smith
Newman Crawford Taylor
Doris Louise Veronica Tharp (A.B.)
Mary Ella Vincent
Charles Wesley
Henerine Rosola Woods
Helen Gladys Wright

CLASS OF 1930*
Jonathan Henderson Brooks
Charles Frank Ervin
Lewis Hill
Mildred Henrietta Hill
Albertine Hopkins
James Molette Hopkins
Fannye Bernice Johnson
Laura Delle McLaurin
Herdesena Dora Moman
Elma Senthia Slaughter
Grace Lee Smith

*Beginning with the 1930 list, all named
graduates received college degrees.

CLASS OF 1931
William Jolly Clark
Carrie Lee Coleman
Dan Edward Hall, Jr.
Dollye Lee Holmes
Wilson Alexander Howell
Richard Leroy Moore
Hugh Sidney Nash
Odessa Wesley
Beatrice Williams
Hannah Rachel Woods

CLASS OF 1932
Mary Magdalena Hall
Willie Marvell Harp
Vina Mae Jackson
Charles Jarrett
George Lee Jefferson
Stella Emma Johnson
Thelma Almeda Johnson
Mary Lee Jones
Bessie Maye Lindsey
Thelma Eloise Lowe
George Washington Lucas
Roy Alexander Mazique
Lawrence Courtney Moman
Willie Clarice Powe
Peter Coleman Rucker
Mabel Estella Smith
LaPlace Franceno Turner
Florice Middria Williams

CLASS OF 1933
Ida Mae Buckley
Eva Lydia Crawford
John Thomas Hall
Leora Winifred Holmes
Nannie Leona Hopkins
Leora Louise Jones
Lillie Heloise Lee
Irdelle Victoria Love
Richard Temple Middleton
Marion Estelle Poe
Thomas Roosevelt Sanders
Alverson Joel Smith
Henerine Rosola Woods

CLASS OF 1934

Alfonso Milton Clark
Fulton David Hill
William Edward Lucas
Samuel Clements Malone
Beula Alberta Marr
Hazel Mae Doris Moman
Leon Albert Nash
Wendell Hampton Page
Florence Johnnie Anna Patterson
Ethel Bernice Stewart
William James Stewart

CLASS OF 1935

Vivian Madelene Daniels
Lucius Andrew Hayden
Floyd Ausburn Jones
Portia Marguerite Lucas
Ira Kalantha McCoy
Beatrice Dorothy Mercer
Edith Margaret Norwood
Carl Tapley Robinson
Effie Mae Sims
Ruth Modena Taylor
Charles Wesley

CLASS OF 1936

James Cornelius Brown
Louise Bernice Cranford
Irma Frozene Dixon
Veola Evelyn Franklin
LaFayette Garrett, Jr.
Dolores Marguerite Greene
William Clyde Haralson
Richard Blackmond Harris
Edward Herbert Jackson
Leon Sidney Jones
(Miss) M. V. Manning
Lillie Mae Montgomery
Edwina Marie Myles
Mildred Lynell Nash
Newman Crawford Taylor
Mabel Sadye Thomas
H. McFarland Thompson

CLASS OF 1937

James Earl Anderson
Louise Rita Bruce
Vernon Cosmo Cade
Ruby Roberts Clarke
Maxcine Katherine Cotten
Edith Rae Davidson
Anne Olivia Garrett
Robert Walker Harrison, Jr.
LeRoy Nolan Jackson
Ellen Miller Johnson
Bernard Crabb Jones
Juanita Alterine Kirksey
James Lawrence Lowry, Jr.
Carey Belle Maddox
Wendell Benjamin Pierce
Lusta Adams Prichard
Edward Jordan Walker

CLASS OF 1938

William Henry Allen, Jr.
Rosa Leola Belle
Bonnie Earl Berry
Frank Henry Blalock
Leon Talmadge Britton, Jr.
Jessie Pearl Brown
Dorothea Beatryce Carter
Edmund Douglas Taylor Cook
Bina Rozelle Crawford
Walter Ambrose Cunningham, Jr.
Leona Beatrice Harris
Ira David Henderson
Eugenia Ernestine Holmes
Samuel Patrick Hoskins
Henry Wilfort Johnson, Jr.
Naomi Elvira Johnson
A. Dee Clara Kenard
Eugene Gilford Mason, Jr.
Austin Claiborne Moore, Jr.
Anna Elizabeth Nichols
Lehman Edward Parrish
Nannie Beatrice Peterson
Fred Mercer Rollins, Jr.
Henry Alexander Talbert
Robert Alexander Thompson

Solly Bylis Ward
James Sherick Watkins
Jacob Wesley
Doretha Lillian Woods

CLASS OF 1939
Inez LaVerne Bozeman
Vernon Braddock
Theresa Marie Bridges
Maude Eliza Brown
Ralph Warrnes Coleman
Annye Lee Cranford
Joe Lee Davenport
Roscoe Benjamin Dixon
Jessie Mae Franklyn
Evelyn Hill
Olivia Beatrix Holmes
Jesse James Johnson
Willie Daucie Johnson
Delores Frances Moman
Martha Mae Mosley
Emile Coleridge Nash
Morris Lewis Romans
Jeanette Elizabeth Wilkes
Henry Joseph Williams

CLASS OF 1940
Theo Malvern Chenier
Eddie Lee Clark, Jr.
Naomi Esther Coleman
Marylena Cotten
Richard Edward Daniel
Mae Isom Davenport
Annie Maenette Gaston
James Luther Howard
George Walton Irving, Jr.
Dorothy Brunetta Jackson
Coleridge Taylor Moman
Dorothy Helen Moman
Fred Edward Pinson, Jr.
Maurice Larnie Sisson
Nora Lee Spencer
William Henry Thomas
Zelma Inez Turner
Tamara McClain Webster
Wilhelmina Wesley

CLASS OF 1941
Essie Mae Ethel Adams
Will Robert Anderson
Rosalie Leslie Armstrong
Amos Griffin Cranford
Edna Allyne Fletcher
John Louis Hamilton
Lee Edna Hamilton
Alma Lilla Harris
Berenice Newman Hunter
John Robert Hutchinson
Helen Camelia Lee
Selma Mae Mackel
Barbara Marion Moman
Doxie Mesetta Montgomery
George Washington Moore
George Albert Owens
Leonard DeQuincey Proctor
Robert Austin Spates
Andrew Jackson Topps
Victoria Elizabeth Webb
Velma Louise Wesley
Mary Gladys Wilkerson

CLASS OF 1942
Bachelor of Arts
John Reuben Amos
Gladys Noel Bates
Ernest Lee Braddock
Thelma Elizabeth Bradford
Avery Roberts Crawford
Evelyn Marva Donelson
Mildred Zulu Franklin
Alvin Clifton Freeman
Mildred Louise Hamilton
Stella Delores King
Earl McKinley Lewis
Napoleon Bonaparte Lewis
Minnie Lee Marsh
Rebecca Eloise Moore
Alice Mae O'Reilly
Earl Shaw
Junius Welton Verdine
Mary Lee Warddles
Bachelor of Science
Claudia Cornell Berry

Rita Hazel Glover
Ruby Ann Hosey
Ida Lee Jones
Ernestine Elizabeth Randall
Mildred Smith
Melba Ruth Thompson
Ethylene Oclamena Topps
Mary White
Venora Deloris Witherspoon

CLASS OF 1943
Bachelor of Arts
Annie Christine Boone
Mary Buenya Gordon
George Washington Greene, Jr.
Carolyn Gloria Hunter
Eddie Mae Jackson
Maryella Jones
Rose Yvonne McInnis
Juanita Hortense Overstreet
Kathryn Carnella Shirley
Willie Henerene Smith
Rubie Alene Smith
Juanita Willie Thomas
Mary Estelle Turner
Oscar Whillington White
Bachelor of Science
Albert Bazaar Britton
Lee Ethel Lojoetta D. Robinson

CLASS OF 1944
Bachelor of Arts
Rosie Lee Brocks
Hilda Claier Burton
Phoebia Violet Hill
Bessie Bernice Lee
Annie Lee Smith Moffett
Edna Yvonne Moore
R. C. Ola McWilliams
Lucille Walker Price
Ernestyne W. Topps
Ella Lois Woods
Bachelor of Science
Mahala Aldean Cole
Ruth Eva Johnson

Alin Jeanette Magee
Ernestine Cornelia Pendleton

CLASS OF 1945
Bachelor of Arts
Marjorie Geraldine Ayers
Annie Lillian Bates
Princess Ella Beasley
Burnette Clarence Dickens
Maggie B. Cheatham Dunson
Annette Craft Fields
Annie Laurie Harris
Charles S. Harrison
George Melvin Hayes
Lydia Kate Johnson
Violet Joyce McInnis
Mildred Evelyn Osborne
Bachelor of Science
Elva Theresa Howard
Norma Kathleen Mosely
Annie Ernestine Seaton
Mattie Elizabeth Vines
Ida Mae Wesley

CLASS OF 1946
Bachelor of Arts
Patricia Frances Beasley
Robert Hunter Campbell
Esther Louyse Cobbins
Ruth Lillian Cobbins
Anna Vernice Cunningham
Mamie Lee Daniels
Merlyne Juanita Jones Graves
Alma Jean Jacobs
Ida Ruth Johnson
Ruth D. A. McDowell
Howard Blanchard Moman
Dorothy Mai Oliver
Mary Louise Robinson
Vivian Belle Romans
Jean Rowe
Jordan J. Scott
Nawassa Wardell Scott
Doris Evelyn Smith
Freddie Belle Stansberry

Armatha A. Thompson
Henryne Marie Topps
James Wesley Vines, Jr.
Gertrude Webster
Bachelor of Science
Hilda Ione Archie
Alda Ruth Blackwell
Rachelle Lavert Bradford
Wilma Lorraine Brooks
Maggie Dora Burkhead
Thelma Louise Caldwell
Anna Jane Crisler
Ernestine Delois Hilliard
Fredia Mae Howard
Gloria Swanson Hullum
Alyce Mabel Moore
Henrietta Thigpen
Nerissa Virginia Wilkerson

CLASS OF 1947
Bachelor of Arts
Mildred Portia Berry
Annabel Blake
Henry Earl Briggs
Thomas Edward Brooks
Cora Inez Brown
Curtis Campbell
Anna Louise Clemons
Ethel Berenia Cobbins
Jerry Madison Edwards
Doxye M. Foster
Arthur Edmond Franklin
Geneva Etta Franklin
Melvin Lee Loper
George Edgar McCall
Pauline Mayfield
Delores Louise Mitchell
Georgia Montgomery
Elvira Oranell Jackson Morris
Ruth Celestine Murry
Matilda Teareise Myers
Olivia Patton
Mary Lou Quinn
Beatrice Joyce Sanders
Mary Alice Scott

Ruth Lee Shirley
Willie Lee Clarence Slaughter
Hazel Mirthlee Stamps
Walter L. Tilles
Mamie Louise Vincent
Kline Emerson Wilkerson
Ambrose Talliaferrio Williams
Thomas Ellen Young
Bachelor of Science
Mary Alice Moman
Jessie Louise Singleton
Miriam Elizabeth Thomas
Nellye Luberta Turner
Jessie Mae Williams

CLASS OF 1948
Bachelor of Arts
Sophia Ruth Baggett
Leroy Percy Bass
Jonas Elbert Bender
Benjamin Franklin Bullock, II
Willis Carroll
Clarence Benderson Clark
Doris Marionette Clemons
Joseph Samuel Cobbins
Thelma Alice Cooley
Garland Damon Davis
Mary Jeane Davis
Leroy Hellems Ellis
Dorothea Gibson
Emmitt Hayes
Lovie Ree Herron
Vernon Anthony Horne, Jr.
Mary Houze
Gloria Patricia Kirkmon
Morris Kenard Lewis
Melvin Lee Loper
Thelma Alice Maddox
Classie Angeline Mayfield
Jones Ambrose Moore
Henry James Mosely, Jr.
Charles C. Mosley, Jr.
Henry Ward Nash
Constance Mary Peters
Juanita Beatrice Reed

Girtie Marie Saddler
Ollie Sylvester Scott
Yolanda Ercelle Sephus
Lurley Henderson Sims
Leroy Terry Smith
Mahala Ervin Smith
Bessie Jone Stephens
Avery Cox Topps
Benjamin Glenn Vines
Walter G. Washington
Ruth Lee Welch
Odis Lee Wicks
Vivian Eugene Wiggins
Henry Coleman Wilkerson
Albert Dumas Wilson
Dora Spencer Woodson
Bachelor of Science
Nova Anderson
Beatrice Butler
Carolyn Pearl Carter
Edna Earl Jones
Lorraine Dewitt Mason
Luther Belle Miller
Ollie Beatrice Newell
Eliza Thigpen
Mary Elizabeth Young

CLASS OF 1949
Bachelor of Arts
Henry Alexander
Helen Louise Archie
Willie Mae Benson
Nathaniel Anthony Boclair, Jr.
Ophelia Caston Bradford
Pearlena Lorraine Briscoe
Gloria Mae Broussard
Marie Cade Calbert
Benjamin Franklin Caston
Annie Jane Cistrunk
Harold William Clay, Jr.
Sylvester Sidney Coleman
Arthurine Beatrice Davis
Berniece Deloice Donald
Derrick Winston Dunning, Jr.
Leonell William Ellis

Essie Hertysyne Gee
Helen Marie Hamilton
Frankye Elise Hillery
Willie Lee Hoover
James Ingram
Juanita Valda Jackson
Ardee Johnson
Olivia Gwyndetta Jones
Joseph McEwen
Cleo McGee
Mary Lois McWilliams
Katie Mae Miller
Merdis Marie Miller
Norma Ruth Miller
Andrew James Moore
Wilbur Daniel Moore
Ida Marie Nimock
Major Lamar Nimock
Essie Beatrice Patton
Luvenia Pickens
Christine Carr Pullum
Catherine Davis Rance
Terrel Julius Rance
Lygia Saulny
Minnie Ruth Butler Seaton
Jessie Josephine Smallwood
William Irving Townsend
Rachel Ann Vincent
Julia Lee Walker
Verma Cellestine Weathersby
Lucy Levern Webster
Percy John Williams
Strand Willis
Derrick Gelston Woods, Jr.
Bachelor of Science
Virginia Ethel Brown
Hettie Mae Canonge
Alene Hunt
Ethel Lee Jones
Equilla Terrelle
Irma Lee Thigpen

CLASS OF 1950
Bachelor of Arts
David Alford

Van Sizar Allen
Stonewall Jackson Alston
Hargrow Barber
Robert Emmitt Bates
Eddie Pearl Black
Simmie Samuel Blakney
Ray Brooks
Joe Hanna Brown
Bertha Manotha Brownlee
Thelmon Campbell
Mary Ella Castillo
Albert Ulysses Clark
Alice Mae Clark
Leroy Coleman
William Calvin Collins
Heartha Canan Cullins, Jr.
Lora Wilvon Davis
Eleanor Warrick Dean
Wallace Lampton Dillon
Henry Thornton Drake
Marian Elliott
Willie Pearl Elmore
Loretta Valeree Expose
Ben Raymond Fielder, Jr.
Will Kent Gee
Edward Earl Gibson
Gwendolyn Louise Greene
Emanuel Hall
Catherine Marie Harris
Mildia Evelyn Harris
Mildred Eloise Harris
Opsy Lee Hill
Howard Hobson
Benjamin Ernest Hodge
Milton Neal Howard
Walter Howard
Marguerite Hopkins Hudson
Margaret Jamie Lee Hughes
Emery Aguinaldo Irving
Gage Johnson
George Albert Johnson
Margaret Johnson
Mable Norman Jones
Marzelle Latham Jones
Robert Lee Jones

Thelma LaVerne Jones
Gilbert Lewis Kelly, Jr.
Ruth Audrey Kimball
Anna Jeralena Latimore
Ethel Lee Lewis
Mannie Lewis, Jr.
Leroy Lucas
Eugene Mattox
Mildred Wilma Jean Mercer
Catherine Lera Miles
Anderson Miller
Calvin Burney Miller
Veronia Mae Moore
Willie Ed Morgan
Jimmie Vaughn Morris
Ethel Marie Nichols
Effie Mae Noel
Florence Hicks Owens
Luther Clearence Patton
Felton Clyde Pilate
Clinton Robinson
Oscar Allan Rogers, Jr.
David Eugene Ross, Jr.
Lillian Narcissus Shirley
Lesly Francis Simmons
Willie Singleton
Willie Frank Slaughter
Joe Henry Smith
Lloyd Vernonearl Smith
Alyce Louise Stribling
Myrtle Floree Terry
Levonne Thompson
Sammye Earl Wansley
Charles Herbert Washington
William Lewis Wayne
Emmett Milburn White
Oscar Bernard Whitehead
Marcus Harold Whitfield, Jr.
Kathryn Lynette Wiggins
Leo Williams
Lois Latham Williams
Vivian Prudence Williams

Bachelor of Science

Pauline Jacqueline Buckley
Mary Louise Harris

Gay Bonita Johnson
Bessie Louise Mott
Jether Lee Walker

CLASS OF 1951
Bachelor of Arts
Alice Ruth Alderman
Beatricx Pearl Barrett
Irma Lee Benson
Vennie Ruth Boler
Bernice Blanche Brookins
George Ester Brown
Hazel Lola Brown
Mary Ruth Brown
Matthew Burks
Ruth Pearl Cooper
Leon Eugene Cramer
Josie Lee Davis
Ida A. Dent
Vanessa Neely Ellis
Delma Juan Gibson
Levandis Headd
Georgia Louise Johnson
Horace Lafayette Jones, Jr.
Wilhelmina Ozell Jones
Herschel Clarence Latham, Jr.
Beatrice Juanita Littlepage
Helen Beatrice Loveless
Mary Elizabeth McGee
James Clifton Polite
Maurice Montello Radcliff
Curlie Mae Ransom
Inez Robinson
Josie Lorraine Robinson
Roosevelt Robinson, Jr.
James Williams Rogers, III
Arvarh E. Strickland
Evelyn Sutton
Rosa Berenice Thompson
Hazel Ruth Washington
Ermin Cleo White
Celia Etta Williams
John Henry Woodard
Bachelor of Science
Henry Chrysler Adams, Jr.

Allie Louise Almore
James Lee Boykins, Jr.
Roy Brewer
Theodore Roosevelt Brooks, Jr.
Eugenia Brown
Walter Edward Carr
Robert Turner Clark
Sidney Lawrence Clark
Paul Coleman
James Marion Dunnings
Emmett Atley Gambrell
Andrew Douglas Graffenreidt
Doris Deloris Hall
Sylvester Brule Hamilton, Jr.
Willie James Harrington
Norma Fay Harvey
Vernon Henderson
Reuben Christopher Hicks
William Robert Horton
Joseph Hutcherson, Jr.
Clarence Bernard Johnson Jr.
Orsmond Jordon
Geraldine Odessa Lacy
Edgar Lewis, Jr.
Lena Mae Lewis
Florida Eva Lusk
Frankye Lucy Mackey
Strown Martin
Elmer Elihu Moses
Ozellia Mosley
Dorothy Louise Naylor
Elsie Pauline Norman
LaHarry Norman
Frankye Lee Parker
Joseph Cornelius Robinson
Gladys Marie Rose
Dorothy Slaughter
Charles Wesley Smith
John Lewis Smith
Doris Louise Thompson
Sammie Tuck, Jr.
Basil Shaw Twyner
Hubert Lawrence Wallace
Ezell Nathaniel Wicks
Robert William Wilkerson, Jr.

Carrie Cotton Williams
Alma Hildreth Winston
Chris Young

CLASS OF 1952
Bachelor of Arts
Theester Berenice Allen
Thomas Daniel Barnes
Annie Lee Bedford
Floyd A. Boclair
James Lowry Bolden
Martha Hollins Cotton
Clifton Curtis Currie
Henry Lee Davis
Lyda Davis
Marion Leora Davis
Cora Denis
Leontyne Jeannette Dorsey
Katie Earnestine Ford
Charles Alexander Gee
Annie Elizabeth Hamilton
Martha Jane Hardy
Golden Harris
Sinclair Oscar Lewis
Mavle Lorenda Jenkins Lindsey
Willette Miller
Phyllis Joan Mills
Fannie Ruth Mosby
Gwendolyn Malinda Nero
Mary L. Foster Peaches
Ellistene Hermione Pilate
Daisy Pearl Radcliff
Delores Louise Ratliff
Bertha ElLoyd Roberts
Jerelyn Keeling Terry
Clara Noble Thompson
Shirley Marie Turner
Bachelor of Science
Thomas Carl Almore, Jr.
William Anderson
Edward Ben Barnes, Jr.
Ruth Kathryne Bradley
Grace Deloris Britton
Joseph Carson
William Webster Collins

Harry A. Cooley
Winchester Davis, Jr.
John Claude Grant
Esther Bernice Harris
James Otis Harrison, Jr.
Wilhelen Haynes
Ernestine Holloway
Stephen Foster Howard
Marjorie Valentine Jackson
Willard Earl Johnson
Charles Louis Jones
Joseph Jones, Jr.
Talmadge Dewitt Kirkmon
Hattie Sherrod Lewis
James Daniel Mahaffey
Eula Theresa Morgan
Willie G. O'Reilly
Matthew Page
Douglas Parris
Annie Laura Polk
Rudolph Valentino Sellers
Opaline Simmons
Marjorie D. Stamps
Ernest Stewart
Alice Sullivan
James Earl Thomas, Jr.
Alberta Harkness Vines
Alma Edith Williams
Henry Jefferson Williams
Mary Kathryne Woodson

CLASS OF 1953
Bachelor of Arts
Valentine Ashmore
Nellie Mae Barnes
C. Donald Beall
Richard E. Benson
Bettye Jean Blackburn
Ollye Luvervia Brown
Willmer T. Buchanan
Booker Taliaferro Cole, Jr.
Mae Frances Hilliard
Margaret Young Lewis
Addison L. Perkins, Jr.
Cora Marie Smith

Nausead Stewart
Alfreta Jean Thompson
Almeta Earlene Thompson
Myrtle L. Smith Wiley
Linda Lee Williams
Bachelor of Science
Tommie Marie Anderson
Martin Luther Beard
Martha Jean Denham
Ruby Gorman
Myles Bishop Harris
Laura Lee Johnson
Willard Lewis Johnson, Jr.
Barbara Elizabeth Jones
Jesse Cornelius Lewis
Felix Liddell
James H. Lockett, Jr.
Dora Coleman McWaine
Eugene Patterson
Willie James Perry
Dola High Walker
Eugene R. Ware
Henrene Williams
Josiepearl Williams
Vivian Marie Williams
Mayo Donald Wilson
Rosa Mae Woods

CLASS OF 1954
Bachelor of Arts
Rosentene Bennett
Dorothy Mae Boclair
Johnnie Ruth Buckley
Alpha Pearlene Cole
Georgia B. Dawson
Alpha Lockett George
Daisy Miller Greene
William McNeamer Harvey
Albess B. Hines
Dorothy Nell Hobson
Johnnie Belinda Hubbard
Irma Mandess Johnson
Flora Claudette Lawrence
Connie De'Lein McCaskill
Jessie Mason Mahaffey

Betty Mae Mallett
Commie Lee Nelson
Edward Kendall Newsome
Annie Belle Pendleton
Dorothy Eichelberger Pickens
Charlene Joyce Smith
Chrystiana Smith
Daisy Marie Smith
Lenora Fulton Stampley
Yvonne Sylvia Wilson
Bachelor of Science
Alma Barnes
James Collins
Mattie Gates Currie
Alice Elizabeth Ellis
Geni-Evelyn Jewel Fields
Harold Clarke Fouche, Jr.
Marion Claude Garrett
Flora Grace
Lille Cistrunk Henderson
Jesse Elmer Jacobs
William Juan Jones
Carolen Moncure
Delores Jeraldine Moore
Carlean Manning Owens
Vivian Miller Patton
Harry Penquite
Roland H. Powell
Dorris Oddessa Renfroe
Ross Earle Simms
John Wesley Spates
Clarence Thompson
Olivia Moore Townsend
Marguerite Grace Varnado
Lillian Montora Welch
Earlene Whitaker
Ernest Luther White, Jr.
William Rodney Wiley
Booker T. Winford

CLASS OF 1955
Bachelor of Arts
Rose Marie Bell
Blandye Dinkins Brooks
Martha George Hopkins Hall

Bessie Burleigh Hawkins
Mary E. Jackson
Willa Lucille Norris McClendon
Joyce Geneva Martin
Ora Lee Nelson
Bernell E. Smith
Robert Teague
Mary Eleine Thompson
Bachelor of Science
Margaret Virginia Alexander
Willie Roy Banks
Herman Bennett, Jr.
Sarah Brown
Alfred L. Carr
Darline Louretha Carter
Dave Britton Coleman
Gus C. Coleman
Andrew D. Collins
Verlean Delaney
Kelly Graham, Jr.
Thelma Wacile Harris
John Ira Hendricks, Jr.
Joseph Marchon James, Jr.
Dorothy Louise Jones
James Jones, Jr.
Luvercia McCormick Jones
Royal Leon Jordan
Chester Arthur Leigh
Mildred Logan
John Elbert McCoy
Collins Attaway Marshall, III
Phillip Roosevelt Norman
Florence Pearl Perkins
Ira Sylvester Polk
Aaron Shirley
Edgar Eugene Smith
Inez Oree' Wiley Smith
Leroy Burns Vinson
Quincy Charles Walker
Pauline Elouise Waters
James Edward West
Joffre Trumbull Whisenton
Vandon Ellaquient White
Benny Kate Whitfield
Katiedelores Williams

Nancy Marshall Williams
Ruthana Wilson
Wardell Wilson
Nola Jean Wynn

CLASS OF 1956
Bachelor of Arts
Iva Nell Abram
Albertine Amelia Boclair
Helen Brown
Samuel Cole
Lillian Earlene Eichelberger
Marie Slaughter Fouche
Russell Daniel Hawkins
Sam Hawkins
O'Nell Hobson
Lou Emma Holloway
Shirley Odette Jones
Isaac Leon London
Mattie Lee Robinson
Bennie Cleveland Russell
Alma Mae Boyd Taylor
Hattie Mae Davis Williams
Ora Lee Winston
Bachelor of Science
Bessie Scruggs Alexander
Hattie Anderson
Zadie Elizabeth Bedford
James Herman Bernard
Daisy Elizabeth Bishop
Nancy Lee Owens Burenstine
Seleana Montgomery Clark
Elzora Louise Collins
Louise Geraldine Dillard
Fred Charles Fielder
Carrie DeBruce Giles
Albertha Jerome Harris
Maudelle Alice Harris
Della Louise Hodge
Alvan Emerson Jagbandhansingh
Roy Carl Johnson
Vivian Louise Johnson
Cornelius Bernard Lawyer
Evangeline Walker Lee
Joshua Leonard Lee, Jr.

Charles Lindberg McNair
Josephine Anntonnye Nichols
Willie Mack Perryman
James Roland Plunkett
Sondra Custard Powell
Webster Slaughter
James Stanton
Clinton Teague
Annette Marie Tillman
Hilton McClain Travis
George Monroe Vincent
Mary C. Terry Walker
Idella Blanche Washington
DeWitt Talmadge Webster

CLASS OF 1957
Bachelor of Arts
Dorothy Jean Anderson
Rachel Harper Camphor
Kay Frances Cooper
Charlie M. George
Amazine McBride Haynes
Bobbie Ruth Holloway
Johnnye Mae Kirk
Melvin Lonnette McKinney
Ernestine Poindexter
Edward P. Pope
Hazel Blanche Prentiss
Ever Lee Hoffman Presley
John W. Reed
Geraldyne Deloys Smith
Ruth P. Smith
Rosa Lee Wells
Rosie Eva Williams
Bachelor of Science
Juanita Adams
Essie Thelma Alston
Arcola Marolyn Barber
Leonard C. Battle
Christine P. Brown Bingham
Maude Zella Brown
Violet Olivia Brown
Pauline Buckley
Hozy Burnestine, Jr.
Lawyer Henry Chapman

James Williams Coleman
Clifford Dealist
Norris Edney
Sylvia P. Fields
Emerson Foster
Helen Marie Frazier
David Edward Garrett
Juanita June Green
Eula Phillips Harris
Madye Frazier Hayes
Emogene Hendricks
Charles G. S. Hill
Julius C. Hughes
Joseph J. Johnson
Dannie B. Jones
Elbert Levi Jones
Thelma Lillian Jones
Thomas Ray Lawrence
Robert Lindsey, Jr.
Kemper Louise McCree
Ethel Lee McGee
Charles E. Middleton
Gloria Jefferson Nichols
Jimmie E. Perryman
Shirley Collier Polk
Fannie C. Hayden Rainey
Samuel Jerome Roberts
Thelma Lynnette Robinson
Theodore R. Rollins
Lula LaVerne Parker Ross
Bonnie Christine Rushing
Erma Jean Sias
Fannie Ruth Smith
Henry B. Smith
Robert Smith
Wilbert L. Smith
Luke Spencer
Thomas Delono Sulton
Benjamin F. Turner
Ollie Hicks Vick
Retha Mae Walker
Mamie B. Williams
Eva Delores Woodard
Hattie Maye Young

CLASS OF 1958
Bachelor of Arts
Richard L. Brooks
Jerry Ann Cole
Marie Cole
Ollie Bell Justice Coleman
William L. Coleman
Hilda Tucker Harris
Charlie Ruth Jewett
Alton Herman Joseph
Annie J. McGhee
William A. Marshall
Marvin L. Pickett
James W. Rollins
Thelma Silas
Georgia Seaton Slack
Jesse L. Trotter
Betty Ann Williams
Lena Mae Wright
Bachelor of Science
Annie Lou Thompson Bell
Marva Myers Coleman
Shirley Coleman
Joseph Warren Custard, Jr.
LoLee Johnson Denton
Poynton Flagg
Louisa Flowers
Zenova Garrett
Eugene M. Gaston
Willie Myles Shelton Hamilton
Laurette Harris
Lorraine Young Jackson
James L. Jones
Nancy Houston Keyes
Bobbie J. Anderson Lawrence
Quenious Merrill
Shirley Lynn Nance
Barbara M. Overton
Everett Parker
R. C. Parker
Beulah Patton
Mary Louise Chandler Perkins
Norval B. Powell
David Rixter
Charlene Rouser

Samuel Rouser, Jr.
Johnnie Warren Rushing
Dannette Salone
McCoy Smith, Jr.
Shirley M. Steward
Oscar C. Tanner
Alpha Ray Thompson
Avenue Buckley Thompson
Herbert Alphonso Thompson
Terrell Waters
Gwendolyn M. Wiggins
Cleveland Williams, Jr.
Mable S. Woods

CLASS OF 1959
Bachelor of Arts
Alice Johnson Allen
Annette Ames
Clara Logan Bedenfield
Alvin Lee Benson
Gloria Anne Bolton
Milton John Bondurant
Virginia Patterson Braden
Mary Mallard Bradford
Eddie Belle Bully
Rachel Lee Bully
Patricia Regina Chandler
William M. Cornelius
Judy Ann Harris
Tommy E. Harris
Arlene Knowles
Itelia Marie McLin
Fred Truman Nolan
Russel Pope
Eva Christine Ross
Marva Anderson Shelby
Gala Deloris Smith
Annie Ruth Thomas
Mary Elizabeth Thompson
FleurdeLis McLaurin Ulmer
Edna Mae White
Suewilla Irene Wright
Bachelor of Science
Helen Jean Artis
Annie Rhodes Bell

Lynette Braddy
Lessie Parrott Branson
Lenora Briggs
Clemontine Brown
Steven Johnanthony Brown
Ruby Jewel Burkett
Mariah Griffin Carroll
Franklin D. Ceruti
Freddie Milton Champion
Clotee Marie Clark
Lillian Theresa Clark
Jacqueline Marie Cober
Alberta Cole
George C. Collier
Octavia Cotton
Jacquelyn Duckworth Cowan
Jessie Geraldine Davis
Eugene DeLoatch
Cornell Claudine Edwards
Samuel Lewis Ellis
Mae Bradford Evans
Richard Arthur Evans
Katherine Faulkner
Mollie Marie Fields
Pearlie Jean Gray
Lenora Vick Hampton
Albertine Harris
Joseph C. Hawthorne
Lewis Helm
Fannie Carolyn Holmes
William Irving
Luella Bender Johnson
Lillian Burrage Jones
Rosa Mae Jones
Earnie Mable Jordan
Ozzie Patrick Lang
Samuel Peter McCann
Ernest Carl Magee
Gurline Callie Moore
Percy Moss
Julius Myers
Essie Lee Myricks
George W. Nauflett
Oscar C. Peace
Dixie Lee Perryman

Gloria Gray Peyton
Charles Pickett
Violet Doreatha Pickett
Annie Ruth Poindexter
Susie Hartzog Polk
Rossie Pierce Powe
Charetha Miller Powell
Samuel Lamar Rhone
Charles Herman Robinson
Laurence Clifton Ross
LaVerne Savage
Leon Slack, Jr.
Ethel Willett Smith
Gloria Jene Smith
Kisiah Bertha Waller
Elizabeth Perry Washington
Grace Evelyn White
David Williams
Marjorie Smith Williams
Robert Thomas Woods
Pearl Young

CLASS OF 1960
Bachelor of Arts
Alice Brown
J. B. Carter
Myrna L. Crawford
James E. Darley
James W. Davis
Minnie Merle Davis
Floreada M. Harmon
Arnetter Hill
Richard Jones
Richard E. Jones
Claude LeFlore
Willie McPherson
Hilda Ann Overton
Alvia Louise Randall
Annie R. Roberts
Robbye Jewell Robinson
Julia K. Shaw
Lannie Slaughter
Mary Jordan Smith
Pearl J. Stephens
Ann Marie Turner

Annie M. Watson
Loretta Wiley
James Wilson, Jr.
Marvie B. Winfrey
Bachelor of Science
Willie M. McGee Adams
Luella Black Anderson
Melverline Archie
Bernice Armstead
Clyde Janet Baker
Kathryn Sue Bates
Archie A. Casher
Marque J. Chambliss
Beatta Cole
Willie E. Collier
Alzenia E. Cotton
Doris Lee Davis
Ida Frances Davis
Ruby Alma Dawson
Sarah Seaton Douglas
Patricia Ann Evans
Rosie Lee Fields
Davis Fitzgerald, Jr.
Willie Foster
Jimmie Mae Goodloe
Mary Louise Green
Georgia E. Hand
George C. Harris
Richard B. Harris
Ethel M. Henderson
G. W. Henderson
Arthur J. Hicks
Hortense M. Hinton
Hazel Prentiss Holt
Virilla W. Hoover
Ruth Helen Houze
Ethel Lee Ingram
Annie R. Jackson
Izola Jackson
Iona Agnes James
Silas James, Jr.
Dorothy Jefferson
Joseph W. Knox
Alice D. Lattimore
Grover L. Lett

Rosetta King Lewis
James Lockhart
Christine A. Long
Ruth Lynch
Quinten T. McCall
Marion Harland Mackie
Winfred Magee
John Martin
Modestine Mervin
Robert Moman
Elsie Hall Mosley
Fannie D. Mosley
Barbara A. Myles
Allie V. Patterson
Willie Benetta Patton
Sceola Scott Phillips
Johnnie Eugenia Porter
Olivia C. Porter
Josephine McLaurin Powell
Mary Stella Rand
Henry C. Redmond
Betty Reynolds
Katherine S. Robinson
Myrtis Brunson Rue
Aaronette M. Seaton
Marie L. Sidney
Teareasy Beatrice Stewart
Alma W. Summers
Martha Rice Vaughn
Esmene D. Waithe
Willie Walker
Walter Welch
Robert White
Josephine G. Woods

CLASS OF 1961
Bachelor of Arts
James Abram
Richard Fulton Anderson
John Albert Bivins
Eleanor Elizabeth Blackmon
Patricia Ann Campbell
Mary Elizabeth Champion
Jeannetta Cole
Mattie Lee Cook

Theo Vanette Davis
Eddie Eugene Dawson
Clarence West Ewell
Earnestine Gant Farris
Jerrye Yvonne Gray
Nelda Ruth Hobbs
Mildred Jean Hubbard
William Henry Jefferson
Lou Emma Jones
Lonnie Davis King
Roland Hayes Luckett
Sarah C. McGowan
John Henry McKelphin
Detella Florence McLeod
Delores Lockett Powell
Cora Lee Sampson
Forrestine Seiferth
Esther Deloris Sherrod
Gloria Ann Simpson
Delores Jan Singletary
Bettye Jean Smith
Easter Lee Smith
Ruth Mae Thompson
Sarah Louise Warren
Patricia Annette Watts
Sidney L. Webb
Dan Walter Williams
Katherine Williams
Bettye Jo Woods
Emma Lee York
Myrtis Lenora Young

Bachelor of Science

Geraldine Davis Anderson
Walter Elbert Beamon
Crimea Bell
Willie Denson Belt
Thelma Thompson Bennett
Vernon Lynwood Blakely
Bettye Ruth Blakney
Everett Dean Branson
Willie John Carr
Annie Pearl Carter
Senia Durcella Collins
Lillian C. Conway
Bobby Gene Cooper

Marjorie Marie Course
Katherine Johnson Dunbar
James Daniel Fitch
Hazel Lewis Fletcher
Ida Yolanda Fouche
Christine Jackson Grant
Kattie Miller Greer
Roy Harris
Robert Walker Harrison, III
Robert J. Hawthorne
Rosalie Herndon
Bobie Ruth Hudson
Eddie Lee Irions
Ruby Lee Jackson
Don Ellwood Jennings
Charles Henry Johnson
Florine Mack Johnson
Mamie Wilson Johnson
Joyce Cellestine Jones
Lillie Dell Jones
Mary Hill Jones
Norma Jean Jones
Jerry Will Keahey
Lena Pearl LeFlore
Alphonse Rene Lewis
Cora Lee Lovelace
Hattie Lyles
Earma Jean Lynch
Catherine B. McCloud
Mae Frances McCoy
Margie Mae McGowan
Clarence Reubin Mason
Minnie Lee Mathis
Artemese Mills
Shirley Jane Moody
Emma Ree Moore
Freddie Clay Moore
Josie Moore
Frank Lee Myers
Henry C. Odom
Alberta Perry Palmer
Ineta Palmer
Ardelia C. Parker
Gwendolyn Vilkki Phipps
Margie Juanita Pope

Elmore Harris Porter
Blondell Thomas Richardson
Robert Lee Sampson
Howard R. Sanders
Benjamin Arthur Shepherd
Leroy Slack
Helen Belinda Smith
Horace Smith, Jr.
William Hamp Taylor
Willie Currie Thomas
Mary Eliza Thompson
Annie Bell Thurman
Vivian B. Turnipseed
JoAnn Vicks
Fitz Herbert Waithe
Clara Mae Wallace
Eva Washington
Emma Pinkey Webster
Neley Webster
Carolyn J. Whisenton
Delores Jean White
Rose Knowles White
Maggie Morris Wilder
John Smith Williams
Adelaide Marvet Wilson
Annette M. Wilson
Lessie Anthony Wilson
Peter C. Wong
Hilda Janette Young

CLASS OF 1962
Bachelor of Arts
Minta E. Aldrige
Glennis Earl Barnes
Willeva Lindsey Barnes
George M. Bender
Carl E. Bickcom
Leslie L. Daniels
Dorothy Ducksworth
Lonnie Haynie, Jr.
Melvin Jennings
Ira C. Lanier
Joseph P. Lewis
Roy Long, Jr.
Bobby McDowell

Lonnie Banks McGill
Bobbie Jean Martin
Roosevelt Matthews
Elizabeth Ransom
William Richardson
Tommie Ross
William M. Ross
Eunice V. Rouser
Ethel Sawyer
Ramona Jackson Sutters
Arthur Tate
Barbara Jean Thompson
Rosie Lee Thompson
Ruby Lee Thompson
Alma L. Tyler
Garfield Warren
George F. West, Jr.
James D. Winters
Bachelor of Science
Mary C. Allen
Julia I. Ames
Allease G. Boose
Alice Branson
Gladys Brown
Ruth Brown
Kinnard N. Bryant
Virginia Campbell
Edith Hill Cannon
Lucille Carter
Lillie D. Chaffee
James C. Coleman
Joan Collins
Emma Conley
Ruth E. Cummings
Alice Davis
Sarah McAdory Davis
Frances Dier
Annie Dulaney
Ruby Mae Dupree
Yvonne Amerson Etheredge
Rosa Farrar
Henry C. Frazier
Ethel Gibson
Annie Gregory
Lou Willie Griffin

James W. Harris
Mable P. Harris
Mary M. Harrison
Jean E. Herron
Cassie Lee Hicks
Clara Lee Horne
Roy A. Hudson
Bernice Hughes
Florence Luella Jackson
Janice LaJune Jackson
Arthur I. Johnson
Carolyn Johnson
Naomi E. Johnson
Dave Jones
Della Ruth Jones
Sue E. Jones
Theodore C. Jones
Carl E. Jordan
Gene L. Lee
Jerry H. Lewis
Alice Luckett
Vivian Lyles
Margaret Martin McEwen
Levi Sam McKelphin
Tommy McKey
Virginia C. McKinney
James McLaughlin, Jr.
Harold L. Moman
Girtie L. Moore
Robert Moreland
Ronald E. Mosley
Sandra Needham
Eunice Parrott
Ruby Patterson
Doris Peace
Eugene Perry
Terlena Perry
Maude Pickett
Anna Polk
Cozetta Smith Poole
Donald Prentiss
Joe Carl Reed
Frank Reid
Mackey Sampson
Bessie Sanders

Alfred Simms
Juruthin Rosetta Smith
Charles Spann
Emilie Steele
Portia Steele
Mazalene Roberts Towner
Gloria Tuggle
Maeola Little Turner
Charlotte Valentine
Gene Douglas Vinson
Roberta Carr Walker
Carlton Wilson
Mamie Sudduth Wise
Weaver Woodson, Jr.
Bettye Marie Young

CLASS OF 1963
Bachelor of Arts
Gloria Jean Amerson
Bettye Jean Andrews
Deloris Singleton Barnes
Charity Beamon
Alice McIntosh Beard
Fredna Louise Bell
Mary A. Berry
Alma Ruth Bland
Mary Valean Bradley
Verna Julimairis Brown
Freddie Fifer Burnett
Bertha Mae Butler
Clarence Chinn
Geraldine Edwards
Barbara Jean Ferguson
Roscoe C. Foreman
Doris Owens Fuqua
Solomon Eugene Gibbs
Rudolph Gregory Graham
Mariah Shaw Griffin
Coleman LeRoy Hacker, Jr.
Willie Joyce Hall
Gloria Brown Harris
Linnie McCoy Harris
Dorothy Mae Henderson
Beatrice Dilla Hicks
Sylvester Hillard

Martha Susie Hunter
Bessie Jackson
Carol Jefferson
Gloria Jean Joffrion
Annie Lee Johnson
Herbert Johnson
Leslie Johnson
Dorothy Kimbrough
Joe Ruby Leatiker
Bobbie Jean Lewis
Allie Houston McCullough
Patricia Williams McGill
Carolyn Beatrice Mann
Lillie Thompson Martin
Charles Moss
Irene Nichols
Eddie Sylvester O'Neal
Nedra Jean Patterson
Ethel Moore Phillips
Orthella Polk
Juanita Brown Robinson
Imogene Roots
Thelma Sadberry
Annie Dotson Scott
Mary Carolyn Scott
Georgia Morris Simmons
Truddie Gray Smith
Lona Campbell Taylor
George Lee Thomas
Jean Esther Torry
Alberta Trotter
Willie Etta Walker
Jeraldine Ward
Linda Ann Wells
Thornell Williams
Carolyn Celeste Wise
Bachelor of Science
Delores Adams
Dorothy L. Alexander
Bruce Columbus Allen, Jr.
Juanita Theresa Amos
Lynette Cecilia Anderson
Jimmie Armstrong
Hugh Earl Bell
Calvin Leon Bradford

Clark Cathey
Curtis Cathey
Etha Camile Coleman
Vera Mae Collins
Gartha DeWitt Dansby
Norman Preston Forester
Myles Foster
Galileo Greer
Lawrence Thomas Guyot
Riley Alexander Hamilton
Juanita Harris
Herbert Stanley Hurd
Thomas Louise Jones
Samuel Charles Jordan
Mahalia Nelson Little
Annette McLaurin
Dindial Mahabri
Willie Teretha Marshall
Madelyn Clayton Martin
Willetta Mitchell
Mary Elizabeth O'Neil
Jerry Dancy Redmond
John Henry Roberts
Blanche Davis Robinson
Betty Jean Savage
Ruby Esther Smith
Thomas Jefferson Summers
Sylvester Eddie Tape
Fred Douglas Thompson
James Roy Todd, Jr.
Carl Lee Watts
Earl Lee Watts
Robert Ellison Woodruff

CLASS OF 1964
Bachelor of Arts
Sadye Elizabeth Almore
Reuben Vincent Anderson
Shirley Beatrice Barnes
Shirley Ann Berry
Margaret Jean Blue
Freddie Brooks
Johnnie Mae Brown
Lilyan Cober
Hattie Boyd Cooperwood

Eugene O'Neil Cross
Jerrodean Delois Davis
Adia Pearl Day
Joe Thomas Elliott, Jr.
Bobbie Jean Gray
Clarissa Griffin
Delores Vernell Gross
Rosie Hales
Annie Josie Hankins
Geneva Honeysucker
Robert Eugene Honeysucker, Jr.
Arthur Horton
Lessie B. Hunt
Clintoria Inge
Betty Jo Johnson
Lavern Johnson
Tommie Ann Johnson
Gertrude Jones
Theodora Smith Joor
Doris Evelyn Kendrick
Joyce Ladner
Carrie Dean Lapsky
Sallie Mitchell
Brenda Lucille Moman
John Andrew Nichols
Memphis Norman
John Sheridan Page
Marva Cecillia Peace
Norweida Rayford
Gloria Smith Reed
Gwendolyn Rogers Ross
Stephen Manson Rutledge
Mattie Jean Sampson
Camelia Rose Shephard
Lenora Sims
Rosie Singleton
Margaree Webb Smith
Mary Louise Smith
Otis Thames
Calvin E. Thomas
Melinda Thomas
Joan Harris Trumpauer
Shirley Marlyn Wells
Mozella B. West
Vealie West

Dorothy Camille Wilburn
John Wesley Wilson
Ruby Lee Wilson
Ruby Yarbrough

Bachelor of Science

Shirley Lee Applewhite
James McHenry Armstrong
Carlyle Juslyn Baker
Jerry Bennett
Thomas Breland, Jr.
Calvin J. Brown
Doris Brown
Robert Carpenter
Margaret Decell Champion
Bennie Cohran, Jr.
Sylvia Annithia Davis
Walter Lee Evege
Louis Hamilton, Jr.
Annie George Hardaway
Jessie Breashears Hartfield
Doris Hayes Hawthorne
Gwendolyn Hill
Robert Wallace Jennings
Emma Lillian Joffrion
Charles Kenneth Jones
Howard Cleveland King
Albert Earl Lassiter
Frank B. McCune
James Earl McQuirter
Floyd Clifford Minor, Jr.
Annie Mae Moody
Ruth Moody
Will Earl Moorehead
Charles E. Quinn
Wallace Stover Randle
Israel Bernard Robinson
Bettie Jean Rouser
Nettie Belle Smith
Louis Jean Stallworth, Jr.
Peter Stoner
Edna Thompson
Lee Joe Thompson
Sharron Faye Tuggle
Gloria Lee Waller
Esther Ruth Ward
Jerry Washington Ward, Jr.

CLASS OF 1965
Bachelor of Arts
Arverna L. Adams
Blanche E. Allen
Lindberg Arnold
William M. Bailey, Jr.
Arlene Bell
Frances Bell
Earline M. Ammons Bishop
Nellie D. Cargin
Cloteal M. Carter
Eugene M. Carter
Dorothy Williams Claiborne
Willye Myrtle Cooke
Rosa L. Crockett
Douglas V. Davidson
Earnest Devine
Willie B. Donerson
Emma P. English
Lela Mae Garner
Joyce Ann Gatlin
Naomi F. Golf
Willie Mae Gray
Mary Ann Hall
Nayland Hayes
Rita Delores Huddleston
Roberta Irving
Clarence S. Johnson, Jr.
George M. Jones, Jr.
Marge Von Kelley
Eliza M. Lewis
Eloys H. Long
Elsie Burnett McLaughlin
Flora Hall Magee
Bettye J. Moore
Lucy D. Moore
Victoria P. Moreland
Junious Morgan
Powell Odie
Mary J. Penny
Mary Body Pepper
Effie Peters
Jetha Pinkston
Annie Lee Potts
Bennie Beatrice Powell

Audrey Jean Prentiss
Mary L. Quinn
Alfred H. Rhodes, Jr.
Reva L. Richards
Benny K. Richmond
Geneva Robinson
Lucille Johnson Robinson
Evelyn Sadberry
Evia M. Simelton
Elinder Smith
Grace Washington Smith
Sarah Frances Smith
Donald Wayne Thompson
Bobby Joe Turner
LaVerne Adams White
Annie B. Williams
Dianella B. Williams
Melinda L. Willis
Ernestine Wilson
Gloria Washington Woodard
Bachelor of Science
Herbie C. Banks
Ikie Haynes Beamon
Reva J. Bender
Dorothy J. Chapman
Johnny I. Course
Slayton A. Evans
O. B. Farish, Jr.
Gwendolyn D. Gary
Glake A. Hill
Brenda Summers Hosey
Ernestine Price Kornegay
Frankie D. Matthews
Shyrl A. Miller
Freddie G. Moore
Leothas E. Nichols
Jesse Seiferth, Jr.
Mary Liddell Spann
Sylvester Spann
Robert L. Thompson

CLASS OF 1966
Bachelor of Arts
Betty Bardwell
Judith LaVerne Bell

Rosa Bradley
Mary Brown
Rebecca Ann Brown
Tommie Virginia Brown
Emily Jean Campbell
Charlene Catchings
Rupert Crawford
Ralph Davis
Linda Darnell DeLoach
Mattie Bivins Dennis
Mamie Lucille Dunmore
Lisa Gail Fielder
Minnie Vee Garrett
Doris Moore Hall
Mattie Beatrice Hicks
Nina Hogan
Thomas Hogan
Gloria Mae Inge
Etta Mary Jackson
Patricia Ann Jackson
George W. Jamison
Fredna Jenkins
Patricia Deloris Jenkins
Josie Lee Jiles
Macie Johnson
Theodore T. Jones
Lawrence Jonathan Jordan, III
Gershon N. Konditi
Lewis Watts Lovelace
Helen M. McDowell
Joyce Evelyn McFarland
Jerome McLaurin
Leontyne Mathis
Altamese Rutledge Merchant
Ruth O. Moore
Albert Obuya Onyach
Marvin Lydell Palmore
Alice Marie Patterson
Sophie Jackson Powe
Edith Earlene Betha Rice
Arduria Jean Robinson
Josie Rosenthall
William Francis Route
Rosie Marie Sias
Patricia Rose Smith

Mildred Spaulding
Walter Jake Turnbull
Lucell Walker
Jacqueline Frances Wallace
Mattie Belle Waller
Frankie Saralyn Walton
Paulette Ford Welch
Josetta Williams
Dora Wilson
Julius Wilson

Bachelor of Science
Sarah Mae Alexander
Henry Lee Armstrong
Estella Letitia Ball
Dorothy Faye Bankhead
Charles Bracey
Fannie Mae Coats
Jo Ann Coleman
Bobbie Ann Cooper
Georgianna Dean
William Earl Duckworth
Alice Laverne Forrest
Carter Glass
Victoria Ann Goon
Atlanta Verlena Harris
Edna M. Harris
Cuvator Harvey
John Lewis Henderson
Patricia Ann Hoskins
Helene Lima Huang
Janet Patricia Jones
Sherrilyn Johnson Jordan
Cyrus Jefferson Lawyer
Sammie Inez Long
Willie Lee McArthur
Hazel Scott McGee
Stanley Merchant
Edna Moore
Robert M. Odie
Harold Joseph Pearson
Oliver Charles Rice
Albert Dudley Smith
James Alfred Spann
Clarence Stewart, Jr.
Eva Hall Taylor

Betty Jo Walker
Carolyn Voncile Walker
Alexander W. Washington, Jr.
George Oga Williams
Perry Edwin Williams
Delores Wilson
Brenda Marie Wolfe
Lilly Ruth Wyatt

CLASS OF 1967
Bachelor of Arts
Mary Evelyn Beecham
Linda Joyce Bennett
Margaret Anne Bingham
Martha Jean Birch
Sarah Ruth Brown
Jayne Allen Burrows
Miriam Gennell Cathey
Sharon Estelle Coates
George Edward Cole
Rosetta Cross
Walter Louis Davis
Sandra Yvonne Dobbs
Thomas Benjamin Forrest
Nancy Cecile Freeman
Estella C. Harris
Charlotte Lucille Harrison
Willye Yvone Holmes
Cassie V. Horton
Darlene Hudson
Charles Edwin Jones
Sarah Porter Jones
Velma Delores McGhee Kelly
Deloise Lowe
Charlene Ann McGowan
Alma Zean McPherson
Ardath Sue Hutchins McQuirter
Lurline Rice Minor
Willa Mae Moore
Debra Jean Morgan
George Curtis Nichols
Greta Beatrice Peyton
Billye Jean Pinkston
Helen Faye Reed

Evelyn Louise Robinson
Marie Rogers
Gwendolyn Campbell Sanders
Constance Iona Slaughter
Albert Squire
Lenwood Sutters
Eunice Annette Sutton
Andrew Sylvester Thomas
Norris Jesse Thomas
Maxine Yvonne Turner
Shairon Rose Vaughn
Clara Etta Vinson
Hattie Mae Cheeks Washington
Ollie Summers Washington
Willie Benjamin Watkins
Carol Pha Watson
Lorene Weathersby
Carol Dean Hicks Williams
Julian Carroll Williams
Vivian Janet Williams
Emily Anne Young
Henry James Young
Bachelor of Science
Carolyn Jeanette Hayes Amerson
Joyce Gwendolyn Bartley
John Henry Brown
Joyce Marie Combest
Oliver Wendell Cunnigen
Morris Carl Davis
Shirley Marie Davis
Frank Charles Dickey
Susan Lucille Donnan
Eddie Bob Gathright
Ethel Jean McLaurin Gibson
Obie Lee Graves
Charles Earl Griffin
Velma Harris
Delano Rhefeldtnette Heard
Marvin Lee Hochstedler
Edward Huddleston, Jr.
Carrie Pearl Hunter
Ollie Williams Johnson
Leander Atley Jones
Theodore James Lawyer
Cortez Evon McFarland

Teresia Moore
Willie Simpson Mosely
Leatha Ann Page
Linda Ruth Shelby
Rosie Mae Sibley
Curtis West Smith
James Bernard Smith
Jack Rogers Stephens
Joseph Frank Tatum
Sterling Samuel Thompson
Albert Holman Williams

CLASS OF 1968
Bachelor of Arts
Jeanettie M. Abrams
Gertrude Ann Alexander
Lewis E. Anderson
Olen Arrington, Jr.
Shirley Delores Bailey
Elaine Baker
Claudette Smith Black
Delores Bolden
Dorothy J. Boler
Laura A. Bradley
Alma C. Campbell
James L. Campbell
Shelly A. Chatman
Clencie L. Cotton
Margaret Burnham Cotton
Mac Arthur Crawford
Rosa R. Crisler
Ogene L. Davis
Odelle Davis Dockins
Betty Jean Dwight
Clemateen Flagg
Johnny Frazier, Jr.
Albert Garner
Bobbie Lee Gray
Clyde Hardamon, Jr.
Eddie L. Hayes
Barbara Jean Haynes
Geraldine Hines
Patricia Stewart Holland
Freddie M. Hoover
Willie L. Horton

Lee Vance Jernigan
Delores E. Johnson
London J. Johnson
Nathaniel E. Johnson
Thomas D. Joiner
Chester R. Jones
Delores J. Lenard
Moses I. Lewis
Patsy A. London
Doris McClendon
Christine C. McDaniel
Ronald J. Martin
Sandra Hampton May
K. C. Morrison
Marie O. Nichols
Joyce R. Parkman
Rose M. Parkman
Patricia A. Patterson
Lula C. Payne
Sarah Pittman
John W. Pleasant
Benjamin M. Prentiss
Chester L. Rash
Everett Sanders
Mary L. Sawyer
Mable M. Seaton
Lorean Short
Loretta Smith
Rosa L. Smith
Howard H. Spencer
Austin Leroy Taylor
Bennie G. Thompson
Rita Queen Trice
Jacquelyn Tucker
Kenneth E. Turnipseed
Samuel L. Tyler
Udo Essien Udoh
Annie A. Walker
Georgia B. Walker
Dorothy D. White
Bachelor of Science
Mary L. Adams
Lenal Anderson
Grover W. Barnes
Carolyn Bell

Joseph H. Bivins
James C. Black
Walter J. Conley
Beverly E. Cooley
William S. Douglas
Lessie M. Dwight
Rachel P. Fairman
David Ford
Algaria Funchess
Arthur Lee Graves
Milton R. Harrion
Lillian Hunter Davis
Gwendolyn Hicks
Tommie L. Hoskins
Hillary J. Knight
Paul C. Lampley
Louise Lawson
Sherrie A. Martin
Jack Miller
Walter E. Perryman
Vikki B. Roach
Lois V. Roots
James A. Sanders
Carolyn Smith Strete
Bertha Lee Thames
Robert Earl Thompson
Juniper O. Trice
Carl E. Washington
Ethel P. Williams

CLASS OF 1969
Bachelor of Arts
James Princeton Adams
Willie Lee Bailey
Carsella Elaine Barnes
Kenneth S. Barnes
Jacqueline Bartley
Patricia Pullum Bell
James Cleo Bradford
Charlie Brown, Jr.
Elvia Brown
Sandra Faye Brown
Terry Bryant
Evelyn Cannon

Archie Arthur Carlyle
Alfred Chiplin
Shirley Johnette Cox
Cleveland Donerson
Regina Yvonne Drake
Amelia Carolyn Evans
Gary Ford
Barbara Ann Garrett
Herman Glass
Doris B. Griffin
Doris C. Griffith
Malcolm Delano Guyton
Jimmie Ann Hampton
Paulette Patricia Hayes
Ollie M. Hicks
Sarah Ann Hines
Juerdline Hogue
Georgia Marie Holton
Cornelius Horton, Jr.
Bernice Camper Inge
Shirley Ann James
Bobbie Jean Johnson
E. Geraldine Johnson
Lutrician Johnson
Marva Ann Johnson
Andrea Louise Jones
Curley Cleveland Jones
Paul Jones
Varria Louise Jones
Henry Anderson Kerney
Eddie David Lance
Leonard Harry McInnis, Jr.
Patricia Ann McLaurin
Willie Earl Mayfield
Queen Easter Meeks
Mary Alice Miller
Golia V. Mills
Myrtlene Minor
Norman G. Mitchell
Patricia Ann Murray
Johnnie B. Neal
Ed Fawona Nguma
Jerry Wayne Nickens
Minnie Lee O'Banner
Daniel Offiong

James Perkins
Cheryl Zanders Pleasant
Eva Warfield Roberson
Una B. Robinson
Seward Rogne
Phillip Delaney Rowe
Gladys Ophelia Scott
James Short
Joseph Smith
Royce M. Smith
Leonard Stapleton
Mary Ruth Teague
John Calvin Thomas
Mollie G. Thomas
Eddie Mae Thompson
Charles Austin Thurman
Michael Turner
Mary Goines Udoh
Dorothy Ann Vaughn
Charles T. Veal
Lovie L. Vinson
Doris Jean Ward
Irma Jean Watkins
Robert Charles Watson
Kathleen Wells
Claudia Faye Wheaton
Sherry Miller White
Booker T. Winston
William Leon Woods

Bachelor of Science
Annie Patton Anderson
Meredith C. Anding
Jimmy L. Armstrong
Jewell Dean Avery
Merry Robin Bender
Shirley Jean Billups
Joan Ransom Bounds
Henry Brown, Jr.
Jerome Arthur Carroll
Levi Coats
Owen Glenn Coker
Willie Judge Collins
Annie Ruth Cornelius
Willie Warren Craft
Robert D. Cummings

Betty Jean Daniel
Tommy J. Denson
Loretta Donald
Quida Deborah Draine
Lucy Thawe Dumbo
Nedson Paulo Dumbo
Henderson Eugene Fouche
Abraham Gates
Thomas W. Gray
Larry Gene Hanshaw
Melton Harris
Lettie Mae Hartwell
Martha Faye Henson
Leola Elizabeth Hunt
Casandra Faye Jackson
James Auston Jackson
Ann Faust Johnson
Joyce Johnson
Ernest Jones, Jr.
Jewell Boone King
Murlene Anderson Kurtz
Robert Edward Lee
Edward Trussell Lewis
Nathaniel McLin
Joyce Bolden McNair
Wroten McQuirter
Roy Lee Patton
Eliza Mae Porter
Wesley Flewerny Prater
Sylvester Price
Mary Turnbull Seard
Barbara Sias
Arthur Smith
Charles J. Smith
Jo Ellen Smith
Juanita Smith
P. Malcolm Taylor
Ora Lee Williams

CLASS OF 1970
Bachelor of Arts
Faye Shaw Anderson
Ricks Charles Anderson
Ruth Inez Anderson
Peggy Irene Bell

Clara Betha
Jacquelyn Betha
Tommy Billups
Marva Blackman
Mary Smith Blackman
Addie Ruth Boyd
Mary Hunter Brandon
Mildred Yvonne Branson
Joann Terry Breland
Norma Chandler Brown
Mordessia M. Campbell
Charlie Carter
Joan Vernett Clark
Mary Hoskins Coleman
Faye I. Cooley
Eula M. Course
George W. Daniel
Ernestine L. Davis
Claudette Dent
Clotile Wilder Derrick
Basil V. Dillon
Jerome Earnest
Johnny J. Ferguson
Patricia W. Fitzpatrick
Limmie McQuirter Flowers
Arlintha A. Frazier
Milford R. Friar
Mondell V. Funchess
Thomas Funchess
Oleta Garrett
Bonnie J. Gibson
Evelyn M. Gipson
Frances R. Gordon
John C. Gore
Edna M. Graham
Janice D. Griffin
Mary A. Hales
Loraine L. Hamlin
Henry Harris
Lelia R. Harris
Janice Lenoir Henry
David Hill
Julia D. Hines
Harvey W. Holland
Elnora Stamps Horton

Barbara A. Hudson
Tanner B. Joffrion
Leon B. Johnson
Connie M. Jones
Frances M. Jones
Loretta J. Jones
Patricia A. Jones
Joyce P. Logan
Cheryl J. Louie
Marvin E. Love
Billye F. Loyd
Hayes McClendon
Jacqueline McKinnie
Johnnie M. Maberry
Lillie B. Magee
Gwendolyn Matthews
Julia E. Merchant
Ada Mae Miller
David Lee Miller
Ardessa Hill Minor
Charlotte S. Moman
Richard L. Moman
Ina C. Neal
Bobbie W. Nixon
Solomon C. Osborne
Dorothy J. Pepper
Willa I. Perryman
Evelyn T. Porter
Gwendolyn Phelps Prater
Kaaren M. Price
Benjamin M. Priestley
Charles W. Purnell
James Reed
John D. Rhodes
Jacqualyn Brown Roberts
Rosetta Smith Robinson
Janice Rogers
Willie Roy Rogers
Leah Rogne
Faye Anna Russell
Maggie J. Russell
Carolyn C. Scott
Charlene Sharp
Everett E. Snowden
Lannie Ree Spann

Alma L. Summers
Van C. Swanigan
Joanne M. Tate
Patricia A. Thomas
Sharron E. Thompson
Glenda F. Trussell
George W. Tyler
Johnetta B. Wade
Bettye J. Ward
John Curtis Washington
Stanley Weakley
Mary Wells
John M. Wesley
Brenda L. White
George M. Wicks
Essie E. Wilson

Bachelor of Science
Richard Adams
Paul Morris Armstrong
Katie Lucille Bell
Rossie Coats
Elane Coleman
Alvin L. Delk
John Curtis Farmer
Arlington L. Finley
Charlie L. Hamblin
Frederick L. Howard
Peggy J. Johnson
Hilda R. Jones
Wesley E. Jones
Ronald D. Lattimore
Gladys White Love
Jimmy R. Love
Mattie L. Love
Joseph D. McSwine
James Moore
Jesse Murphy
Henry L. Nichols
Aruby Odom
Manorris Odom
Herman E. Pearson
John Allen Rosenthall
Samuel C. Rundles
Alfreda D. Simmons
Johnnie Simms

Dan Emory Smith
Maxine D. Smith
Willie E. Smith
Zachary J. Taylor
Sammy L. Turnbull
Gloria J. Upton
Delores G. Williams
Carl D. Willis

CLASS OF 1971
Bachelor of Arts
Robert Abrams
Myrtle M. Addison
Sylvia J. Alexander
Addie B. Armstrong
Willie H. Bailey
Karl M. Banks
Robert A. Bell
Norma Jean Bentley
Marguerite Billingsley
L. A. Billups
Edward Blackmon, Jr.
Carolyn D. Blackwell
Percy Louis Bland
Ernest K. Brandon
Mary L. Dunmore Brown
Louvenia Bullie
Johnnie Edward Burse
Wilma Ree Byrd
Charles Caldwell, III
Gladys Marie Caldwell
Helen Lucille Calvert
Roslyn V. Caston
Otis Clowers
Jo Ann Collins
Bettye Ruth Cotton
DeLois R. Crawford
Mary Ella Crump
Hattie L. Daniels
Lue Bertha Davis
Peggy Ann Davis
Athalia A. Easterling
Thomas Lee Eskridge
Georgene A. Ewell
Tommye Robinson Finley

James R. Gibson
Ludwig A. Goon
Carolyn Wells Grace
Doris A. Gray
Sandra Hayes
Annie Ruth Hill
Janice Jackson Horne
Annie L. Jackson
Gloria King Jackson
Barbara W. James
Gwendolyn J. James
LeRoy Jenkins
Patricia A. Jernigan
Clarence L. Johnson
Danise Pamela Johnson
James E. Johnson
Morris L. Johnson
Eva L. Jones
Jimmie A. Jones
Lela Bridges Jones
Olivia T. Jones
Jesolyn Larry
Julia Lattimore
Martha LeFlore
Janet Jo Lockhart
Willie A. Lucas
Delois Lynch
Mary L. McGruder
Edward Magee
Elma J. Martin
Kenneth Mayfield
Arlette Miller
Gloria D. Mitchell
Walter Mitchell
Anna M. Nickens
Effiong E. Obot
Francis S. Odom
Patricia A. Odom
Dianne Parker
Cinderella Reed
Doris Richardson
Jeffrey Robertson
Gloria Yvonne Robinson
Florence Russell
Martha A. Shannon

Audrey D. Smalling
Bertha P. Smith
Margie Smith
Peggy Smith
Carolyn A. Stamps
Havis B. Stewart
Beverly Styles
Charles Taylor
David M. Taylor
Tasso Thomas
Alfonso Todd
Roy Tolbert
Horace Turnbull
Emma Pearl Turner
Cyrille Walwyn
Elaine Ward
Marilyn G. Weaver
Melvin C. Weaver
Lenora Brewer Whitfield
Lewistine Young

Bachelor of Science

Tophas Anderson
Mary A. Brown
Daryl Brownlow
Robert Byrd
Terry J. Collins
Otis Dampeer
Ezelle Edwards
Sammie Giles
Terry Gene Henderson
Lovie L. Jackson
Maurice James
Mavis Parkman James
James Kegler
Hattie Lenoir
Katie Ethel McGee
Jewell McKinney
Alfred McNair
Thelma Matlock
Jesse Owens
Carolyn G. Price
Earnest Rankin
Janice B. Reed
Rose M. Rogers
Marion E. Roots

Jessie L. Sherrod
Haywood Stephney
Helen Summers
Lawrence M. Sutton
Carl E. Washington

CLASS OF 1972
Bachelor of Arts
Edwin D. Adams
Janice Lynch Adams
Elverse Alexander
Eddie J. Anthony, Jr.
Frenchie Holton Bailey
Mandie Marie Barnes
Odessa Anderson Barron
Betty Robinson Bass
Leatha M. Bennett
Hilda Gibson Billups
Patricia Ann Blackmon
Edna Jean Body
Betty Jean Bogan
Joann Green Boyd
Willie L. Bridgeman, Jr.
Thelma Calvert
David Louis Carr
Eddie Lee Chambers
Emma Gibson Clowers
Ethel King Coleman
Henry Mason Coleman
Charles Cook
Lillie Morton Cunningham
Gail Ann Davis
Joe Edward Davis
Sandra J. Davis
Clyde E. Dinkins
James Durr
Edward Rudolph Dyson, Jr.
Rubysteen Ephfrom
Mary Artilee Evans
Frank V. Figgers
Jacqueline Joan Funchess
Van Meter Gandy
Evelyn Marie Gibson
Lee Gene Gillard
Jacqueline C. Glover

Fredia Bender Goon
Jimmie Gross
Linda J. Hamilton
Linda G. Hardaway
Peggy Diannie Hardy
Gloria Inez Hawkins
Leroy Hayes, Jr.
Mary Ruth Haynes
Doris Jean Hill
Sophia M. Huff
Gwendol Maethel Hurd
Priscilla A. Isabelle
Carol S. Johnson
Jacqueline Johnson
Zelma Jean Johnson
Zep Carl Johnson
Hercules A. Jones
Juanita Jones
Judith Consuella Jones
Robert Jones
Jean Diane Kelly
Georgette Kimbrough
Archie Lee Langston, Jr.
Evelyn Farrish Lewis
Larry Darnell Lewis
Willie Lyn Lewis
James R. Lindsay
Jeanette V. Lofton
Glenda Logan
Janice Lucas
Emma Lyons
Eligia E. McGee
Carl McNair
David Earl Miller
Lorma Miller
Brenda Joyce Montgomery
Charles R. Murphree
David Lee Nall, Jr.
Josephine Neely
Maxcine Nichols
Mary Belinda Owens
James H. Parker
Otis Pearson
Melvin Phillips
Thelma E. Raglin

Dorothy Rankin
Earl Ratliff, Jr.
Susan B. Rhodes
William J. Rice, Jr.
Juanita Ritter
Selwyn Ross
Lorene Rush
Mittie P. Seals
Lena Mae Seaton
Delores Arnold Shaw
Ava Singleton
Joyce Small
Ardelia Smith
Eric Smith
LaQuita Smith
Shirley Jean Smith
Frankie Sutherland
Gwen Lavell Taylor
Sandra Baker Taylor
Lesly Ann Terry
Harold Thompson
Velma J. Tillman
Dannie Tucker
Melvin Turner, Jr.
Don H. Walker
Roy D. Walker
Joyce Clark Warren
Mary A. Washington
LaVaughn White
Irving Wilkerson
Marilyn S. Wilkerson
Ella Louise Williams
Frankie Elaine Williams
Linda Joyce Williams
Robert Williams, Jr.
Susan M. Williams
Cozette Wilson
Geraldine Clara Wilson
Lynda D. Woods
Ernelle Wright
Bachelor of Science
Willie N. Barksdale, Jr.
Richard Temple Black
Tommy Harold Black
Patricia Trace Booth

Shirley Faulkens Bradford
Bobby Earl Brown
Eunice Carter
Donald Ray Cole
Carolyn Ann Combest
Deloris D. Daniels
Maxine M. Dickerson
Milton Webster Forte, II
Jimmie L. Foster
Howard Wayne Glenn
Helen Marie Hoover
Roy Lee Irons
Vernon James Ivory
Artman Jackson
Jerry J. Jackson
Tommy Lee James
Aurelia Jones
Doretha Lance
Albert Luther Love
Phillip Marsh
James Westley Miggins
Laura Ann Mims
Rufus J. Outley
Edwin H. Quinn
Ruthven Nathaniel Sampath
Robert W. Smith, III
Wilmer Earl Standfield
Roosevelt Turner, Jr.
Joyce Marilyn Weathersby
Primus Wheeler, Jr.
Charles Earl Williams
Ernestine Willis

CLASS OF 1973
Bachelor of Arts
Carolyn Ann Abrams
Patricia Ann Aldridge
Emma Lou Allen
Annie Louise Anderson
Henry E. Anderson
Romona Barney
George Bartley
Donnetta Baylous
Booker J. Bearden
Norman Bennett

Albert Roy Bowman
Acquanetta LaFaye Bracy
Mary LaJoyce Brady
Patricia Ann Brandon
Donna Jean Bridgeman
Marion Joyce Broadwater
Charlie Broady
Mary Paulette Brown
Isaac K. Byrd
Mary Alice Calvert
Emma McCune Carroll
Patricia Pearl Castilla
Marilyn Chambers
Lethaniel Chandler
Dorie A. Ladner Churnet
Doris Jean Clay
Arlena Ruth Clayton
Shirley Ann Cook
Slyvia Marie Crumwell
James T. Davis
Sherry Lynn Davis
Emma Dean Willingham Dixon
Jackie Louise Dotson
Patricia Washington Dyson
Audrae Faye Elders
Carrie L. Gates
Christine Lark Glenn
Hattie M. Johnson Gooden
Tomie Z. Turner Green
Mary A. Hall
Willie Kent Hand
Clara Frances Turner Hayes
Loistine Hines
Beverly Wade Hogan
Mary Lee Howard
George Harold Huff
Catherine L. Adams Irons
Gussie Marie Jackson
Richard Jackson
Samuel Jennings
Bernard Johnson
Isaac Johnson
Marion M. Johnson
Susan Johnson
Verdine Johnson

Albert Arthur Jones
Eddie W. Jones
Lois Todd Jones
Mary Reeves Jones
Geraldine King
Carol Ann Labat
Mathew Lindsay
Ivory Fernando Lofton
Joe Earl Love
Lillie Will McCain
Patricia Ann McClinton
Rita Faye McGill
Sandy Dwayne Martin
Debra Stevenson Miller
Fearrington Miller
Willie Jewel Miller
DeLois Montgomery
Shirley Vernice Montgomery
Grace Marie Moore
Paula Diane Morrow
Terry Morton
Rosamary Murph
Jerretha Parker
Shirley Mason Pearson
Andrew Pennington
Larry Peppers
Gloria Porter
Herman U. Porter
Herman D. Powell
Mary Catherine Rainey
Dennis Ramsey
Clara Faye Reed
Frankie S. Reed
Shirley Ann Roberts
Connie Taylor Sanders
Joyce M. Shelton
Bernice H. Smith
Daisie Mae Smith
Isabella Brandon Smith
Willie Spann
Betty Spraggins
Ezzard Charles Stamps
Marva Paulette Taylor
Perelia M. Thompson Taylor
Ellen Ann Todd

Bernice Turner
Laura Bailey Turner
Randolph Watson
Earlene Jordan Wheeler
Dorothy Marcelle White
Hazel Lee White
Melvin White
Pearlena Wilburn
Beverly A. Williams
Bruce E. Williams
Eugene Williams
Henry Eugene Williams
Johnny Lee Williams
Julius Williams
Wesley B. Williams
Jerry Edwind Wilson
Percy G. Wilson
LaDonna Woullard

Bachelor of Science
Frazier Anderson
Carolyn Donald Bennett
Felicia Joyce Brown
Sharon Ann Brown
Irving C. Comer
John Edgar Davis
Johnny B. Gilleylen
Lionel Graham
Geraldine Chaney Hardamon
Issac H. Hawthorn
Charlie B. Henry
Glenda Huston
Rosie Lynn Johnson
Johnny Ruth Jackson Leach
Larry Lenard Lowe
Rosemary Crump McClendon
Delorise Ann Neely
Joyce Ann Newsome
Ronnie Layne Paige
Joseph Powell
Imbree Charles Richmond
Calvin R. Robinson
Masefield Chesterton Sampath
Jean Smith Sampson
Curtis Shaw
Jimmy L. Simon

Edna E. Stingley
Jimmy Lee Thompson
Shirley Ann Walker
Shirley Jean Williams
Alphonso Willis

CLASS OF 1974
Bachelor of Arts
Armelia Angela Adams
Gearlean Byrd Adams
Joseph L. Adams
Wilma Joyce Alexander
Maxine White Allen
William B. Allen
Lula Mae Anderson
Anna B. Barnes
Larry N. Bland
Carolyn Anita Booth
Doris Jean Gibbs Broadwater
Claudia Ester Brown
Delores Wright Brown
John Earl Brown
Mary E. Buck
Willie L. Buckner
Delores Buford
Emitt Carman
Jo Ann Carr
James Walter Carson
Annie Jean Cason
Mack Earl Chambers
Sandra Chambers
Robert Lester Clark
Mamie L. Clayborn
Linda Ann Cole
Lydia Gail Cole
Hurtistine Collins
Paul Lawrence Cooper
Deborah Hulitt Corner
Donald Cunnigen
Wanda K. Davis
Marvell Donald
Gerald Joseph Donatien
Robert Donnell
Elizabeth Douglas
John Earl Draine

Annie Jean Fains
Yvonne Delores Fairley
Walter Lewis Flood
Patricia Ford
Barry Andre Garner
Sirrinthia Thomas Gilleylen
Linda Ruth Gines
Bernadine Grady
Rubestine C. Hacker
Jacqueline Diane Harmon
Donald Harris
Linda Joyce Hawkins
Mary Louise Hill
Margo Yvonne Davis Hines
Peggy McDonald Hilton
Beulah Bernice Hobbs
Bertha Holmes
Lethaniel Holt
Vivian Holton
Shelia Ann Howard
Eddie A. Hunter, Jr.
Evelyn Hyche
Elizabeth Ann Jackson
Embra K. Jackson, Jr.
Geraldine Logan Jackson
Mary Lynn James
Lois Jean Jernigan
Rosa Ethel John
Mattie Pearl Johnson
Shirlean Jones Johnson
Adonna E. Jones
Annie Mae Jones
Horatio Erwin Jones, Jr.
Jacqueline Jones
Katherine Jones
Linda Carroll Jones
Ruby Mae Burney Jones
Annette Keeton
Willie James Kelly
Fannie Kimbrough
Donna Eleene King
Juanita Kinnard
Jerry Don Langston
Verna Deanne Collins Lee
George A. Levy

Quinella E. Lewis
Michelle Lofton
Ronald Love
Lela Odessa McCants
Leonard McDavid
Tommie McNeill
Emma Pearl Miller
Bettie Mitchell
John Harvey Montgomery, Jr.
Robert Leon Moore
William Yan Quae Mulbah
Carolyn Faye Neal
John Foster Peaches
Shirley Diane Pennington
Alva Ruth Peyton
Alice C. Pickett
Sandra Alyn Quinn
Febbie Jones Ramsey
Josephine Davidson Robertson
Roosevelt Robinson, Jr.
Patricia Ann Rosenthall
Rochella Green Sanders
Mary Banks Shelton
James Parish Smith
Mamie L. Thomas
Worth Hal Thomas
Janice E. Thompson
Fannie Rebecca Turner
Linda Marie Turner
Elizabeth Walker
Linda Marie Walker
Willie Barnard Washington
Hester Leontyne Watts
Stella Webb
Zebton C. Wells, Jr.
Essie Lena Wicks
Beverly Ann Williams
Carolyn Ann Williams
Frank Williams, Jr.
Patsy Tillmon Williams
Mary Lena Windfield
Bessie L. York
Jack Harvey Young, Jr.

Bachelor of Science

Maude Helen Andrews

Yvonne Vivian Bailey
Janie Davenport Beasley
Sterling Coleman Beasley
Elinda Burks
Dennis Lerone Chandler
Larry Lamar Day
Metric Lamar Dockins
Carolyn Dianne Douglas
Dianne Murry Hamblin
Lloyd M. Harrington
Portia Martini Harris
Berkeley A. Jemmott
Julietta Laureen Johnson
Lawrence Jones
Quintus Jones
Patricia King
Charles Lambert
Philson Joseph Lewis
Shun Cheng Lin
Arthur L. Little, Jr.
Clyde Ray McLaurin
Paul Douglas McQuitter
Peter Lun-Yan Ma
Joycelyn Mass
Willie Edward Morgan, Jr.
Wilhelmina F. O'Reilly
Joyce L. Perkins
Melvin Perkins, Jr.
Henry Lee Pippins
Obra Della Harrington Porter
Charity L. Shaw
Ann Elizabeth Stinson
Howard Charles Walls

CLASS OF 1975
Bachelor of Arts
Norma Grice Alexander
Clara Bea Allen
Donnie Ray Allen
Grace Allen
Sarah Ann Allen
Carrie Anderson
Dorothy Jean Anderson
Jacqueline J. Anderson
Margie A. Barnes

Motice Jean Barnes
Daryl Bass
Annie B. Bell
Frances Jean Boose
Shirley Ann Boose
Patricia Myles Bradford
Bonnie Faye Britton
Barbara Brown
Billy Wayne Brown
Edna Earle Buck
Barbara Ann Bulloch
Clova Burks
Jeruthie Arlene Burton
Shirley Clairse Byers
Tillmon Calvert
Eddie J. Calvin
Patricia Laverne Cannon
Joe Louis Carpenter
Jean Farish Carson
Ronnie Melvin Carter
Debra A. Casey
Hattie Mae Coleman
Sallie Mae Coleman
Shirlee Diane Coleman
Tyrone Andre Coleman
Martha Ruth Darden
Calvin Day
Donna Y. Dillon
Diana McClendon Dixon
Linda Davis Dixon
Doris Edna Durr
Deborah England
Linda Gail Esco
Carolyn Louise Evans
Stacy Marie Evans
Charles C. Fouche
Ruth Mae Freeman
Gladys Beatrice Gibbs
Tommie Giles
John A. Grandberry
Gloria Jean Green
Sandra Shelley Harbour
Bernice Harris
Hattie B. Harris
Henry Harris

Emmitt W. Hayes
Jennie Virginia Haynes
Daryl Henderson
Adolphus Henson
Gloria Stine Howard
Linda R. Hunt
Victoria Ivory
Patricia Ivy
Jesse Leon Jackson
Margie Joffrion
Alletia D. Johnson
Carl V. Johnson
Joe Willie Johnson
Willie Charles Johnston
Betty Jones
Tanya D. Lezie
William F. McDaniel
Loretta Shird McLaurin
Stephania Joyce McMullen
Mildred McMurtry
Wilton Allen McNair
Brenda Lynell Mabry
Audrey Z. Martin
Ora Dean Martin
John Edwina Mattix
Linda Jean Moore
Ornell Denis Morris
Steven Njemanze
Harvey Owens
Essie M. Patterson
Linda Yvonne Payton
Shirley Marie Perkins
Willie James Perkins
Jimmy H. Polk
Sherry Ann Polk
James L. Powell
Brenda Sue Putnam
James Randolph
Linda Ratliff
Susan Etta Reed
Debra Richardson
Shirley Mae Roberts
Betty Cathel Robinson
Brentice Robinson
Larry Robinson

Lee Edgar Rodgers
Yvonne Rogers
David E. Ross
Earnestine Russell
Ruth Ann Schnell
Linda Ruth Scott
Archie Rudolph Smith
Charles Edward Smith
Lloyd Smith
Rita Marie Smith
James V. Steele
Luke D. Stowers
Linda Rose Sutton
Charles Edward Taylor
Jesse Lee Thomas
Zolda Tillman
Dorris Lynell Varnado
Carolyn LaJean Wales
Deloris Walker
Jeanie Theresa Walker
Joan Lorraine Walker
Sarah Frances Washington
Patricia A. Watkins
Lucas Nathaniel Watson
Cathy Sias Weaver
Fredia LaVerne Wheaton
Gwendolyn Johnson Wilkes
Cheryl Denise Williams
Michael W. Williams
Shirley Dinell Williams
Arthur Neil Willis
Velma Wilson
Joselyn Wyatt
Deborah Yvonne Young
Lorna Shird Young
Ollie Myrtle Zanders

Bachelor of Science

Willie J. Allen
Michael Jerome Brown
Janice Deborah Farrish
Elliot Wendell Forte
Will Kent Gee
Albert Gibbs
Dianna Grant
Bobby L. Harris

Tyrus A. McCarty
Roslind I. McCoy
Clois Lee McLain
Theodore Morgan
Michael F. Owen
Savannah B. Shelby
Pearl Eunice Smith
Veronica Lake Styles
Rose Marie Thomas
James Howard Webb
Emanuel Wilkes
Cora L. Young

CLASS OF 1976
Bachelor of Arts
Linda L. Adams
Margie Mae Adams
Michael O. Adams
Raynaldo Agnew
Deborah LaNeice Aldridge
Berda Ann Amos
Rosie Elaine Anderson
Carol Annese Armstrong
Georgianne Bacon
Charles Edward Banks
Tumutual Bell
Shirley Bennett
Theresa Coleman Bland
Sally Evans Briggs
Jackie Marie Burtin
Lester Jerrel Carter
Wanda Elizabeth Carter
Rosie Clark
Mary Clayton
Carol Ann Cummings
Laurette Patricia Daniels
Delores Davis
Odessa Day
Vinceson Earl Diamond
Gloria Ann Donelson
Sandra Victoria Douglas
Linda C. Dunham
Donnie Evans
Joyce Marie Farrar
Joe Albert Fleming

Sarah Johnson Gailes
Walter Gant
Genoise M. Gaylor
Robert Lewis Gibbs
Roberta Springwater Gibson
Deborah A. Gordon
Frederick Griffin
Laurinda Denise Hall
Barbara Hobson
Charles E. Holbrook
Joyce Jones Hollins
Grace E. Hood
Richard E. Hopkins
Martha Faye Howell
Diane Hunley
Melvina Hurst
Dorothy Leola Hutchins
Frances Jenell Hutchins
Debra Jean Jackson
J. C. Jackson
Linda Faye Jerdine
Alberta Lynette Johnson
Mary Johnson
Tommie Jones
Quinton Kabi Kargbo
Sandra Lucille King
Joyce Yavatte Kirkmon
Mary Ann Langford
Gladies Lee
Israel Lee
Mildred Juanita LeSure
Leroy Levy
Charles Douglas Lewis
Emery Jerome Lewis
Thallis Lewis
Woodlin W. Lewis
Mamie Evelyn Locke
Betty R. Luckett
Gerthania Luckey
Patrick L. McCray
Carolyn Faye McDonald
Joe Ann Horn McDonald
Shirley Joyce Magee
Evelyn Massey
Mae Katherine Meeks

Terry D. Micou
Angela Elaine Miller
Quincy Charles Moore
Reginald H. Moore
Janice Karen Murph
Annie A. Nash
Annie M. Nash
Jacqueline Bouvier Nelson
Benjamin Nwagaboniwe Omali
Mary L. Owens
Frances Dianne Parkman
Sandra Faye Peaches
Johnny Paul Pickett
Chris Powe
Marshall Regano Powe
Thurgood M. Price
Doris Marie Rice
Gregory Rice
Veola Robbins
Cynthia Gale Russell
Thomas H. Sanders
Gail Bouldin Savage
Elva Jean Smith
James Curtis Smith
Joan Smith
Johnnie Mae Smith
Nollie McIntosh Smith
Pamela Day Sparks
Sandra F. Spencer
Ann D. Stamps
Denise Delores Sweet
Michael Taylor
Regina Marie Thomas
Dianne Marie Thompson
Loistine Thompson
Mary Lee Thompson
Earlie Mae Washington
Betty Jean Watkins
Silas Joseph White
Cynthia Kathleen Williams
Jessie L. Williams
Constance E. Wilson
Shirley Ann York
Dias A. Young
Sharron Oliver Younkins

Bachelor of Science
Gene Mark Baines
Richard R. Bloom
Regan Edwin Fennell
Charles E. Gailes
Milton Grays
Ronnie Hawkins
Jon Kendahl Jones
Mary Gail Jordan
Edna Elaine Mass
Lee Nola Morris
John A. Patterson
Brenda Ann Rogers
Dorothy J. Sallis
Henry Lee Simpson
Willie W. Stapleton
Eddie Summers
David Turner, II
James E. Williams

CLASS OF 1977
Bachelor of Arts
Carrie B. Alexander
Thomisene Anderson
Gloria Barnes
Karen Devriese Bell
Ruby Bennett
Edgar A. Bishop
Josephine Franklin Bowser
Maxine Brandon
Dorothy Rene Brown
Joni Yvette Brown
Natalie Brown
Connie Latrenda Butler
Laura Cappie
Larry Chambers
Patricia A. Cole
Elzie James Collins
Gregory Cotton
Cherrie Davenport
Barbara A. Davis
Mary Celeste Deanes
Frederick Lamar Diamond
Robert Earl Donnell
Diane Ephfrom

Doris Jean Epson
Carrie Robbins Evans
Jimmy Faggett
Alice Patricia Falls
Lorraine Gates
Lavern George
Herbert Ray Gilbert
Debra Jeanette Gray
Willie Griffin
Glenda Ruth Haynes
Barbara Smith Henderson
Odya Herbert
Nadene Houston
Geraldine Hutchins
Linda Deloris Jackson
Annette Cheryl Jacobs
Roy Lee Jacobs
Anthony W. Joe
Betty A. Johnson
Lavern Johnson
Brenda Jones
Janet R. Jordan
Minnie Pearl Joyner
Janice Faye Kennedy
Brenda Denise Lee
Stanley Lee
Kenneth Gibson Lewis
Linda Ann McLaurin
Vernetta Magruder
Marilyn Marie Moore
Sandra Faye Murray
Gwendolyn Newsome
Gertrude Melresse Payne
Sarah Perry
Jearlean Porter
Richard S. Porter
Monica Price
Helen Jean Randolph
Hannah Rankin
Gail Ratliff
Patricia Ann Ray
Minnie Reed
Wanda MacChell Reed
Liza Richard
Coleen Rivers

Clyde Ellis Rogers
Cynthia N. Williams Rogers
Barbara Rouse
Gail Lanette Seaton
Mary Ann Sellers
Isabella Shears
Shirley M. Singletary
Joe C. Smith
Roberto L. Smith
Nathaniel Jerome Stampley
Freddie L. Stimage, Jr.
Wanda Joan Straughter
Nannie Hope Sudduth
Dennis Charles Sweet, III
Burna Dean Thomas
Linda Faye Travis
Maudie H. Tucker
Violet Marie Tyler
Deborah S. Varnado
Hattie Walker
Joyce Lorraine Walker
Maggie Ward
Freddie Gehazi Williams
Irene Williams
Charles Wilson
Terrecia T. Wilson
Teresa Ann Woodard

Bachelor of Science

Alexis Aning
Catherine Thompson Ayewoh
Joseph C. Battle
Lloyd Booker
Michelle Byrd
Arthelis Carson
Deborah Renae Clark
James K. Coleman
Kennedy C. Coleman
Fannie Ruth Collier
Felton J. Daniel
Jonathan Dean
Michael Jerome Gibson
Brenda K. Harmon
George Davis Headd
Rhonda Elaine Hill
Sarah Ann Jackson

De'Andra Johnson
Gloria Ann Johnson
Joseph Johnson, Jr.
Cheryl Denise Jones
Loretta Mae Lewis
Randy S. Love
Deborah Eloise Luckett
Linda K. McAdory
Obie Michael McNair
Jo Helen Minor
Teresa Mixon
Danette Janice Nevels
Isaac Perkins
Linda Faye Queen
Minnie Mae Riley
Bobby Gene Roberson
Steven Robinson
Clara C. Sallis
Shirley Ann Jackson Sanders
Joyce Marie Scott
Minnie Esther Sherman
George Marie Strickland
Linda G. Taylor
Irma M. Thompson
Isaac Tuah-Poku
Dellwyn Michelle Turnipseed
Patricia Ann Wade
William Lloyd Wade
Sheriel Faye Walker
Debbie Williams
Debra Williams

CLASS OF 1978
Bachelor of Arts
Isaac Oluwafemi Adeeko
Mary Vivian Alexander
Rhonda Yuvonne Armstrong
Gwendolyn Buckner Baines
Cheryl Denise Bell
Myrtle Shirley Boglin
Audrey Bousqueto
Connie Jean Brown
Dennis Bush
Sylvia J. Carpenter
DeLinda Carter

Ray Charles Carter
Lucy Chatman
Vernell Clayborn
Breat Nathaniel Coleman
Thomas Frederick Coleman
Mary Louise Lyons Conway
Elbe Patricia Darden
Erma Lee Ferguson
Arlington Lee Fitch
Bessie Funchess
Steven Anthony Gipson
Kenneth Jerome Graves
Garnett C. Gunn
Brenda Dianne Hines
Tyrone Byron Hines
Renay Hinton
Nathaniel Hobbs
Juanita Alicia Hover
Gregory Howard
Bonita Rose Jackson
Michael Albert Jackson
Jacqueline James
Timothy James
Ruben A. Joe
Jean M. Johnson
Keith Johnson
Linda Leggins Johnson
Annie M. Jones
Brian Joseph
Glen Lacey
Marshall Earl Lee
Deborah Faye Linson
Carlton F. McCullough
Virginia Faye McMullen
Marilyn Martin
Thomas Martin
William Wendell Martin
Thaddeus Mayfield
Paul J. Mays
Carolyn Jean Minor
Melissa Ann Mitchell
Tyrone Mitchell
Stanley Lloyd Moore
Kenneth Elroy Morris
Myra Danita Murray

Linda Marie Myles
DeLois Ann Newman
Kathy Laverne Pruitt
Joseph Richardson, Jr.
Mary Riley
Brenda Ruffin
Dorothy L. Webb Salvant
Cynthia A. Dorsey Smith
James Smith, Jr.
Fabvienen Clara Taylor
Carl Edward Thomas
Debra A. Thomas
Mattie Thomas
Shirley Mae Thomas
Charles Allen Thurman
Zonnytta Myrette Vinson
Thurman Wallace
Eddye Belinda Ware
Berthene Washington
Malinda Watts
Deloris Wedlaw
Barbara Jeane Weeks
Jacqueline Wheeler
Maxine Wilkes
Betty Jean Williams
Debra G. Williams
Pamela D. Williams
Andrew James Wilson
Ira Wilson

Bachelor of Science

Sam Davis Adams
Myrna Ellen Alexander

Clement C. Alleyne
Willie Arbuthnot
Gloria Jean Barnes
Debra Denease Bartley
Lewis Blair
Evelyn Marie Brown
Barbara Ann Clark
Fredrick D. Clark
Patricia Ann Cole
Debra Ann Davis
Sam Henry Davis
Diann Grant
Andrea Lynn Green
Mary Ann Hadley
Yvonne Yvette Henderson
Fleta Marie Jones
Bobby Larry
Debra Ann Lee
Brenda Gail Lockhart
Norma Jean Lumpkins
Carolyn Luster
Lee Samuel Lyons
Marion L. McNeal
Shirley Ann Mass
Rose Mary Matthews
Ruth E. Williams Patterson
Percy Lee Price
Sherry Ann Queen
Peter John Reed
Carolyn Sanders
Billie Kay Spurlock

Graduates / 1979–2001

May 13, 1979

Associate of Arts
Mary Battle
Laura Granderson
Rosie Head Howze
Queen E. Howard
Maretta Ross
Hattie B. Saffold
Dixie B. Sparkmon
Carrie Williams

Bachelor of Arts
Alean McIntyre Adams
Dianne Adams
Sandra Backstrom
Barbara Clemetta Banks
James Barnes
Johnny R. Barnes
Kaye Dianne Barnes
Margaret Marcellia
    Barnes
Alex Bellamy, Jr.
Leroy Bennett
Eve M. Blair
Rose Mary Bourn
Annie Mae Brandon
Maggie Buchanan
Earlene Bullock
LaWanda Marcel Burnett
Lee Esther Butler
Kenneth Jerome Calvin

Jeannie M. Coe
Beverly Faye Cole
Johnnie Mae Cole
Don L. Coleman
Mildred Copeland
Willie L. Crowner
Irma Ree Dailey
Regina Marie Daniels
Otho Lee Day
Ruth Lynett Evans
Brenda Foreman
Augusta Gail Forest
Joseph L. Gibson, Jr.
Mirian Peprika Gibson
Helen M. Glenn
Joyce D. Gooden
Carolyn Lanise Grant
Joyce Ann Hankins
Gail Loretta Hall
Gary E. Haynes
Joan Michelle Herron
Mary Alice Hinds
Sonya Denese Hines
Barbara Sharran Jackson
Patricia Elois Jackson
Angelique Michelle
    Jefferson
Frank M. Johnson
Robert E. Johnson
Emma Jean Keeton
Walterine Langford
Deborah Denise LeSure

Eddie H. McCoy
Barbara L. Manning
Brenda Kaye Mitchell
Sadie R. Myers
Patricia Nichols
Ignatius Nwakire Okoro
Alyce M. Osborne
Ruth Osborne
Barbara Jo Payne
Mack J. Addison
    Pendleton
Robbie Blackmon
    Pendleton
Darrell L. Pierce
Sheila Denise Porter
Hattie Laura Randolph
Charles Ranson
Larry Rayford
Ruthie Ann Redfield
Aileen Robbins
Christopher Allan
    Rogers
Eva Voncile Ros
Michael Everett
    Rutledge
Michele Yvette Rutledge
Ronald Sims
Rose Marie Small
James C. Smith
Williette Smith
Walter Stewart
Rufus Taylor

Beverly Ann Terry
Jo Ann Vaughn
Frederick Lewis
  Washington
Louis Joseph West, Jr.
Isabel Elaine Wheeler
Brenda Fay Williams
Ricky A. Williams
Cheryl Danette Wise
Doris Louise Woods
Felix M. Yeboah

Bachelor of Science
Lila Darlene Boddie
Frank Arnold Brown
Detrick Lolether Brown
Melvin D. Burton
Joy L. Buttler
Geneva Cannon
Kurt Roger Cherry
Beverly Bernett Clark
Lindberg Clark, Jr.
Raymond Earl Daniels
Alfred Davis
Bonnie Clarissa Davis
Marsha Ann Douglas
Frankie Elaine Faulkner
Gloria Fields
John C. Flowers
Jean Fry
Lucinda Green
Annie Jeanette Harris
Yvonne Sarah Hart
Gerri Lavonne Hill
Bernice Drusella Jackson
William Theodore
  Jefferson
Elsie Johnson
Faye Acqunita Johnson
Gwendolyn Johnson
Gloria Jean Jordan
Bobby Glen Keyes
Edward Maurice Kitchen
Blanche A. J. Lowry

Melanie Patrice Monroe
Jonas Udeaqbala
  Nwaeme
Michael Anthony
  Reddix
Charles Leonard Rodgers
Diann Sims
Edith Faye Smith
Gala Deloris Smith
Denise Spurlock
Kirk Sheppard Stovall
Mary Alice Thompson
John B. Veasley
Bettye Walters
Don Cornelius Williams
Edith J. Winder
Cheryl Elayne Wright

May 11, 1980

Associate of Arts
Willie D. Frizell
Mary Louise Jones
Laura Moore
Equlla Taylor

Bachelor of Arts
Brenda Blackmon
Kenneth Blackmon
Brenda Celest Bullard
Edith Deloris Cannon
Basil Anya Chukwu
James Ronnell Coleman
Winnie Branch Conway
Gwendolyn Crosby
Sharon Gail Crosby
Frank Lee Crump
Denise D. Crutchfield
Brenda F. Culp
Melba L. Dixon
Norma Jean Dorsey
Janice S. Ellis
Nancy Marie Ellis

Mary McCain Fluker
Phyllis Lenora Garris
Dorothy Ann Glenn
Gloria J. Grace
Evon Grant
Janice Hampton
Derrick Hankins
Joyce Elaine Harris
Kenneth Earl Hollins
Verneta Hampton
  Humes
Martha D'Trellis Irons
Barbara P. Jackson
Dianne Jackson
Gwendolyn Jackson
Jimmie Johnson
Mahalia Johnson
Veranda Lorraine Joliff
Rachel Faye Jones
Joyce Marie Kendrick
Deborah Jennings Lake
Dianne Larry
Verlene Lee
Hurbert Wallace Loper
Pearlie Maurice Magee
Lucille K. Martin
George E. Mass
Brenda Lorraine
  Middleton
Wes Carlton Miller
Alfredia Minor
Sadie Ruth Myers
Betty Jean Norwood
Samuel Ogbonnia Ogbuh
Dorothy Jean Osborne
Beverly Ann Parker
Pamela Denise Perry
Racheal Perry
Lavern Pitchford
Janice Faye Porter
Margrett B. Goodloe
  Prentiss
Debra D. Richmond
Brenda S. Ritter

Freddie Mae Rufus
Eloise Russell
Hattie B. Saffold
Bernita Ann Scott
Carrie Michele Seaton
Virgie Marie Seltzer
Patricia Belle Sims
Essie L. Smith
Herman Smith
Jackie Surrell
Roderick B. Wade
Emma Delois Walker
Lucille Walker
Robert Walker
Debra Ann Waller
Barbara June Warner
Mattie L. Watson
Calvin Weathersby
Bernadean Wells
Barbara Dian Wesley
Lubertha Nash Wilder
Charlene Hazel Wilkins
Tela LeKaye Wilson
Yolanda Denise Wilson

Bachelor of Science
Cheryl Denise Berry
Homer Booth
Sheila Ann Braxton
Natalie Yvette Brookins
Wandalyn Denise Fields
Dianne Hill
Mary Jackson Holbrook
Dianne Johnson
Paul Johnson
David W. Jordan
Derek LaRosa Kelly
Sharon V. Kersh
Edwin A. Lee, Jr.
Karl Dee Moore
Abraham Morris
Romero Nicholson
Godwin Offiah
Peggy S. Oswald
Lee Andrew Palmer

Deborah Kim Parker
Humphrey Planner, Jr.
Doris Elaine Queen
Carl M. Reddix
Gregory Alan Robertson
Stephanie Cecile Smith
Carol Tanner
Ernest Leroy Terry
Rosie Kinzy Thomas
Clifton Burnett West, Sr.
Carolyn J. White
Eddie L. Whitehead
Mavis Theodora
   Williams
Michael LeRoy Williams

May 17, 1981

Associate of Arts
Etta B. Greer
Dorothy J. Long Huston
Elma W. Thompson

Bachelor of Arts
Brenda Faye Armstrong
Jeffrey Claiborne
   Armstrong
Patsy Jo Barnes
Geraldine Barney
Myrna Lynette Beard
Demetriss Almonette
   Bennett
Alesia Gail Booth
Patricia Alice Bradley
Eddie Noel Brown
Roger Bernard Brown
Richard F. Brownlow, Jr.
Peggy A. Jones-Buckner
Wilda Deliece Buie
Sandra Burnett
Cynthia L. Camper
Helen Coleman
Lucille Coleman
Cynthia Varetta Cooper

Emmit Cornelius
Lisa Denise Crawford
Jerry Jerome Davis
Brenda Gale Dennis
Sandra Dennis
Octavia Dubose
Lillie Mae Dulaney
Eric A. S. G. Garnes
Belinda A. Gipson
Dennis Ray Gordon
Adrienne Yvonne Gordy
Eula Ceelia Green
Linda Delories Green
Jacqualine Elaine
   Gregory
Keenan David Grenell
Sherry Dianne Gunn
Jerry D. Hargett
Gloria Jean Hart
Joseph Curtis Haynes
Charlotte Diane Hill
Willie Bee Hinds
Herdie Lee Holloway
Flecha W. Holmes
Linda Faye Horn
Bonnie Lou Jackson
Calvin D. Jackson
Ruth Clarie Jackson
Tracy Annette Jefferson
Cheryl Ann Jones
Earnestine Jones
Yvonne Jones
Alice Louise Joyner
Cassandra Early Leach
April Renolda Levi
Carleen Lynn
Lorraine McDonald
Glenn McMillian
William Earl Martin
Belinda Miller
Linda Murphy
Rose Nichols
Cynthia Jean Norris
Joseph B. Osborne
Helen Vernita Parrish

Walter Payton
Kathy Louise Pugh
Willie Mae Reed
Hattie B. Saffold
Demetrius Sherrod
Carl Shorter
Mary Lee Sims
Vicky Elaine Singleton
Stephanie Crale Smith
Lisa Carol Thomas
Stannette Towner
Donald Eugene Usher
Lolita Vanterpool
Loretta Ward
Charlotte Denise
  Warden
Harry Lee Watson
Gloria Ann Wheeler
Brenda Gayle Whitaker
Deborah Ann Williams
Lenza Williams, Jr.
Anthony Quinn Young

Bachelor of Science
Angela E. Beasley
Vernon E. Bell
Lois Jean Blair
Glenda Ann Bogan
Barbara A. Easterling
  Brown
Janice Brown
Brenda Lynn Carter
Gloria E. Chaney
Anthony Cowart
Shirley Birch Edwards
Vance Albert Evans
Frances Elaine Gaddis
Rylander Ruth Garrett
Marion J. Gibbs
Cassaundra Green
David Oscar Groomes
Samaria C. Hall
Frank Harrell
Rechee S. Huff
Maxine Johnson

Geraldine G.
  Montgomery
Latanja Renee Moore
Philippa Jhean Norman
Gwendolyn O'Neal
Eugene Purry
Linda Diane Ruffin
Linda Ann Slater
Larry James Small
David L. Smith
Loretta Anita Smith
Gloria Jean Stingley
Leonette Jean Thomas
Jesse L. Trotter, Jr.
Errol A.C. Walcott
Lafayette Eugene Wales
Rosie Lucille Walker
Tommye L. Walker
Aaron A. Washington,
  Jr.
Beverly A. Haywood
  Williams
Mack H. Wilson
James C. Winters
Albert Benjamin Wood

May 16, 1982

Associate of Arts
Cora Howard
Dorothy J. Hutson

Bachelor of Arts
Brenda Adams
Debra Denise Allen
Bryan D. O. Andrews
Ruth Frances Arsene
Dorothy Irene Avant
Connie Jose Baird
Benjamin Barnes
Linda Barnes
Linda Kay Bishop
Gwennie Ruth Bouie
Valoree Bowden

Teresa Dianna Cannon
Shirley Jean Carson
Kymmeria Lynette
  Chambers
Annette Rochelle
  Cleveland
Brenda Ann Coe
Rhonda Michelle
  Cornelius
Danny Coverson
Mary Evelyn Dailey
Andrea Denise Davis
Joseph J. Davis
Victoria Davis
Beatrice Edwards
Wanda Joyce Fort
Deboraha Lynn Griffis
Joyce A. Grim
Mavis Harris
Charles A. Henderson
Rita L. Henry
Marilyn Elaine Hill
Chukwuemeka
  Ikeanyionwu
Dwight Jackson
Stephanie Renee Jackson
Brian Anthony Jemmott
Annie Louise Johnson
Aaron Jones, Jr.
Angela Verdia Jones
David Orlando Jones
Vanessa Lofton
Sharon Denise Loggins
Allen Winston
  McClinton
Billy Ray McDaniel
Cheryl Letrice McCleod
Marion La June McNair
Hilda D. Manning
Geraldine Mass
Majorie Louise Mass
Glenda Elaine Moore
Sharon Elaine Newell
Karen Renee Nolan
Carolyn D. Phillips

Sandra Elaine Powell
Thomas Warren Powell
Christopher Darrell
  Robinson
Teresa Deloise Roundtree
Ollie Mae Seals
Gwendolyn Earlene
  Shaw
Lawrence Sledge
Alvin Joseph Smith
Onetta Starling
Charles Otis Streeter
Cynthia Denise Tate
Pamela Rudean Taylor
Daniel Thomas
Gloria G. Thompson
Terwinda Towner
Gregory Earl Travillion
Sylvia L. Turner
Joyce M. Vaxter
Paulette Elaine Wales
Darrell Walker
Mikel D. Walker
Ruben Wallace
Linda Sue Wells
Colvin Williams
Karen Marie Williams
Larry D. Williams
Henry Wilson, IV
Brian Allen Worthy
Mechelle Y. Wright
Perrymon Carl Wright

Bachelor of Science
John Elvin Brandon
Patricia Ann Brown
J. B. Carter, III
Debra Ann Caruthers
Val Clifford Cherry
Leon R. Copeland
Earnest Cox
Tami Denise Daniels
Anita Dorsey
Woody Joe Edwards
Donnie Evans

Naomi Flowers
Clifton Frazier, Jr.
Williams J. Givens, III
Terrald Demar Gunn
Vincent O. Harris
Daryl I. Harrison
Carla Isaac
Evelyn Marie James
Sandra Elaine Jones
Terence Calvin Jones
Sandra Kaye McClinton
Theresa McDaniel
Anthony McKinney
Alvin McQuarters
Mary Magee
Brenda Faye Mallard
Albert L. Mungo
Esther Ruth Ogbuh
Marvita K. Oliver
Norma Gean Phillips
Cynthia Rankin
Verda Jean Sago
Oteria Lynn Starling
Melvin M. Trotter
Valarie Elaine Warner
Sheila Denise
  Weathersby
Sandra Faye Wilson
Franklin Winters
Stephanie Yolanda York

May 15, 1983

Associate of Arts
Alice K. Sellers

Bachelor of Arts
Carolyn Elaine Andrews
Lillian Denise Arnold
Christine Levell Bachus
Carol Michelle Bardwell
Joseph Craig Bell
Clyde Jerome Bennett
Linda Kay Bishop

Katie Ruth Blair
Diana Cunningham
  Bowen
Brenda J. Brown
Joyce Ann Brown
Dianne Buckhaulton
Mardis Williams
  Burnette
Vernette Valaria Byrd
Debra Ann Cain
Darlene Caviness
Karyn E. Clark
Linda Richele Clay
LaVern Crowder
Gina Linette Daniels
Barbara Ann Davis
Linda Day
Alfredia Benita Ellis
Regina Mae Ford
Carolyn Goss
Tylvester Goss
Scott Grady
Charlotte C. Gray
Ida Mae Grayer
Vickie A. Griffin
Cheryl Rene Hayes
Elizabeth Turner Hines
Deborah D. Hopkins
Donald Bernard Jackson
Clarice Yolanda James
Carolyn Ann Johnson
Ronald Kevin Johnson
Theodore Johnson
Hazel Jordan
George Alvin Joseph, Jr.
Branda Kates
Felecia Diane King
Thomas Edward King
Jewel Chantay Lane
Herbert Lee, Jr.
John Willie Lee, Jr.
Freda D. Lewis
Harold Desantis Lewis
Robin Pauline Lockhart
Carl Oswald Lowe

Jennifer C. Lumzy
Shurla Jean Mance
Velma Ann Marshall
C'Ella Meeks
Shirley Dianne Mitchell
Gwendolyn D. Nelson
Ronnie Lewis Nobles
Peter Chidi Nwachukwu
Desiree Prowell
Akpan Rabson
Yvonne Randle
Eddie Columbus
    Rhodman, Jr.
Patricia Roberts
Wilbert K. Roberts
Gloria A. Rodgers
Carla Sonya Russell
Keith Lamarr Sanders
Pamela Diane Singleton
Carmelia Smith
Mary Ann Smith
Wilma Rochelle Smith
Willie Pearl Strickland
Bridget Dolores Taylor
Debra Ann Whitfield
Dexter Duane Whitley
Sammie Willingham
Vincent Lewis Wright

Bachelor of Science
Laurie Adams
Vernessa J. Alexander
Sherrelyn Denise Allen
Linda Jean Amos
Erskin Bell
Robert E. Bradshaw, Jr.
Glenda L. Coleman
Richard D. Davis, Jr.
Sandra Yvette Davis
Catherine Felder
Yolanda Denise Gales
Damita Jo Griffin Jones
Jerry Dean Heard
Anthony Howard
Benita Lawan Johnson

Brenda Darlene Knott
Eric Darnell Lucas
Dwight Luckett
Anthony McKinney
Leli Gail Matthews
James Peter Miller, Jr.
Wayne Darrell Murray
Winifred Ndali
    Osanakpo
Cherry Lynn Ramsey
Phyllis Elizabeth
    Richardson
Christian Shawn Rogers
Jennifer Scott
Karie L. Smith
Sharon Jean Taylor
Debra Ann Thedford
Joyce Marie Tobias
Leilani Maxine Tull
Brigetta Kay Turner
Donnie Durell Verges
Myra Anthonette
    Wheaton

May 13, 1984

Assoicate of Art
Fannie Cameron
Rita Delores Lewis
Gwendolyn McDonald
Earlene McMorris

Bachelor of Arts
Saundra Lynette Adams
Kenneth E. Arnold
Dana M. Barnes
Keith Barnes
Thomas E. Bernard
Barbara Ann Bishop
Michael R. Campbell
Lisa Childress
Glenda Faye Cleaver
Annie Catherine
    Coleman

Abigail Yolanda Renee
    Daniel
Julie Patricia Ealy
Orlando C. Featherstone
Melody Lucretia Fortune
Judy Faye Gipson
Darryl Glenn Graves
Valerie Grim
Jimmy L. Howell
Jacqueline M. Hudson
Stephanie Dennett
    Jackson
Diana Johnson
Walter Thomas Johnson
Frederic C. Keys
Benny Jerome Larry
Joyce Marie Ledlow
Eugene Elias Lenston
Alin Gazell McCarty
DePriest McCary
Alesia Gail McClenty
Gloria Ann McCray
Edna Faye McNeal
Virginia Maxine Martin
Ora Caroline Matthews
Janice Denise Owens
Lydia Ann Perry
Peottra Antione Pickett
Sharon Rena Ratliff
Kathelean Wilder Rucker
Pamela Joyce Sanders
Cynthia Myers Sims
Marie A. Sipp
Melvin L. Smith
Tyrone Smith
Donald Stevens
Eddrena Renee Stitt
Belinda Thornton
Lynda Carol Tillis
Kimberly Yvette Wesley
Rodney West
Darcy Lynette Williams
Janie Mae Williams
Gwendolyn Patrice
    Winters

Carla Elizabeth Woods
Cheryl Angela Wright

Bachelor of Science
Michelle Denise Abram
Carla Buie
Mitchell Wayne Burks
Pamela Olivia Carter
Jacqueline Rena Cleggett
Brenda Faye Coleman
Fred Bernat Cox
Maurice Sebastian Davis
Barbara Janett Dent
Joseph Edward Frazier, II
Doris Gathings
Glenn Green
Jennifer Griffin
Angela Denise Harris
Ranard C. Head
Donnell Jack
Caroline Denise Johnson
Karyne Yollanda King
Donna Michelle
    Kornegay
Lavoris Monia Myles
Bridgett Machell Pelts
Lawrence Lavale
    Roinson
Patricia Elaine Small
Aaron L. Smith
Sonya DeNaye Byrd
    Thompson
Wanda Lynn West
Carolyn Denise Williams
Gregory Willis

May 12, 1985

Associate of Arts
Retha Bates
Hazel J. Bridges
Mary Hellen Daniels
Mary B. Dickey
Paullena Kemp

Dora Richardson
Cleolia Sanders
Bernice Wilkerson Small
Velma Bailey Smith
Billy Joe Wells
Gwendolyn Williams

Bachelor of Arts
Silifatu Lillian Alao
Stanley Edd Amos
David Barrow
Robert Darrell Beamon
Dorothy Ann Brown
William Washington
    Buchanan, III
Sophronia Ann Collins
Mary Alice Cook
Jennice Courtney
Carnella Clarice Crisler
Elizabeth Michele Dent
Adriane Janise Dorsey
Michael D. Dozier
Arthur Mell Eastern
Cynthia T. Franklin
Danese O. Frazier
Shiron Annette Frelix
Louis E. Gilbert
Cherri Green
Priscillia Marie Harrell
Sandra Bernadette Harris
Patricia Ann Kennedy
Enohkpen Ayuk-Takor
Angela Rena Lawrence
Mary Janet Tyler Loper
Jacqueline Braddy Mc
    Dougal
Jesse J. McGowan
Janice Marie Webb
    McMillian
Alleen A. Miller
Sandra Dee Moore
Chuck Murriel
Adrienne Denise Nolan
Lasbrey C. Nwachukwu
Francine Blount Odom

Anthony Owens
Debra Lynn Poe
Linda Irenette Posey
Keith L. Quinn
Melinda Nada Roundtree
Fredericka Sands
Patricia Louise Sheriff
Eddie Mae Sims
Kaye Francis Sly
Patricia Ann Smith
Monique Sneed
Andre' Keith Steward
Mary Ann Stewart
Serry Taylor
Shawn Thomas
Barbara Linda Wade
Danny Walker
Pamela S. Washington
Valeria H. Wheatley
Danny Hugh Young

Bachelor of Science
Sheilia Diane Abby
Vallee' Michelle Adams
Marsha Elaine Anderson
Percy L. Anderson, Jr.
Yolanda Anthony
Curtis Bell
Rickey Bolden
Marvette Brown
Eddie L. Caruthers, Jr.
Lucy W. Clabon
Samuel Anthony Cole, Jr.
Glenford E. Darbeau
Harold Davis
Rosita Denise Griffith
Richard Joseph Hairston
Jacqueline Lavern
    Hampton
Gwendolyn Denise
    Harris
Edmond E. Hughes, Jr.
Marcus K. Jackson
Rose M. Jackson
Darryl Lambert Jordan

Barbara Jean Kinsey
Maxine Lee
Eric A. Leggette
Kathleen Mckinney
Bettye R. Moody
Stephen Planer
Thomas William Porter
Melissa Bridgett
  Richardon
Jerry L. Smith
Darryl Stewart
Shwanda Juanita
  Thompson
Diana Powell Trim
Alvernica Whitfield
Antrunette Whittington
Brenda Louise Woodruff

May 18, 1986

Associate of Arts
Rosa Lee Sanders

Bachelor of Arts
Frederick D. Alexander
Tammie Diane Allen
Trenia LaShelle Allen
Don Antonio Alleyne
Joe Edward Brown, Jr.
Sylvia Lynette Burkhead
Donald E. Butler
Ollie Mae Butler
Judia Lorraine Coleman
Clint L. D. Copeland
Evangelia J. Crisler
Yolanda Ann Foster
Barbara E. Fullard
Trina Lavette Galloway
Abram Fitzgerald Green
Michael D. Griffin
Beverly Patrice Harris
Tim Haynes
Andrea Denise Hollis
Valarie Jean Kendrick

Sanford Knott
Reynoir Ray Lewis
Gwendolyn Denise
  Lymon
Frances Marshall
Regina Lynne Massey
Robert E. Middleton
Diane C. Neal
Veda Lanell Russell
Curtis Lionell Shears
Donna Stewart
Joy Ugwuanyi
Helen Louise Ware

Bachelor of Science
Audrey Armstrong
James Vincent Beamon
Sherman Basil Bernard
Glynis A. Burns
Patricia Ann Conner
Brian Rodrick Dorsey
Beverly A. Harris
Joyce Ann Hill
Roger Huey
Clark J. Hymes
Sonya Dee Lewis
Alfrenett Ranae Rodgers
Cheryl D. Smith
Louis Wesley
Regenia Denese White
Andrew Wayne Wilson
Carolyn Joyce Wright

May 17, 1987

Bachelor of Arts
KoJo Allen
Aldoria Anderson
Sharon Veronica Arnold
Donald T. Benson
Cassandra Blackmon
Youlanda Garmaine Blair
Carmelita Lyshelle
  Brackett

Debbie R. Brown
Phyllis Ann Burkhead
Elaine Burrell
Roy Burton
Sturleen D. Butler
Jennifer Renee Byrd
James Charles Coleman,
  II
Brenda K. Dale
Arnita T. Davison
Joycette Apasra Dockins
Katrina Ellis
Patricia Wanda Green
Marion Rossi Hudson
Michael Kendrick
  Hutchins
Malcolm Chenier
  Jackson
Calvin Christopher
  Johnson
Beverly R. Thompson
  Jones
Sharon Jeanette Jones
Yolanda Mechell Jones
Paulleana Kemp
Desiree Wilmetta
  Kilcrease
Angela Antoinette
  Lockett
Paul McGerald Luckett
Dwitte Leploean
  McDougle
Rosie Corrine McElroy
Sandra Faye McGhee
Darlene Denise
  McKeplin
Angela Moore
Daniel Okwuchukwu
  Ofoegbu
LaVern Wilson Powell
Tonelle Andrea Ricard
James Richardson
Debra Lynne Rogers
Brenda Venessa Smith
Stephanie LaNita Smith

T. Derrell Swilley
Pieter J. Teeuwissen
Godwin C. Ugwuanyi
LaRessa Beverlyn Walker
Shelia Gail Warren
Billy Joe Wells
Barbara J. White
Ruby A. Williams
Mary Evelyn Young

Bachelor of Science
Eugena M. Anderson
Karen Michelle Bryant
Elisa Gale Bunch
Jimmie Denise Clark
Deborah Ann Coleman
Patricia Ann Conner
Ronald Davis
Larry B. Foster
Youlanda Green
Tammie Sue Griffin
Claretta C. Jackson
Loretta E. Jackson
Emily Joyce Jones
Stanley Conroy Jones
Stanley James Jossell
Hope J. Lindsey
Audrey LeJean McAfee
Jacqueline F. McMorris
Jeffery Allen Parker
Kevin Wade Shelby
Emma Mariah Simmons
Debra Suzette Smith
Rosie Marie Starks
Reginia Lynn Taylor
Bobby K. Taylor
Ronald DeWitt Thomas
Amye Charaille Veal
Angelia Anita Wade
Chandra F. White

May 15, 1988

Bachelor of Arts
Darlene Adams

Bobby J. Allen
Patricia Rotonia Allison
Karen Latrice Brown
Kimbley R. Burbridge
Constance R. Burns
Christy Legreta Burton
Roderick Emil Johnson
  Byrd
Joyce A. Cole
Nona Eileen Coleman
Phyllis T. Cooper
Alkamessa Dalton
Vera Ann Davis
Mitee Echols
Beverly A. Ford
Armena Foster
Lauretta Ann Gavin
Karen Renee Gilbert-
  Hutchins
Melcenia Jones Gilbert
Tressie L. Gill
Audrey Earl Gilmore
Valerie Michele Green
Lucretia Denice Griffin
LaDonna Monique
  Harrell
Andre' Pierre Hartwell
Douglas E. Henderson
Dexter Hogan
Clarence Hulett
Kevin Antionne Jackson
Sharon Renee Jefferson
Sonya Caprice Jenkins
Veronica A. Johnson
Jennifer Julious
Janice Renee Lathan
Teressa Jo Lewis
Carla Yvette Lucas
Svetlana Zenobia Lucas
Shannon Demetra
  McElroy
Johnny Earl Magee
Sheri Michelle Merrill
Angela Denise Mickey
Delores Micenhamer
Laura Moore

Lorraine Owens
Cherelyn A. Poe
Carl James Powe
Troy Lorenzo Price
Cassandra Lattress Reed
Pamela Alicia Reed
Daphne Renee Robinson
Phyllis Delise Ross
Lillie R. Sims
Chiquita Yvette Sterling
Doris Anita Thedford
Stephen Wesley Todd
Reba Gigesle Topps
George Timothy Vaughn
Toni Patricia Walker
Lori Anne Watson
Jeanette Smith
  Whisenton
Wendy Bernadette White
Daphne Whittington
Herron Earl Wilson
Carlon Denice Winder

Bachelor of Science
Vernon Anthony
  Alexander
Mariea Antoinette Banks
Cynthia Koran Barnes
Irving Glen Beamon
Radecki James Burns
Veronica Faye Chambers
Dwight Dwayne
  Coleman
Karyn L. Collier
Marcia de'Carlo Eley
Dewin Bender Govan
Darryl Vanrich Grennell
Philip Dean Hairston
Juanelma Alvinette
  Harrion
Michele Carolyn Huff
Reginald D. Jenkins
Dion D. Jones
Leneise Cheri Lynn
Sonya Renee' McElroy
Vallery Mechell Magee

Keith Caesario Miller
Tracie L. Newsome
Charles Pickett, Jr.
Cheryl A. Powell
Donnell Washington
 Roach
Millard Gerald Robinson
Sophia Dwanna Stewart
Tarence Earl Wade
Shirley Lee Warfield
Debra A. Washington
Pamelia Michelle
 Watson
Anna Carol Williams
Minnie Vera York

May 14, 1989

Associate of Arts
Joann Rush Parks
Betty Jean Tolliver
Lois Vinson

Bachelor of Arts
Marian Arnita Allen
Ramona L. Anderson
Evelyn Bankhead
Ann Marie Beckworth
Sinetra Ann Bowdry
Geraldine Brown
Carrie Johnson Carson
Nada Ruth Banks Clark
John Derrell Cobbins
Bonita Ruth Coleman
Evelyn Deloise Coleman
Tracie Lynn Cooper
Danita Colette
 Whisenton Dillard
Sterling A. Dunkley
Stephanie D. Esters
Marvin Maurice Furdge
Linda Diana Gibbs
Johnny Cordell Greer
Delbra F. Haney
Kevin Harvey

Susan M. Hardy
Grangerette Haynes
Karen Harris Hobson
Barbara A. Holmes
Ronda L. Hooper
Nedra A'Faye Jenkins
Clementine R. Woodard
 Johnson
Evette Faye Kincaid
Bernard Emanuel
 Kitchen
Addie LeFlore
Zenobia F. Lewis
Pamela Yvette Loftin
Teia Denise McGee
John Henry Marshall
Phoebe Clara Martin
Shantha K. Moorthy
Kathy Yvonne Mosley
Aurila Dykes Nash
Mary Jo Newman
Nancy Nelson
Charles Erik Pickering
Lillie Pearl Portis
Okolo Rashid
Angela Donnette Reed
Angela Marie Rice
Stacy Marcell Seevon
 Roach
Mercer Maxceria
 Robinson
Ralph L. Russell
Ulrich David Schnell
Ramona Lashell Seabron
Robert E. Shield
VaNessa Phylis Singleton
Felicia Roshurl Slater
Jacqueline Smith
David Lee Thomas
Marzlinn Levette
 Thompson
Gerald L. Walker
Linda Marie Washington
Charles Anthony
 Watson
Veronica Denise Wiley

Carolyn Ann Williams
Gwendolyn W. Williams
Michael Conell Wolfe
Frankie Andrea Woods
Marc Jacob Woods
Chauncy Wright
Antoinette Young

Bachelor of Science
Michelle Lazette Badon
Felicia Marie Brown
Evelyn Pernice Clark
Anthony Clay Coleman
Deidre Dionne Brown
 Gordon
John M. Grady
Diane Nevette Greer
Galen V. Henderson
Angela Colette Jamison
Ingrid Gwyn Jenkins
Tanya T. Kelly
Tina Charlette Lucas
Musa Ali Mahamud
Robert Irving Moore
Angie Martin
Lavetta Lache Newell
Formeka Dinette LaMon
 Russell
Yul L. Shelton
Tommy C. Short
Glinda Smith
Linda F. Smith
Jacqueline Marie Spann
Teresa ReShae Spencer
Deidre Yvette Talley
Brenda D. Taylor
ReNita Ann Thomas
Paula M. Tucker
Mike C. Watkins
Angelia Michelle
 Watson
Rhonda Lenoria Watts
Kenya Delisa
 Weatherspoon
Leonard Gleen Webster
James Edward Williams, Jr.

May 20, 1990

Associate of Arts
Dorothy Blackmon
Elizabeth Singleton Clay
Stella Dixon
Barbara Francis
Mamie Johnson
Robert Johnson
Willie Ruth Johnson
Francine Adams Joyner
Sylvia Mackey
Willie Mae Myers
Sarah Singleton
Peggie J. Turner
Katherine Washington

Bachelor of Arts
Valarie T. Beamon
Bonna Deneise Bishop
Lynda L. Blair
Willie Bolden
Na'Son S. Brown
Sheron Buchanan
Odie Eugene Cannon
Curtis Clay, Jr.
Marva DeChantal
  Courtney
Denard Crawford
Charrita Deonne Danley
Ursula M. Davis
Imogene Dickey
Rosa L. Dixon
Emma L. Dorsey
James Edward Fountain,
  III
Angelia Denese Gipson
Floyd Green, Jr.
Theresa LaShawn Harris
Frances Annette Henry
Nathaniel Holmes
Sharon Michelle Hoye
Sidra Carol Jackson
Camille Johnson

Kimblyn Johnson
Rachelle E. Johnson
Davelyn Maria Jordan
Jerry Howard Lewis, Jr.
Miranda Aretha
  McCants
Sandra L. McDaniel
Susan L. McDaniel
Shelia Renay McDonald
Annette McLaurin
Christopher X. Polk
Keith Prenell Posley
Julia Corinne Simmons
Jacqueline Denise Slater
Andrew LaVel Smith
Charles A. Smith
Donna Ann Summers
Linda Lee Thomas
Anthony Laddon
  Thompson
Terrence Leon Vinson
Angela Michelle
  Webster
Helean Wheat
Delano Leviticus White
Darren Lydell Whitehead
Ernie Tyrell Williams
Geraldine H. Williams
Gretta Pinilles Winters
Carla Lennail Woodley
Marc Jacobs Woods
Tracey Laverne Young

Bachelor of Science
Angela Kermetta Ball
Anthony Joseph
  Chambers, Jr.
Stephanie Denise Collier
Carol Kowiada Cox
Samuel Croff, Jr.
Lathan Charles Dabbs
Kervin Orlando Evans
Teresa Carol Foster
Leslie Gene Harmon

Sheryl D. Harris
Demetria Cledith
  Howard
Adrienne Maxine
  Jackson
Monique Renee' Johnson
Terry D. Johnson
Angela Martin
Romonita McDowell
Robbye Delores McNair
Patricia Ann Oneal
Athena Pennington
Joy Chantele Poe
Sean D. Smith
Betty L. Spann
Mary Ann Stewart
Rita Denise Usher
Tanya LaWanda
  Washington
Francesca Amelia
  Wilkins
David Christian
  Williams

May 1991

Associate of Arts
Annie Allen
Elcena H. Bouldin
Johnny Ruth Brown
Alma Drinker
Janice M. Grant
Victor Cunningham
JoAnne Malone

Bachelor of Arts
Cynthia Denese Allen
Vera A. Armstrong
Sandra Aretha Artis
Delora LaWita Banks
Felicia Renee Barnes
Michael James Bolden
Brenda Gale Brinston

Angela Renee Brown
Shundra Denise Brown
Tomasinia Annette
　Brown
DeAndra Rachelle
　Carter
Rosa Dixon Clark
Kimberly Clemons
Jocelyn R. Connor
David Cousin
Gloria Jean Cross
Michael Crouther
Monica Jeanette Darden
Laquita M. Davis
Monica Rochelle
　Galloway
Stephen M. Gavin
Lisa Grass
Reginald Green
Schella V. Wilkerson
　Hairston
Sharron D. Haralson
Pamela Gisele Harrion
Felicia Harris
Bridget Aletha Hathorn
Karen Henley
Vickie D. Hewitt
Katrina Neciette Hicks
Cheryl Denise Hunter
Felicia Denise Jenkins
Claire Johnson
Louida M. Johnson
Robert Lee Johnson
Charlene William Jones
Joyce O. Jones
Lisa Diane Jones
Elisa Mae Kincaid
Mabvudza Kuziwa
Jacqueline Smith Lacey
Dorothy Levy
Hannis Longino
Vanessa Maberry
Dennis J. Martin
Ginger Felice Martin

LaCheryl P. May
Ethel Renee Milton
Jerry Moore
Roddrick Murray
Carletta M. Noland
Kevin D. Patterson
Gaither T. Pope
Evelyn Cooper Powell
Laverne A. Rankin
Freeman Richmond
Dexter Jerome Robinson
Yolanda Rodgers
Margaret Elaine Saffold
Brenda Smith
Tonya D. Holly Spann
Sharon Thompson
Azande Makeba Wallace
Llewellyn Watkins
George F. West, III
Charlene Wiley
Debra Elaine Williams
Emily Elaine Willis
Robin K. Wilson
Wendy Schenique
　Wilson
Andrea R. Wright
Samuel T. Young

Bachelor of Science
Joyce Buchner Brown
Sonji Brown
Rosalyne Michele Davis
Laurencin Dunbar
Sharon Ferguson
Sonya Yvette Hamilton
Tracie Quilette Hampton
Renee Harris
Tharrow Pegues
James E. Plummer, Jr.
Sherri L. Richmond
Yvette Sanders
Angela Sherry
Susan Stamps
Beverly Machell Stewart

Karen D. Stokes
Veda Vedette Thames
Stacie D. Tyler
Danurius Williams

May 1992

Associate of Arts
Dorothy Jean Anderson
Mary Jean Myles
Margaret Ross
Stanley Travis
Edna Watkins

Bachelor of Arts
Velma Luri Allen
Margaret M. Arrington
David Patrick Bickham
Lynell Bolden
Elcena Bouldin
Patricia Ann Brown
Roderica Brown
Priscilla Cage
Pamela Carr
Yolanda M. Clay
Daphney Darlene Cole
Tina Louise Cooks
Rochell G. Cottingham
Boris Broderick Cousin
Willie Barnett Cowan,
　Jr.
Mosetta Elaine Crosby
Jerri Dean
Prinn L. Deavens
Sandra Dortch
Flora Ann Eskridge
　Bennett
La'Loria Fontaine
Renee' R. Graham
Meauchelle Huddleston
Cassandra Ann Hart
Jacqueline R. Hawkins
Jennette Hudson

Petrina Huff
Roslyn Marie Jackson
Debra Arlean Jenkins
Katie Johnson
Sheila Benese King
Edward Tyrone Knight
Kana Koide
Tammy La'Vette Lanier
Juandalynn W. Lymon
Greta Denise Mack
Valerie Nicole Matthews
Zandra ReFaye
  McDonald
Michael Saunte'
  McLendon
Venetia Ann Miller
Terence Maurice Nimox
LaRhonda Rethier Owens
Terra Payne
Calvin Posley
Idella Loretta Redmond
Pamela Garnett Rogers
Janet Shumaker
Maxine Simmons-Bolden
Roberta Simmons
Caroline Louella Smith
Donna Elizabeth Smith
Nicole Southward
Valerie Lousie Spann
  Robinson
LaTonya Lenise Thames
LaDonis DeShannon
  Toney
Peggy J. Turner
Loretta Wales
Williamenia Miranda
  Walker
LaWanda Cherie
  Weatherspoon
Verchele LaTrease
  Wiggins
Charlie Williams
Darfeis Drake Bells
  Williams
Tina Williams
Lisa Wyatt

Anne E. York

Bachelor of Science
Teaster Thomas Baird, Jr.
Anthony Bennett Bell
Carol L. Calloway
Paula Carr
Annette Davis
Quenyatta Echols
Leigh Krystina Hawkins
Deborah L. Hunley
Hollye R. Johnson
Anthony Warwick Jones
Patricia A. Jordan
Denzil Leroy Kelly
Melvin Charles King
Tammy D. McMillian
Clyde McMorris, Jr.
Yolanda Alysia Rankin
Angelia M. Reed
Shinita Yewonde Reed
Dannielle Kavitria Sharp
Anita Yvette Spencer
Shondra Wilkerson
Angela D. Woods

May 16, 1993

Associate of Arts
Louella Cole-Allen
Alma Marie Epps
Dorothy A. Harris-Bell
Gwendolyn M. Love
Sarah J. Mack
Brenda Martin
Linda K. Martin
Thelma Spivey
  Wedgeable

Bachelor of Arts
Donna Abram
Brian E. Anderson
Derrick Romon Austin
Theona Michelle Barney
Howard Bartee, Jr.

Genise Reba Beamon
Henrietta Lamonica
  Bowen
Glenda Faye Brinston
Deesha Brown
Lori Ann Brown
Oona Tryphonsa Carr
Linda M. Coates
Katrina Lavett Coleman
Wanda L. Conway
Kenneth Dottes
Lashonda Yvette Dukes
Vanessa E. Elliott
Alex Jerome Finch
Tonie R. Francis
Daphne Gray-McDonald
Benita M. Grayson
Monica Alisa Green
Wanda Danita Green
Mario D'Andre Harris
Tifarah Lynette Lawrence
Tamia P. Herndon
Margaret Lolita Holiman
Shelia Rene Hoskins
Dorothy S. Hull
Launita Jacobs
Carmalena Jefferson
Tanya Lafranze Jefferson
Felicia R. Jennings
Leroy Duke Jennings, Jr.
Frank Caswell Jones, III
Deborah Jordan
Arthea Kendrick
Michelle Yvette King
Joe Anthony Knott
Donovan Marchand
  Lang
Crystal D. Lewis
Amy Denise Lofton
Renee' McDavis
Miranda Denease
  McDonald
Stephanie Daniela
  McNeil
Lisa Michelle Moorehead
Cheryl D. Moreland

Willie Mae Myers
Chantrese L. Neal
Gail Lorraine Newbill
Sharlette Norwood
Howard Hosea Payne
Rhonda Sharone Pippins
Pamela Renee Poplar
Leona Demethia
  Richards
Tasha Amina Roberts
Tammi S. Saddler
Yolanda M. Small
Angela Michelle Smith
Felicia L. Smith
Robert Shuler Smith
Frances Denise Starr
Shereese Ravitt Taylor
Shelia L. Thompson
Alicia Louise Upson
Andrea Monique Viel
Angela L. Walker
Daryl Dewayne
  Washington
Stefan Michael
  Wheelock
Temekka R. Williams
Trina Sharese Wise

Bachelor of Science
Patrina Leshan Beard
Franklin Earl Bennett
Marla Y. Brown
Vanessa Larose
  Chambliss
Pamela Vernetta Clayton
Valeria Cornell Cohran
Adero A. Corner
Cleotha Arnell Dinkins
Aretha Shontell Green
Valerie Diane Holden
Shunte' Monique Jones
Ronnie Phineas
  McMillian
Carl Michael Otis
Deborah Denise Parker
Laura Carol Pratt

Mercedes Jo Sanders
Lenore Saulsberry
Tonya S. Spells
Jefforey A. Stafford
Phaedra Aviv Steward-
  Scott
Thomasena Dillon
  Stuckett
Niema Pythia Tillman
Marcus Lemar Ware
Sonji Joell Wells
Elliot Andre' Wheeler
Michelle Yolanda
  Williams

May 15, 1994

Associate of Arts
Glenda Hill Harden
Ruth Silas

Bachelor of Arts
Sonja R. Abrams
Teresa Elaine Alexander
Royce M. Allen
Shonda R. Allen
Tomekia Rena Allen
Brian E. Armstrong
Stephanie D. Barnes
Katina Baugh
Angelia Diane Bell
Penny Renee' Bell
Jacqueline Denise Bills
Carla Benita Boudlin
Greta Jeanette Bradford
Aaron Torhaan Branch
Paheadra Dionne
  Bratton
Deitra Brown
Reginald Buckley
Shannon Leigh Carr
Jabal L. Chase
Marcus E. Cheeks
Amanda Coleman
Mechelle Collier

Zatanya Derrayna L.
  Coney
Yvette Michelle Devine
Nakisha Delynn
  Ducksworth
Stephanie Annyces Ellis
Kimberly Vonshell
  Franklin
Erica Jasmine Gee
Theresa Renae Godwin
Keisha L'Faye Graham
Ronda N. Grays
Luther C. Griffin, Jr.
Gloria Denise Guilty
Angela Rochelle Holmes
Donovan Lafon Horton
Victor Deshone Hubbard
Jennifer D. Hunt
Winna Isiahrena Hyche
Pauline Jenkins
Derrick T. Johnson
Clarence W. Jones, Jr.
Donald Jones
Linda Faye Jones
Vann George Clinton
  Jones
Jeanne Julious
Dana Patrice Kendrick
Nsombi Ayanna
  Lambright
Tammie Shereia
  Lawrence
Kecia Dehaven Lowe
Demetrese Evette
  Luckett
Yvette Deloria Mackel
Carolyn J. C. Manyfield
Precious Tyrone Martin
Kenith Wayne Matthews
Cassandra Ann McClure
Sabrena McQueen
Teselyn Afrique Melton
Veronica Latrice Milton
Rita Moore
Lizwi X. Mtumtum
Sean D. Nichols

Pamela Denise Palmer
Kelvin C. Pickett
Kwanza Ayanna Price
Bennie Lenard Richard
Malcolm E. Robertson
Albertine Robinson
Quinton Curt Robinson
Stephen Dewayne
  Sanders
Ronald Dwayne Sayles
Leo Darnell Simmons
Rachel Denise Sims
Titus Snell
Lashonda Stewart
Dawn Lavern Stough
Terrilyn Tate
Jessica Dashanna Taylor
Carol A. Thompson
Wanda Denise Tolbert
Jacqueline Patrice
  Vickers
Erika Jon Washington
Toya S. Washington
Darrell Lemond Wells
Tonia Faye Wells
William White
Jetaune C. Williams
Toni Marshea Williams
Yvetta Lynette Williams
Arlandra Shauntel
  Winters
Lashun Alexandria
  Young

Bachelor of Science
Andrea Maderia
  Andrews
Bruktawit Tesfaye Asfaw
Eddye Jean Bullock
Tavetia Cheryl Davidson
Erick Antoine Falconer
Sonya Alicecia Forbes
Henry Shun Goss
Frederick Theodore
  Holley, II

Yonka Flechette Holmes
Jacqueline Denise
  Hudson
Erika Faye Jackson
Heidi E. Jones
Frank McCune, III
Melanie J. McEwen
Berthrone LaCalvin
  Mock
Antonio Chandrea
  Oliver
Earl D'Wayne Robinson
La'Toya Natrea Ross
Natascha R. Ruffin
Patrick Brandon Simon
Lashondra S. Singleton
Patrice N. Smith
Adrienne Nicole Spells
Jerrod Taylor
Kristie Michele Thomas
Debra Michelle
  Townsend
Garrett Jacobey Verser
Marva Mercedes Walker
Fatissa Inez Washington
Karita Dawn Williams

May 1995

Bachelor of Arts
Perry B. Allen
Loretta Anderson
Ronica D. Arnold
Victoria Benjamin
Katie C. Blakely
Rian E. Bowie
Marjorie Brookins
Diane Brooks
Mary Catchings Brown
Santeria C. Brown
Monique Buckhaulter
Jill V. Burgess
Sandi Carroll
Quemardo M. Castilla

Angela Lee Charleston
Stephanie D. Clark
Undra Lavon Collins
Nia Ayodele Corner
Sandra Kay Covington
Eyvon D. Curry
Rodney Dixon
Tarcha L. Elkins
LaGrand V. Elliott
Fredia D. Elmore
Valarie R. Evans
Mweni Udowah Ekpo
Malinda Vernell Fuqua'
Nelda Yvette Fuller
Chandar TeJauna Gilbert
Reginald Anton Gray
Monica Delicia Green
Nikisha Shontelle Green
LaShawn Denise Griffin
Reginald Paul Harrion
Ivory Harris
Myckycle Munri Hart
Donald Hewitt
Katina Lorraine Hicks
Daffonie Himes
Jeffery Dwayne Holiday
Melba Marcia Hollins
Stevan M. Hooper
Jennifer Deloise Hoskin
Adriane Sophia Jackson
Cathy Rochelle Jenkins
Anita Regina Johnson
Barbara Ann Johnson
Damani Kobie Johnson
Lemzel Ballard Johnson
Nicole Viana Johnson
Sharon Johnson
Gary Lydell Jones
Myrtle Deloice
  Arbuthnot-Jones
Willie Henry Jones, Jr.
Ingrid Renae Larkin
Makeaba Rochelle
  Latiker
Christina Leflore-Armon

Ko Nessia Locke
Angie N. Lockhart
Robert Love, Jr.
Lorraine Yvette Loving
Kendric Earl Kenyatta
  Lucas
Ranessa Ontrae' Maberry
Kermit R. Madison
Juandalyn D. Magee
Lesa Lashun McBride
Angela Marie Miller
Stacy L. Moore
Milton L. Moore, Jr.
Kema B. Nichols
Shauna Latice Nicholson
Terrence L. Packer
Keith A. Palmer
Fernanda Onderal Parish
Latessa Marie Pearson
Theresa Marie Phillips
Paula Jo Pollard
Shelia Lavelle Ramsey
Tarryn Lashawn
  Rutherford
Darrell D. Scott
Sharon D. Sims
Kenyatta Shantell Smith
LaShonda F. Smith
Demond L. Spann
Ruth Deann Stark
Moleendo Sundiata
  Stewart
William James Summers,
  II
Erica Adantae Taylor
Khary Malcom Jamal
  Taylor
Tamiko Sha'ron Thames
Sylvia J. Thomas
Daniel Dwayne
  Thompson
Deidra S. Thompson
Johni Annette Trigg
Lachandrea Nicole
  Turnbull

Beverly Jane Turnage
Anslem S. Turner
Iris Turner
Jeffrey Kerrence Turner
Justin Terrence Turner
Lashara D. Varnell
Terrell Demond Wells
Byron Anthony Williams
Christina Williams
Valerie Latrice Williams
  Cyonne Wilson
Samantha Shuntil
  Wilson
Toeshia Shanta Winfield
Crystal L. Young

Bachelor of Science
Reeshemah N. Allen
Bennie L. Brown
Hope C. Brown
Sandra Carr
Cynthia Charleston
Carolyn Faye Cohran
Regina P. Cooper
Dereck B. Davis
Antonio Ali Gamble
Catherine D. Garner
Kevin Lutrelle Gaylor
Carman N. Hall
Kamiti U. Harden
Natasha Nichole
  Hardeman
Audray Kenkay Harris
Carldell Hudson
Kimberly Lynett Jackson
Walter Jackson, Jr.
Theodore Lorenzo
  Johnson
Roshunda Michelle
  Leach
Marcus Duane Lewis
Laketia M. Marshall
Merton H. Masterson
Patrick Edward McGee
Ruthie Moman-Sayles

Sandra Renee Nash
Leothas E. Nichols, II
Oyinlola Olabode
Dianna Denease Payne
Karen V. Phillips
Erica L. Quinn
Dameta Joi Richardson
Patreece Le'Shune
  Sanders
Reginald Wyatt Silas
Maurice Starks
Deandra Lashelle
  Thompson
Umoja Shanu Turner
Undrea K. Walker
Danita A. Williams
Tangela M. Williams
Lecretia Antoinette
  Wilson
April Renee Wise
Johnny C. Wright
Marilyn D. Wyatt

May 19, 1996

Associate of Arts
Sabah Al-Fadhli
Greta Williams

Bachelor of Arts
Donovan D. Adams
Chynee Allen
Michael D. Ayers
Frizell Bailey
Shanda Barrett
Tanya Y. Bartee
Erica Keyonta Bell
Sharra L. Belt
Idetra M. Berry
Benita C. Best
Larry Bland, Jr.
Tamala R. Boyd
Arnetra O. Brent
Eric Levern Brooks

Kidada N. Brown
Kinberley D. Brown
Lenell A. Brown
Marcus Ray Brown
Shekita L. Brown
Shunda L. Brown
Kedra K. Carter
Marqwell R. Carter
Lorenda R. Cheeks
Katina M. Christian
Michael T. Clayton
Bethaney M. Coleman
Chastity Coleman
Melissa Coleman
Reggie D. Cooper
Shi Angelia Copeland
Keith B. Craig
Mary E. Crosby
Princess A. Cry
Cassaundra Danley
Tony C. Davis
Angel L. Day
A'Drienne Dillon
Torkwase Dyson
Chandar M. Fleming
Karamu Dami Ford
Sylvette Ford
Elliot Lenard Forest
Regina Fults
Chirvona Gary
Janet M. Gibson
Ayanna Gill
Seletta E. Goodall
Angela R. Gray
Walter L. Greer, Jr.
Lusondra C. Griffin
Nickia Griffin
Yolanda Harris
Latonia Hart
Gwennetta Holloway
Vandy R. Hopson
Sonia Kay Idleburg
Ava D. Jackson
Kimberly R. Jackson
Shana Jackson

Tawonder Jackson
Mary M. Jacobs
Latonya Jenkins
Kerry C. Johnson
Shannon Jones
Teshia L. Jones
Erica C. Journey
Glenda F. Kelly
Latonya Chenise King
Eric E. Lawson
Tiffany Love
Tonya D. Mahone
Adrienne Manning
Deverio Manning
Shatanner C. McFarland
Carl D. McNair, II
Kawanda P. McNeil
Keisha Moore
Tommy A. Morris
Abdul Muhammad
Regina Murphy
Jennifer L. Neal
Shundreia Neely
Ebonie N. Newton
Lanice O'Hara
Kai Tiombe Osborne
Fredricka Owens
Portia M. Patton
Annette Pickett
Lara A. Ray
Tawanda Reed-Ferrill
Tevaria L. Rhodes
Kidada M. Rice
Nikisha Ross
Raphael Sample
Yolanda Savage
Randi K. Scott
Timothy Scott
George Derek Shavers
Sheletha E. Shelton
Letitia Simmons
Alyssa J. Simpson
Adrian Smith
Derrick M. Smith
Erick D. Snyder

Kimberly Spann
Tenicia L. Speech
Latoshia Stamps
Tiffany Stewart
Stacy Swazy
Natoya V. Taylor
Demetrice Thompson
Lenika Thurman
Daphne D. Trigg
Ketina Walker
James A. Washington, Jr.
Tina Elizabeth
    Washington
Latashia Wells
Lakitta Westmoreland
Keshia T. Williams
Psonya C. Wilson
Marion Ange Woods
Jameca S. Woody
Brenda Greer Young
Tonya Young-Oddman

Bachelor of Science
Romond M. Arnold
Timothy Beacham
Amanda Bell
Catouche Body
Ako D. Bradford
Gregory D. Brown
Shontell Credit
Jaynida M. Ellis
Krysti Laketha Evans
Tikeshay J. Fleming
Marcus A. Freeman
Corinda Govan
Shari Natarsha Hart
Glake Hill, Jr.
Shunda R. Irons
Erica M. Laury
Kentrell Liddell
Ashalla Magee
Veronica M. McDonald
Angela T. Murphy
Amy V. Pitts
Angela Elaine Powell

Shaneka Profile
Caramah J. Quiett
Stacey L. Rhodes
Jonas D. Richard
Alfred DeBruce Ross
Sheila Rushing
Juana E. Scott
Efrem Sharp
Lucretia A. Speech
Toni Walker
Jerremey Willis
Sheldon Willis
Latasha A. Willis
Gwenzetta R. Wilson
Lora A. Wilson
Anitra Witherspoon
Cathy Yarn

May 18, 1997

Bachelor of Arts
Kimberly Shawaun
  Alford
Maceo R. Allen, Jr.
Raina M. Anderson
Emily Nichole
  Armstrong
Brian K. Baird
Kelvin Leroy Banks
RoSusan DorNiece
  Bartee
Craig N. Belton
Adrienne Charisse Bester
Jeffrey Dawon Blackmon
Tiffany Yvette Bledsoe
LaShondia Adree'
  Boclear
Marquita Fannisa Brown
Shaft Vondell Brown
Warren Marshall Brown
Tawana Marie Buchanan
Pierre Concepcione Buler
Katrina D. Carr
Robert Z. Carr, Jr.

Angela D. Clifton
Sharon L. Coleman
Talisa Monette Cox
Electra Manuel Crisler
Trinette Crump
Althea Lynn Davis
Maria Andrenette Dillon
Heather Lynne Douglas
Felice L. Dowd
Derricka DeShawn
  Drake
Stephen E. Draper
Kara Dione Edwards
Alma Marie Epps
Tondia Mischelle Evans
Vanessa Rochelle Exum
Ronnie C. Ferdinand, Jr.
LaDreana L. Freeman
Donnie Dion Graves
Lynnette Marshea
  Gilbert
Shelbi Lynn Griffin
Pythia L. Griggs
Tiffany Miran Hardy
Toya Vatrina Harrell
Lemika Christia Hayes
Jeffrey erome Hudson
Clarence Hopkins
Doressia L. Hutton
Margaret Olivia Hutton
Kashelia BriAnne
  Jackson
Shonnett M. Jackson
Yolanda Katrice Jackson
Lashundria R. James
Shelton Kenvion James
Jarvis Jernigan, Jr.
John Courtney Johnson
Kenya Nakia Johnson
Marquis Johnson
Schantate Ofelicia
  Johnson
Veronica Renee Johnson
Victoria Lynn Johnson
Karrin N. Jones

Kristen Michelle Jones
Octavis D. Lampkin
Tony Latiker
Dionna G. Lewis
Whittie Lockett, III
Stacy Lynette Lodge
Candice Nicole Love
LaShanda Martin
Shondra V. Mason
Zanah L. McCune
Mahalia Denise
  McDonald
Shalanda McLin
Chiquita Luceshia Minor
Samecia Andrianov
  Minter
Dawn Elizabeth Moore
Monica Denise Nelson
Iesha C. A. O'Deneal
Danya Ladwana Orey
Latoya Teneka Owens
Vicki Lynn Patterson
Tonya Danielle Parks
Shaninum F. Pittman
Rodneeka Polk
Lanetta Lavicka Powe
Sharon Posley
Brenda Linette Robinson
Litasha M. Robinson
Adrienne LaShawn
  Russell
Carrie C. Russell
Kamisha Jontee Shannon
Keesha L. Shaw
Kamili D. Smoot
Stophen L, Spencer, Sr.
Clemie Roger Stewart
Zachary T. Summers
Connie Larissa Tate
Tosha Novuya Taylor
Latonya Sherce Thomas
Roderick Dannell
  Thomas
Marcus Darweshi Turner
Jose' Benedict Watson

Tiffany Yvette White
Angela Delores Williams
Charlene Williams
Thea Hayes Williams
Crystal Na'Shay
  Wordlaw
Jamie Terrell Wright
Ester D. Young-Stamps
Kimberly Young

Bachelor of Science
Jacqueline Novelle
  Aldridge
Nicole Athena Allen
Angela Felicia Barnes
Daphne Meshea Bilbrew
Catrina Rene' Bogan
Tracee Lynne Booker
Stacy Nicole Cameron
Nicholas Alexander
  Chamers
Natasha Jeanette
  Champion
Kimberly Denise Clark
Eric Marcel Coleman
Marilyn Joy LaGene
  Coleman
Alicia Maria Dillon
Sheletha Mekella
  Dunning
Johnnie Mae Evans
Rashonda L. Edwards
Kimberly Roshella
  Ferdinand
Laviesta Leshan Ferrell
Laronda Sherice Fisher
Alicia Antionette
  Fleming
Kanika Anquanette
  Fleming
Kerry R. Fleming
Rodney D. Franklin
Isaac T. Friday
Angela Denise Givens

Candice Demisses
  Graham
Trulaine Greene
Rolanda L. Gustavis
Tonyatta Tarachi'
  Hairston
Derrick Dewayne Rush
  Hamilton
Kurt Holmes
Shontia Vashe' Jackson
Sonja Arlyce Jackson
Edward Dwayne Jones
LaTonya Jordan
Jerry Lewis
Everett Kenyon Lockhart
Kimberly Anitra
  McCullough
Erica Lashawn Parkman
Katina Robbins
Tammie Rudd-Hampton
Parthrenia Ninasa Smith
Latanya Deshae Thomas
Lynn Kendell Tuggle
Rochelle Weatherspoon
Iva C. White
David Demetrius Wilson
Latasha Patrice Wright

May 16, 1998

Associate of Arts
Mylinda P. Boles
Jeannette Travis Esco
Margelet Fields
Athenia B. Jefferson
Delores Fay Potts
Lettie Roberts
Lorraine Rose

Bachelor of Arts
Renee Antoinette
  Adams
Elliott M. Anderson

Grover Alfred
  Applewhite, Jr
LeTonia M. Bailey
Andrea' Renee' Barnes
Felicia Reshanda Barnes
Lakeitha Bassett
Brynder Carolyn
  Billingsley
Jumanne B. Brisby
Alicia Michelle Brooks
Sonya Tonnette Brown
Jeredith DeKe Brown
Kauvonda Buie
Patrice D. Burks
Genia L. Butler
Ganita R. Cohran
LaSandra Coleman
Erica D. Collins
Audrey L. Cone
Tara T. Cooper
Kimberly Michelle Cosby
Melissa Ann Cowan
Brian Shawn Creal
Roslyn Nicole Daniel
Charlotte D'Juana
  Danley
Leo A. Dixon
David Lesean Domino
Dwan Shamelle Ellis
Tiffany Cheri Francis
Dieema Ada Foley
Natasha Ni Forbes
Dashanka Latrice Friar
Desmond Gaddis
Dawana Gholar
Gregory Paul Glenn
Amanda E. Green
Brian Bernard Henderson
Amy Denise Hill
Byron Duane Hooper
Helen Hutcherson
Brian Dion Johnson
Erdelle Nicole Johnson-
  Edwards

Stephanie Johnson
Tarik Omari Johnson
Felicia Leshay Jones
Wesley Jones, Jr.
William Jean Jones-
    Strickland
Wilton Muakuidi Jones
Marsha L. Kennedy
Sanette Leakett
    Langston
Mollie Leflore
Carpia Marie Lewis
Eddie R. Martin
Valerie Lynn Mattox
Sheri Tajuana McKinney
Otis Leon Miller
Roderick Fernando
    Miller
Mauda LaShandra
    Monger
LaTanya Denise Ann
    Montgomery
LaToya Latrice Nance
Clemon Marie Nichols
Carlos Diallos Palmer
Tiffaney Scheryl
    Parkman
Harold D. Patton
Rhondalyn K. Peairs
Natasia Petrice Rucker
Shanna Simone Saddler
Paul Scott
Kobie' D. Singleton
Roy Kenionne Smith
Nneka Mariama Stringer
Andre' Lamar Terrett
Brian B. Terry
Ricardo Rian Thomas
Fredrick Marquise
    Thorns, III
Tanya Andrea Thurman
Natasha Denise Tucker
Brandi Veasley
Tiffany Walker

Christopher Washington
Yolanda Renee
    Washington
Anasa Watts
Erika Louise Williams
H. Andre R. Williams
Theodore R. Williams,
    III
Verlonda Faye Wilson
Corneda Yvette Winston
Chandra E. J. Wise
Crystal Renee' Woodard
Carlos LeRoy Woodson
Stephanie Young

Bachelor of Science
Chudney Dionne
    Andrew
Edward C. Bell
Chaddrick Perez Bibb
Cherise Renae Bowen
Cheryl Denise Brent
Angela Y. Brooks
Torrance Tramel Brown
Marilyn Brownlow
Shantwania Areonesia
    Buchanan
Lea Rosel Bush
Terralon Jamila Cannon
Jennifer Le Esther
    Chandler
Shalawn Kozet Clark
Dana Helene Evans
Sonja Rena Evans
Lori Angela Genous
Laronda Denise Giles
Portia M Grayson
Shannon Rolanda
    Hopkins
Loretta Jackson
Michele L. Jackson
David Depriest Johnson
Kesi Yvette Johnson
Patrice Shunte Johnson

Valerie Lakesa Jones
Robert L. McField, II
Zeita Merchant
Tiffaney Twonia Monroe
Shannon Dione Pittman
Lashondra Marquet
    Powell
Sholunda J. Rucker
Tameka Lashun
    Simmons
Dederic Yevette Taplin
Jason F. Tate
Kendria Valencia Ward

May 16, 1999

Associate of Arts
Jannie Lavern McMorris
Stephanie Whittington
Bessie R. Wright

Bachelor of Arts
MaKesha Lorraine
    Adams
Sabah Hamad Al-Fadhli
Christina S. Allen-Henry
Anwar Lenal Anderson
Von Lerue Anderson
Honoray Vashawn Ard
Jennifer Janee' Armon
Corey L. Armstrong
Nikki L. Arrington
Denise Lachelle Banks
Joi Njiiri Barnes
Chancey Ka Bass
Katrina Lynette Bates
Clemon Diamond
    Beamon
Carolyn R. Blackmon
Janessa E. Blackmon
Tiffany Phana Blackmon
Tasha Le'Toya Blevins
Shelia Denise Bonner

Amechi Bowser
Nishaon A. Bridges
Gowon Brisby
April Anjanette Brown
Toya Telesia Brown
Sonya Mechelle Buckley
Khari Kenyatta Butler
Shathal Janeen Butler
Brenda W. Campbell
Jason C. Campbell
Jennifer Christmas
Demarquis Johntrelle
  Clarke
Crystal Coleman
Yolanda Yvette Culver
Mary Helen Daniels
Alysia Davis
Kesha Lontonya Davis
Van Edward Davis, III
Yarnelle Monique Davis
Kelly Rashida Dominick
Sheena M. Dowe
Monique Shuniell
  Edmond
Marvis E. Green
Terri L. Griffin
Tiffany Cheryl Griffin
Cedric M. Hammond
Chad Re'Shad Hampton
Charlotte Bridgette
  Hardy
Rhonda L. Hardy-
  Harmon
Nakeitha Denise Harges
Tanyeka Shanay Harris
Angela Tamekia Harvey
Amy Melissa Henderson
Nikki L. Hillard
Jeremy Wayne "Chico"
  Hodge
Marsha Minyette Hollins
Nathan Trey Hunter, III
Maanami F. Irving
Hubert Jackson

Athenia B. Jefferson
Tiffanni C. Jerdine
Carolyn D. Johnson
Keisha Monique Johnson
Sharron Natasha
  Johnson
Stephen Mandrell
  Johnson
Chilsea Joy Jones
De'Andra Jones
Eddie L. Jones, Jr.
Titania Latersa Jones
Darvis Redeneatto
  Jordan
Ebonie Nicole Kennedy
Cynthia Lacy-Evans
Michael Lowe
Betty Ann Poole Marsh
Petrena Retonya McCoy
Paquita Shawnetta
  McCray
Sembene Bian
  McFarland
Joshua Bernard McGee
Venetra Erin McKinney
Sharon Moncure
Catrina Letrece Murry
Peggi Ann Patterson
Kella Lacoya Pleasance
Jacqueline Denise Potts
Tonia Luaricia Powell
Venita Roshea Powell
Katrenia M. Proby
Howard Rambsy, II
Terrica Lashun Redfield
Willie D. Richardson
Christopher Robinson
Kenneth Rodgers
T'Juan Tyree Rucker
LaTonya Rene' Sutton
Delvin Donyale Taylor
Kimberly Ann Taylor
Philip Anthony Taylor
Khira Janell Turner

Kemba Adero Ware
Yumekia Shuntay Ward
Johnnie Mae
  Washington
Edward Owens Watson
Reginald D. Weary
Bobby Martize Wilder
Ryan Frank Wilkins
Donrandra Marie
  Williams-Cowan
Nyeta Timiza Williams
Johnny E. Wilson, Jr.
Angela Windham-Blakley
Shalondia Winston-
  Johnson
Malcolm Horace
  Woodland
Heather Renee' Woods
Tiffanie Young

Bachelor of Science
Kimberly L. Anderson
Siddeeaah D. Bilal
Cassandra Terrell Brown
Sherry L. Caldwell
Lakisha A. Crigler
Latanya Rodanna
  Dunbar
Karyn Danita Dunlap
Vanessa Doanchell
  Finklea
Aletha Arnette Fletcher
Garrick Lanoris Florence
Yolanda Marie Gordon
Danny Latrell Green
Dionne D. Griffin
Kerry Ledon Griffin
Umekei W. Griffin
Tammy M. Harris
Zerra V. Harris
Kisha S. Jennings
Adisa Jamil Jones
Sheikilya Rochandra
  Lewis

Amoni Matthews
Claurice Wonkesha Nash
Monica Adrienne Peeler
Teresa Lashay Poindexter
Jason K. Taylor
Felicia Wynette
  Thompson
Tekeeta S. Washington
Carlos D. White
Corey Bartlett Wilder
Cressinda Verel Young

May 21, 2000

Associate of Arts
Michelle A. Mosley

Bachelor of Arts
Kashonda L. Anderson
Louella Cole-Allen
Tamaria La'Reese Barnes
Zandra N. Bender
Delicia Nicole Bennett
Christy Lynn Berry
Kristie Marie Betts
L.S. Bishop, Jr.
Alfred Boyd, Sr.
Michellia A. Bridges
Kenecha Shanice Brooks
Chad William Brown, Jr.
Greta Brown Bully
Tiffany Reagana Burks
Eric Burton
Kammilla Patrice Burton
Keneisha Bush
Gayla Larita Carpenter
Tracy A. Carr
Stacy Denese Chislom
Lawrence M. Clark
Milton John Clark
Natasha Michelle Collins
Tiffany M. Cooper
Larry L. Day

Camila Joy Ducksworth
Shunessa Meless Ealey
Anitra LaShanda
  Eubanks
Tekemia O. Evans
Margelet Fields
Melody Teracita Fisher
Damertric Shantel
  Fletcher
Kiana LaFaye Foster
Munirah A. Foster
Charles H. Gailes, Jr.
Pamela Gibson
Celestial M. Gordon
Jacqueline Meeks Griffin
Sharelle Antoinette
  Grim
Christopher Alex
  Harmon
De'Mario L.M. Harris
Althea LaShay Hart
Constance O. Harvey
Angela Denise Hill
Nicholas J. Hill
Orlando Adrain Hill
Erica Jamelle Hopkins
Kimberly Shenis Irvin
Emleigh Marilyn Jacobs
Ayhana Michelle Jackson
LaShundra Jackson
Jacqueline Dianne Evans
  James
Cicely Dionne Jefferson
De'Sheria Le'Trecia
  Johnson
Madisa Jorett Johnson
Trinita Marcelle Keeler
  Johnson
Willie Ruth Johnson
Jamie Jennifer Joiner
Coletta Joy Jones
Marsha Rhnee Jones
Edshundra Shinell
  Jordan

Kimberly Nicole Jorden
Felicia LaToya Kincaid
Stephanie M. King
Terriny Nakitta Knox
Cynthia Nicole Lawson
Anchanese Levison
Lakesha Lashea Lewis
Bieannya Leverne
  Cheree' Lockhart
Lisa Maria Lynch
Danelle Renee
  McClellan
Derrick McCoy
Petrena Retonya McCoy
Renita LaShaun
  McGee
Nakia Deltreje
  McGlothen
Preamiller Inilia
  McKinney
Tijuana Michelle Miller
Christine Morgan
Takela Jones Morris
Tina Michelle Murray
Monica Michelle
  Nichols
Alisha Rochell Nickson
Tinitia S. Patterson
Carlos Antonio Payton
Becky Poindexter
Delores Fay Anderson
  Potts
William D'Wayne
  Purnell
Tomeeka F. Robbins
Lettie E. Roberts
Deunderia T. Smith
Kevin Charles Smith
Ruby Shenell Smith
Zurick Tiant Smith
Sylvester Spann, Jr.
Geoffrey Marcus
  Stansberry
Luticia Sharlet Staple

Patrick LaDonis Sutton
Cassandra Jani
  Theobalds
April Necole Thomas
Demarcus Fitzgerald
  Thomas
Charlotte Shanae
  Thompson
Rosalind Vanessa
  Thompson
Charles A. Wansley
Shaunte' Denise
  Washington
Dameon Demil Williams
Demetric Dyann
  Williams
Diana L. Williams
Gregory C. Williams
Greta Williams
Maleka G. Williams
Adrienne Bertille
  Woodard

Bachelor of Science
Shenetra Necole Burse
Charley A. Cheney, III
Kimberly Cotrell
  Claxton
Willie Warren Craft, Jr.
Shalana Lynette Donald
Misty Necol Ducksworth
Naisha-Nyoka Shanett
  Fuller
Katrina Renee Gaines
Kendra Yvette Gee
Tekka Laureen Cosby
  Herron
Albert Benjamin
  McClemore
  Jackson
Lenessa Rispba Jackson
Hosea Rafeal James
Ayanna Kafi Jenkins
Chandler R. Johnson

Stefen Leo King
Bernadette Knight
LaKeyra G. McCoy
Sonya Makeba McGee
LaShonn L. McNair
Nicole Christina
  McPhearson
Rosalind Suzanne
  Ramsey
Aisha Reed
Fannie Latrice
  Richardson
Valerie Jenora Robinson
Vonda Charmaine
  Robinson
Jennifer Rose Rundles
Tyronza Daniell Sharkey
LaTonya Benittress
  Washington
Lafarra Young

May 20, 2001

Associate of Arts
Mary Mays Gary
Donna Nichols Green
Brenda Joyce Thompson
Doris Ann Williams

Bachelor of Arts
Charae Elizabeth Adams
Shanetta Danielle Akins
Lishonlynn E. Akporido
Charles L. Alexander
Khambraya Charnelle
  Anderson
Latoya Corinne
  Anderson
Melissa Michelle
  Anderson
Donald Bailey, Jr.
Justin Ray Bailey
Kimberly C. Banks

Lawanda M. Bell
Franzetta Viola Bester
Robert A. Bettis
Melissa Lynn Bills
Tristan Phelance
  Blackmon
Stacey Scharlene Blalock
Mylinda Phillips Boles
Jenelia Krishaun Bracey
Vernita Latisha Bradley
Antwyn Shawntez
  Brown
Tayarta Lawillette Brown
Kathy J. Bryant
Bertha L. Buck
Geneva Hannah Burton
Marlow Kendrell Butler
Shugana Levetta
  Campbell
Elizabeth Ruby Carr
Daphne Rochelle
  Chamberlain
Jeana Clark
Kanika Fatima Collins
Tashana Rene' Coleman
Jennifer Danielle Davis
Laquita Shonne Davis
Shanna Tamiko Davis
Zaritta Ja'Net Davis
Ebonye' Dawn Debose
Khiedrae Meikelle
  Deloach
Virginia Dixon
Chevis Devon Earle
Lala M. Eddie
Christopher William
  Espy
Sandra Diane Evans
Laquanda Sha' Ron
  Fields
Cyril D. Fisher
Aisha Shekina Fowler
Gwendolyn Clanton
  Franklin

Andrea Deprea Galloway
Ginnie T. Gill-Cox
Antoinette Gooden
Thomas J. Gordon
Kianca Latrelle Guyton
Kenji Lammon Haley
Shana Senise Harper
Roslyn Hartwell-Smith
Deltrinae Rayann
  Hodges
Annie Lois Holmes
Felicia Marie Holmes
Simea Roshanda Howard
Vick L. Hudson
Kandi Deshell Hunter
Chazeman Shenetta
  Jackson
Roderick Jermaine
  Jackson
April Tershekia James
Nacola Rae James
Louella Frazier Jenkins
Trymunda Germae
  Jenkins
Latishe Dianne Johnson
Rashid Ahmad Johnson
Daniel Augustus Joiner
Chandra Marie Jones
A. Pierre Keys
Sherieda Kenyatta King
Felix Stephen Lawson
Jamie Carol Lewis
Tamaria L. Liddell
Catherine G. Lipsey
Makeisha L. Logan
Dalton M. Lovelock
Kim Lonnell Luckett
Rukia Kai Lumumba
Tristan Van Ness
  Marshall
Joe L. Martin, Jr.
Paula Diane McCarthy
Crystal Kaye Miller
Patrick James Miller

Styra Lashay Monger
Dana M. Moore
Shanika A. Moore
Gertrude Atoinette
  Mosley
Alphia Ralondra Myers
Hasina Nailah Neal
Norma W. Neal
Kuwana Sheree Paschal
Michael Jackson
  Penquite
Letitia Vonnda Plummer
Latonya Renelle Reed
Ericka Denise Rice
Frederick Tyrone
  Richards
Tobias Robinson
Christie De'Andra
  Rogers
Mary Frances Rose
Saran Tene' Savage
Lawanda Tunesia Scott
Renada C. Singleton
April Shavette Smith
Delmon D. Smith
Dina Suzanne Smith
Kanisha Smith
Shawonda Shanta' Smith
Sheata Shaunta
  Southern
Anna T. Stanley
Anthony L. Thomas
Chasity Ladonya Tillman
Misty Lashay Trunnell
Sharon Darlene Wallace
Javin R. Walker
Gail Denise Ward
Shalom Fatima Watkins
Carlyle Creswell White
Gail Marthette White
Quinn Alecia White
Kristy Michelle Wiley
Dwaynia Kenise
  Wilkerson

Crystal Devoe Wilson
David R. Winters, Jr.
Krissy Michelle Wright

Bachelor of Science
Qwantina Barlow
Dana Moray Blair
Alisha Marquita Brinson
Tedric D. Campbell
Kristy Naomi Cochran
Jason Craft
Shondra Renee' Forbes
Jeremiah Gates, Jr.
Carlie Yvonne Gaunty
Gachavis M. Green
Kimaleshia Moniche
  Harper
Ayatti Dunjuni Hatcher
Pierre D. Leaks
Alice Rozena Love
Raven Haynes McCoy
Angeletta Nakeya
  McCraney
Willie Perkins, Jr.
Shanna Briann Pettie
Jacqueline Y. Samuel
Fredria Carlynette Shaw
Alyce Stewart
Latesha Quinshun Swilly
Dennis J. Tanner
Charlon Edward Tolliver
Pamela Townsey
Latonya S. Ware
Tameka Lashun Wilder
John M. Woodard, Jr.